Sociology of Europeanization

Sozialwissenschaftliche Einführungen

Series Editor
Rainer Schützeichel

Volume 3

Sociology of Europeanization

Edited by
Sebastian M. Büttner, Monika Eigmüller
and Susann Worschech

DE GRUYTER
OLDENBOURG

ISBN 978-3-11-067362-3
e-ISBN (PDF) 978-3-11-067363-0
e-ISBN (EPUB) 978-3-11-067383-8
ISSN 2570-0529

Library of Congress Control Number: 2021946997

Bibliographic information published by the Deutsche Nationalbibliothek
The Deutsche Nationalbibliothek lists this publication in the Deutsche Nationalbibliografie;
detailed bibliographic data are available on the internet at http://dnb.dnb.de.

© 2022 Walter de Gruyter GmbH, Berlin/Boston
Typesetting: Integra Software Services Pvt. Ltd.
Printing and binding: CPI books GmbH, Leck

www.degruyter.com

Preface

The numerous and far-reaching socio-political transformations that have taken place on the European continent since the mid-20th century have stipulated the emergence of new approaches and research fields in the social sciences. One of these is the development of a Sociology of Europeanization during the 1990s and 2000s against the backdrop of major political changes in Central and Eastern Europe from 1989, the establishment of the European Union (EU) in 1993, and more general processes of transnationalization and globalization. Since then, the long-term processes of European integration and corresponding dynamics of Europeanization have intensified tremendously: The EU expanded within a relatively short period from a community of 12 member states at the beginning of the 1990s to a community of 28 member states by 2013. Today it consists of 27 member states, since with the so-called 'Brexit' of Great Britain in 2021 after the 2016 referendum we have also witnessed the first withdrawal of an EU member state from EU membership. Apart from its huge territorial expansion, the thrust of European integration since the 1990s has also nurtured the social, cultural, and economic diversity of the EU. Beyond this, the establishment of the EU during the 1990s with the enforcement of its four major freedoms (the free movement of goods, capital, services, and labor), the expansion of European policy coordination, and the implementation of a common currency have stipulated multifaceted institutional changes and social transformations that are neither easy to grasp nor to comprehend. Furthermore, during the past decade, Europe has been shaken by several serious and far-reaching economic, social, and political crises, bringing about new social conflicts, strong disintegrative forces, and putting into question overly rosy prospects of a united Europe and shiny visions of an ever-integrating union.

This reflection of major social and societal transformations in Europe is at the center of this book. It is one of the first and most comprehensive introductions to major terms and concepts, theories, topics, and discussions of the Sociology of Europeanization, a dynamically evolving research field within the wider arrays of sociology, and more general sociological reflections on social change and societal transformations. This book comprises 14 chapters, each covering one particular theme of the multifaceted explorations, reflections, and debates of the Sociology of Europeanization – ranging from more general conceptual discussions to the examination of the numerous socio-spatial, cultural, economic, political, judicial, and socio-structural implications of Europeanization. While reading and studying the 14 chapters of this book, it should become clear that the scope of analysis of the Sociology of Europeanization is

https://doi.org/10.1515/9783110673630-202

limited neither to the territory of the EU nor even to the 'territory' of the European continent in the proper sense. The sociological exploration of Europeanization comprises and requires much more than just focusing on the EU and its member states. In fact, it comprises reflections of the long-term socio-spatial and socio-cultural history of Europe and the tremendous transnational and global implications of 'Europeanization' in both the past and the present. All these different dimensions and aspects of Europeanization are addressed in the 14 chapters of this book, which were written by experts on the different themes and topics that are presented.

All of the chapters are compiled as introductory texts into major topics, terms, and concepts of the Sociology of Europeanization. This textbook is particularly designed as a fundamental reading in study programs and modules particularly focusing on sociological aspects and implications of Europeanization. It can be used as an introductory reading in sociological study programs and in European studies both at B.A. and M.A. levels. Moreover, the book can also serve as a general introduction and information source for those interested in learning more about Europe, European society, and major topics of the Sociology of Europeanization.

While based on experiences from our own lectures and seminars, it strongly and heavily relies on the experience and expertise of all contributors who were open to our ideas about the structure and the style of this textbook from the very beginning. Hence, our first big 'thank you' goes to all authors and contributors, without whom this book would not have come into being. We are grateful for all their efforts, their engagement, and their patience. We are grateful for their openness to adapt their texts in accordance with the format of this textbook and for investing huge effort in compiling highly informative and legible chapters.

Furthermore, we would also like to say 'thank you' to Lucy Jarman from De Gruyter for her support throughout the entire project and to Rainer Schützeichel, the editor of De Gruyter's series *Sozialwissenschaftliche Einführungen*, who approached us initially and encouraged us to edit this textbook. As always, there are many more people and organizations involved in producing, compiling, and editing a book such as this. Hence, we are highly grateful as well to Ahmet Celikten, one of our student assistants, who very much helped us with the copy-editing of the individual chapters, and to Inke Kühl for her final check-ups. Moreover, we would like to thank Tom Alterman and Laura Cunniff for their thorough editing. Our sincere thanks go also to the Viadrina Institute for European Studies (IFES) at the European University Viadrina and the Interdisciplinary Centre for European Studies (ICES) at Europa-Universität Flensburg for having supported the language editing. Finally, we would also like to thank our students for their interest in the topics of our classes and their valuable contributions which, in one way or the other, also influenced the development of this book. This book was made for you and for all students to come, being eager to learn more about Europe and the sociological implications of Europeanization.

Some final remarks on the didactical concept of this textbook: As this book is divided into 14 chapters, it is conceptualized as background reading for an introductory course or lecture for a duration of one semester or trimester. All texts have about the same length and contain introductions to major concepts and key references. Moreover, they usually also contain overviews of key developments and major empirical findings in each of the different presented areas of study. All texts are written in an accessible style and no in-depth knowledge of sociology or sociological theory is required; however, we invite and encourage everybody who wants to learn more about sociology, and some of the major figures, debates, and concepts mentioned in this book, to learn more about it in further classes and readings. We hope that this book stimulates the interest and curiosity to go further and learn more. Therefore, all chapters end with a short didactical section, in which key learning points, further readings, and major web sources for further explorations are provided. In some of the chapters, you will find a short glossary with explanations of major keywords and concepts. The keywords that are further explained in the glossary of a chapter are usually printed in **bold type** (like this) when they first appear in a chapter.

Finally, we want to point out explicitly that this book is neither designed as an introduction to the EU and to EU politics nor to the history of European integration or the history of Europe in general. However, some background knowledge on the EU, its major organizations, and the history of European integration can be helpful indeed for a deeper understanding of some of the topics and debates addressed in this book. If you need more background information on key developments and facts, we strongly recommend to look at the further readings presented at the end of the chapters and deliberately searching for relevant information online, since most of the basic facts and information – especially key facts and background on European integration and the structure of the EU – are easily accessible. You will find many hints to relevant web sources and background readings throughout this book. Moreover, we have also integrated some extra-recommendations for basic readings and basic information provided online to the didactical section of the first chapter, the introduction to the Sociology of Europeanization. Hence, you can use this first introductory lesson as an occasion to enrich your knowledge on Europe and the history of European integration right at the beginning of this book. We hope that our readers will enjoy their journey throughout the Sociology of Europeanization and that this book will be an inspiring starting point for your course through this fascinating topic.

Erlangen/Berlin, Flensburg, and Frankfurt (Oder) in July 2021,
Sebastian M. Büttner, Monika Eigmüller, and Susann Worschech

Contents

Part I: **Introduction**

Susann Worschech, Monika Eigmüller & Sebastian M. Büttner

1 Sociology of Europeanization: An Introduction

When, a century ago, Max Weber defined sociology as a science that "attempts the interpretive understanding of social action in order thereby to arrive at a causal explanation of its course and effects [. . .]" (Weber & Heydebrand 1999), his key analytical focus was the capitalist nation state and the social consequences of its advancing consolidation. And not without cause: Weber and his contemporaries were deeply fascinated by the growing entanglement of capitalist economics, democratic political systems, and increasingly powerful and efficient bureaucracies in the early 20th century. One core question for intellectuals of that time was how modern nation states and national societies developed vis-à-vis new institutions, and the resultant emergence of new interaction patterns, social identities, and socio-structural features.

A century later, the nation state itself underwent a massive transformation in and beyond Europe, due to increasing internationalization and globalization on the one hand, and far-reaching European integration on the other hand that has led to the establishment of the European Union (EU). Propelled by international political arrangements and new institutional settings, such as freedom of movement and permeable borders between EU member states, European integration gave rise to new (supranational) political and institutional orders – i.e., developments that led scholars to interpret 'Europeanization' mainly in terms of the impact of EU-level politics on national political processes in European countries (Börzel & Risse 2003; Vink 2003). Yet the process of European integration has not only led to the emergence of a new supranational layer of government, that is mainly represented by 'the European Union'; it has also spurred, in fact, the 'Europeanization' of national institutions and social structures in EU member states (Bach 2008; Mau & Verwiebe 2010). In contrast to the understanding of Europeanization as a domestic adaptation of political structures to EU processes, this second set of issues – the Europeanization of societal change, and the question of how local, regional, national, and transnational social action can shape societies within a European and Europewide framework – have only gained serious scholarly attention in the past two decades. For contemporary political sociologists, the challenge is to comprehensively explain the course and effects of social action within the context of Europeanization. A sociological perspective of Europeanization as both a top-down and bottom-up process of social change and transformation is one that considers the

https://doi.org/10.1515/9783110673630-001

construction, dissemination, and institutionalization of both formal and informal norms, institutions, and lifestyles at different levels of society (Radaelli 2003).

While it only recently emerged as a relevant sub-discipline of sociology, the Sociology of Europeanization has its own developmental history. The scholarship of modernization, transformation and social change has tended to adopt a *longue-durée* perspective and a European focus when looking at processes and events.[1] Increasingly established in intellectual debates since the age of Enlightenment, the idea of political and societal modernization – which emerged more or less in parallel to the rise of nation states, national economies, and new social orders in Eastern and Western Europe in the 20th century – has long been a major point of reference for sociology. The very concept of modernization, therefore, is inherently linked to the concept of Europeanization and to 'becoming European'. Underpinning this understanding of a (Western) European societal role model is the often proclaimed 'return to Europe' of post-socialist countries in Central and Eastern Europe after 1989–1991. The implicit connection between Europeanization and modernization is further reflected in critical studies on (post-)colonialism (Boatcă 2006; see also Chapter 5 in this volume) and in processes such as the development of individualization and the emergence of post-modernity or post-democracy. Consequently, sociological perspectives on Europeanization offer far more than a mere societal background in political and economic integration. We also distinctly reflect ideas and interpretations that shaped the evolution of Europe and our contemporary understandings of *Europe, European society*, and *Europeanization*.

Today, the Sociology of Europeanization has its own major research foci and perspectives. Eigmüller and Mau (2010) have outlined the following two major approaches being fundamental to the Sociology of Europeanization: The first approach focuses on *comparative analyses* of a specific social situation within the context of European regions, states, or territories; it derives from classic social structure analysis, which has been a core subdiscipline of sociology since its beginnings. It implies a scale-shift of classical macrosociology (which was and still is oriented towards the nation state) towards the comparative analysis of cases within a supranational entity. The second approach involves a sociological *exploration of the emergence of new European societal constellations* – that is, in short, the exploration and reflection of the emergence of a European society. Examining linkages and interactions among European individuals, societies, and/or states to find out whether and how European identities, belongings, and collective

---

1 For a more in-depth explanation of the concept of *longue dureé*, see Info-Box 4.3 in Chapter 4 of this volume.

action can take shape, this second approach rests on an understanding of Europeanization that differs fundamentally from the first one. Rather than juxtaposing individual (often national) cases, this second approach explores the particular 'transnational' or 'European' factors in light of current changes and transformations of European society. While the first approach might compare social inequality in two European regions or societies, for example, the second perspective can illuminate how and to what extent 'Europeanization' leads to new societal formations and constellations (like cross-border networks of social welfare, the rise of new NGOs in border cities, or new networks and communities of cross-border work migration). In this sense, the second perspective of Europeanization studies moves away from a particular "methodological nationalism" (Beck & Grande 2007: 94f.) that has predominated in sociology and especially in sociological conceptions of what makes up a 'society' until recently.

Against this background, we propose that the Sociology of Europeanization focuses on three major elements constituting the social world and therefore underpinning much of sociological analysis: institutions, interaction, and interpretation. All three of these factors can be approached from either a comparative or a transnational perspective. While the former marks a scale-shift of sociological analysis from the regional or national to the supranational level, the latter can be identified as an approach that stresses the *European* (or *transnational*) elements of societal formation. Table 1.1 outlines this classification:

Table 1.1: Sociology of Europeanization: Objects and approaches.

	Comparative Perspective: **Scale Shift**	**Transnational Perspective:** **Transformation**
Institutions	Institutional settings in selected regions or countries often affected by the European level	Transnational institutions and governance; new structures or institutional settings
Interaction	Networks, action patterns and social organization with reference to Europe	Emergence of new social configurations, networks, patterns; transformation of (national) societies and social patterns
Interpretation	Habitus, identities, interpretations, and frames on European issues from a domestic perspective	Transnational habitus, identities, interpretations, and frames as new social dynamics across borders linked with Europe/Europeanization

Based on this systematization, two insights in the field and history of the Sociology of Europeanization merit some comment here. First, institutions, interaction and interpretation represent different angles of research, but also different phases in the development of our research field. Second, the step from a comparative to a transnational perspective is neither self-evident nor compelling, but it marks an important step in the advancement of sociological thinking on Europe and globalization (Beck & Grande 2007). This evolution of the different paradigms within sociology will briefly be outlined in the following section.

Two Perspectives and an Interdisciplinary Research Field

European studies constitute an interdisciplinary research field. It is and has been strongly shaped by perspectives and approaches from the political sciences, law, and economics – especially those areas of European studies that deal with core issues of EU integration and EU policymaking. Moreover, the field of European studies also has strong roots in the humanities and different branches of the cultural sciences, such as history, philosophy, and philology. In this area of European studies, the cultural, historical, and philosophical dimensions of European society, as well as its interaction and interpretation patterns, are at the center of attention. Sociology certainly has its own place within this wide array of approaches and traditions, taking an intermediary position in the field by combining institutional, interactionist, and interpretative approaches. While sociologists raise questions that are relevant to core *institutionalist* fields in European studies, they also contribute to the humanistic and culturalist pole when reflecting *interactions* and *interpretations* thanks to the discipline's strong hermeneutic, socio-historical, and theoretical traditions.

Yet, the explicit study of Europe and the distinct focus on Europeanization emerged quite late in sociology, i.e., during the late 1990s and even more intensely since the beginning of 2000. However, this does not mean that Europe and European issues were completely absent from sociology before. Quite to the contrary, sociologists have long studied and reflected on features of European society. These studies and reflections were often framed differently than they are now, or at least not referred to in connection with a *Sociology of Europe* or a distinctly 'European' perspective. After World War II and until the late 1980s, social scientists systematically described and analyzed – often comparatively – major political institutions in Europe as well as social, economic, and cultural characteristics of 'Western' societies. By the end of the 20th century, when European integration started to intensify, the perception of a stronger 'Europeanization' and 'globalization' of national societies began to draw sociologists' attention. Accordingly, we can roughly trace the emergence of the *Sociology of Europeanization* at the edge of two major periods: the period before its formation as an own research field, and the period since the 1990s, when Europeanization started to intensify and sociological attention to these processes started to grow.

The Classical Sociological Perspective: Transformation and Social Change

The emergence of contemporary Sociology of Europeanization has strong historical roots that have significantly influenced and shaped current conceptions and specific research perspectives. Although we mentioned in the beginning that classical sociology emerged during the era of nation-building in the 19th and early 20th centuries, some of the classical sociological concepts and perspectives are still instructive for scholars and students of sociological European studies (Münch & Büttner 2006; Wobbe 2009; Münch 2016). A look at these classical texts shows that those early sociologists were much more engaged with general reflections about the emergence of modern society in Europe and the distinctive features of modernity than with analyzing the features of nation states or particular national societies. Karl Marx (1818–1883), for instance, focused on the emergence of capitalism in general, even traveling around Europe to study the origins and distinctive features and expansion of the industrial society in Europe and beyond. Likewise, Max Weber (1864–1920), despite having been educated primarily in national law, national economics, and history, was not exclusively referring to German society (or any other national background) in his analysis of the cultural foundations and central features of modern capitalism, government, and bureaucracy. Throughout his professional life, Weber was mainly preoccupied with the emergence of *European* modernity – or rather of a major cultural logic, in a process that he called 'occidental rationalization' (and one that he also analyzed extensively in detailed historical comparisons to other world regions). Émile Durkheim (1858–1917), moreover, another frequently proclaimed classical sociologist, mainly focused on the historical evolution of French society in his groundbreaking work *The Social Division of Labor*; however, he also described modernization as a transformation of the collective consciousness of societies. In his concluding remarks, Durkheim explicitly envisaged the formation of a European society in 1893, a moment of vigorous nationalism and nation-building: "We have already seen that among European peoples there is a tendency to form, by spontaneous movement, a European society which has, at present, some idea of itself and the beginning of organization." (Durkheim [1893] 1960: 405). Today, this quotation and Durkheim's general approach towards the analysis of large-scale processes of social change are regarded as a major point of departure for an emergent Sociology of Europeanization (Münch & Büttner 2006; Mau & Verwiebe 2010).

Like Marx, Weber, and Durkheim, none of the other major classical sociologists, such as Ferdinand Toennies (1855–1936), Georg Simmel (1858–1918), Herbert Spencer (1820–1903), or Vilfredo Pareto (1848–1923), focused their work on a specific country. While these thinkers represented different national sociological traditions, they were also interested in more general reflections and analyses of societal transformation, especially on the European continent. In the same vein, a generation later, Norbert Elias (1897–1990) analyzed the emergence of European modernity and the rise of modern statehood in his extensive socio-historical and psychogenetic study *The Civilizing Process* (Elias [1939] 2000). Focusing on the concept of *civility* (or rather of *civilité* as in the French original) in France and Germany, this is one of the first sociological studies to explicitly carry out a historical cross-country comparison of differing cultural understandings and interpretations of a major underlying theme in European society. Elias's study offered a prototype of a distinctly trans-local study of long-term socio-cultural developments that, even today, is instructive as a model for multi-sited cultural analyses, transnational network approaches, and socio-historical studies of larger social configurations. Taken together, these works of classical sociological inquiry prepared the ground for the emergence of what we have already defined as a second thematic perspective within the Sociology of Europeanization: namely, the study of broader societal transformation and the emergence of new social configurations.

The Focus on Institutions

In the period after World War II, sociology and the social sciences in general were increasingly influenced and dominated by the concepts and approaches to social research coming out of the United States and by US American adaptations of classical modernization theory and the expansion of empirical research methods. Against this backdrop, comparative analyses increasingly came to be seen as standard practice for social inquiry in general. Concomitantly, the rise of survey research brought about new data and novel research designs that made possible new types of comparisons among European or 'Western' countries. A standard reference for this period is the work of sociologist and political scientist Seymour Martin Lipset (1922–2006), who strongly influenced the emergence of political sociology during the post-war era, especially with his seminal work *Some Social Requisites of Democracy: Economic Development and Political Legitimacy* (Lipset 1959). Lipset's work and similar studies published during the post-war period inspired a surge of research on political parties and attitudes during the second half of the 20th century which continues to represent an important branch of political sociology and comparative research (Skocpol 1992; Marks & Wilson 2000; Hooghe & Marks 2008). Another key contribution to institution-oriented political sociology with a distinctly pan-European focus (although mainly in terms of Western Europe) was put forward by the Norwegian sociologist Stein Rokkan (1921–1979), who also closely cooperated with Lipset, especially while developing the so-called *cleavage theory* (see Chapter 13 in this volume). In his writings on nation-building and party systems in Europe, Rokkan provided an impressively detailed yet highly generalized description of modern European social history. His book *State Formation, Nation-Building, and Mass Politics in Europe* (Rokkan 1999) represents a major reference point for the founding period of sociology-grounded European studies and the gradual emergence of the Sociology of Europe. This development has also been spurred by the development and expansion of 'area studies' in post-war social and cultural sciences. Hence, a major driving force of the emergence of contemporary Sociology of Europeanization has been the emergence of 'European studies' (next to the exploration of other major world regions, such as East Asia studies or Latin American studies and the like) and the development of distinct geographical foci in social and cultural sciences, such as the development of special foci on 'Eastern Europe', 'South-Eastern Europe', or 'Southern Europe'.

Equally emblematic for this era of comparative political research are analyses of welfare states. Between the 1980s and 1990s, the debate over different institutional settings of economic systems strongly dominated comparative political research, political economy, and political sociology. Outstanding examples of research and publications in this context were Gosta Esping-Anderson's 1990 monograph *The Three Worlds of Welfare Capitalism* and the multi-faceted debate over the *Varieties of Capitalism* (Hall & Soskice 2001; for the late 2000s, see also: Crouch & Streeck 2006; Streeck & Thelen 2009).

It was during this period, marked by the emergence of comparative, institution-oriented sociological research, that transnationalist approaches first gained a foothold within the growing scholarship on Europe. Two major research strands were decisive for the consolidation of this transnational, distinctively European perspective in sociology: The first strand was mainly influenced by scholarship on the emerging structures of international politics, international relations, and supra-national institution-building in the aftermath of World War II. Ernst B. Haas's book *The Uniting of Europe*, first published in 1958, is often referred to as one of the prototypical works of both contemporary European studies and the Sociology of Europe (Fligstein 2008;

Favell & Giraudon 2011). The second more general approach was laid out by social and political scientist Karl W. Deutsch (1912–1992), who studied the distinctive features and conditions of international cooperation and institution-building. Neither of these scholars focused solely on political actors and processes; rather, they were interested in the larger social repercussions of such cooperation for European politics and society.

Driven to acquire a broader understanding of the socio-historic foundations of nationalism in Europe, Deutsch was also one of the first scholars to focus on economic integration in Western Europe since its emergence in the 1950s, and on the relationship between growing international interaction and international institution-building (Deutsch et al. 1957). His study later gained prominence as the 'transactionalist approach', which can be seen as the analytical counterpart to the comparative perspective (see Chapter 12 in this volume). Apart from this early scholarship on international relations and cooperation, genuine pan-European perspectives and research agendas also evolved within the sphere of historical and socio-historical research on European civilization. In this regard, French historian Fernand Braudel (1902–1985) and other members of the so-called *Annales School* merit special mention (see Chapter 4 in this volume). Distinctly European perspectives in socio-historical research have also prominently evolved in the German context, especially in the contributions by M. Rainer Lepsius, Jürgen Kocka, and Hartmut Kaelble.

After a period of stagnation of European integration during the 1970s, often referred to as 'Eurosclerosis', European integration virtually soared during the 1980s and 1990s. Driving this shift were a number of key developments that worked to increase diversity in the EU and laid the grounds for stronger cooperation between its member states: the *southern enlargement of the European community (EC)* through the accession of Greece (1981), Portugal, and Spain (both in 1986); the *establishment of the Common European market and the European Union (EU)* with the treaty of Maastricht in 1993; the *further enlargement of the EU* through the accession of Austria, Sweden, and Finland in 1995; and the *creation of an Economic and Monetary Union* during the 1990s, leading to the introduction of the *Euro* as the common currency of the EU in 1999. In addition, and most importantly, the fall of the Iron Curtain and the breakdown of Soviet communism by the end of the 1980s fundamentally changed the political landscape of post-war Europe. In the aftermath of this historic sequence of events, Central and Eastern Europe rapidly became areas of systemic transformation and far-reaching political reform, leading the EU to take on a significant *Eastern enlargements in 2004 and 2007*. In political economy and political sociology, many researchers directed their attention to analyzing and debating the conditions and consequences of the far-reaching transformations in Central and Eastern Europe (see Chapter 6 in this volume). These developments, and especially the enlargement process, spurred increasing comparative and transnational reflection on the different conditions and dimensions of Europeanization. The new studies mainly looked at institutional alignment to the EU's *acquis communautaire* as the prerequisite for EU accession and explored the structural-institutional adjustments taking place in Europe's dynamically progressing integration process. Broadly speaking, the major reflections and sociological research on Europeanization of this period tended to cluster around scholarly debates over the social effects and deeper sociological implications of institution-building beyond the nation state (Lepsius 1992, 2006; Bach 1999). At the center forefront of these reflections was the question of whether a new social order is emerging in Europe, and the struggle between national and European forces that accompanied the formation of European institutions (Delanty & Rumford 2005; Heidenreich 2006; Beck & Grande 2007; Vobruba 2008: 48).

Increasing Focus on Interaction

These pioneering sociological works on European integration were still strongly influenced by predominating political science approaches. Nevertheless, during the first decade of the 21st century, a research agenda specific to the Sociology of Europeanization increasingly began to take shape, spurred by the major theoretical contributions of Richard Münch, Maurizio Bach, Georg Vobruba, Ulrich Beck and Edgar Grande in the German context, and by the emergence of internationally renowned publications such as *Rethinking Europe* by Gerard Delanty and Chris Rumford (2005), Neil Fligstein's book *Euro-Clash* (2008), or *The Sociology of the European Union* edited by Adrian Favell and Virginie Guiraudon (2011). The sociological turn in EU studies was late and more than overdue. It was already in 2010, 53 years after the signing of the treaty of Rome and 18 years after the Treaty of Maastricht, when Sabine Saurugger and Frederic Merand (2010) asked in a special issue of *Comparative European Politics*: "Does European integration theory need sociology?".

Ultimately, developments within European integration itself – in particular, the establishment of EU citizenship in 1992 and the increasing public attention to European issues – put new topics on the research agenda and made clear the need for new analyses, especially sociological ones. These developments gave rise to increasing questions not only about institutions and their social consequences, but about the emergence of a European society as a legitimate subject of sociological inquiry.

The growing awareness of transnational and transformative processes across Europe gave increasing salience to the major national and transnational political actors and movements such as trade unions, civil society, and social movements (Della Porta & Caiani 2009). In parallel, researchers began to see not only actors, but also *interactions* and *networks* as driving forces of Europeanization and thus as relevant subjects of study (Fligstein 2000). The shifting perspective on networks, interaction, movement actors and the emergence of transnational public spheres went hand in hand with a general boom of globalization research in sociology during the late 1990s, when the discourse on globalization, transnational protest campaigns and the recognition of increasing inter- and transnational interdependencies started to noticeably flourish in sociology. In this context, 'Europeanization' has been interpreted as a specific symptom and manifestation of a more general trend towards increasing transnational and global connectivity (Della Porta et al. 1999).

In the ensuing scholarly debates, decisive questions were raised regarding the formation of a European civil society and a European public sphere (Gerhards 2001; Trenz 2005; Eder 2006; Koopmans & Statham 2010), on trans-European social movements and collective mobilization (della Porta & Caiani 2009), spatial mobility within and between European cities (Le Gales 2002; Favell 2008), and transnational European solidarity (Ciornei & Recchi 2017; Lahusen et al. 2018; Gerhards et al. 2019). Furthermore, building on the long tradition of comparative welfare research, the *social* dimension of the European Union – defined in terms of welfare politics and social policy but not, however, solely focused on institutions – also moved into the scholarly spotlight (Heidenreich 2006; Bernhard 2010; Börner 2013; Eigmüller 2021).

A further innovative approach brought up by sociologists in European studies was to move the focus of interest away from the EU decision-making procedures, political legitimacy and institutional competences (Moravcsik 2006; Hix 2008; Scharpf 2003), towards the political struggles, social practices, and symbolic representations in which the European multilevel governance system's various actors are embedded (Büttner 2012; Schmidt-Wellenburg 2017). Profound and systematic studies of the social, professional, and sociodemographic backgrounds of the actors involved in European integration, a rather neglected topic of study until then, provide for a deeper understanding and interpretation of Europeanization processes (Georgakakis & Rowell 2013; Büttner et al. 2015). The focus on institutions and interactions led to new research approaches and new reflections of the formation of political communities beyond the nation state (Elias [1939] 2000; Tilly 1992), on social interaction (Boltanski & Thevenot 2006) and on political sociology (Bourdieu 1998; Kauppi 2003).

These approaches also spurred the development of relational methods, such as network analyses, extensive field work, pattern analyses and the like.

Thus, sociology not only brought about a conceptual shift in European studies – from comparative to (increasingly) transnational analysis, and from a focus on institutions to one geared towards interaction and interpretation. It also gave rise to new research methods (see Favell & Giraudon 2011). Hence, sociology's contribution to the field of European studies has enabled new questions not only to be asked, but also – and above all – to be answered.

Interpretative Approaches in Europeanization Research

The sociological view of Europeanization processes is marked by a more comprehensive understanding drawn from a systematic broadening of the scope of research beyond that traditionally used in other disciplines. In contrast to political science or legal studies research on Europe, which observes and analyzes EU institutions *from afar* mainly through the lens of institutional change, sociologists can work with methods (such as fieldwork or ethnography) that bring them closer to their research subjects. They allow them to direct their gaze away from institutions towards those who actually *do* Europeanization: the actors who take part in Europeanization processes as well as the interpretative approaches, narratives, and framings employed by those actors (Diez Medrano 2003; Fligstein 2008; Merand 2008; Mau & Verwiebe 2010).

This characteristic *'zooming in'*-approach within the Sociology of Europeanization means that sociologists view European integration as historical process (that is, one that unfolds over time) that involves multiple actors. A case in point is Kathleen McNamarra's 2010 study of EU institutional change (and especially European symbolic politics) with reference to the macrosociological work of Charles Tilly (1992) in connection with Bourdieu's theory of symbolic power (Bourdieu 2015). Adopting a historical-sociological view of these developments, McNamarra asks to what extent they lead to what she calls "banal Europeanization". For many authors, this raises the question of what these observable historical developments can tell us about similar developments in European society-building today, and, in particular, about the emergence of a European identity, as well as concerns about how best to approach such diachronic comparisons (Bartolini 2005; Fligstein 2008; Eigmüller & Börner 2015).

Another strong contribution to sociological analysis of Europeanization – one that points to the increasing relevance and prominence, within European studies, of interpretative analyses of Europeanization and of framings/interpretation itself – has been the emergence of a field concept that combines structure and action.

Drawing on Bourdieu's field theory as well as pragmatic sociology, and informed by political science analysis of European institutions, the field concept enables scholars to see EU integration as a field, where social structures and cultural repertoires are produced and reproduced by the social actors involved in integration (that is, EU citizens, politicians, and bureaucrats) (Georgakakis & Weisbein 2010, among others). In this context, the idea of *European fields*, initially invented by Fligstein and Stone Sweet (2002), draws on both historical institutionalism and organizational sociology, which enables the authors to look at the interactions between various actors within the field. In *Euroclash*, Fligstein (2008) shows impressively that European integration has been successful because the actors' creation of new transnational social fields around European institutions has given rise to new European social fields that extend beyond the scope of the national (see also Chapter 9 in this volume).

This so-called '*horizontal Europeanization*'-approach (Beck & Grande 2007; Mau & Verwiebe 2010; Heidenreich 2019) not only focuses on institutions and the ongoing processes of institution-building shaped by various actors, but also on individual European citizens. Scholarship in this vein seeks to identify the actors that are relevant for integration and to discover how their ideas and interests impact on integration processes. The underlying idea is that (Beck & Grande 2007; Mau & Verwiebe 2010; Heidenreich 2019) not only political representatives, but also individual European citizens play a key role in European integration processes – not only through their interactions and common understanding, but also through general support for or rejection of EU policies and the further integration process. Understanding the actions and attitudes of individual Europeans is thus crucial to explaining the successes as well as the failures of the European integration project (Teney et al. 2014). Furthermore, sociological research on Europe has shown that Europeanization produces winners and losers, with success depending on the degree to which an individual has gained access to the political and/or symbolic fields of action within Europe (Fligstein 2008; Haller 2008; Recchi and Favel 2009; Kuhn 2015; Heidenreich 2019).

Some Problems in Europeanization Studies and a Definition

As this brief excursion through the history of sociological research on Europe and European integration shows, scholarship in this field is now extremely diverse and rich in topics, methods, and research questions. However, the Sociology of Europeanization faces numerous challenges. First and foremost, when talking about the

Sociology of Europeanization, it is often unclear what scholars actually mean by 'Europe' and 'Europeanization'. Studies of 'Europeanization' mainly focus on processes related to the European Union as a core political frame. Without calling into question the empirical relevance of all social processes related to EU integration, it is worth noting that Europe is obviously more than the EU. The term 'Europeanization', therefore, should not only be used to denote processes happening within the EU. However, it is equally problematic if we extend it to include processes that take place within the European continent, in a geographical sense. Post-colonialist studies in particular show that Europeanization targets extracontinental regions and societies – for example, the French overseas territories or international trade partners who adopt their procedures to European rules (see Chapter 5). Hence, the first central question is: What exactly do we mean when we talk of Europeanization? What constitutes the 'European' aspect of our analyses, and how does the term Europeanization differ from transnationalization or comparative internationalism?

The second problematic aspect of such scholarship concerns the overwhelming centrality of the EU integration process and its consequences as a topic within the broad field of Europeanization research. While EU member states' political and economic integration into the EU can be seen as driving forces of societal change in those states, this strongly integration-oriented focus prevents Europeanization scholars working from focusing on other core issues, such as the causes and effects of conflicts, contestation, and crises. In most studies on Europeanization, integration processes are described in rather positive terms (or at least as something that moves on and further); by contrast, crises and conflicts are given a *disintegrative connotation* and portrayed as breaks or ruptures in an otherwise more or less linear process of development towards an ever-closer union. Sociology, however, has a great potential to identify and analyze conflicting or contradictory aspects of Europeanization and uncover their consequences (Vobruba 2017). As a feature of Europeanization, such ambivalence underlines the unpredictable, chaotic, and contingent nature of social change processes. This contingency and ambivalence requires its own and genuinely sociological perspective (Worschech 2018).

Third, but not less importantly, although Europeanization is often interpreted as a process of harmonization involving the adaptation of institutional arrangements, rules, and procedures, it is equally important to recognize Europeanization as the making of Europe through interactions, networks, and shared understandings between individuals. Europeanization *from below* or 'horizontal Europeanization' describes an approach that sheds light on these community-based processes, which are often rooted in direct interaction. It can be argued that institutional alignment and integration such as freedom of movement within the EU is a relevant precondition for these processes that constitute the emergence of new societal entanglements based on interpersonal linkages in and beyond Europe.

With these three factors in mind, we propose that 'Europeanization' can be seen as a multiplicity of simultaneous structural, cognitive, and relational mechanisms of social change which link the national or sub-national to the trans- or supranational level of European societies (see also: Worschech 2018, 64). Accordingly, analyzing Europeanization necessarily involves analyzing processes and mechanisms of social change that may have transnational roots, courses, and consequences. Going back to the three research categories introduced earlier in this chapter, those underlying mechanisms may be structural (*institutional*), cognitive (*interpretative*) or relational (*interactive*). Together, they form the core of empirical observation and theoretical reflection on the subject.

With its focus on social processes and dynamics from a micro- to a macro-level, and interest in the *making* of Europe – be it in the everyday life of citizens, societal movements and processes or rituals and styles among elite members of society – sociology has much to offer to European studies. Following the sociological classics Weber, Simmel, and Durkheim, we can interpret sociological conceptions of social phenomena as constructed via interaction, interpretation, and institutionalization.

The Sociology of Europeanization also holds out a key advantage to sociology itself. Studies of transnationalism are a relevant, although not a core issue of sociology today. Criticism of methodological nationalist approaches has already helped to shift the focus of much sociological inquiry beyond borders, and border studies themselves have flourished in recent years. However, because of the inherently ambivalent, conflictual, or contradictory character of Europeanization as a fluid, contentious and often violent negotiation of societal past and futures in Europe, the Sociology of Europeanization provides a particular frame for the causes and effects of transnational sociation (Beichelt et al. 2019, 5; Beichelt et al. 2021). Europeanization processes are complex, non-linear, ambivalent, and even contradictory; they can both cause and be caused by crises, conflicts, and ambivalence. This very ambivalence tends to direct the attention of the sociologists who study Europeanization towards conflictive transnational sociation processes in and beyond Europe.

Final Remarks and Brief Outlook to the Content of this Book

As we hope to have shown in this chapter, there is not *one* Sociology of Europeanization, but rather a range of questions and perspectives arising from researchers' differing theoretical and methodological points of anchorage within the discipline. The kinds of questions and perspectives that any given study will cover is partly a function of its theoretical orientation – whether it draws on the ideas of Marx, Weber, Durkheim, Bourdieu, or other thinkers. The same can be said of methodology: here again, we find quite significant diversity and a multitude of methodological paradigms and methods, depending on the specific objects of research. In all cases, however, the following applies: everything is useful that helps to explain the process of Europeanization. Thus, in this introductory volume we have sought to represent the great diversity that underpins European sociology and tried to leave space for a variety of theoretical and methodological approaches. – Following an introductory section that outlines the various theoretical strands of European sociological research and its methodological traditions (Chapter 2), this volume is structured along three core questions:

The *first question* asks how Europe is characterized in terms of space, territories, and borders, including the question of what Europe actually *is* in geographical, cultural, and social terms – that is, where it starts and where it ends. This is by no means a trivial question, but one that goes to the heart of European studies. After all, the EU is still far from being a clearly defined, socio-political ruling body with clearly demarcated political, social, and economic boundaries; due to the EU's particular political and social configuration, its external borders are still more blurred than those of the classical nation state. This is evidenced, above all, in the "concentric border structures" (Bös 2000: 438) that have risen in different degrees of integration within the EU and the EU's specific forms of association with non-EU countries (Vobruba 2007). – The question of *finalité*, however, goes beyond merely expanding the EU's integration and membership area. The way we define the EU borders, and the nature of these borders, depend on what kind of union we wish to be, and the shape that we want it to take in the first place. Thus, it is not only the geographical concept of Europe that is still fuzzy; our very definition of Europe remains vague in other respects. Speaking of a society in view of this indeterminate entity remains difficult.

In the post-national space of a politically unified Europe, the clarity of national reference systems is replaced by the ambiguity of different membership spaces and still negotiable territorial spaces (Bös 2000). Thus, the spatial binding of collective identities (Bach 2008), which could only take shape through the invention of the nation, is now beginning to falter. But are these spatial bonds – the coming together of the territorial, the political, and the social – now being erased without replacement in the post-national era, or will they be transformed? And if so, how and to what end will they change? These are the essential questions that are addressed in Part II of this volume, especially in Chapter 3 (space) and in Chapter 4 (culture). It also points towards post- and decolonial perspectives on Europeanization and the necessity to focus on the global and historical context when looking at Europe and Europeanization (Chapter 5). Finally, a look at transformations studies reflects more recent historical developments of Europeanization in the European 'peripheries'. (Chapter 6).

A *second question* addressed in this volume concerns how Europe is manifested in economy, law, and politics and what a specific sociological perspective on the Europeanization of these fields should look like (Part III). For a long time, European integration was understood exclusively as a political and economic process that is implemented and driven forward by law; hence, the perspective of the national societies that are directly affected by these changes was ignored. This situation only changed after it became clear that support for the European integration process among some parts of those populations had begun to wane. Thus, sociological work on the Europeanization of economy (Chapter 7), law (Chapter 8), and politics (Chapter 9) – core fields of European integration – has two sides: On the one hand, it emphasizes the societal implications of integration; on the other, it uses an expanded actor concept to develop a completely new approach to those fields.

The societal effects of these Europeanization processes – in terms of social policy and solidarity (Chapter 10), the social structure of the European societies (Chapter 11), migration and mobility (Chapter 12) – presented in Part IV underpin the volume's *third research question*. Europeanization is reflected in these key fields and topics as a new trans- and supranational social order that arose with the EU more than half a century ago and continues to have a lasting impact on how we live in Europe. This applies to questions of mobility as well as to questions of social security and social cohesion alike.

The final part of this volume (Part V) addresses recent developments within European society – increasing Euroscepticism (Chapter 13), the emergence of a European civil society and European social movements (Chapter 14) – and the microsocial processes of Europeanization. This view is fundamental to a holistic understanding of the processes of Europeanization, and an essential feature of sociological research on Europe.

Of course, the individual contributions stand on their own and can be discussed in different sequences within the context of a course. To facilitate classroom discussion of the issues and questions that may arise in connection with the

Sociology of Europeanization, we recommend consulting the didactical sections at the end of each chapter, in some chapters you can even find questions for further reflections. We hope that this introduction to sociological European studies will not only prove useful to our readers, but also that it will inspire them to adopt a sociological perspective on the core issues presented in this volume.

Didactical Section

Key Learning Points

- The Sociology of Europeanization has its own developmental history. It emerged during the 1990s and by 2000 as a sub-discipline of general and political sociology, and it has its own place within the larger field of European studies.
- In contrast to political, juridical, and economic approaches the Sociology of Europeanization focuses less on specific aspects and outcomes of European integration and on the numerous facets and implications of EU politics, but on the broader sociological and societal implications of the project of European integration. This essentially implies considering and exploring the construction, dissemination, and institutionalization of both formal and informal norms, institutions, and lifestyles at different levels of society.
- Two major perspectives dominate research endeavors of the Sociology of Europeanization: Firstly, comparative perspectives in terms of comparing of social structures and phenomena in a European or European-wide social context. Secondly, generic transnational (European) approaches focusing on newly emerging social structures, social practices, and institutions resulting from ongoing and far-reaching Europeanization. This does not mean that 'Europeanization' is only conceptualized in teleological way as a one-directional path, but this only entails exploring disintegrative tendencies, the emergence of new conflicts, cleavages, and counter-movements.
- We propose in this introduction that the Sociology of Europeanization mainly focuses on three major elements or dimensions of sociological analysis: *institutions*, *interaction*, and *interpretation*. All three of these factors can be approached from either a comparative or a transnational perspective.
- Drawing on Worschech (2018) we propose to see 'Europeanization' as a multiplicity of simultaneous structural, cognitive, and relational mechanisms of social change which link the national or sub-national to the trans- or supranational level of European societies.

Further Readings

Haas, E. B., 1958: *The Uniting of Europe: Political, Social, and Economic Forces 1950–1957.* Stanford: Stanford University Press.
Davies, N., 1998: *Europe: A history.* New York: Harper Perennial.

Delanty, G. & C. Rumford, 2005: *Rethinking Europe. Social Theory and the Implications of Europeanization*. London: Routledge.

Beck, U. & E. Grande, 2007: *Cosmopolitan Europe*. Cambridge: Polity.

Haller, M., 2008: *European Integration as an Elite Process. The Failure of a Dream?* London: Routledge.

Fligstein, N., 2008: *Euroclash: The EU, European identity, and the future of Europe*. Oxford University Press.

Roche, M., 2009: *Exploring the Sociology of Europe. An Analysis of the European Social Complex*. London: Sage.

Rumford, C. (ed.), 2009: *The SAGE Handbook of European Studies*. London: Sage.

Favell, A. & V. Guiraudon (eds.), 2011: *Sociology of the European Union*. Basingstoke: Macmillan.

Koniordos, S. & A. Kyrtsis (eds.), 2014: *Routledge Handbook of European Sociology*. London: Routledge.

Bigo, D., T. Diez, E. Fanoulis, B. Rosamond & Y. A. Stivachtis (eds.), 2020: *The Routledge Handbook of Critical European Studies*. London: Routledge.

Additional Web-Sources

Brief overview of the history of European integration: https://europa.eu/european-union/about-eu/history_en

Information about the Council of Europe, an intergovernmental organization that is NOT part of the European Union, but stands at the beginning of European integration in post-war Europe: https://www.coe.int/en/web/about-us/

The European Union in brief: https://europa.eu/european-union/about-eu/eu-in-brief_en

Institutions and bodies of the European Union: https://europa.eu/european-union/about-eu/institutions-bodies_en

Webpage of the European Commission, where you can find information on all policy areas and executive bodies of the Commission: https://ec.europa.eu/info/index_en

Overview of all European treaties that were relevant during the history of European integration: https://europa.eu/european-union/law/treaties_en

Webpage of the Council for European Studies, a major academic organization dedicated to European studies hosted at Columbia University, New York (USA): https://councilforeuropeanstudies.org/

Digital library of research in European Studies: https://www.cvce.eu/en

European history primary sources: http://primary-sources.eui.eu/

References

Bach, M., 1999: *Die Bürokratisierung Europas: Verwaltungseliten, Experten und politische Legitimation in Europa, vol. 751*. Campus Verlag.

Bach, M., 2008: *Europa ohne Gesellschaft. Politische Soziologie der Europäischen Integration*. Wiesbaden: Springer VS Verlag für Sozialwissenschaften.

Bartolini, S., 2005: *Restructuring Europe: Centre Formation, System Building, and Political Structuring between the Nation State and the European Union.* Oxford: Oxford University Press.

Beck, U. & E. Grande, 2007: *Cosmopolitan Europe.* Cambridge: Polity.

Beichelt, T., C. M. Frysztacka, C. Weber & S. Worschech, 2019: Ambivalences of Europeanization: Modernity and European Integration in Perspective. *IFES Working Paper Series* 1/2019.

Beichelt, T., C. M. Frysztacka, C. Weber & S. Worschech (eds.), 2021: *Ambivalenzen Der Europäisierung.* Stuttgart: Franz Steiner Verlag.

Bernhard, S., 2010: From conflict to consensus: European neoliberalism and the debate on the future of EU social policy. *Work Organisation, Labour and Globalisation* 4(1):175–192.

Boatcă, M., 2006: Semiperipheries in the World-System: Reflecting Eastern European and Latin American experiences. *Journal of World Systems Research* 12(2):321–346.

Boltanski, L. & L. Thévenot, 2006: *On justification: Economies of Worth.* Princeton, NJ: Princeton University Press.

Bourdieu, P., 1998: *The State Nobility: Elite Schools in the Field of Power.* Stanford: Stanford University Press.

Bourdieu, P., 2015: *On the State: Lectures at the College de France 1989–1992.* Cambridge: Polity.

Börner, S., 2013: *Belonging, Solidarity and Expansion in Social Policy.* Palgrave Macmillan.

Börner, S. & M. Eigmüller, 2015: *European Integration, Processes of Change and the National Experience.* London: Palgrave Macmillan.

Börzel, T. A. & T. Risse, 2003: Conceptualizing the Domestic Impact of Europe. In: Featherstone, K. & C. M. Radaelli (eds.), *The Politics of Europeanization*, pp. 57–80. Oxford: Oxford University Press.

Bös, M, 2000: Zur Kongruenz sozialer Grenzen. Das Spannungsfeld von Territorien, Bevölkerungen und Kulturen in Europa. In: Bach, M. (Ed.): *Die Europäisierung nationaler Gesellschaften.* Kölner Zeitschrift für Soziologie und Sozialpsychologie, Sonderheft 40, pp. 429–455. Wiesbaden: Westdeutscher Verlag.

Büttner, S., 2012: *Mobilizing Regions, Mobilizing Europe: Expert Knowledge and Scientific Planning in European Regional Development.* London: Routledge.

Büttner, S., L. Leopold, S. Mau & M. Posvic, 2015: Professionalization in EU Policy-Making? The topology of the transnational field of EU affairs. *European Societies* 17(4):569–592. https://www.tandfonline.com/doi/abs/10.1080/14616696.2015.1072229.

Ciornei, I. & E. Recchi, 2017: At the source of European solidarity: assessing the effects of cross-border practices and political attitudes. *JCMS: Journal of Common Market Studies* 55(3):468–485.

Crouch, C. & W. Streeck (eds.), 2006: *The diversity of democracy: corporatism, social order and political conflict.* Edward Elgar Publishing.

Delanty, G. & C. Rumford (2005): *Rethinking Europe. Social Theory and the Implications of Europeanization.* London: Routledge.

Della Porta, D. & M. Caiani, 2009: *Social movements and Europeanization.* Oxford University Press.

Della Porta, D., H. Kriesi & D. Rucht (eds.), 1999: *Social Movements in a Globalising World.* London: Palgrave Macmillan.

Deutsch, K. W., S. A. Burrell, R. A. Kann, M. Lee Jr., M. Lichterman, R. E. Lindgren, F. L. Loewenheim & R. W. Van Wagenen, 1957: *Political Community and the North Atlantic Area.* Princeton: Princeton University Press.

Diez Medrano, J., 2003: *Framing Europe: Attitudes to European Integration in Germany, Spain, and the United Kingdom*. Princeton University Press.

Durkheim, É., [1893] 1960: *The Division of Labor in Society*. Glencoe, IL: The Free Press.

Eder, K., 2006: Europe's borders: The narrative construction of the boundaries of Europe. *European Journal of Social Theory* 9(2):255–271.

Eigmüller, M., 2021: *Sozialraum Europa. Der Einfluss der europäischen Bürgerinnen und Bürger auf die Entwicklung einer EU-Sozialpolitik*. Wiesbaden: VS-Verlag.

Eigmüller, M. & S. Mau, 2010: Gesellschaftstheorie und Europapolitik. Eine Einleitung. In: Eigmüller, M. & S. Mau (eds.), *Gesellschaftstheorie Und Europapolitik: Sozialwissenschaftliche Ansätze Zur Europaforschung*, pp. 9–29. Wiesbaden: VS Verlag für Sozialwissenschaften.

Elias, N., [1939] 2000: *The Civilizing Process: Sociogenetic and Psychogenetic Investigations*. Wiley-Blackwell, 2nd edition.

Esping-Andersen, G., 1990: *The Three Worlds of Welfare Capitalism*. Princeton, NJ: Princeton University Press.

Favell, A., 2008: *Eurostars and Eurocities: Free Movement and Mobility in an Integrating Europe*. Oxford: Blackwell Publishing.

Favell, A. & V. Guiraudon (eds.), 2011: *Sociology of the European Union*. Macmillan International Higher Education.

Featherstone, K. & C. M. Radaelli (eds.), 2003: *The Politics of Europeanization*. Oxford: Oxford University Press.

Fligstein, N., 2000: The Process of Europeanization. *Politique européenne* 1(1):25–42.

Fligstein, N., 2008: *Euroclash: The EU, European identity, and the future of Europe*. Oxford University Press.

Fligstein, N. & A. Stone Sweet, 2002: Constructing polities and markets: An institutionalist account of European integration. *American Journal of Sociology* 107(5):1206–1243.

Georgakakis, D. & J. Weisbein, 2010: From above and from below: A political sociology of European actors. *Comparative European Politics* 8:93–109.

Georgakakis, D. & J. Rowell (eds.), 2013: *The Field of Eurocracy: Mapping EU Actors and Professionals*. Basingstoke, UK: Palgrave.

Gerhards, J., 2001: Missing a European public sphere. In: Kohli, M. & M. Novak (eds.), *Will Europe Work?* pp. 159–172. Routledge.

Gerhards, J., H. Lengfeld, Z. S. Ignácz, F. K. Kley & M. Priem, 2019: *European Solidarity in Times of Crisis: Insights from a thirteen-country survey*. Routledge.

Haas, E. B., 1958: *The Uniting of Europe: Political, Social, and Economic Forces 1950–1957*. Stanford: Stanford University Press.

Hall, P. A. & D. Soskice, 2001: *Varieties of Capitalism: The Institutional Foundations of Comparative Advantage*. Oxford University Press.

Haller, M., 2008: *European Integration as an Elite Process. The Failure of a Dream?* London: Routledge.

Heidenreich, M. (ed.), 2006: *Die Europäisierung sozialer Ungleichheit: Zur transnationalen Klassen- und Sozialstrukturanalyse*. Frankfurt a.M.: Campus.

Heidenreich, M. (ed.), 2019: *Horizontal Europeanisation: The Transnationalisation of Daily Life and Social Fields in Europe*. Abingdon, Oxford and New York, NY: Routledge.

Hix, S., 2008: *What's Wrong with the Europe Union and How to Fix It*. Cambridge and Malden, MA: Polity Press.

Hooghe, L. & G. Marks, 2008: European Union? *West European Politics* 31(1/2):108–129.

Kauppi, N., 2003: Bourdieu's political sociology and the politics of European integration. *Theory and Society* 32:775–789.

Koopmans, R. & P. Statham (eds.), 2010: *The making of a European public sphere: Media discourse and political contention.* Cambridge University Press.

Kuhn, T., 2015: *Experiencing European integration: Transnational lives and European identity.* Oxford: Oxford University Press.

Lahusen, C., M. Kousis, U. Zschache & A. Loukakis, 2018: European solidarity in times of crisis: Comparing transnational activism of civic organisations in Germany and Greece. *Österreichische Zeitschrift für Soziologie* 43(1):173–197.

Le Galès, P., 2002: European Cities: Social Conflicts and Governance. Oxford: Oxford University Press.

Lepsius, M. R., 1992: Beyond the Nation-State: The Multinational State as the Model for the European Community. *Telos* 1992(91):57–76.

Lepsius, M. R., 2006: The ability of a European Constitution to forge a European identity. In: Blanke, H. J. & S. Mangiameli (eds.), *Governing Europe under a Constitution*, pp. 23–35. Berlin and Heidelberg: Springer.

Lipset, S. M., 1959: Some Social Requisites of Democracy: Economic Development and Political Legitimacy. *The American Political Science Review* 53(1):69–105.

Marks, G. & C. J. Wilson, 2000: The past in the present: A cleavage theory of party response to European integration. *British Journal of Political Science* 30(3):433–459.

Mau, S. & R. Verwiebe, 2010: *European Societies: Mapping Structure and Change.* Bristol, The Policy Press.

McNamara, K. R., 2010: Constructing Europe: Insights from historical sociology. *Comparative European Politics* 8(1):127–142.

Mérand, F., 2008: European Defence Policy: Beyond the Nation State. Oxford: Oxford University Press.

Moravcsik, A., 2006: What can we learn from the collapse of the European constitutional project? *Politische Vierteljahresschrift* 47:219–241.

Münch, R., 1993: *Das Projekt Europa: Zwischen Nationalstaat, regionaler Autonomie und Weltgesellschaft.* Frankfurt a.M.: Suhrkamp.

Münch, R., 2016: *The global division of labour: development and inequality in world society.* Springer.

Münch, R. & S. Büttner, 2006: Die europäische Teilung der Arbeit. Was können wir von Emile Durkheim lernen? In: Heidenreich, M. (ed.), *Die Europäisierung sozialer Ungleichheit: zur transnationalen Klassen- und Sozialstrukturanalyse*, pp. 65–107. Frankfurt a.M.: Campus.

Radaelli, C. M., 2003: The Europeanization of Public Policy. In: Featherstone K. & C. M. Radaelli (eds.), *The Politics of Europeanization*, pp. 27–56. Oxford: Oxford University Press.

Recchi, E. & A. Favell (eds.), 2009: *Pioneers of European integration: Citizenship and mobility in the EU.* Edward Elgar Publishing.

Rokkan, S., 1999: *State Formation, Nation-Building, and Mass Politics in Europe: The Theory of Stein Rokkan.* Edited by Peter Flora. Oxford: Oxford University Press.

Saurugger, S. & F. Mérand, 2010: Does European integration theory need sociology? *Comparative European Politics* 8(1):1–18.

Scharpf, F. W., 2003: Problem-solving effectiveness and democratic accountability in the EU. *MPIfG working paper* No.03/1.

Schmidt-Wellenburg, C., 2017: Europeanisation, stateness, and professions: What role do economic expertise and economic experts play in European political integration? *European Journal of Cultural and Political Sociology* 4(4):430–456.

Skocpol, T., 1992: State formation and social policy in the United States. *American Behavioral Scientist* 35(4/5):559–584.

Streeck, W. & K. Thelen, 2009: Institutional change in advanced political economies. In: Hancké, B. (ed.), *Debating varieties of capitalism: A reader*, pp. 95–131. Oxford University Press.

Teney, C., O. P. Lacewell & P. De Wilde, 2014: Winners and losers of globalization in Europe: attitudes and ideologies. *European Political Science Review* 6(4):575–595.

Tilly, C., 1992: *Coercion, Capital and European States, A.D. 990–1992*. Cambridge, MA: Basil Blackwell.

Trenz, H. J., 2005: The European public sphere: contradictory findings in a diverse research field. *European Political Science* 4(4):407–420.

Vink, M., 2003: What Is Europeanisation? And Other Questions on a New Research Agenda. *European Political Science* 3(1):63–74.

Vobruba, G., 2007: *Die Dynamik Europas*. Wiesbaden: VS Verlag für Sozialwissenschaften.

Vobruba, G., 2008: Die Entwicklung der Europasoziologie aus der Differenz national/europäisch. *Berliner Journal für Soziologie* 18:32–51.

Vobruba, G., 2017: *Krisendiskurs. Die nächste Zukunft Europas*. Weinheim, Basel: Beltz-Juventa.

Weber, M. & W. V. Heydebrand, 1999: *Sociological Writings. The German library v. 60*. New York: Continuum.

Wobbe, T., 2009: Vom nation-building zum market-building. Der Wandel von Vergesellschaftungsformen im europäischen Integrationsprozess. *Mittelweg 36*, Heft 3 Juni/Juli 2009:3–16.

Worschech, S., 2018: The 'Making' of Europe in the Peripheries: Europeanization Through Conflicts and Ambivalences. *Culture, Practice, and Europeanization* 3(3):56–76. https://www.uni-flensburg.de/fileadmin/content/seminare/soziologie/dokumente/culture-practice-and-europeanization/cpe-vol.3-no.3-2018/worschech-2018.pdf (accessed July 15, 2021).

Hans-Jörg Trenz

2 Outline of a Sociology of Europeanization

Europeanization is a widely used term across disciplines in the description of processes of Europe's social and political integration. In their overview article, Exadaktylos and Radaelli (2015: 206) distinguish three different meanings: Europeanization as *project*, Europeanization as *process* and Europeanization as *outcome* or as *effect*. In its most generic use, Europeanization refers to the long history of the expansion of Europe: the mutual interdependencies of European culture, politics and society and the impact of European civilization on other parts of the world (Delanty 1995; Stråth 2002; Beck & Grande 2007; Kaschuba 2008). The project of Europeanization is seen here as overlapping or largely identical to the project of European modernity (Passerin D'Entrèves & Benhabib 1996). Political science has made key contributions in narrowing down the notion of Europeanization to the study of European integration and its effects on member states (Bache 2008; Börzel & Risse 2011; Radaelli 2004). Political scientists agree to use Europeanization as a relational term to describe an institutionally confined process of change (such as the process of implementing an EU regulation). This can apply to:

a) case-specific cause and effect relationships within an emerging common market and a system of regulatory governance, for instance the domestic impact of EU regulation on national law and policy making (Börzel & Risse 2006; Haverland 2006).

b) linear processes of adaption of (sub)national level units to common rules and standards, usually graded in terms of more or less Europeanization or accelerated Europeanization of particular policy fields or whole sectors over time (Heritier 2007), for instance, by sustaining that the field of agricultural policy is highly Europeanized whereas degrees of Europeanization within the field of cultural policies are still low.

c) specific outcomes (such as a harmonized policy or the application of an EU rule at (sub) national level) or effects of European integration such as Europeanized forms of behavior or identities (Checkel & Katzenstein 2009; Risse 2014).

How does a sociology of Europeanization position itself in light of these varied usages of the term? The answer is that no genuine sociological tradition to the study of Europeanization is readily available. Europeanization is not linked to any particular theory but instead gives rise to an empirical research agenda with a broad field of application. Through empirical insights and studies, sociologists

https://doi.org/10.1515/9783110673630-002

have contributed to both our generic understanding of Europeanization as the process of creating new social arenas for regular, intensified, and institutionalized interactions among actors (states, organizations, firms, and individuals) and to all its specific subfields of understanding process, institutional change, mechanisms, and impact/effects (Fligstein 2000). Even though there is no precise sociological usage of the term, sociology can nevertheless be useful as a discipline that can reflect on the various usages of the term Europeanization and their underlying narratives (Trenz 2016). Broadly speaking, sociologists would not only analyse exchanges within a regulatory state or multi-level governance system but also changes in state-society relationships. Europeanization is therefore useful as a term that shows the ways in which the EU relates back to pre-existing national societies and/or might even trigger a process of European society building (Delanty 1998; Delanty & Rumford 2005; Beck & Grande 2007; Fligstein 2008; Münch 2010; Heidenreich 2019). The purpose of this chapter is to elaborate a comprehensive theoretical understanding of Europeanization in terms of both polity and society building. Europeanization thus comprises social and political changes at national or subnational level as triggered by EU policymaking (the pushing factors of European integration) and opportunities and constraints for EU institution-building and governance as driven by political mobilizations, societal demands, and expectations (the pulling factors of European integration). As shown in Table 2.1, a range of theoretical toolkits are available within the disciplinary tradition of sociology for the development of a more nuanced understanding of this nexus between supranational European integration, domestic change and societal transformation in a combination of macro, meso and micro models of social analysis (Trenz 2011).

Table 2.1: Sociological approaches to Europeanization.

macro	meso	micro
The interlinkage between market integration, political integration, and social integration	Processes of intermediation between the supranational, national, and subnational arena	Transformations of people's lifeworlds and every-day practices
System building and structural configurations	Vertical and horizontal exchanges	individual and collective preference building, identity, and agency formation
Delanty & Rumford 2005; Fligstein 2008	Mau & Verwiebe 2010; Recchi and Favell 2019	Delhey et al. 2014; Favell et al. 2014; Scalise 2015

Theoretical Perspectives

A sociology of Europeanization, broadly speaking, does not consider the processes of legal, political, economic, and social Europeanization in relative isolation from each other, but instead contributes to our generic understanding of the context, conditions, mechanisms and effects of Europeanization across these different arenas (Fligstein 2000). This raises the question of the *why*, *what*, and *how* of Europeanization (Olsen 2002).

Why Europeanization?

Why do we need a new research agenda of Europeanization that is distinct from the existing study of European integration? Sociologists typically justify their engagement in studies of Europeanization through the limited explanatory power of political science approaches that specialize in the study of EU bureaucracy and multi-level governance. EU integration studies are based on institutional analyses of EU policy actors and policymaking, yet they rarely take into consideration the variety of social responses and knock-on effects at member state level. Europeanization studies are therefore necessary in order to highlight the broader implications of European integration on other sectors of social life, such as culture, education, family or everyday life (Favell & Guiraudon 2009).

Europeanization studies are also distinct from EU integration studies in that they question the assumption of a linear and necessary development of the European Union towards 'deeper integration'. EU integration theory not only asked why states integrate, but also provided well-developed arguments on a regular basis as to why they *should* integrate (Dobson 2006; Wiener & Diez 2004). Therefore, many sociologists have preferred the more dynamic concept of Europeanization over the conventional and normatively loaded term of European integration (Delanty & Rumford 2005: 6). They would instead pose the question: Why do societies converge or diverge within the geographical and political space of Europe? And which factors or mechanisms drive these processes of exchange, adaptation and diffusion (Olsen 2007)?

Europeanization of What?

To approach 'Europeanization' we require a reference point. The second question to be addressed by sociologists is therefore the *Europeanization of what*? The typical answer refers to national or subnational units as objects (or subjects) of Europeanization. The process of Europeanization applies to nation states and national societies that undergo a specific transformation in adaptation to European rules, norms, and standards. If sociologists promote the study of Europeanization outside the context of formally established EU politics, this should therefore not mean sidestepping or disregarding the political dimension of the issue. Both within and beyond the borders of the EU, contemporary Europe is a politically constructed space and its internal and external dynamics of exchange are shaped by power and conflicts (Delanty & Rumford 2005; Olsen 2007). Processes of Europeanization unfold in symbiosis with political integration and are confined in their relationship to Europe's nascent political order, the various opportunities related to it (such as mobility, free movement, and common market exchanges), and the collective experiences and interpretations of the Europeans living under a shared authority. In processes of Europeanization, EU institutions of governance (*polity*) interact with multiple layers of society (*constituency*) (Fossum & Trenz 2006). As the *what* of Europeanization, these layers can be variably addressed by research as citizens, civil society, stakeholders, social interest groups or business and corporations. However, it is rare that societal groups are merely passive recipients taking a subordinate role or simply bowing to EU authority. The 'objects' and 'subjects' of Europeanization are also responsive; they raise their voices, and their voices are heard, thus shaping the emerging European social and political order in several meaningful ways (Imig & Tarrow 2001; Ruzza 2004; Trenz et al. 2015). Strictly speaking, the 'what' of Europeanization therefore refers to the dynamic interlinking between multi-level polity and society building, not to be understood in a linear way or as a one-directional exchange but as a structured coupling between state (political institutions) and society. Enhanced and intensified Europeanization would result from the mutual reinforcement of these state-society relationships, while differentiations or rollbacks would result from opposition or resistance. It is then not too far-fetched to say that Europeanization research focuses on the interrelated processes of EU state and society building. To a degree, a sociology of Europeanization is thus always political, approaching the question of social order through the lens of the political (Favell & Guiraudon 2009; Guiraudon et al. 2015; Kauppi 2014).

Responses to the question of the 'what' of Europeanization further refer to its vertical or horizontal, and internal and external dimensions. Within EU studies, the focus was on the expansion of markets and regulation, and the subsequent repercussions for lower-level entities. Therefore, the 'what' of Europeanization mainly comprised the vertical exchanges within a market and a multi-level polity. This agenda has been expanded upon by cultural sociologists, media and communications scholars, migration and mobility scholars and ethnologists, all of whom emphasize the importance of horizontal exchanges triggered by

European integration, such as the exchange of goods, media information and culture, but also of people moving across borders (Recchi & Favell 2009; Recchi & Favell 2019). A key differentiation is further introduced by distinguishing between the internal and external dimensions of Europeanization. In a multi-level governance system Europeanization can be internal (in the form of the direct impact of EU law and policies on member states, for instance) or external (the effects of the EU on non-member states) (Lavenex 2007). The external dimension of Europeanization has been investigated from multiple perspectives. From a political economy perspective, the emphasis is placed on the structuring of new inequalities as an effect of free exchange in neoliberal markets and its impact on the transformation of welfare states, social and public policies or on education (Bologna Process) in Europe and beyond (Dale & Robertson 2009; Hay & Wincott 2012). From a postcolonial perspective, the perceived imposition of Europe as a form of political and cultural domination with exclusionary effects on what is defined as the non-European 'other' is elaborated upon (Bhambra 2009). From a world society perspective, Europeanization is conceptualized as one of several forms of regional integration within a global context (Rumford & Buhari-Gulmez 2016; see also Chapter 5 in this volume).

How does Europeanization Unfold?

Various processes of Europeanization at member state level do not simply occur in terms of states developing their own distinct patterns of responses; such responses are meaningfully related to each other. The common perception of Europeanization as a process of directional and accelerated social change has been stated previously in this article. Therefore, models that explain *how* Europeanization unfolds are often based on mechanisms as pathways towards specific outcomes. Such mechanisms of Europeanization identified in the literature range from coercion, learning, adaptation, or diffusion (Auel & Benz 2005; Börzel & Risse 2011; Exadaktylos & Radaelli 2015; Knill & Lehmkuhl 2002). They are distinguished in terms of conditionality, making either a strong or weak causality assumption. The primary method employed to test such mechanisms is process-tracing; identifying chains of events or recurrent effects over time (Moumoutzis & Zartaloudis 2016). Technically speaking, Europeanization is standardization, which in turn leads to convergence, causing European societies to become more similar. Europeanization is further seen as progressing and intensifying by imposing European standards, forms of behavior, rules, and norms over time.

Apart from such harmonizing processes, more recent theoretical approaches have emphasized how Europeanization can also lead to internal differentiation and, as such, is manifested in new heterogeneous practices that give rise to an increase in diversity. In legal-political terms, the relationship between the supranational delegation of authority and the differentiated impact of integration on national and subnational units has been analyzed (Bátora & Fossum 2019; Gänzle et al. 2019). In socio-cultural terms, the manifestations and expressions of 'European society' and 'European culture' measured against the persistence of national or local cultures have been explored (Heidenreich 2014; Münch 2010; Outhwaite 2013; see also Chapter 4 in this volume). The sociological challenge here is to theorize Europeanization as a form of social integration at a new level of abstraction and differentiation (Münch 2010: 233; Trenz 2011 & 2016).

In this sense, Europeanization need not be conceived in contrast to EU integration, but it does allow for the highlighting of particular processes in European integration through both harmonization and differentiation. The challenge faced by the EU over the last decade has been the development of Europeanization more in the form of differentiation both internally, concerning the EU's institutional set-up and contractual arrangement, and externally with regard to the EU's relations with the rest of the world (Fossum 2019). Differentiated Europeanization also triggers increasingly varied social responses, in terms of patterns of support and opposition, and overall increasing levels of conflict, which is commonly referred to as the 'politicization' of the EU (Statham & Trenz 2012).

The Drivers of Europeanization

Taking a closer look at the drivers of Europeanization identified in the literature, we can distinguish three main approaches: a) Europeanization as driven by collective action, b) Europeanization as driven by functional needs, and, c) Europeanization as norm-driven.

Collective Action

A first account is to say that Europeanization is driven by actors' strategies and interests. The American sociologists Neil Fligstein and Dough McAdam have formulated a general theory of strategic action fields that can be used to conceptualise the linkage between Europeanization and collective action (Fligstein & McAdam 2011). Action-driven Europeanization differs from state actor and government driven interest politics, as this has been framed within EU studies by the so called liberal-intergovernmentalist approach of European integration theory

(Moravcsik 1993). A strategic action field is an institutionalized form of collaboration involving a set of actors such as governments and EU institutions who meet regularly, build and exchange knowledge from within a range of common understandings on the goals of the field (such as EU agrarian policy), their relationships and obligations and the rules specified in the field (as established by EU law, but also other formal and informal conventions) (Fligstein & McAdam 2011: 3). The theory is thus aware of the limits and restrictions of rational choice and interest-driven behavior, acknowledging that collective action is always embedded in social structures and processes. Such a perspective of a so-called 'field' thus enables a recombining of agency and structure in an analysis of social process and change. Europeanization typically takes place within such strategic action fields for institutionalized and goal-oriented cooperation. Interactions within this field are not simply interest-driven, but are also shaped by socialization experiences, shared knowledge or norms on what are considered to be appropriate strategies, and norms to be followed (Fligstein 2008). At this juncture the actor-driven approach to Europeanization overlaps with institutional and normative accounts, as will be discussed below. In contrast to these other approaches, the emphasis here rests on the explanation of how Europeanization proceeds, due to the fact that actors engage with Europe and occupy a European field of strategic interaction to respond to opportunities offered by European integration or to achieve common goals (Marks & McAdam 1999). Striving to take advantage of the opportunities within the EU, these collective actors can engage in interest-driven collaboration, such as professional groups, market actors or economic experts (Georgakakis & Rowell 2013; Büttner et al. 2015; Schmidt-Wellenburg 2017), or in knowledge-driven cooperation, as with scientists (Amaral et al. 2009). At professional and civil society levels, European cooperation often takes the form of networks, such as the informal networks in transnational journalism that account for the dense collaboration within investigative journalism and a convergence of news coverage (Heft et al. 2019).

A further distinction in actor-driven approaches is drawn between vertical Europeanization, which can either be from above or below, and horizontal Europeanization. **Vertical Europeanization** from above views governments or EU elites as the main promoters of European standards, which are formulated in EU elite circles and then imposed from above, through the authority of EU regulation and law, or through soft modes of policy transfer (Radaelli 2004). In accounts of vertical Europeanization from below, a key role is played by civil society and social movements (Della Porta & Parks 2015). This is often reflected in more critical perspectives of European integration and the promotion of an agenda for an 'alternative Europe', such as the European social forums analysed by Della Porta (and colleagues) that gathered thousands of social movement organizations and activists in the early 2000s to promote 'another Europe' (Della Porta 2009). Lastly, **horizontal Europeanization** is regarded as being linked to the establishment of social fields of interconnectedness and interdependence between particular groups of actors who institutionalise specific forms of co-operation, such as specific professional groups including architecture, public administration or academia (Heidenreich 2019). Horizontal Europeanization can also be driven by individuals enacting their rights of EU citizenship; for instance, by making use of new opportunities for mobility in education or in their professional lives (Carlson et al. 2018; Favell 2008).

Functional Needs

A second account views Europeanization as being driven by the functional needs of markets, law, or intertwined societies. Functionalist explanations were originally developed as one of the main approaches of European integration theory. When Ernst Haas ([1958] 2004) theorized about the dynamics of European integration in the late 1950s, he expected integration to occur through *functional spill-over*; once a common market was established, the need to maintain and expand that market would trigger further integration. Neo-functionalism, as this early theoretical strand was labelled, is sociological in the sense that it assumes a link between economic, political, and social integration, and describes the social forces that determine societal change. It thus postulates the existence of endogenous social laws that promote the unity of Europe. The European economic community, as it was still called, did not simply follow a market logic; it also followed a social logic (Fligstein 2008).

If neo-functionalism was ideologically inspired by the federal thinking of Jean Monnet, it was intellectually inspired by the grand social theory of Talcott Parsons. In this sociological tradition, society is conceived as an internally differentiated and externally delimited social system. It is stabilized through the interchange between different sub-systems, each contributing to the maintenance of social order: the economic system through adaptation to the environment, the political system through goal attainment, the societal community through membership, and the cultural system through value attachment (Parsons 1967: 3ff.). The European Union is a social system to the extent that it provides services with regard to each of these sub-systems. Neo-functionalism could therefore postulate the emergence of a European society as a structured entity in line with national society. European society would evolve as a new layer in a federal model of social and political order.

In the classic definition by Ernst Haas, the concept of *integration* was used in this broad sense, comprising both political and social integration: "Political integration is the process whereby political actors in several distinct national settings are persuaded to shift their loyalties, expectations and political activities toward a new centre, whose institutions possess or demand jurisdiction over the pre-existing national states" (Haas [1958] 2004: 16). The optimism of early integration theorists referred to a societal perspective of European integration: "The end result of a process of political integration is a new political community, superimposing over the pre-existing ones." (Haas [1958] 2004: 16)

Norms and Understandings

Lastly, Europeanization can be viewed as being driven by shared norms and understandings concerning long-term goals, projects, and identity (Delanty & Rumford 2005). A 'normative turn' in the study of European integration was marked with the Single European Act of 1986, which set out the schedule for completing the common market with encompassing free trade arrangements, the free movement of workers and capital, and a monetary union (Bellamy & Castiglione 2000). These accelerated dynamics of integration had a deep normative impact on perceptions of the European project's legitimacy. Legitimacy could no longer be derived from the permissive consent of citizens, who profited from the outputs of the common market in terms of welfare and security (so-called 'output legitimacy'); it also had to be generated by providing specific inputs in the form of aggregating citizens' preferences and engaging them in political will formation (so-called 'input legitimacy') (Eriksen & Fossum 2000). In this sense the legitimacy base of the EU is not simply based on shared interests but on the normative foundations of shared European values (Foret & Calligaro 2018).

It is thus significant to note how Europeanization research emerged in response to this concern with the normative deficits of European integration. As shown by Barbara Hoenig, the use of Europeanization in sociology has always been linked to a critical agenda along specific pathways towards deeper integration (Hoenig 2019). For instance, standards for critical assessment of processes of Europeanization are found in the notion of a 'European social model' or the 'Europe of solidarity', in which the critical yardsticks are the reduction of social inequalities and regional disparities. In the same vein, a long tradition of criticism of the democratic deficits of the European Union can be found, and Europeanization is assessed as part of the 'unfinished democratization of the EU, for instance in its capacities to re-couple EU level decision-making with practices of national and supranational democracy (Eriksen 2009).

Sociological research can contribute to shedding light on the ideational power of Europeanization as related to a specific European set of norms and values that simultaneously claim universal validity (Delanty 2009). The transfer of norms and worldviews is not simply linked to the mobilization efforts of specific actors, but often takes place through what has been labelled 'discursive Europeanization' and can be measured through the spread of discourse, popular culture and identities (Motschenbacher 2017; Schmidt 2009). Examples of the spread of European worldviews through discourse are the promotion of gender equality policies (Lombardo & Forest 2015; Seibicke 2019) or the EU's vocation as a 'normative power' in its external relations (Manners 2008). From a long-term historical perspective, Europeanization as 'democratic norm setting' can also provide a retrospective explanation for the progressive democratization of post-war Europe and the democratic transition of countries such as Greece, Spain and Portugal in the seventies and eighties and Central and Eastern Europe in the nineties and early 2000s (Schimmelfennig & Sedelmeier 2005; Schmidt 2006).

In response to such a normative project, Europeanization is sometimes described as a hegemonic strategy to supplant competing projects and impose no-alternative choices (Bulmer 1993). However, it is part of the European self-understanding that notwithstanding these historical processes of Europeanization as value consensus and convergence, the core set of European values must be kept within a pluralistic framework (Olsen 2019). In other words, there is an inbuilt mechanism of conflict in 'discursive Europeanization' through the competition of the validity of norms and their application in specific contests (Eigmüller & Trenz 2020). One more recently tested possibility in sociological research is, in fact, that the contentiousness of European integration has increased over time and that we are currently assisting a process of politicization of European integration that is aimed at reversing it (Grande & Hutter 2016; Statham & Trenz 2012). Furthermore, the politicization of the EU could, however, be seen as a further indicator of Europeanization that triggers resistance, polarizes public opinion and generates specific counter-discourses, for instance in the form of Euroscepticism (Guerra & Trenz 2019; see also Chapter 13 in this volume).

Europeanization of Everyday Life

A sociological research programme of Europeanization will show further interest in processes of European integration through institutions, programmes, norms, and rules, and the ways in which they shape citizens' daily lives as well as their relationships with each other. Europe is a new social context for common experiences, shared values, and dense interactions that enter the familiar context of the national. This is implied in the discussion of the Europeanization in the European free movement area; cross-border exchanges are no longer exclusive to migrants but encompass various practices of mobility, such as educational exchange, intermarriage, and travel, which involve a growing number of ordinary citizens in everyday trans-border activities (Mau et al. 2008). Along these lines, cross-border mobility and education have been analyzed as key dimensions of European social integration, which involve 'ordinary citizens' as movers within the common market (Recchi & Favell 2009; Mau 2010). The everyday reality of Europe is best represented by the EU regime of citizenship and free movement, which, in the words of Favell, Reimer and Solgaard Jensen (2014: 283), has become a "mass middle-class phenomenon". He observes how free movement has become part of Europeans' banal consumption through holidays, short-haul travel, knowledge of other places, and expanded networks of friendships. Everyday interactions and social relationships across borders are an example of Mau and Verwiebe's (2010: 303) description of 'horizontal Europeanization' (see also Chapter 12 in this volume). For instance, the infrastructure of horizontal Europeanization becomes tangible in the numerous transport projects that connect Europeans (such as the Øresund Bridge and the Channel Tunnel), the well-developed road and air traffic networks, the preferred hotspots of European tourism, and the transnational friendship and family networks (now more easily maintained through social media and other means of communication). Mau (2010) provides a socio-structural analysis of these emerging transnational social life worlds, based on Eurobarometer data, which posed the following questions: "In the last 12 months, have you visited another EU country?" and "In the last 12 months, have you socialized with people from another EU country?" He then identifies a mix of explanatory variables, based on social factors, which either strongly or slightly affect Europeanization: education, social class, age, gender, and citizenship are all positively correlated to the likelihood of having foreign social relationships. Structural factors such as size of the country of origin (people from Luxembourg are more likely to travel abroad than people from France), degree of modernization, and length of EU membership further help to explain differences in social transnationalism among European populations.

Building on Mau's survey, Favell et al. (2014) measure social transnationalism within the following dimensions: transnational travel and mobility, social relations (friends and family abroad), communication and consumerism, and human capital (knowledge of languages and watching foreign-language television). Their findings confirm that the everyday reality of horizontal Europeanization is not restricted to certain privileged countries or strata of the population, but can also be found at a high scale and intensity, providing evidence of a broader diffusion of opportunities for mobility among Europe's middle and lower classes (Favell et al. 2014: 166).

The intensification of transnational interactions gives rise to what can be called a European culture of everyday life. This is related to the cognitive learning of individuals who are exposed to transnational experiences, knowledge, and information. We can find traces of such everyday socio-cultural involvement in a number of low-level engagements through which EU citizens identify with the EU in unremarkable ways: carrying passports or driver's licences, conforming with legislation, walking past EU flags, and not waving national flags (Cram 2012: 79). There is a presence of Europe that reminds citizens of "being involved in the larger EU system whether for good or ill" (Cram 2012: 79). There are many daily reminders of the presence of Europe: we automatically walk through the EU nationals' lane at customs; we watch a movie in the theatre that is supported by the EU media programme; we drive on a road that has been financed by EU infrastructure network funds; we eat Italian ham that has an EU guarantee of origin; however vague it may be, we have an awareness of EU rights in relation to equal pay or access to health care. The EU becomes normalized as individuals stop noticing the presence of these daily reminders.

All of the studies on everyday transnationalism find strong evidence that the degree to which ordinary people are involved in everyday transnational practices correlates with their adherence to more European and cosmopolitan values (Favell et al. 2014; Mau et al. 2008). They thus help us to shed light on the mutual interdependence of Europeanization from below and Europeanization from above. The sociological research agenda of Europeanization needs to focus precisely on this interrelationship between Europeanization as an 'impact' of institutional transformation on the micro-structures of society (the political science approach) and Europeanization as an impact of the transformation of society on the institutionalization of the EU (see also: Díéz Medrano 2008). European citizens' changing lifeworlds and experiences further result in **subjective or cognitive Europeanization** (Lahusen & Kiess 2019), referring to "Europe's growing role in the cognitive, affective and normative perceptions and orientations of people and the weakening of the fixation on the nation state" (Mau & Verwiebe 2010: 329).

In many instances, Europeanization as social transnationalism is not restricted to Europe but also involves dense interchanges with other parts of the world. How can the European and the global be distinguished in social transnationalism, and does this distinction matter? According to Delhey et al. (2014), to speak of Europeanization would imply that these networks of interactions are also geographically confined and distinguished from other (global) networks, at least to some degree. From this perspective, Europeanization is a relational term that involves processes of external closure from the world and processes of internal opening towards the national. To capture this interwoven character of place-bridging and place-building practices, Europeanization must be operationalized in relative rather than absolute terms, according to Delhey and collaborators. We must not only address Europe's salience vis-à-vis the national (the measure of *absolute* Europeanization) but also its salience vis-à-vis the rest of the world (the measure of *relative* Europeanization). To develop such an understanding of 'relative Europeanization', it is necessary to take systematic account of 'external closure', namely the ways in which transnational practices are consolidated within the European social space and how this European space becomes demarcated against the outside world as an effect of such practices.

After Europeanization

The purpose of this chapter is to shed light on the different uses of the term Europeanization as a diffuse and multidimensional concept. As a discipline, sociology enjoys no distinct and privileged access to the study of Europeanization, yet it does allow us to sketch linkages between existing approaches and accumulate empirical knowledge from different disciplines. Europeanization research can then be taken as an opportunity to activate the sociological imagination of reflection on the possibilities of a European society and its relationship with existing national societies (Trenz 2011). Unlike European integration or nation-building, Europeanization is neither wilful design nor a 'project'. It is not a progressive force based on the shared values of Europeans in search of self-realization, but a by-product of European market building and the social and structural effects of Europeanization on citizens' changing lifeworlds.

Europeanization proceeds as a quiet revolution of markets, political institutions, and everyday life, through which an increasing number of Europeans are entrenched in a dense network of vertical and horizontal exchanges, living under a new type of political authority and developing similar lifestyles and expectations. New generations of Europeans acquire similar knowledge of Europe and go through the same experiences of socializing in a European context of travel, education, social and cultural exchanges, and labor. Nonetheless, in most of its empirical manifestations, the contours of Europeanization remain rather blurred in the wider context of denationalization, transnationalization, or globalization.

Sociologists should always keep in mind, however, that Europeanization is not a harmonious process. There is no linear path of development and Europeanization could face several turning points or ruptures. In post-crisis Europe, Europeanization is facing challenges from numerous nationalist backlashes against the perceived threats of identity loss through transnationalization. The current crisis-ridden liberal market Europe points to another trend of Europeanization that increasingly shapes inequalities throughout the market of free movement and thus divides European populations into specific groups of winners and losers (Hooghe & Marks 2009). Europeanization as forced adaptation, as a *deus ex machina*, or even worse, as an 'iron cage of bureaucracy' (Weber) and hegemony, creates resistance.

An intriguing question for sociological analysis concerns whether Europeanization can be reversed when particular elements disintegrate; for instance, when popular conflicts become divisive or antagonistic, or states decide to opt out. While an abundance of theories on EU integration are available, theory of disintegration is noticeably lacking (Zielonka 2018). Attempts to draft such a theory mainly emphasize dysfunctional developments (Hooghe & Marks 2009), states of anomaly or crisis (Webber 2018), or a negative spiral of discrimination that successively undermines the goals of integration in terms of equality of opportunity and life chances (Jones 2018). However, the question remains open as to whether a possible reversal of European integration would also necessarily imply a reversal of Europeanization. To answer this question, we would need to define what the opposite of Europeanization is. For instance, one could identify recent re-nationalization trends as a reversal of Europeanization. The problem with this account is that re-nationalization does not stand in simple diametric opposition to Europeanization, but rather forms a symbiotic relationship with Europeanization or even continues it in different forms, such as the convergence of the mobilization strategy of the Eurosceptic opposition during European Parliamentary elections (De Wilde & Trenz 2012). There may even be a correlation between Europeanization and re-nationalization, and that the two processes cannot be disentangled but will rather remain interdependent. In the case of Brexit, such a rupture with European integration is paired with the sobering experience that there is indeed no way to escape the iron cage of Europeanization by plebiscite. Ironically, Brexit is not a one-time decision and solution but has turned itself into a process that can only develop into differentiated forms of Europeanization without escaping it (Outhwaite 2017).

For more in-depth readings of sociologists' key contribution to the establishment of Europeanization research as a distinct research field, students should be able to distinguish between the organizational analysis of Europeanization of governance in terms of the domestic impact of EU politics (Börzel & Risse 2006), and the study of Europeanization as dynamic state-society relationships and long-term societal transformation at macro, meso and micro level (Delanty & Rumford 2005; Trenz 2016, 2011). In the EU's post crisis conundrum, close attention should be paid to processes of differentiated Europeanization and its controversial effects on contestation and EU politicization (Bátora & Fossum 2019; Statham & Trenz 2012). While EU polity-society relationships are still far from being settled, there is also a need to deepen our understanding of horizontal and **everyday Europeanization** that involves citizens who increasingly find themselves in transnational social relationships and lifeworlds (Heidenreich 2019; Recchi & Favell 2019).

Didactical Section

Key Learning Points

- Europeanization studies are needed to the broader implications of European integration on other sectors of social life, like, for instance, culture, education, family or everyday live.
- The effects of Europeanization can be internal (for instance in the form of the direct impact of EU law and policies on member states) or external (the effects of the EU on non-member states).
- Europeanization is neither a harmonious process nor a linear development that leads towards further integration, but can be also driven by enhanced conflicts and politicization.

Glossary

Vertical Europeanization: mainly formal and institutionalized processes of exchange between EU-institutions and the EU's member states (Börzel & Risse 2006).

Horizontal Europeanization: both formal and informal processes of exchange between member states involving public and private actors (citizens) (Mau & Verwiebe 2010).

Everyday Europeanization: the intensification of transnational interactions among citizens, giving rise to a European culture and identity (Heidenreich 2019).

Subjective or **Cognitive Europeanization**: the cognitive and affective perceptions of Europe and of European belonging (Mau & Verwiebe 2010: 329).

Further Readings

Favell, A. & V. Guiraudon, 2009: The Sociology of the European Union: An Agenda. *European Union Politics* 10(4):550–576.

Fligstein, N., 2008: *Euroclash: The EU, European Identity, and the Future of Europe*. Oxford: Oxford University Press.

Heidenreich, M., 2019: *Horizontal Europeanisation: The Transnationalisation of Daily Life and Social Fields in Europe*. London: Routledge.

Kauppi, N., 2014: *A Political Sociology of Transnational Europe*. Colchester: ECPR Press.

Recchi, E. et al., 2019: *Everyday Europe: Social Transnationalism in an Unsettled Continent.* Bristol: Policy Press.
Trenz, H. J., 2016: *Narrating European Society: Toward a Sociology of European Integration.* Lanham: Rowman and Littlefield, Lexington Books.

Questions for Discussion

- How can the concept of Europeanization be applied at the macro, meso and micro levels of sociological analysis?
- What is the difference between Europeanization as project, Europeanization as process and Europeanization as outcome or as effect? Provide examples for each.
- What does *horizontal* and *vertical* Europeanization mean? Can you find examples for each?
- What kind of sociological research programme can be formulated with reference to everyday processes of Europeanization?

References

Amaral, A., G. Neave, C. Musselin & P. Maassen, 2009: *European Integration and the Governance of Higher Education and Research.* Dordrecht: Springer.
Auel, K. & A. Benz, 2005: The Politics of Adaptation: The Europeanisation of National Parliamentary Systems. *Journal of Legislative Studies* 11(3/4):372–393.
Bache, I., 2008: *Europeanization and Multilevel Governance.* Lanham: Roman & Littlefield.
Bátora, J. & J. E. Fossum, 2019: *Towards a Segmented European Political Order: The European Union's Post-crises Conundrum.* Basingstoke: Palgrave.
Beck, U. & E. Grande, 2007: *Cosmopolitan Europe.* Cambridge: Polity Press.
Bellamy, R. & D. Castiglione, 2000: The Normative Turn in European Union Studies: Legitimacy, Identity and Democracy. University of Exeter Department of Politics RUSEL Working Paper No. 38, http://ssrn.com/abstract=1530444 (accessed June 21, 2021).
Bhambra, G. K., 2009: Postcolonial Europe: or, understanding Europe in times of the post-colonial. In: Rumford, C. (ed.), *The SAGE Handbook of European Studies*, pp. 69–86. London: Sage.
Börzel, T. A. & T. Risse, 2006: Europeanization: The Domestic Impact of European Union Politics. In: Jørgensen, M. B., A. Pollack & B. Rosemond (eds.), *Handbook of European Union Politics*, pp. 483–503. London: SAGE Publications Ltd.
Börzel, T. A. & T. Risse, 2011: From Europeanisation to Diffusion: Introduction. *West European Politics* 35(1):1–19.
Bulmer, S., 1993: The Governance of the European Union: A New Institutionalist Perspective. *Journal of Public Policy* 13(4):351–380.

Büttner, S. M., L. Leopold, S. Mau & M. Posvic, 2015: Professionalization in EU Policy-Making? The topology of the transnational field of EU affairs. *European Societies* 17(4):569–592.

Carlson, S., M. Eigmüller & K. Lueg, 2018: Education, Europeanization and Europe's social integration. An introduction. *Innovation: The European Journal of Social Science Research* 31(4):395–405.

Checkel, J. T. & P. J. Katzenstein (eds.), 2009: *European Identity*. Cambridge: Cambridge University Press.

Cram, L., 2012: Does the EU Need a Navel? Implicit and Explicit Identification with the European Union. *Journal of Common Market Studies* 50(1):71–86.

Dale, R. & S. Robertson, 2009: *Globalisation and Europeanisation in Education*. Oxford: Symposium Books.

De Wilde, P. & H. J. Trenz, 2012: Denouncing European Integration: Euroscepticism as Polity Contestation. *European Journal of Social Theory* 15(4):537–554.

Delanty, G., 1995: *Inventing Europe: Idea, Identity, Reality*. London: Macmillan.

Delanty, G., 1998: Social theory and the European Transformation: Is there a European Society? *Sociological Research Online* 3(1):103–111.

Delanty, G., 2009: *The Cosmopolitan Imagination*. Cambridge: Cambridge University Press.

Delanty, G. & C. Rumford, 2005: *Rethinking Europe. Social Theory and the Implications of Europeanization*. London: Routledge.

Delhey, J., E. Deutschmann, T. Graf & K. Richter, 2014: Measuring the Europeanization of Everyday Life: Three New Indices and an Empirical Application. *European Societies* 16(3): 355–377.

Della Porta, D. (ed.), 2009: *Another Europe*. London: Routledge.

Della Porta, D. & L. Parks, 2015: Europeanisation and Social Movements: Before and after the Great Recession. In: Börner, S. & M. Eigmüller (eds.), *European Integration, Processes of Change and the National Experience*, pp. 255–278. London: Palgrave Macmillan UK.

Díez Medrano, J., 2008: Europeanization and the Emergence of a European Society. *IBEI Working Paper* No. 2008/12, https://ssrn.com/abstract=1086084 (accessed June 21, 2021).

Dobson, L., 2006: Normative Theory and Europe. *International Affairs (Royal Institute of International Affairs)* 82(3):511–523.

Eigmüller, M. & H. J. Trenz, 2020: Value conflicts in a differentiated Europe: The impact of digital media on value polarisation in Europe. In: Leonardi, L. (ed.), *Shared Values and Global Challenges*, pp. 21–46. Bologna: Il Mulino.

Eriksen, E. O., 2009: *The Unfinished Democratization of Europe*. New York: Oxford University Press.

Eriksen, E. O. & J. E. Fossum (eds.), 2000: *Democracy in the European Union. Integration through Deliberation?* London: Routledge.

Exadaktylos, T. & C. M. Radaelli, 2015: Europeanisation. In: Lynggaard, K., I. Manners & K. Löfgren (eds.), *Research Methods in European Union Studies*, pp. 206–218. London: Palgrave Macmillan UK.

Favell, A., 2008: *Eurostars and Eurocities: Free Moving Urban Professionals in an Integrating Europe*. Oxford: Blackwell.

Favell, A. & V. Guiraudon, 2009: The Sociology of the European Union: An Agenda. *European Union Politics* 10(4):550–576.

Favell, A., D. Reimer & J. Solgaard Jensen, 2014: Transnationalism and Cosmopolitanism: Europe and the Global in Everyday European lives. In: EUROCROSS (ed.), *Final Report:*

The Europeanisation of Everyday Life: Cross-Border Practices and Transnational Identifications Among EU and Third-Country Citizens, pp. 138–168.

Fligstein, N., 2000: The Process of Europeanization. *Politique européenne* 1(1):25–42.

Fligstein, N., 2008: *Euroclash: The EU, European Identity, and the Future of Europe*. Oxford University Press.

Fligstein, N. & D. McAdam, 2011: Toward a General Theory of Strategic Action Fields. *Sociological Theory* 29(1):1–26.

Foret, F. & O. Calligaro (eds.), 2018: *European Values: Challenges and Opportunities for EU Governance*. London: Routledge.

Fossum, J. E., 2019: Europe's Triangular Challenge: Differentiation, Dominance and Democracy. EU3D Research Papers No. 1. https://ssrn.com/abstract=3505864 (accessed April 5, 2021).

Fossum, J. E. & H. J. Trenz, 2006: The EU's fledgeling society: From deafening silence to critical voice in European constitution making. *Jounal of Civil Society* 2(1):57–77.

Gänzle, S., B. Leruth & J. Trondal, 2019: *Differentiated Integration and Disintegration in a Post-Brexit Era*. London: Taylor & Francis.

Georgakakis, D. & J. Rowell, 2013: *The Field of Eurocracy: Mapping EU Actors and Professionals*. Palgrave Macmillan UK.

Grande, E. & S. Hutter, 2016: Beyond authority transfer: explaining the politicisation of Europe. *West European Politics* 39(1):23–43.

Guerra, S. & H. J. Trenz, 2019: Citizens and Public Opinion in the European Union. In: Cini, M. & N. Pérez-Solórzano Borragán (eds.), *European Union Politics*, pp. 219–232. Oxford: Oxford University Press.

Guiraudon, V., C. Ruzza & H. J. Trenz, 2015: Introduction: The European Crisis. Contributions from Political Sociology. In: Trenz, H. J., C. Ruzza & V. Guiraudon (eds.), *Europe in Crisis: The Unmaking of Political Union?* pp. 1–23. Basingstoke: Palgave Macmillan.

Haas, E. B., [1958] 2004: *The Uniting of Europe. Political, Social, and Economic Forces, 1950–1957*. Notre Dame: University of Notre Dame Press.

Passerin D'Entrèves, M. & S. Benhabib (eds.), 1996: *Habermas and the Unfinished Project of Modernity: Critical Essays on The Philosophical Discourse of Modernity*. Hoboken: Wiley.

Haverland, M., 2006: Does the EU cause domestic developments? improving case selection in Europeanisation research. *West European Politics* 29(1):134–146.

Hay, C. & D. Wincott, 2012: *The Political Economy of European Welfare Capitalism*. Basingstoke: Palgrave Macmillan.

Heft, A., B. Alfter & B. Pfetsch, 2019: Transnational journalism networks as drivers of Europeanisation. *Journalism* 20(9):1183–1202.

Heidenreich, M. (ed.), 2014: *Krise der europäischen Vergesellschaftung? Soziologische Perspektiven*. Wiesbaden: Springer.

Heidenreich, M., 2019: *Horizontal Europeanisation: The Transnationalisation of Daily Life and Social Fields in Europe*. London: Routledge.

Heritier, A., 2007: *Explaining Institutional Change in Europe*. Oxford: Oxford University Press.

Hoenig, B., 2019: 'Critique as a vocation': Reconstructing critical discourses on Europeanization in German sociology, 1990–2018. *Culture, Practice & Europeanization* 4(2):37–58.

Hooghe, L. & G. Marks, 2009: A Postfunctionalist Theory of European Integration: From Permissive Consensus to Constraining Dissensus. *British Journal of Political Science* 39(1):1–23.

Imig, D. & S. Tarrow (eds.), 2001: *Contentious Europeans: Protest and Politics in an Emerging Polity*. Lanham: Rowan & Littlefield.

Jones, E., 2018: Towards a theory of disintegration. *Journal of European Public Policy* 25(3): 440–451.

Kaschuba, W., 2008: Europäisierung als kulturalistisches Projekt? Ethnologische Beobachtungen. In: Jaeger, F. & H. Joas (eds.) *Europa im Spiegel der Kulturwissenschaften*, pp. 204–225. Baden-Baden: Nomos Verlagsgesellschaft.

Kauppi, N., 2014: *A Political Sociology of Transnational Europe*. Colchester: ECPR Press.

Knill, C. & D. Lehmkuhl, 2002: The National Impact of European Union Regulatory Policy: Three Europeanization Mechanisms. *European Journal of Political Research* 41(2):255–280.

Lahusen, C. & J. Kiess, 2019: 'Subjective Europeanization': do inner-European comparisons affect life satisfaction? *European Societies* 21(2):214–236.

Lavenex, S., 2007: The External Face of Europeanization: Third Countries and International Organizations. In: Faist, T. & A. Ette (eds.), *The Europeanization of National Policies and Politics of Immigration*, pp. 246–264. Berlin: Springer.

Lombardo, E. & M. Forest, 2015: The Europeanization of gender equality policies: A discursive–sociological approach. *Comparative European Politics* 13(2):222–239.

Manners, I., 2008: The normative ethics of the European Union. *International Affairs* 84(1): 45–60.

Marks, G. & D. McAdam, 1999: On the Relationship of Political Opportunities to the Form of Collective Action: the Case of the European Union. In: Della Porta, D., H. Kriesi & D. Rucht (eds.), *Social Movements in a Globalizing World*, pp. 97–111. Basingstoke: Macmillan.

Mau, S., 2010: *Social Transnationalism. Lifeworlds beyond the Nation State*. London: Routledge.

Mau, S. & R. Verwiebe, 2010: *European Societies: Mapping Structure and Change*. Bristol: Policy Press.

Mau, S., J. Mewes & A. Zimmermann, 2008: Cosmopolitan Attitudes through Transnational Practices. *Global Networks. A Journal for Transnational Affairs* 8(1):1–24.

Moravcsik, A., 1993: Preferences and Power in the European Community: A Liberal Intergovernmentalist Approach. *Journal of Common Market Studies* 31(4):473–524.

Motschenbacher, H., 2017: *Language, Normativity and Europeanisation: Discursive Evidence from the Eurovision Song Contest*. Basingstoke: Palgrave Macmillan.

Moumoutzis, K. & S. Zartaloudis, 2016: Europeanization Mechanisms and Process Tracing: A Template for Empirical Research. *JCMS: Journal of Common Market Studies* 54(2):337–352.

Münch, R., 2010: *European Governmentality: The Liberal Drift of Multilevel Governance*. Basingstoke: Palgrave.

Olsen, J. P., 2002: The Many Faces of Europeanization. *Journal of Common Market Studies* 40(5):921–952.

Olsen, J. P., 2007: *Europe in Search of Political Order. An Institutional Perspective on Unity/Diversity,Citizens/their Helpers, Democratic Design/Historical Drift, and the Co-existence of Orders*. Oxford: Oxford University Press.

Olsen, T. V., 2019: The EU defending liberal democracy in a liberal democratic way. In: Malkopoulou, A. & A. S. Kirshner (eds.), *Militant Democracy and its Critics*, pp. 150–168. Edinburgh: Edinburgh University Press.

Outhwaite, W., 2013: *European Society*. Oxford: Wiley.

Outhwaite, W., 2017: *Brexit: Sociological Responses*. London: Anthem Press.

Parsons, T., 1967: *Sociological Theory and Modern Society*. New York: Free Press.

Radaelli, C. M., 2004: Europeanisation: Solution or problem? *European Integration online Papers (EloP)* 8(16), http://eiop.or.at/eiop/texte/2004-016a.htm (accessed June 21, 2021).

Recchi, E. & A. Favell (eds.), 2009: *Pioneers of European Integration: Mobility and Citizenship in the EU*. Cheltenham: Elgar.

Recchi, E. & A. Favell, 2019: *Everyday Europe: Social transnationalism in an unsettled continent*. Bristol: Policy Press.

Risse, T., 2014: *European Public Spheres*. Cambridge University Press.

Rumford, C. & D. Buhari-Gulmez, 2016: *Europe and World Society*. London: Routledge.

Ruzza, C., 2004: *Europe and Civil Society. Movement Coalitions and European Governance*. Manchester: Manchester University Press.

Scalise, G., 2015: The Narrative Construction of European Identity. Meanings of Europe 'from below'. *European Societies* 17(4):593–614.

Schmidt, V., 2006: *Democracy in Europe, The EU and National Polities*. Oxford: Oxford University Press.

Schmidt, V. A., 2009: Re-Envisioning the European Union: Identity, Democracy, Economy. *Journal of Common Market Studies* 47(Annual Review):17–42.

Schmidt-Wellenburg, C., 2017: Europeanisation, stateness, and professions: What role do economic expertise and economic experts play in European political integration? *European Journal of Cultural and Political Sociology* 4(4):430–456.

Schimmelfennig, F. & U. Sedelmeier, 2005: *The Europeanization of Central and Eastern Europe*. Ithaca, NY: Cornell University Press.

Seibicke, H., 2019: Gender Expertise in Public Policymaking: The European Women's Lobby and the EU Maternity Leave Directive. *Social Politics: International Studies in Gender, State & Society* 27(2):385–408.

Statham, P. & H. J. Trenz, 2012: *The Politicisation of Europe. Contesting the Constitution in the Mass Media*. London: Routledge.

Stråth, B., 2002: A European Identity: To the Historical Limits of a Concept. *European Journal of Social Theory* 5(4):387–401.

Trenz, H. J., 2011: Social Theory and European Integration. In: Favell, A. & V. Guiraudon (eds.), *Sociology of the European Union*, pp. 193–214. Basingstoke: Palgrave Macmillan.

Trenz, H. J., 2016: *Narrating European Society: Toward a Sociology of European Integration*. Lanham: Rowman and Littlefield, Lexington Books.

Trenz, H. J., V. Guiraudon & C. Ruzza (eds.), 2015: *Europe's Prolonged Crisis: The Making or the Unmaking of a Political Union*. Basingstoke: Palgrave Macmillan.

Webber, D., 2018: *European Disintegration?: The Politics of Crisis in the European Union*. Basingstoke: Macmillan Education UK.

Wiener, A. & T. Diez, 2004: Taking Stock of Integration Theory. In: Wiener, A. & T. Diez (eds.), *European Integration Theory*, pp. 237–248. New York: Oxford University Press.

Zielonka, J., 2018: *Counter-Revolution: Liberal Europe in Retreat*. Oxford: Oxford University Press.

Part II: **Where and What is Europe: Spatial, Cultural, and Socio-historical Perspectives**

Nikola Tietze & Camille Noûs

3 Space, Territories, and Borders in Europe

Space, territories, and borders "are created in action and [. . .] embodied in institutions that pre-structure action" (Löw 2016: xiv). The dual movement from structure to action and from action to structure, which is generally a feature of spatial constructions, is exemplified in the European Neighborhood Policy (ENP) implemented by the European Union (EU) in 2004. With the creation of the ENP, the governments of the EU member states established structures for a **space** in the sense of the French word *espace*, which not only refers to distance and time but also to "place", "site", "area", "surface", or "region" (Shields 2006: 147). Drawing on this spatial construction, the ENP regulates, finances, and legitimates (as well as delegitimates) actions, for example, in the realm of cross-border economic and workplace relations or in infrastructural networks such as rail transport or wastewater collection systems connecting the EU and several nation states that border on the EU to the south, southeast, or east (apart from Turkey and Russia). Furthermore, this EU program is an essential element of the European **border** regime. The neighborhood space establishes the framework for administering and controlling migration on the so-called external borders of the EU and creates interaction between the EU member states and the nearby states. By creating such interaction, the ENP highlights the general features of political constructions of space that define areas, **territories**, and borders. Such definitions determine who belongs and has access to rights and thus who is included or excluded; they also legitimate domination and the sovereignty of power. With respect to these general features of political constructions of space, the EU is characterized by a unique additional trait: the EU is founded on the principle of supranational governance. In other words, the Union's spaces intersect with the territorial sovereignties of the EU member states. As a result, in many policy areas, the competence of the European communities and the EU and those of the member states do not constitute "distinctly separate spheres" (Patel & Röhl 2020: 217). This complex interplay also results in flexible redefinitions of state borders.

For sociologists investigating Europeanization, space, territories, and borders are revealed in the codification of laws, in the architecture of institutional regimes, in the organization and regulation of markets, in the ways infrastructure is generated, in the coordination of social security systems, in the harmonization of criteria, standards, and administrative procedures. In the EU, legal,

Note: We thank Paula Bradish for translating our text into English.

https://doi.org/10.1515/9783110673630-003

institutional, administrative, economic, and social processes, practices, and structures reveal specific ways in which space construction overlap with respect to the member states' integrity and identity and to fluid EU borders (Jureit & Tietze 2018). Nonetheless, EU spatial governance is built on **phantom geographies** – "the traces left in contemporary societies by defunct territorialities" (von Hirschhausen 2017: 107). Such phantom geographies intersect with contemporary EU spatial constructions, be it in the realm of the European neighborhood policy, with respect to the enlargement of the European communities (Vobruba 2003), issues related to labor migration, to Spanish cities in Morocco, to French *départements* in the Carribbean, or to privileged economic cooperation, for example between Polish and Ukrainian companies.

Space, territories, and borders are not only objects of social science research; they are also categories of sociological observation and explanation. As such they offer opportunities for discovering and elucidating the interdependencies, interactions, and discontinuities between various realms of actions related to phantom geographies, as well as between distinctive territorial scales of political and economic power or between different domains of governance. This perspective focuses on social relations that are ordered by spatial constructions, territorialization, and the drawing of borders. These three spatial categories for observation reveal inequalities and tensions that generate the architecture of a political order or an actor's activities that run counter to such architectures, for example, in the form of illegal border crossings.

In this chapter, the double character of space, territories, and borders – first, as an object of study in the sociology of Europeanization and, second, as a category for observing and explaining Europeanization – is outlined in two steps. After briefly sketching the historical origin of the three categories of spatial governance just mentioned, this chapter will focus on what spaces, territories, and borders have been established in the EU by means of law, institution building, and markets. The following sections consider the spatial categories of sociological observation and explanation and discuss two methodological approaches: the scalar structuration approach (Brenner 2001) and the *jeux d'é-chelles* approach (Revel 1996).

Info-Box 3.1: Space as a concept in the social sciences and humanities
In his book *La production de l'espace* (1974), which appeared in English in 1991 as *The Production of Space*, the French philosopher and sociologist Henri Lefèbvre referred to space as a complex social construction consisting of meanings, ideas, and practices. As meanings, ideas, and practices, spatial concepts become the basis for action and instruments for structuring interactions. According to Lefebvre, they are thus tools for social control and the enforcement of domination and power. Lefebvre's thinking has had a major impact – first in France and, from the late 1980s, in the English-speaking world – in particular

on human and economic geography, which studies the interactions and interdependencies between social, cultural, economic, and political activities and the environments in which they occur. This is reflected in the work of critical urban theorists, among others, who address urbanization and capitalist governance from the point of view of social justice (Brenner 2011; Brenner & Elden 2009; Döring & Thielmann 2008). A continent, a place, a mountain range, a country, a district, a river, a border, etc. are terms used in the social sciences and humanities to denote relations: (i) between actors and structures, (ii) between different activities, and (iii) between activities, actors, and the earth's surface. In this sense, space is a form of order, observation, and communication (Jureit 2012). In the realm of political relations, where power, domination, and control are at stake, the concept of space has found its expression historically in territories and borders. This means, for example, that the designation of a 'natural' border (for instance the Pyrenees) naturalizes a relationship of domination. Legal regulations, control devices, and the othering found on either side of the border materialize the definition of the border; physical features on the earth are not what materializes border.

Space, Territories, and Borders from the Perspective of the History of Political Ideas

The term space, which is used in this text in the sense of the French term *espace* as outlined above refers to geographical features, that is, "specific arrangements of objects and people" (Löw 2016: xii) and sets social interactions in relation to a specifically constituted environment. The political meaning of space emerged in the early modern period and refers to the territorialization of state rule. In the late Middle Ages in Europe, rulership was tied to a place that was the seat of a ruler such as a castle, fortification, or marketplace. But this was frequently accompanied by uncertainties about the limits of domination. Such uncertainties accelerated a process in which governance was territorialized. With the development of the European territorial states, territory became the basis for the organization of rule and its expansion.

Since the 19th century, *political spatiality* has become intrinsically intermeshed with the spatiality of national territory and of state sovereignty. One result of this development is the emergence and ongoing significance of the sovereignty of nation states. According to Charles S. Maier, territoriality represents the central concept of European governments in the 20th century. "Territoriality means simply the properties, including power, provided by the control of bordered political space, which until recently at least created the framework for national and often ethnic identity" (Maier 2000: 808). The control of 'bordered political space' has not only led to the establishment and consolidation of border regimes (Eigmüller & Vobruba 2016). During the 19th century and in the European context, national territory also increasingly framed economic relations, industrialization and infrastructure policies, resource extraction and the energy supply, and, last but not least, the development of social security and health care systems.

In the 20th century, the control of bordered political space found its expression in two different forms of territorial domination, which nevertheless refer to one another: the European nation state and European colonial empires; that is, the attempts to establish regional spheres of influence or, in Carl Schmitt's terminology, *Großräume* [*greater areas*] (Jureit 2012). The conflicts as well as the cooperation of European governments after World War I were based on the understanding that a nation state consists of and is a territory. Thus, the integrity of a state is damaged when its borders are crossed without permission or when other ruling groups hinder it in exercising its sovereignty. An almost corporeal understanding of law underpins the right to self-determination of peoples, which was of fundamental importance for decolonization processes until well after 1945. The European states, which simultaneously drew on and were in competition with the nation state understanding of territoriality, nevertheless consolidated and expanded their political power because of their colonial empires and the creation of regional spheres of influence. The first half of the 20th century was therefore also a period in which hegemonic theories of large spaces like Carl Schmitt's highly controversial theory were taken up and developed. These theories, which are rooted in particular in European imperial traditions, have been instrumental in demarcating an imagined Europe of civilization or culture that was perceived as different from other regions.

The concept of Europe gained political significance during the 19th and 20th centuries in a context marked by the tension between the two territorial forms of rule that enacted competing national and ethnic identities – the European nation state, on the one hand, and the expansion of their spheres of influence in the form of colonial empires and metropolitan policies, on the other. The competition among nation states for economic and technical progress as well as for social modernization, cultural development, and the realization of perceived standards of civilization measured in terms of nation state parameters shaped the spatial experience of European political and economic actors and established the spatial image of a Europe that was seen as being too crowded. Moreover, within the framework of the European nation state model and in the aftermath of World War I, the understand emerged and was reinforced that social relations can be planned and spatially ordered on the basis of scientific arguments, for example by population resettlement or transfer (Bernhardt 2017; Rosental 2006). With Europe perceived as 'too crowded' to allow for the competition among European nation states that was deemed necessary to achieve progress and modernization, compensation was found in the expansion of colonial empires, in the establishment of colonial trading posts and settlement projects, in the transfer of civilization and culture, and so on. Constitutive for this policy was the idea and production, with the use of force, of 'empty areas', '*espaces de peuplement*', 'areas of exploitation', and of 'frontiers' as transition spaces (Jureit 2016).

The contradictions and violent conflicts in the interwar period can be seen as responses to profound changes in global power balances. New nation states with claims to global political and economic leadership such as the United States had entered the international arena, and South American states that became independent in the 19th century demanded a say in international organizations and negotiations. Moreover, economic interdependencies intensified and expanded to the extent that economic processes could no longer be controlled based on national territoriality. These developments, which continued long after the end of World War II, have meant that the market, and above all the world market, has become increasingly relevant for the territorial organization of state rule.

Against the backdrop of these changes, the establishment of the first European communities in the 1950s reflects the attempts of Western European states to respond to global economic interdependencies as well as to wartime devastation by creating common European markets, asserting their place in the emerging bloc formation of the Cold War, and countering the consequences of decolonization (not least of their own colonial empires) for acquiring raw materials, for trade, and for labor markets (Milward 1992). With this attempt, the governments of the founding states of the European communities at the same time clearly rejected the historical models of hegemonic and violent control of a bordered political space (Wobbe 2005) – not only on the discursive level, but above all by forming a body of European law and building European institutions.

As the history of political ideas outlined here suggests, the sociology of Europeanization encompasses issues that transcend by far, in both temporal and spatial terms, the founding of the European Communities and the European Union. However, in the following I will limit myself to addressing spatial constructions, territoriality, and definitions of border regimes in the context of these legal institutional arrangements.

Spatial Constructions, Territories, and Borders: Three Interdependent Objects of Sociological Research on Europeanization

The European Coal and Steel Union (1951) and especially the European Economic Community (EEC) founded in 1957, laid the groundwork for the "area without internal frontiers", as it is called in Article 13 of the Single European Act (1986). On the one hand, this spatial construction of a European area overcomes the model of the European nation state based on a contractually guaranteed and shared sovereignty in certain policy areas. These policy areas are constantly expanding during the European integration process, which has accelerated as a result of the Single European Act. This act replaced the principle of unanimous decision making by member states with qualified majority voting rules. The member states have thus abandoned the paradigm of harmonization of regulations in social relations and facilitated legislative processes on the European level. The area without internal frontiers is founded on European laws that aim to combine and coordinate divergent national legal orders (Patel & Röhl 2020: 81–91). On the other hand, this European area consists of the sum of the national territories of the members of the European Communities and today's European Union (EU). Article 4 of the Consolidated Version of the Treaty of the European Union states as follows: "The Union shall respect the equality of Member States before the Treaties as well as their national identities [. . .] [and] their essential State functions, including ensuring the territorial integrity of the State, maintaining law and order and safeguarding national security". Thus, the structural core of the EU's current spatial construction is the way in which both nationally and supranationally guaranteed claims to power and sovereignty and nationally and supranationally guaranteed economic and social orders and forms of solidarity overlap. Because of these overlaps, a complex and flexible European border regime has emerged at multiple locations, some of which are extraterritorial; this regime has various instruments of control at its disposal (Eigmüller 2007; Mau et al. 2012). What is more, this regime created opportunities for the European Communities and the EU to expand their sphere of influence, following the logic of 'tiered levels of integration' (Vobruba 2004). Under this regime, implementation of classic forms of border control on the periphery of the member states' territories has become a sign that states of emergency are in effect (for example, following terrorist attacks or during pandemics).

Law and Institutions

The overlapping of supranational and national claims to power and sovereignty and of economic and social orders constitutes 'spatialities of Europeanization' (Clark & Jones 2008) that shape and influence the relationship between the territories of the member states as well as the territorial frames of social relations and interactions in the area without internal frontiers. The 'spatialities of Europeanization' – which are marked, from a sociological perspective, by the dialectic between Europeanization as a process of opening and as a process of national closure (Münch 2008) – are based to a decisive extent on the legal codifications set out in European primary law, i.e., on European treaties, and secondary law, i.e., European directives, and regulations. The member states that signed the Treaty of Rome in 1958 agreed to four fundamental principles: free movement of goods, free movement of capital, freedom to provide and establish services, and the free movement of persons. By establishing these four liberties, they outlined a European legal space (Vauchez 2015). At the core of this legal space is the prohibition of "any discrimination on grounds of nationality" (Article 7 EEC). These principles ensure equal access to the national legal orders of the member states for companies, investors, service providers, and employees and form the basis for the development of a constitutional framework for the European Union. The legal space thus not only frames and legitimates the supranational regulation of relations between the sovereign powers of the member states and the hierarchies between European norms and national legal systems. It also enables the institutions that represent this space to define fundamental legal norms, install European citizenship, and enact laws and monitor compliance with them.

From a sociological perspective, the European legal space generates interactions and interdependencies between representatives of the respective member states' governments and public authorities, but also among various groups of non-governmental actors such as market participants, experts, workers, persons covered by different national security schemes, students, etc. The tensions and conflicts associated with these interactions and interdependencies, due to clashes of interests, claims to hegemony, or uneven social developments, shed light on the fractures and discontinuities in the area without internal frontiers. One indicator of these shifting fractures and discontinuities is the extent to which mobile EU citizens do or do not have access to tax-funded social benefits in other member states. In various rulings handed down since 1998 (judgement of the ECJ C-86/96 *Sala v. Freistaat Bayen*), the Court of Justice of the European Union has recognized that EU citizens who reside, because of their job or education, in a member state other than the state whose nationality they have are entitled to social benefits. Such claims to social benefits have nonetheless repeatedly been challenged by national social welfare offices and social courts. Since 2014 (judgement of the ECJ C-333/13 *Dano v. Jobcenter Leipzig*), the European Court of Justice has itself negated such claims in three cases (Blauberger et al. 2018; Tietze 2018). These conflicts of solidarity (Farahat & Krenn 2018) highlight contradictions that have emerged in the legal space of the EU area without internal frontiers as a result of inconsistencies between the right to free movement for workers and trainees and their right to social security, on the one hand, and the social rights guaranteed for mobile EU citizens, on the other. Tax-funded social benefits as a core element of welfare state policies have remained within the domain of member states (Ferrera 2003). Allocation of benefits to mobile EU citizens who become unemployed or require assistance during their training is subject to the European process called coordination among member states (Pataut 2018), which means that, since 2014, access to benefits for mobile EU citizens not recognized as workers or trainees depends more and more on discretionary decisions reached by individual member states.

Nevertheless, precisely the tensions and conflicts in the area without internal frontiers highlight the potential of law to Europeanize political, economic, and social relations and to institutionalize European forms of conflict management. Both the founding of institutions with a material presence in a specific locale – such as the establishment of the Court of Justice of the European Union in Luxembourg (as part of the Treaty of the European Coal and Steel Community of 1952) and the Common Assembly that has become the European Parliament with directly elected deputies since 1979 in Strasbourg and Brussels – and the establishment of normative institutions such as the prohibition of discrimination on the basis of nationality, the portability of social rights and benefits, and the prohibition of double taxation of mobile EU citizens are all part of these processes.

The European institutional order, in which the area without internal frontiers intersects with the territories of the member states, regulates the formal relationship between the EU institutions and the institutions of the member states, and determines which decision-making competence is assigned to what authority. A complex regime of different layers of regulation structures the European area without internal frontiers and determines the details of, for example, the 'free movement of persons' that is constitutive of European citizenship and the area without internal frontiers. A differentiated system of EU and member states' regulations stipulates who is included in or excluded from the area without internal frontiers under what conditions, for what period, and with what options for taking action. The various categories of mobile workers (cross-border workers, posted workers, workers who reside in another member state than their nationality, third-country workers, etc.) shape both contrasting mobilities taking place within this area and distinctive access to the rights that establish it. In this respect the European legal space and the institutional orders associated with it led to multiple unequal 'spatialities of Europeanization' – not only in the domain of the labor relations within the European area.

Markets and Social Protection

Such differences and inconsistencies in Europeanization contradict the unity and especially the uniformity suggested by the spatial constructions of the European Union and its predecessors, the European Communities. An example of such a spatial construction that suggests uniformity is the single market. The latter was established with the Single European Act 1986 and builds on the free trade zone (1960) and the customs union (1968), which were also spatially constructed. The introduction of the Euro on January 1, 1999 highlighted the symbolic unity of this single market. In reality, however, it established a new space within the single market – the Eurozone. The "spatial image" of the market invokes the "dream" of a society that bases its cohesion on egalitarian exchange relations and the interdependencies of supply and demand (Kracauer 1990: 186). In this respect, the political decisions of the member states and the legal codifications that materialize the single market represent, among other things, the attempt of the governments of the member states to reduce the complexity of global economic interdependencies and to find an adequate response to economic globalization processes beyond territorially constituted national economies.

"Speaking as one voice, the EU carries more weight in international trade negotiations than each individual member would", according to an official statement on the official webpage of the European Union.[1] The EU trade balances, which Eurostat compiles annually based on exports and imports of member states to and from countries outside the EU, demonstrate the existence of the single market and the associated global flows of goods. They also reinforce the importance of the single market for European and non-European economic actors, such as companies, investors, national governments, employees, etc. Eurostat statistics and data materialize the construction of space in a market economy by classifying political economic action based on European categories and simultaneously create reference points for political and economic action.

---

1 "Trade. Towards open and fair world-wide trade". Official website of the European Union. https://europa.eu/european-union/topics/trade_en (accessed January 22, 2021).

In this respect, the statistical office of the European Union reproduces the dual history by linking statistics to the establishment of the European nation state model and the public policies decided on in the name of the nation state. On the one hand, statistics serve decision-makers as evidence of the sphere in which specific policies apply, and, on the other hand, as an instrument of justification for their scope (Desrosières 1998; Bartl et al. 2019)

Eurostat statistics and data reveal the basic structure of the single market, which consists of the sum of the economies of the member states (Fink & Lammers 2018). For example, the external trade balances not only inform us that, between 2003 and 2017 (a period in which several Eastern European countries joined the EU, and which also includes the 2008/09 economic and debt crisis), extra-EU exports increased by 117.9 per cent, while extra-EU imports increased by 98.7 per cent. Data also shows that, during this period, Germany was the largest EU exporter with EUR 532 billion, far ahead of the United Kingdom (EUR 204 billion), Italy (EUR 199 billion), France (EUR 195 billion), and the Netherlands (EUR 143 billion) (Bundeszentrale für politische Bildung 2019).

Despite its member-state structure, the single market has undoubtedly transnationalized corporate structures, labor markets, infrastructure development, knowledge and technology production, educational pathways, and individual biographies within the EU, thus contributing significantly to a convergence of living standards as well as to converging GDPs. The Commission notes in a report published in 2007 an "increase in welfare of € 518 per head in 2006 compared to the situation without the single market (corresponding to a 2.15% increase of GDP over the period 1992–2006)" (European Commission 2007). However, the growth in wealth generated on the single market has both produced and reinforced an uneven distribution of resources and opportunities to participate in the market exchanges. This development could be observed before the EU enlargements of the 2000s, as well as in the aftermath of the economic and financial crisis of 2008–2009 (Beckfield 2009; Heidenreich 2016). The *European Observation Network for Territorial Development and Cohesion* (ESPON), for example, observed two dividing lines on the single market in 2011, in particular with respect to competitiveness. These divisions were between regions in the East of the 'marketplace' and those in the West and between regions in the South and those in the North.[2] Furthermore, the increase of prosperity and the converging living standards in the EU have not abolished the large differences between member states in the portions of their populations that are at risk of poverty. These relative

---

2 See for example "Lisbon performance and regional economic development, 2001–2011": https://mapfinder.espon.eu/mapfinder/?p=2432 (accessed February 16, 2021).

differences have increased significantly in the wake of the economic and debt crisis since 2010. The territorial cohesion of the single market and social inclusion into the European area without internal frontiers are accompanied by large social inequalities, which follow the two dividing lines just mentioned and intersect the prosperous zones of economically strong member states.

Figure 3.1 illustrates how economic competitiveness follows regional dividing lines and highlights the uneven topography of converging standards of living. This uneven topography is also found in countries with generally more equal levels of income and distribution of income, in particular in Germany, and countries with large intra-national disparities such as Italy, where economic inequalities reflect underlying weaknesses in the construction of the Italian nation state. Also, the map illustrates that the single market in part ends at the borders of the member states. Although several border areas – for instance, the region along the Rhine between France and Germany, the area between the Belgian city of Antwerp and the Dutch city Rotterdam, or the Spanish and French Basque region – have low ARoP rates, the ARoP rates of other border areas such as the Catalan region or the German-Polish Pomerania region point to the impacts of national borders on the capacity of regional actors to take part in competitive single market exchange.

The intra-European asymmetries that the single market generates, perpetuates, or deepens are an indication of the unequal bargaining power of the member states. These inequalities are, to a large extent, a result of the member states' different shares of intra-European trade in goods. Figure 3.2 summarizes the differences in import and export among the EU member states in 2019.

The interstate framework of the single market contributes to promoting asymmetric power relations between the member states, due to unequal participation in intra-European trade leads, which in turns leads to uneven bargaining power (Lechevalier 2018). As a result, economic and social inequalities between member states tend to be reproduced, because the basic structure of the market construction in the member states for the most part prevents processes in which political differences are balanced out at the level of other territorial differentiations.

Regulation of the market is largely in the hands of the governments of the member states and is therefore based on the power of a government to assert itself in negotiations on market regulation in intergovernmental councils. Furthermore, decisions on market regulation are made in relation to other policy areas, which are differentiated according to the division of competences between the EU and the member states. These policy areas include business and industry, competition, education, training and youth, employment and social affairs, energy, agriculture, environment, regional investment and solidarity

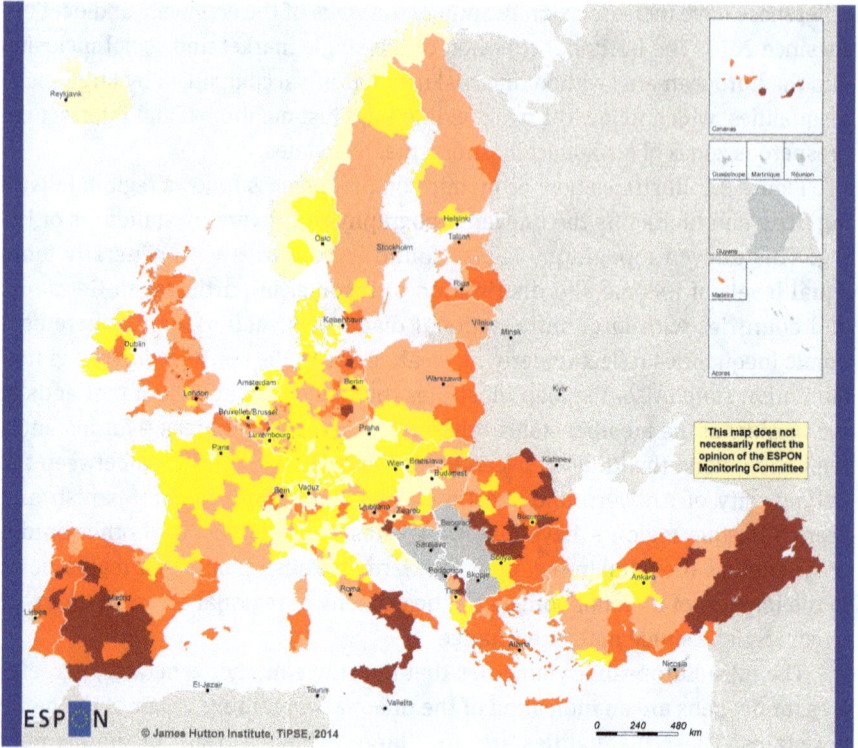

Regional ARoP Rates, 2011

(Percentage of population in households with <60% of the national median equivalised disposable income)

- No Data
- < 9.9
- 10.0 - 14.9
- 15.0 - 19.9
- 20.0 - 29.9
- 30.0 - 63.4

Sources:
BE, DE, EL, ES, IT, AT, PT, TR, CH - ESPON TiPSE project.
DK, SE, FI, NO, IE, NL, FR, UK, HR - National Statistical Institutes
LV, HU, RO, SI, SK - World Bank
BG, CZ, EE, CY, LT, LU, MT, PL, LI - Eurostat Regio Database (NUTS 0-2)

Figure 3.1: Regional at-risk-of-poverty (ARoP) rates (2011).
Source: ESPON 2013 Programme, https://mapfinder.espon.eu/mapfinder/?p=2520 (accessed June 21, 2021).
Copyright: EuroGeographics Association for administrative boundaries.

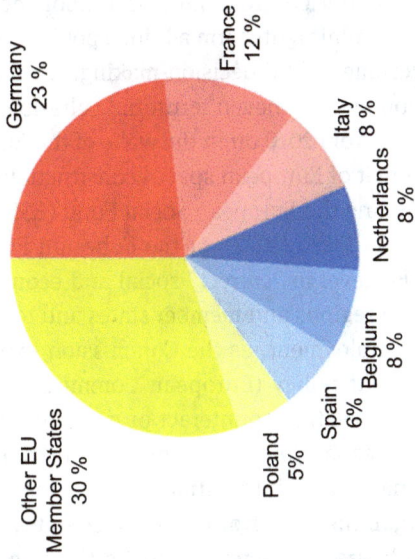

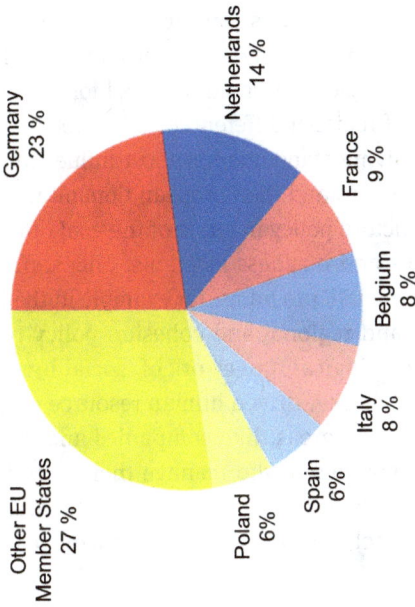

Intra EU-27 trade in goods, 2019
(% share of EU-27 exports/imports)

Exports

Imports

Source: Eurostat (online data code: ext_lt_intratrd)

Figure 3.2: Intra EU-27 trade in goods, 2019.
Source: Eurostat (2020: 8).

and others. The interdependencies and interactions between the European single market, the Eurozone, the European area without internal frontiers, the Schengen area in which border controls have been abolished, and the European legal space of fundamental rights form a blind spot in the institutionalized organization of intergovernmental EU decision-making. However, they give rise to inequalities of inclusion and to uneven territorial cohesion. Indeed, the austerity policies implemented from 2010 on in the wake of the Euro and debt crisis highlight this political deficit of European spatial constructions.

Various funds – including the European Social Fund (ESF) (1958), the European Regional Development Fund (1972), or the Cohesion Fund (1994) – have been established at the EU level to "correct" social and economic "disparities" and "imbalances" between regions and member states and to mitigate the problems associated with unemployment, as the Commission explains on its webpage in the EU's investment policy (European Commission 2021). But these funds do not initiate processes that counteract or dismantle the power hierarchies between member states and/or implement the redistribution of social resources on a supranational and or intranational level. Moreover, a significant cause of the uneven bargaining power of the member states is the policy context in which these funds are implemented. Since the late 1970s, measures taken to enhance social welfare and mitigate economic inequality between structurally weak and economically strong regions have more and more frequently been designed to serve the market (Lechevalier 2018). Policy approaches that run counter to market logics or uphold the need for the protection of social welfare and the leveling of regional differences as by-products of an increase in the GDP and converging living standards have lost influence in the single market. Instead, the member states and the European Community as well as the EU define social and infrastructure policy in terms of the goal of increasing the competitiveness of companies and business locations. This shift became apparent from the 1990s on, when the ESF programs, for example in the field of vocational training and retraining, and regional and cohesion policy funding assistance were placed within the ideological framework of 'social investment' and 'activation'. In the context of "market-driven human resource management" (Bode 2019: 136), regions and urban areas, like companies and employees, are perceived as individual entrepreneurs who manage their own man- and womanpower. In this perspective, the resources of regions, urban areas, and employees are "mobilized" with the help of business management instruments (Büttner 2012).

Observing and Describing Europeanization: Space, Territories, and Borders as Perspectives for Sociological Research

The previous section referred to statistics and maps to elucidate EU spatial constructions, the intergovernmental relations between member states, and the redefinition of border regimes. Statistical categories and cartography are part of the toolkit employed in the social sciences and historical research to observe and describe social realities. However, the intention behind the use of statistical and cartographical instruments in research is to avoid reproducing the power relationships embedded in space, territories, and borders by reflecting on and comparing statistics and maps. By interpreting statistics and maps, social scientists aim to study the processes triggered by the social and political constructions of space, territories, and borders as well as the domination, hierarchization, differentiation and de-differentiation, and, last but not least, (in-)equalities associated with these processes. When space, territories, and borders become devices for the sociological investigation of Europeanization, then such work focuses on the actors who act out and realize the intersections of space, territories, and borders – for instance, mobile workers, street-level bureaucrats in the authorities that deal with applications for political asylum, or experts who establish and elaborate categories for Eurostat or European guidelines (Büttner 2012; Hassenteufel & Palier 2014; Kazepov 2010; Lahusen & Wacker 2019). Utilizing spatial categories for sociological observation and description enables researchers to relate processes on the macro-theoretical and on the micro-theoretical level to one another. The sociological challenge is to integrate the multiple layers of interactions, mobilities, and regulations that inform social relations and power relationships within the EU into a coherent interpretive framework.

Describing the 'Politics of Scales'

The scalar-structuration approach proposed by geographer and political scientist Neil Brenner, drawing on Fernand Braudel and Henri Lefebvre, offers a means of studying these multiple layers. This approach focuses on the question of how **'geographical scales'** create vertical orders and in doing so (re-)hierarchize market economic exchange between states or regional or urban actors in the context of capitalist globalization (Brenner 2001, 2011). A geographical scale represents a site for economic and political action and, according to Brenner, should be distinguished from other social science spatial concepts such as space, place, locality, and territory. In building descriptions of the construction of the European legal space, of the institutionalization of the area without internal frontiers, or of the single market on the analysis of "scaling processes" and "politics of scales," researchers shed light on the "changing positionalities" in Europeanization (Brenner 2001: 603) and on the multiple 'spatialities of Europeanization' (Clark & Jones 2008). The scalar-structuration approach facilitates researchers' efforts to identify the opportunities that emerge (or fail to emerge) for economic and political actors when their activities interact with European border definitions or with the European intersections between transnational spaces, on the one hand, and respect for the "national identities" of "Member States" (art. 4 TEU), on the other. By taking changing positionalities seriously, such approaches bring into focus the uneven distribution of bargaining power of EU member states as well as the hierarchies and power relations that exist, for example between multinational companies and medium-sized or small companies or between metropolitan areas and border areas or areas with low population density. The sociological observation and description of rescaling processes makes it possible to highlight shifts in power that result, for example, from the re- or decentralization of financing structures in a member state or in the Euro area.

Taking up the Actors' jeux d'échelles

The **jeux d'échelles** [*games of scales*] approach developed by French historians and anthropologists as a tool for observing and describing interconnections in social relations also creates a perspective for the study of multiple layers in the processes of Europeanization and their discontinuities (Revel 1996; Marung & Middell 2019). In contrast to Brenner's concept of scales, proponents of the *jeux d'échelles* perspective conceptualize scales as yardsticks for gauging action. These yardsticks are not only based on territorially defined scales, like administrative levels of public action, but also on scales defined by professional socialization, by income, by social or legal status, or by historical experience. Depending on the configuration of the social relations, the interactions involve a certain variety of scales that mirror the multilayered character of social relations. According to the *jeux d'échelle* approach, the significance that an EU institution, a single-market freedom, the law of a member state, trade unions, the action of an NGO, etc. assumes in the process to be described arises in each case from experiences on different territorial scales and from the actors' socialization in specific contexts of interaction. In this perspective, the historical, anthropological, or sociological observation of the interdependencies and the structures of interactions is based, as a methodological principal, on the intentional variation in the scale focused on, in order to consider the layered structure of the social. This methodological principle is of interest for research on Europeanization in three ways. First, processes on the micro- and the macro-theoretical level can be empirically and analytically conceptualized as interconnected. For example, on the basis of an intentional scale variation, it is possible to relate the construction of the European legal space to the practices of freedom of movement or to the organization of a company, to the work in a local authority, or to access to social benefits in actual practice. Second, an intentional scale variation makes it possible to observe how territorial levels – for instance, European guidelines or the European production of expert knowledge – affect various occupational groups in different ways and to a different extent. Third, the methodological principle of scale variations is associated with a 'mobile perspective' (Amelina & Vasilache 2014). This perspective enables researchers to reflect on the flexible ways in which spatial constructions, territorial levels, and border definitions are related to the 'immobile'; that is, they can employ this approach to structure the character of political regimes and take into account the regulation of social interactions as something that is always situated in a specific place. Finally, the *jeux d'échelles* approach brings into focus the relations between mobile elites in the EU and population groups that are tied to 'locales'. The methodological principle of utilizing various focal points and scales induces researchers to reflect on their own position in the research process as sociologists of Europeanization and to integrate their position vis-à-vis the respective objects or subjects of their work into the analysis of over-lapping spaces, territories, and borders.

Concluding Remarks

Both the intersections of EU spatial constructions and respect for the identity of member states and their territorial integrity (Article 4, Treaty on European Union), on the one hand, and the overlapping of new shifting border definitions and traditional member states' borders, on the other hand, create variations and differentiations in the process of Europeanization. As this chapter has elucidated, the multiple forms of Europeanization result from asynchronous processes of legal and economic integration and transnationalization of criteria and standards for public policies. At the same time, the multiple forms of Europeanization are an expression of contradictions in the process of dismantling and constructing borders. The EU asylum regime is one of the most Europeanized policy areas. The construction of European external borders at times resembles a frontier – for instance, within the European Neighborhood Policy – at times, a control site in the style of historical *comptoir colonial* [*colonial trading posts*], and at times a border fence. Together they constitute a series of *spatialities of Europeanization* inside and outside of the EU. Another contradiction emerges from the discontinuities between transnational harmonization in the domain of the four freedoms (free movement of goods, free movement of capital, freedom to provide and establish services, and the free movement of working persons) and interstate coordination in welfare state affairs. For example, whereas regulations pertaining to the internal market are 'harmonized' across EU territorial borders, social security systems are differentiated and coordinated within the framework set by member states' borders and, last but not least, by national egoism. One of the consequences of these contradictions is the threat that Europeanization, as a political integration project, will increasingly be limited to a focus on market efficiency and performance.

Didactical Section

Key Learning Points

- Political space is mirrored in the territorialization of governance and the establishment of border regimes. Spatial constructions serve as a means of structuring social interaction and as such become an instrument of social control, domination, and power. Space, territories, and borders define membership and access to rights, determine inclusion and exclusion, and legitimate the sovereignty of rule.
- The EU is based on a specific spatial construction, in which nationally and supranationally guaranteed sovereignty as well as nationally and supranationally guaranteed economic and social orders and forms of solidarity are intertwined. The result is that, on the one hand, the member states of the EU share their sovereignty in certain policy areas, which have been steadily increasing in the course of political integration. On the other hand, the EU consists of the sum of the territories of the member states.
- A complex regime of different layers of regulations structures social interactions in the EU. This leads to multiple and uneven '*spatialities of Europeanization*'. These spatialities of Europeanization result, among other things, in unequal opportunities for participating in the "area without internal frontiers" and in the single market, as well as in unequal protection of the right to free movement through social policies. The interstate framework of EU spatial constructions, on the one hand, and the almost exclusively market-based understanding of territorial and social cohesion, on the other hand, prevent measures aimed at mitigating the multiple uneven 'spatialities of Europeanization'.
- Sociological observation and description in spatial categories focus on interactions and interdependencies between actors, their actions, and a specifically constituted or structured environment. Spatial approaches offer opportunities for researchers to relate processes on the macro-theoretical to those on the micro-theoretical level.
- When space, territories, and borders become devices used in sociological investigations of Europeanization, the focus is on the actors who act out and realize *the intersections of space, territories, and borders*, such as *mobile workers*, *street-level bureaucrats* who deal with asylum applications, or *experts* establishing and elaborating categories for Eurostat or European guidelines. The sociological challenge is to integrate the multiple layers of interactions, mobilities, and regulations informing social relations and power relationships in the EU into a coherent interpretive framework.

Glossary

Border: the main instrument for implementing a monopoly on defining legitimate modes of movement and for governing transnational interaction

Geographical scale: a site for economic and political action (Brenner 2001)

Jeux d'échelles: the interplay of yardsticks for gauging action (Revel 1996)

Phantom geographies: the "traces left in contemporary societies by defunct territorialities" (von Hirschhausen 2017: 107)

Space: refers, in the sense of the French word espace, not only to distance and time but also to "place", "site", "area", or "region" (Shields 2006)

Territory: represents, in the 20th century, the central concept of European governments for framing economic relations, industrialization, infrastructure policies, and welfare protection (Maier 2000)

Further Readings

Desrosières, A., 1998: *The Politics of Large Numbers: A History of Statistical Reasoning.* Cambridge, MA: Harvard University Press.

Lechevalier, A., 2018: Social Europe and Eurozone crisis: The Divided States of Europe. *Culture, Practice & Europeanization* 3(3):5–29. https://www.uni-flensburg.de/fileadmin/content/seminare/soziologie/dokumente/culture-practice-and-europeanization/cpe-vol.3-no.3-2018/lechevalier-2018.pdf (accessed December 12, 2020).

Löw, M., 2016: *The Sociology of Space: Materiality, Social Structures, and Action.* New York: Palgrave Macmillan.

Mau, S., H. Brabandt, L. Laube & C. Roos, 2012: *Liberal States and the Freedom of Movement: Selective Borders, Unequal Mobility.* Basingstoke: Palgrave Macmillan.

von Hirschhausen, B., 2017: The Heuristic Interest of the Concept of "Phantom Borders" in the Understanding of Cultural Regionalization. *L'Espace géographique* 46(2):106–125.

Additional Web-Sources

Borders in Motion is a research center at the European University Viadrina Frankfurt (Oder). The website of the center gives an overview of research focused on territorial, supranational, and non-governmental borders in the context of migration, work, and conflicts: https://www.borders-in-motion.de/profil

Website of the European Commission on the EU's Regional Policy: https://ec.europa.eu/re
gional_policy/en/2021_2027
Official information on the EU's Neighborhood Policy: https://ec.europa.eu/info/policies/euro
pean-neighbourhood-policy_en
Eurostat is the statistical office of the European Union: https://ec.europa.eu/eurostat/web/
main/home
ESPON is a cooperation program, co-financed by the European Regional Development Fund, this
program aims at "promoting and fostering a European territorial dimension in development
and cooperation": https://www.espon.eu – ESPON also provides a database of numerous
interesting representations of the EU's space: https://mapfinder.espon.eu/mapfinder/
*Mobilités, Migrations, Recomposition des espaces | Mobilität, Migration und räumliche
Neuordnung* is a blog published by the research group of the same name at Centre Marc
Bloch to report on its activities. Focal point is the transformation of spaces and forms of
mobility such as migration: https://rm2.hypotheses.org/

References

Amelina, A. & A. Vasilache, 2014: The Shadows of Enlargement: Theorising Mobility and
Inequality in a Changing Europe. *Migration Letters* 11(2):109–124.
Bartl, W., C. Papilloud & A. Terracher-Lipinski, 2019: Governing by Numbers – Key Indicators
and the Politics of Expectations. Special Issue. *Historical Social Research* 44(2).
Backfields, J., 2009: Remapping Inequality in Europe, The Net Effect of Regional Integration on
Total Income Inequality in the European Union. *International Journal of Comparative
Sociology* 50(5–6):486–509.
Bernhardt, C., 2017: Governance, Statehood, and Space in 20th Century Political Struggles:
An Introduction. *Historical Social Research* 42(2):199–217.
Blauberger, M., A. Heindelmaier, D. Kramer, D. Sinbjerg Martinsen, J. Sampson Thierry,
A. Schenk & B. Werner, 2018: ECJ Judges Read the Morning Papers: Explaining the
Turnaround of European Citizenship Jurisprudence. *Journal of European Public Policy*
25(10):1422–1441.
Bode, I., 2019: Let's Count and Manage – and Forget the Rest: Understanding Numeric
Rationalization in Human Service Provision. *Historical Social Research* 44(2):131–154.
Brenner, N., 2001: The Limits to Scale? Methodological Reflections on Scalar Structuration.
Progress in Human Geography 25(4):591–612.
Brenner, N., 2011: The Urban Question and the Scale Question: Some Conceptual
Clarifications. In: Glick Schiller, N. & A. Çağlar (eds.), *Locating Migration: Rescaling Cities
and Migrants*, pp. 23–41. Ithaca, NY: Cornell University Press.
Brenner, N. & S. Elden, 2009: Henri Lefebvre on State, Space, Territory. *International Political
Sociology* 3:353–377.
Bundeszentrale für politische Bildung, 2019: Außenhandel der EU. https://www.bpb.de/nachs
chlagen/zahlen-und-fakten/europa/70555/aussenhandel-der-eu (accessed December
23, 2020).
Büttner, S., 2012: *Mobilizing Regions, Mobilizing Europe: Expert Knowledge and Scientific
Planning in European Regional Development*. Abingdon: Routledge.

Clark, J. & A. Jones, 2008: The Spatialities of Europeanisation: Territory, Government and Power in 'EUrope'. *Transactions of the Institute of British Geographers* 33(3):300–318.

Desrosières, A., 1998: *The Politics of Large Numbers: A History of Statistical Reasoning.* Cambridge, MA: Harvard University Press.

Döring, J. & T. Thielmann (eds.), 2008: *Spatial Turn: Das Raumparadigma in den Kultur- und Sozialwissenschaften.* Bielefeld: transcript.

Eigmüller, M., 2007: *Grenzsicherungspolitik. Funktion und Wirkung der europäischen Außengrenze.* Wiesbaden: VS.

Eigmüller, M. & G. Vobruba (eds.), 2016: *Grenzsoziologie.* Wiesbaden: VS.

European Commission, 2007: *The single market: review of achievements.* Accompanying document to the Communication from the Commission to the European Parliament, the Council, the European Economic and Social Committee and the Committee of the Regions – A single market for 21st century Europe. SEC/2007/1521 final.

European Commission, 2021: *The EU's main investment policy.* https://ec.europa.eu/re gional_policy/en/policy/what/investment-policy/ (accessed June 23, 2021).

Eurostat, 2020: International trade in goods. Statistics Explained. https://ec.europa.eu/euro stat/statistics-explained/pdfscache/1188.pdf (accessed January 21, 2021).

Farahat, A. & C. Krenn, 2018: Der Europäische Gerichtshof in der Eurokrise: Eine konflikttheoretische Perspektive. *Der Staat* 57:357–385.

Ferrera, M., 2003: European Integration and National Social Citizenship: Changing Boundaries, New Structuring? *Comparative Political Studies* 36(6):611–652.

Fink, M. & A. Lammers, 2018: Ungleichheiten harmonisieren: Lohngleichheit und Sozialstatistiken in den Europäischen Gemeinschaften (1957–1978). In: Fertikh, K., H. Wieters & B. Zimmermann (eds.), *Ein soziales Europa als Herausforderung. L'Europe sociale en question,* pp. 117–140. Frankfurt a. M.: Campus.

Hassenteufel, P. & B. Palier, 2014: Still the Sound of Silence? Towards a New Phase in the Europeanisation of Welfare State Policies in France. *Comparative European Politics* 13(1): 112–130.

Heidenreich, M. (ed.), 2016: *Exploring Inequality in Europe: Diverging Income and Employment Opportunities in the Crisis.* Cheltenham, UK: Edward Elgar.

Jureit, U., 2012: *Das Ordnen von Räumen. Territorium und Lebensraum im 19. und 20. Jahrhundert.* Hamburg: Hamburger Edition.

Jureit, U. (ed.), 2016: *Umkämpfte Räume. Raumbilder, Ordnungswille und Gewaltmobilisierung.* Göttingen: Wallstein Verlag.

Jureit, U. & N. Tietze, 2018: Postsouveräne Territorialität. Die Europäische Union als supranationaler Raum. *Der Staat* 55:353–371.

Kazepov, Y., 2010: Rescaling Social Policies towards Multilevel Governance in Europe: Some Reflections on Processes at Stake and Actors Involved. In: Kazepov, Y. (ed.), *Rescaling Social Policies: towards Multilevel Governance in Europe.* Volume 1, pp. 35–72. Farnham: Ashgate.

Kracauer, S., [1926] 1990: Über Arbeitsnachweise. Konstruktionen eines Raumes. In: Kracauer, S., *Schriften.* Vol. 5, pp. 185–192. Frankfurt a. M.: Suhrkamp.

Lahusen, C. & M. Wacker, 2019: A European Field of Public Administration? Administrative Cooperation of Asylum Agencies in the Dublin system. In: Heidenreich, M. (ed.), *Horizontal Europeanisation: The Transnationalisation of Daily Life and Social Fields in Europe,* pp. 153–174. London: Routledge.

Lechevalier, A., 2018: Social Europe and Eurozone Crisis: The Divided States of Europe. *Culture, Practice & Europeanization* 3(3):5–29. https://www.uni-flensburg.de/fileadmin/content/seminare/soziologie/dokumente/culture-practice-and-europeanization/cpe-vol.3-no.3-2018/lechevalier-2018.pdf (accessed December 12, 2020).

Lefèbvre, H., 1974: *La production de l'espace*. Paris: Editions Anthropos. [English translation: 1991: *The production of space*. Oxford: Basil Blackwell].

Löw, M., 2016: *The Sociology of Space: Materiality, Social Structures, and Action*. New York: Palgrave Macmillan.

Maier, C. S., 2000: Consigning the Twentieth Century to History: Alternative Narratives for the Modern Era. *American Historical Review* 105(3):807–831.

Marung, S. & M. Middell (eds.), 2019: *Spatial Formats under the Global Condition*. Berlin: De Gruyter Oldenbourg.

Mau, S., H. Brabandt, L. Laube & C. Roos, 2012: *Liberal States and the Freedom of Movement: Selective Borders, Unequal Mobility*. Basinkstoke: Palgrave Macmillan.

Milward, A. S., 1992: *The European Rescue of the Nation-State*. London: Routledge.

Münch, R., 2008: *Die Konstruktion der europäischen Gesellschaft: Zur Dialektik von transnationaler Integration und nationaler Desintegration*. Frankfurt a. M.: Campus.

Pataut, E., 2018: Securité sociale, assistance sociale et libre circulation: remarques sur les frontières de la solidarité en Europe. *Cahiers Européens* 11:169–189.

Patel, K. K. & H. C. Röhl, 2020: *Transformation durch Recht. Mit einem Kommentar von Andreas Wirschung*. Tübingen: Mohr Siebeck.

Revel, J. (ed.), 1996: *Jeux d'échelles. La micro-analyse à l'expérience*. Paris: Gallimard-Le Seuil.

Rosental, P. A., 2006: Géopolitique et Etat-Providence: Le BIT et la politique mondiale des migrations dans l'entre-deux guerres. *Annales, Histoire, Sciences Sociales* 61(1):99–134.

Shields, R., 2006: Knowing Space. *Theory Culture Society* 23(2–3):146–149.

Tietze, N., 2018: Legal Imagination am Europäischen Gerichtshof: Erzählungen europäischer Richter über Gleichbehandlung und Kategorisierungen, pp. 323–350. In: Fertikh, K., H. Wieters & B. Zimmermann (eds.), *Ein soziales Europa als Herausforderung. L'Europe sociale en question*. Frankfurt a. M.: Campus.

Vauchez, A., 2015: *Brokering Europe: Euro Lawyers and the Making of a Transnational Polity*. Cambridge: Cambridge University Press.

Vobruba, G., 2003: The Enlargement Crisis of the European Union: Limits of the Dialectics of Integration and Expansion. *Journal of European Social Policy* 13(3):35–49.

Vobruba, G., 2004: Grenzen des Projekts Europa: Von der Expansionsdynamik zur abgestuften Integration. *Osteuropa* 54(5–6):61–74.

von Hirschhausen, B., 2017: The heuristic Interest of the Concept of "Phantom Borders" in the Understanding of Cultural Regionalization. *L'Espace géographique* 46(2):106–125.

Wobbe, T., 2005: Die Verortung Europas in der Weltgesellschaft: Historische Europasemantik und Identitätspolitik der Europäischen Union. In: Heintz, B., R. Münch & H. Tyrell (eds.), *Weltgesellschaft. Sonderheft der Zeitschrift für Soziologie*, pp. 348–373. Stuttgart: Lucius & Lucius.

Sebastian M. Büttner & Monika Eigmüller
4 Europe and Culture: Perspectives of Cultural Sociology

The analysis of culture is indeed a very prominent topic of sociology. Culture itself, however, is a complex and multifaceted concept, one that is neither easy to grasp nor to define (see Info-Box 4.1). Because of its inherent vagueness and the general "semantic confusion" (Kroeber & Parsons 1958: 582) surrounding its very meaning, some researchers have even suggested that we abandon the term 'culture' altogether from the canon of major sociological conceptions in favour of more concrete and precise analytical terms and concepts (Luhmann 1995). Yet the idea and meta-concept of culture has not only persisted, but has gained increasing popularity in recent decades, both in everyday life and in scientific discourse, especially in the humanities and in social sciences (Reckwitz 2000; Jacobs & Spillman 2005; Bachmann-Medick 2016). This more general **cultural turn** (Alexander 1988: 91) is partly also associated with processes and dynamics that are at the heart of this textbook: the increasing transnationalization and global integration of society, and, in particular, the process of Europeanization (Tomlinson 1999; Ritzer 2010: 171–197).

Just as diverse as usages and definitions of culture are the numerous different references to culture in the European context. Culture is often used as an integrative concept, referring to commonalities amongst Europeans – i.e., shared cultural characteristics, values and experiences and a common *European cultural heritage* (Rietbergen 1998). But it is also frequently used as a key indicator of social distinction, to mark differences amongst nations, regions, ethnicities, local traditions, and religious groups within Europe. This is particularly pertinent in Europe, where national, regional, and local traditions are often fervently put forward as markers of cultural identity. Aptly capturing this dual meaning of culture is the phrase "united in diversity", which since around 2000 has been an official slogan of the European Union, a reference to the persistence of national cultural peculiarities and the huge variety of cultures and traditions all around Europe (Calligaro 2014, see also: https://europa.eu/european-union/about-eu/symbols/motto_en, accessed January 24, 2021).

Info-Box 4.1: The meaning(s) of culture
Etymologically, the term *culture* derives from the Latin verb *colere*, meaning "to reside", "to cultivate" or "to worship". It is also strongly linked to basic religious practices, since the word 'cult' directly derives from the Latin word *cultus*, denoting the performance of certain

https://doi.org/10.1515/9783110673630-004

religious rites or simply worship service. Hence, the concept of culture is fundamentally associated with the development of humankind, marking a distinction between *cultivated*
human practice and *non-cultivated*, ("raw"), nature (Lévi-Strauss 1983).

In the humanities and social sciences, the concept of culture mainly characterizes the
basic expressive and **symbolic** dimension(s) of human nature. Hence, culture is used an
umbrella term for a whole range of human expressions that are shared and 'cultivated', in
the literal sense, in collectives. These expressions can be both *material* (e.g., certain practices, techniques, artefacts, and concrete tangible symbolic expression) and *immaterial*
(such as ideas, norms, beliefs, or values). Moreover, they encompass a whole range of different expressions from mundane everyday customs, habits, and traditions (e.g., styles of
clothing and cooking, tool usage, housing construction) to more complex, abstract, and so-
phisticated systems of knowledge, symbolic systems, and practices of meaning-making
(such as literature and arts, philosophy and sciences, religion and other types of fundamental mythologies and belief systems, etc.).

The distinction between more complex *cultural systems* and mundane elements of *everyday
culture* has also found its expression in *evaluative* and *normative* distinctions between different
kinds of culture, such as the distinction between *advanced* and *folk cultures, classical* and *pop
culture*, or numerous other hierarchical distinctions of 'taste' and 'cultural consumption' (Bourdieu 1985). Beyond that, conceptions of culture also differ in their scope: On the one hand, we
find *narrow* definitions of culture as just one of many spheres to be found in society next to
other spheres, i.e., a distinct sphere of cultural production, encompassing the arts, theatre,
literature that is independent of other major spheres of society, such as politics, economy, or
the domain of sciences (Kroeber & Parsons 1958). In marked contrast, *broader* definitions of
culture rather see culture as an omnipresent phenomenon that is not limited to a certain area
or realm of social life, but rather fundamentally structures the development and conduct of
human beings, social relations, society, and (to some extent) even what we consider as 'nature'. This is the conception of culture that widely predominates in the contemporary cultural
sciences and cultural sociology (Reckwitz 2000; Alexander 2003; Adloff et al. 2014).

It is important to keep in mind this conceptual ambiguity and versatility of culture while exploring and describing Europe's cultural dimension and the cultural
implications of Europeanization, since conceptions of culture always carry certain
political and normative implications (Welsch 1999; Brubaker 2002). Significantly,
the concept of culture can be used in a highly selective and even exclusionary
way, as a fundamental marker of social belonging and strong **collective identity,**
i.e., to distinguish people who share similar cultural characteristics (e.g., certain
habits, traditions, customs, symbols etc.) from those who do not. This rather *static*
and **essentialist** conception is usually associated with historical conceptions of
culture common during the 18th and 19th centuries, such as the so-called '**ball
model of culture**' ("*Kugelmodell der Kultur*") proposed by the German poet and
philosopher Johann Gottfried Herder (1744–1803). Yet culture can also be conceived as a relatively *dynamic* phenomenon that changes constantly over time and
may encompass a variety of different and even conflicting cultural elements. This

constructivist conception of culture is standard in contemporary approaches to cultural sociology (Reckwitz 2000; Alexander 2003). Nevertheless, essentialist ideas about culture have not yet disappeared. They are still to be found in the social sciences and, especially, in contemporary political debates and reflections on culture and collective identities (Brubaker 2002).

The distinction between *static* and more *dynamic* conceptions of culture also resonates with the varying interpretations of sociality and collectivity used in the fields of sociology and social psychology. Groups and societies with a strong sense of social belonging and clear-cut *in-group* and *out-group distinctions* are usually defined as highly 'cohesive' or even 'closed' collectives, as opposed to more pluralistic, multi-cultural, cosmopolitan, or even transcultural societies (Welsch 1999). The degree of cultural diversity usually (but not necessarily!) increases with the size of a collective (Durkheim [1893] 1997). This is particularly characteristic within the context of Europeanization, which brings together a huge number of different ethnic and national traditions and promotes a relatively high level of cultural diversity. Hence, analyses of on culture and cultural dynamics are at the heart of sociological reflections on European social history and the changing patterns of 'societalization' (in the sense of the German notion of *Vergesellschaftung*) brought on by more recent processes of Europeanization (Delanty & Rumford 2005; Beck & Grande 2007). Consequently, it is a major challenge for scholars working on the sociology of Europeanization to engage in these reflections without tacitly presupposing a dominant understanding of *European culture* or making essentialist assumptions about 'European' cultural characteristics. On the other hand, distinctive cultural features and dynamics shape European **civilization**, and it is the task of sociology and the related social and cultural sciences to capture major cultural developments and patterns.

Europe and Culture = European Culture?
A Distinction of Five Major Understandings

Attempts to identify distinctive features of European culture are at least as manifold as attempts to determine the meanings of culture. To date, scholars have put forth quite different ideas and understandings of *European culture* – all of which influence how we perceive and narrate the cultural history of Europe and the cultural evolution of European civilization(s). In exploring the discourse on European culture, the Dutch sociologist Jan Berting (2006: 52) has identified at least five different prevalent concepts: European culture as a common *European cultural heritage* with a specific cultural identity (1), European culture as a *totality of national cultures* (2); European culture as a *totality of cultures* (3); Europe as a sphere comprised of different *historical culture areas* (4); and Europe as a *modern culture in the making* (5). In one way or another, all five of these different ideas are used in explorations of European history and reflections on Europe's cultural development. In the following pages, we draw on this distinction and briefly portray each of the five conceptions referring to major developments, concepts, and approaches of sociological reflections about European culture.

(1) *European culture as Europe's common 'European heritage'*: This is the idea about Europe's cultural development that we often find in history books and in general introductions to European cultural history (Davies 1996; Rietbergen 1998; Ostergren & Le Bossé 2011). It is also strongly linked to the political conceptions of a common 'European heritage' put forth, for example, in various international conventions since the beginning of European integration, and by major European political organizations like the Council of Europe, the European Commission, or the European Parliament (Council of Europe 2018; EPRS 2018; European Commission 2019).

According to Berting (2006: 53), official conceptions and understandings of European cultural heritage usually tend to focus on the "noble elements" of European history. Hence, definitions and conceptions of a common European cultural heritage have often reflected a rather generalist stance, one that highlights major 'cultural developments' within European civilization and the distinct cultural practices and 'achievements' that are widely and commonly regarded as typically 'European'. These ideas about European culture come up most often in studies of major historical cultural developments and cornerstones (the Greek and Roman heritage or the rise of Renaissance culture); however, they can also be found in scholarship on the evolution of principles of modernity (such as liberty and human rights) during the European Enlightenment of the 16th to 18th centuries (Davies 1996; Delanty 2019). We also find numerous references to the development of a canon of typically 'European' cultural expressions and representations, such as the evolution of typical architectural styles and traditions, the pan-European development of arts and styles of music, or the development of certain general cultural standards and practices (Ostergren & Le Bossé 2011).[1] Historically, the development and spread of common European cultural 'achievements'

---

1 Many of the numerous cultural products and expressions that are commonly referred to as outstanding representations of European heritage are also officially listed and promoted as part of the collection of World Heritage by the UNESCO (see: http://whc.unesco.org/en/eur-na/, accessed February 25, 2021).

were strongly embedded in clerical and aristocratic structures (Elias [1939] 1994) and spurred by various forms of pan-European trade and other historical types of pan-European mobility and exchange. In fact, it has been shown that cities and major cultural centres emerged along the lines of major historical trade routes from Northern Italian cities, through the central European regions up to Britain and Northern Europe (Braudel 1981; Rietbergen 1998).

Often disregarded in narrations of European cultural history, however, are the multiple foundations and diverse historical roots of European culture. Without doubt, the history of Europe and European culture stretches back to far before Greek and Roman civilization and reaches far beyond the current official borders of the European continent (Rietbergen 1998; Delanty 2019). Both the Mediterranean Sea and the Eurasian territory have always been zones of dynamic social exchange and cultural transfer (Braudel [1949] 2002; Hann 2016). The distinction between the 'European Occident' (in the west) and 'the Orient' (in the east), which is fundamental to the rise of a common European self-understanding (Said 1985), has undergone many semantic changes and shifts throughout history.

More striking still, scholarly reflections on Europe's cultural heritage still largely ignore the strong colonial history of many European empires and the role that colonialism and imperialism have played in the emergence of European culture and self-understanding (Said 1993; Osterhammel 2005). As British sociologist Gurminder Bhambra has noted, scholars' failure to address the colonial histories of Europe, "enables the dismissal of the postcolonial and multicultural present of Europe and the associated populations. A properly cosmopolitan Europe [. . .] would be one that understood that its historical constitution in colonialism cannot be rendered to the past simply by the denial of that past" (Bhambra 2017: 396). The debate on this topic is just about to emerge in contemporary European studies and in sociology in the wake of an increasing reception of global history and post-colonial thought (see also Chapter 5 in this volume).

(2) *European culture as a totality of 'national cultures'*: In marked opposition to the first understanding of European culture that we just outlined above, this second conception points to the huge variety of cultures along the lines of national boundaries, rather than the cultural commonalities shared by Europeans. Here, Europe is not conceived as a common cultural cosmos or entity, but rather as an agglomerate of distinct national cultures and traditions – a Europe of nation states, so to speak. Underpinning this perspective are strong conceptions of national sovereignty (and, especially, a strong valuation of national cultural sovereignty) and the idea of the nation as an 'original' refuge of social belonging and cultural identity. Without a doubt, national cultural traditions, national demarcations, and national cultural distinctions still have a major

impact on our understanding of society and overall structural differences amongst European people. In Europe, politics, public discourses, and public life in general have been structured along the lines of national borders and pronounced national distinctions for almost two centuries now (Therborn 1995).

At the same time, however, we must be sensitive to the constructed character of national cultures and to their numerous divergences and ambivalences. The assertion and establishment of national cultural patterns is usually not self-evident, unfolding instead within an overly complex and conflictual social process. Even today, one finds in many countries no single predominant majority culture, but rather a variety of different ethnic cultures and traditions, which coexist with varying degrees of consensuality (Brubaker 1996). In fact, research on the formation of modern nation states has shown that many national traditions and regional cultural characteristics that seem quite 'natural' and 'self-evident' today were consciously put forward and promoted by cultural elites, mainly during the nation-building between 1800s and early 1900s (Gellner 1983; Anderson 1983; Hobsbawm 1990). It was with this understanding that Benedict Anderson (1936–2015), a figurehead of constructionist studies about nationalism and nation-building, developed the seminal concept of nations as "imagined communities" (Anderson 1983) – in strong juxtaposition to the fictitious idea that nations, national history, and traditions are naturally given.

Moreover, nation-building and the establishment of predominating ideas of national sovereignty were often violently imposed through very rigid, patronizing, and deadly policies (Therborn 1995; Bourdieu 2013). Thus, it would be problematic to take for granted the existence of nations, national cultures, and alleged long-lasting 'national' traditions. At the same time, the significance of national cultures, institutions, and societal structures can neither be denied nor underestimated. Despite ongoing Europeanization and global integration, the idea of national sovereignty and national political institutions still play a central role in contemporary society. Therefore, the distinction of European culture and society along the lines of national characteristics and conducting country comparisons are still highly relevant and justified in contemporary Sociology of Europeanization (Lepsius 1999; Gerhards 2007; Immerfall & Therborn 2010).

(3) *European culture as a totality of cultures*: The understanding of European culture as a totality of cultures represents a "much wider concept than that of the European culture as a whole of national cultures" (Berting 2006: 56). Instead of emphasizing national cultural differences, it addresses 'cultural diversity' in a much broader and wider sense. Scholarship in this vein stresses local and regional differences, and the variety of ethnic traditions and cultural differences within and across existing national borders that result from the long-term development of historical regions and from the distinct cultural

traditions of ethnic groups and cultural minorities (Panayi 1999; Cole 2011; Mishkova & Trencsényi 2017). Here, European culture is seen as an agglomerate and amalgam of all these different cultures (Hann 2016; Delanty 2019: 241–263; Murphy et al. 2020).

In ethnological anthologies, but also in numerous everyday cultural encounters, we indeed find a huge variety of European folk traditions. Ranging from traditional costumes and styles of music and dance to culinary traditions, local customs, everyday routines, and languages and dialects, most of these contrasting cultural characteristics are strongly influenced by and associated with the vast array of longstanding ethnic groups and traditions in Europe (see Info-Box 4.2). Nevertheless, definitions of ethnicities and minorities are highly contested (European Commission 2017; Pan et al. 2018a: XXXI) and issues regarding the recognition of ethnicities and cultural minorities continue to fuel numerous political disputes and conflicts (Alcock 2000; Pan & Pfeil 2018; Pan et al. 2018a). Sociological reflections of ethnicities and ethnic cultures must necessarily address these disputes, questions of classification and categorization, and processes of ethnicity-based *boundary work* and *group-making* (Brubaker 1996, 2002). Beyond that, it is also important to be aware of the frequently stylized and constructed character of cultural or ethnic traditions. As Hobsbawm and Ranger (1983) have shown, even most cherished and hallowed (ethnic) traditions have been adapted and re-adapted over time, and many have simply been (re-)invented in modern times.

Info-Box 4.2: Ethnic groups, minorities, and languages in Europe
Definitions of ethnicities, ethnic groups, and other types of culturally defined groups and communities (for example, certain language groups) are highly contested (European Commission 2017; Pan et al. 2018a: XXXI). What is clear, however, is that the ethnic distribution of the about 770 million people living on the European continent between the Atlantic and the Urals is not congruent, by and large, with Europe's political division of states (Pan & Pfeil 2018: 3). On the European continent there are currently 47 'acknowledged' nation states, but the number of 'acknowledged peoples' and 'national minorities' dispersed throughout Europe amounts to 104. Furthermore, the absolute number of cultural minorities is significantly higher, since the definition of a *minority* is not necessarily linked to the concept of ethnicity or to a certain ethnic identity. In addition, cultural minorities are usually counted on a country basis, such that we often find duplicate references in official statistics.

Since *language* is one of the most important markers of social and cultural distinction – and an important denominator of local, regional, and national culture and identity – language politics have traditionally constituted a crucial feature of cultural politics (Anderson 1983; König 2002). It is estimated that there are almost 150 (143, in fact) actively spoken languages on the European continent (Haarmann 2011). In comparison to that of other continents and countries, such as Indonesia (701), Nigeria (427), India (418), Brazil (236), the USA (224) and China (206), this number is surprisingly low. This is not what one would expect against the backdrop of strong evocations and perceptions of Europe's cultural diversity in political proclamations and in public discourse. Yet 48 of Europe's languages are spoken by more than a million people – this number is higher than in any other region worldwide (Haarmann 2011; for an overview of major European languages and language families, see: Pan et al. 2018b: 40ff.)

(4) *European cultural areas*: Defining culture and cultural differences in Europe in terms of *cultural areas* is another major approach to European culture that we find both in everyday life and in academic research. One popular distinction aligns cultural areas to major linguistic traditions, distinguishing 'Roman countries' for instance, from 'Germanic', 'Slavic' or 'Scandinavian countries' (see also Info-Box 4.2 above). Similarly, historical-cultural areas and societies with comprehensible common historical experiences are often clustered together. Accordingly, we often find the categorization of 'Mediterranean countries' that are distinguished, for instance, from 'Celtic' or 'Northern European countries' and 'post-soviet' countries from Central and Eastern Europe. Another important aspect of this approach is the identification of cultural areas along the lines of major religious affiliations – such as, above all, the distinction between historically 'Catholic', 'Orthodox', and 'Protestant' cultural areas, many instances of which can still be found in Europe's economic geography and cultural landscape (Panther 1997; Inglehart 2006; Gerhards 2007, 2010).

Underlying these approaches is the assumption that language, religion, and politics have a long-term effect on mentalities, habits, and every cultural practice of 'European civilization'. One of the main classical authors to deeply reflect on the long-term effects of culture on the evolution of larger 'cultural circles' ('*Kulturkreise*') was Max Weber (1864–1920). In his famous essay *The Protestant Ethic and the Spirit of Capitalism* (Weber [1904] 2002) and in his unfinished *Comparative Studies of Religious Ethics* (Weber 1920), he analysed the relationship between everyday social practice and religion in different cultural areas. Another important classical reference is the idea of the *longue dureé* proposed by the French historian Fernand Braudel (1902–1985), a major figure of the so-called *Annales School* of socio-historical research (see Info-Box 4.3). A third major concept from historical sociology that is also highly relevant for understanding the long-term cultural developments and differences in Europe is that of **path dependency**, introduced by institutionalist scholars (Thelen 1999). Institutionalist concepts are often used to account for continuities of social structures and the influence of culture and **institutions** on the structuration of social differences throughout Europe (Lepsius 1999; Münch 2010).

Yet, just as we must exercise caution vis-à-vis simple reifications of national, local, or ethnic cultures, we should also be careful not to simply presume the existence of long-term cultural patterns and cultural areas. There is always a certain risk of oversimplification and misinterpretation when we take for granted the persistence of cultural logics and larger cultural areas. Scholarly analysis of long-term cultural factors and structures, it is safe to say, always requires a certain level of "reflexivity" (Bourdieu 1990; Brubaker 2002) on our underlying analytical assumptions and how we conceptualize the persistence of long-term cultural structures and logics.

Info-Box 4.3: The Annales school and Fernand Braudel's concept of the longue dureé
The so-called *Annales* school of socio-historical analysis was one of the most influential socio-historical research movements of the 20th century. It was named after the scholarly journal the *Annales d'histoire économique et sociale*, founded by a group of prominent French historians including Lucien Febvre (1878–1956), Henri Hauser (1866–1946), and Marc Bloch (1886–1944). One of the most important figures of the second generation of the *Annales* school, Fernand Braudel (1902–1985), studied the long-term cultural evolution of civilization around the Mediterranean Sea and the development of trade and culture along the lines of historical trade routes (Braudel 1981), among other topics. He was interested in how socio-historical analysis captures the relationship between time and space. Braudel's approach to social history strongly influenced the development of other major paradigms in social history, such as, above all, the development of Immanuel Wallerstein's (1930–2019) world-systems-approach.

In his book *The Mediterranean and the Mediterranean World in the Age of Philip II*, Braudel ([1949] 2002) proposed a tripartite division of historical time. At one level, he saw the so-called *histoire événementielle* ('event history') – a perspective that continues to predominate in historical scholarship, especially in its perception of history as a constant flow of events. At a second level and at the opposite end of his conceptual paradigm, Braudel identified the relatively stable *histoire quasi immobile*, that is, those dimensions of reality that mainly appear as constants, or for which change is so slow as to be almost imperceptible. This level is mainly associated with long-term geological and geo-cultural formations, such as the Mediterranean Sea in southern Europe, the Alpes in Central Europe, or the Baltic Sea in the North, and the emergence of typical socio-economic and cultural structures around these stable and distinctive geological formations. In between these two dimensions or levels, Braudel identifies structures of *longue dureé*: relatively stable cultural, economic, and political formations that are shaped by certain socio-cultural conditions, but that slowly change and transform over time (for a more extensive discussion, see Harris 2004).

(5) *Europe as a modern culture in the making*: The fifth and final concept in Berting's classification is, first of all, strongly linked with classical debates within sociology regarding the larger socio-economic and cultural effects of industrialization and modernization since the end of 18th century. These debates often draw on Weber's cultural sociology and on his theory of **cultural rationalization**, as well as on issues, topics, and reflections of other classical sociologists, such as Karl Marx, Émile Durkheim, Ferdinand Tönnies, Georg Simmel and

many more. The so-called 'founding fathers' of sociology extensively explored and sought to identify the typical cultural features and sociological implications of a European modernity that has emerged since the 14th-century Renaissance and, even more powerfully, since the European Enlightenment of the 18th and 19th centuries. Proponents of this approach often see the current era of Europeanization as having strong cultural roots in the historical nascence of European modernity (Münch 1994, 2010; Müller 2010; Strath & Wagner 2017).

Scholarly reflections on Europe as a *modern culture in the making* is also linked with other, more recent debates in sociology and related disciplines. Within these, one cluster of studies focuses on processes of cultural rationalization in a global context; a good example here are recent discussions about the global diffusion of a highly rationalized and scientized expert culture that is strongly embedded and institutionalized in practices of international organization (IOs) and similar political entities, such as the European Union (Meyer 2010; Krücken & Drori 2010; Rumford & Buhari-Gulmez 2018). Studies from this perspective interpret European integration as a specific expression of cultural rationalization whose values, principles, and practices are constantly being evoked and upheld in official legal documents and in the everyday routines of EU policymaking (Büttner 2012; Foret & Calligaro 2018). A second major group of studies focuses on the larger transformations of modernity during the second half of the twentieth century. These more recent reflections on the advent of the 'post-industrial network society' (Castells 2009), the rise of new societal challenges and risks in a new era of 'reflexive modernity' (Beck 1999) and increasing 'cosmopolitization' are also intricately linked to considerations on the cultural logics and effects of Europeanization (Delanty & Rumford 2005; Beck & Grande 2007; Heidenreich 2019).

Even more, the European integration project is one of unprecedented transnational society-building: a distinctive political project that entails an exceptional degree of political integration and supranational institution-building, as well as an extraordinarily open and contingent process of transnational society-building (in the sense put forth in Simmel's concept of *Vergesellschaftung*). Nowhere in the world has economic, political, and societal integration gone as far as it has in Europe in the aftermath of World War II, and especially since the fall of the Soviet communism near the end of the 20th century. In effect, Europeanization represents a kind of real-life experiment in transnational society-building, and may thus even mark an epochal watershed in the history of modernity, as Ulrich Beck and Edgar Grande (2007: 31) point out in their seminal book *Cosmopolitan Europe*:

[T]he process of Europeanization can and must be understood as part of a comprehensive 'epochal break' in the development of modern societies. Only in this way can the potentials, dynamics, contradictions, crises and impacts of the European project be grasped completely and classified correctly. This project is about much more than the removal of toll barriers, the introduction of a common currency, the construction of new bureaucracies, etc. Europe's reflexive modernization gives rise to the structures of a new, transnationally interconnected society that breaks out of the container of the nation state and simultaneously transforms its own basic institutions.

As during the classical era of modernity, however, contemporary Europe is far from meeting the high normative ambitions and expectations that are often associated with Europeanization. On the contrary, the multiple crises of the past decade – the Euro crisis, the refugee crisis, the Brexit and, not least, the rise of anti-European movements – clearly show the ambivalences and flipside of the bold and ambitious utopia of a 'cosmopolitan Europe' (Bhambra 2016, 2017; Wagner 2017; Outhwaite 2017). Hence, the European project is always at risk of failing or being dismantled (Beck & Grande 2007: 224–230), as the widening disparities amongst the EU member states and growing 'dismantling' and 'disintegration' of the European Union threaten to upside the ambitious dream of a cosmopolitan Europe (Krastev 2017).

Major Topics and Debates of the Cultural Sociology of Europeanization

When surveying the major sociological topics and research approaches on European culture, we find four key thematic fields: explorations of values and value changes in European societies; analyses of an emerging European public sphere; studies of changes in collective identifications and of the traits and characteristics of European identity; and finally, explorations of European collective memory and other dimensions of European cultural policy. Since cultural research is highly interdisciplinary, many of the following debates strongly intersect with debates and discussions from neighboring disciplines, especially modern European history, political sciences, culture and media studies, and cultural anthropology. Moreover, in all four thematic fields the five conceptions of European culture that we discussed before keep popping up in the debates and research programs of cultural sociology in light of Europeanization.

Values and Value Change in European Societies

Explorations of values and value differences amongst European societies have long stood at the centre of a cultural sociology of Europeanization (Diez Medrano 2003; Gerhards 2010). Many of the research approaches on this subject use quantitative methods to explore cultural differences amongst European countries or amongst groups of countries (see concepts two and four, above). Scholars have also engaged in lively discussion about European values in historical sociology, social theory, and political philosophy (Joas & Wiegandt 2005; Habermas 2009; Strath & Wagner 2017). These discussions are thematically linked to the debates discussed above under concepts one and five.

Reflection of the role values in society has a strong tradition in sociology. In classical sociological approaches, values were seen as an important basis of social integration, setting the moral foundations for a well-functioning society (Durkheim [1893] 1997). Surprisingly, however, although the concept of values has gained salience in academia and public discourse there is no solid agreement as to what values actually are. According to van Deth and Scarbrough (1998: 22), values are "non-empirical – that is, not directly observable – concepts of the desirable [. . .] with a particular relevance for behavior." However, whether values directly influence behavior has always been hotly debated by sociologists. While a Weberian interpretation would indeed give values an impact on behavior insofar as they "determine the tracks along which action has been pushed" (Weber 1991: 101), Niklas Luhmann emphasizes in marked contrast that values are far too abstract to guide concrete action, since they "are not like fixed stars, but rather like balloons, whose covers are kept for blowing them up on occasion, especially at festivities." (Luhmann 1997: 342).

However, whether something is seen as valuable or not differs within and across societies. This is particularly significant for the sociology of European integration. The European Union has often been described as a "community of values" (Foret & Calligaro 2018) at the core of which lie democracy and a liberal understanding of the rule of law, laid down in the treaties and the Charter of Fundamental Rights of the EU. Initially, it was considered necessary to intensify the economic links between member states to secure a lasting peace between members while at the same time broadly anchoring the liberal consensus of values in EU member societies, across social classes and national cultures (Eigmüller & Trenz 2020).

Whether and to what extent the EU has fostered value convergence across the continent has been the subject of heated debate amongst sociologists. On the one hand, we can observe that the Europeanization of Western democracies has contributed to a long-term cultural shift towards liberal values. Inglehart

(1971) described this as a "silent revolution", a transformation "altering the basic value priorities of given generations, because of changing conditions influencing their basic socialization." (Inglehart 1971: 991) Accordingly, empirical sociological studies show that the EU member states from Western Europe have developed similar value patterns over time, anchored in similar sets of 'modern' values (such as rational secularism and tolerance) (Gerhards 2007). On the other hand, however, we still see significant cross-country diversity with respect to certain values, such as those associated with self-expression or religion (Diez Medrano 2003; Inglehart & Welzel 2005). In line with Inglehart's assumptions, Gerhards (2007, 2010) argues that these differences are not primarily cultural, but rather related to the differing levels of 'modernization' within the European societies. Democratic values and gender equality in the family and workplace, he argues, gain strength in tandem with increases in prosperity.

Apart from this still remarkable persistence of value differences between the EU member states, we can also observe growing value differences *within* European societies, namely the newly emerged cultural cleavage between 'liberal cosmopolitans' and 'protectionists' which – at least in part – replaces and overlays the old societal cleavages between the political right and left (Zürn & de Wilde 2016). It is remarkable, however, that these growing internal value cleavages within EU member states refer to newly emerging transnational value cleavages across European societies. The significance of these cleavages within and across European societies has become particularly apparent in recent years in the face of growing value conflicts in Europe, culminating in the so-called 'Brexit vote' in Great Britain in 2016, the loud call for closed EU-borders and growing influx of populist parties and movements all over Europe. Whether the increasing support of "authoritarian values" (Norris & Inglehart 2019) in many European countries marks a persistent "cultural backlash" within the EU is still undecided (see also concept five, above). From a European studies perspective, however, it is particularly noteworthy that we can observe transnational European movements and a growing European public sphere along the lines of these value conflicts (Eigmüller & Trenz 2020).

The Emergence of a European Public Sphere?

For a long time, the question of the emergence of a European public sphere determined sociological discussion on European integration, which gained critical momentum as the EU's democratic deficit became a subject of public and scholarly discourse (Eder 2000; Trenz 2008). Nevertheless, sociologists were deeply divided over the importance (and even existence) of this deficit. Some saw it as a logical consequence of the lack of a European public opinion and thus as an insuperable obstacle inherent to the EU – a conclusion that they empirically corroborated in several research studies (Gerhards 2001). Others offered much more positive visions of the EU, empirically demonstrating the emergence of a European public sphere (Trenz 2004; Koopmans & Statham 2010). Nevertheless, the existence of a nascent European public sphere only began to gain broad scholarly acceptance with the onset of the major fiscal and economic crisis that swept through the EU in 2008, which brought on a flurry of reporting on Europe and prompted EU member states to pay closer political attention to developments in other EU member states. Not least because of a thoroughly changed media landscape (especially the existence of social and digital media), but also because of an increasingly interwoven political and economic European Union, a European public sphere can no longer be denied – at least regarding specific topics. Concurrently, a European media landscape has also developed, supported by a steadily growing number of recipients, and equipped with essentially its own transnational infrastructure of communication operating through myriad channels and agents, from *Arte* and *EuroNews* to the dense network of European media correspondents in Brussels (Aldrin 2013).

Yet the original expectation that such a European public sphere would have a positive impact on European integration – by increasing democracy in the EU and promoting public participation, social connectedness, solidarity, and so forth among EU citizens – has yet to be fulfilled. Rather, the emergence of a European public sphere has by no means led Europeans to automatically self-identify positively with the EU or to an overall sustained increase in democracy in the EU. On the contrary, it has become evident that the emergence of European media discourses and European social movements have also promoted anti-European and anti-democratic sentiment, and we can assume that it is above all the EU critics and opponents who connect transnationally to create a common counter-public sphere (Eigmüller & Trenz 2020).

Explorations of European Identity

This leads directly to one of the core questions of the sociology of Europeanization, namely: is there a European society emerging, and if so, what are its characteristics? Initially, sociological debate on the conditions of social integration within the EU – that is, the question of the prospect of developing of a European society – was clearly divided into two camps: Some scholars pointed to a "Europe without society" (Bach 2008) and thus to a design that was still inadequate in comparison to that of national society; others, especially those who offered empirically-based studies, soon began to investigate the social imprinting power of the European institutional project and drew conclusions that suggested that it could shape future European society *sui generis* (Lepsius 1999; Kohli 2000). The inspiration for this somewhat empirically oriented European research was initially Karl Deutsch's transactionalist theory (Deutsch et al. 1957), according to which so-cieties would emerge from a condensation of the processes of communication, interaction, and exchange. This inspired sociologists to ask whether greater con-tact with foreigners brings with it a more cosmopolitan view of the world, whether the increased cross-border transfer of goods, money, communication, and person-nel lead to increased mutual trust, and whether all of this leads to a stronger iden-tification with the EU and the formation of a European identity (see also Chapter 12 in this volume).

Conceptually, these debates point to the general question of whether and in what form a European identity exists (Kohli 2000), and whether the develop-ment of relatively stable (positive) attitudes towards the European integration process is predicated on such a European identity (see conception one, above). While the overall impact of EU politics on EU citizens has become more and more significant during course of the Single European Market Programme, sev-eral treaty reforms, and the implementation of EU citizenship, research has also increasingly focused on attitudes of Europeans regarding the European Union. The end of the so-called **permissive consensus** (Hooghe & Marks 2009) set the starting point for scholarly analysis of European identities and attitudes to-wards the EU integration process (Risse 2015).

Faced with steadily declining public support for the European integration process since the 1990s, researchers have started to ask, what conditions are needed to sustain the European integration project in the long term. Often this research rests upon the more or less implicit normative background assumption that the EU citizenry must develop a collective identity, if the EU is to function as a stable democratic system.[2] This particularly European collective identity is mainly understood as a product of common experiences, memories, and inten-sifying transnational communication (Eisenstadt & Giesen 1995; Eder & Spohn 2005; Beck & Grande 2007). Scholarship on collective identity has highlighted the cognitive, affective, and evaluative dimensions of identity (Brubaker & Coo-per 2000), each of which can be associated with various levels of attachment to

---

2 It is also in this context that Habermas argues for a European identity must necessarily be based on 'constitutional patriotism', that is, on a form of civic identity that emphasizes demo-cratic citizenship as an integrative force (Habermas 2009).

the EU. It was highlighted, against this backdrop that a) to qualify as collective identity, not all dimensions must be met; b) multiple identities can coexist, with European identity rather complementing than replacing national and/or regional identities; and c) that all identities are "based on the similarity to some people and differences (perceived or actual) from others" (Hjerm 1998: 337). In accordance with the fifth conception of European culture discussed above, European identity-building is now primarily seen as a longitudinal process in the making. Hence, sociological research mainly seeks to identify the cultural preconditions of Europeanization and European identity formation, and to find out who participates in this process and to what extent (Fligstein 2008; Fernández et al. 2016). In his seminal book *Euroclash*, Neil Fligstein (2008) diagnosed a growing polarization between supporters of Europeanization and those strata of European societies who perceive Europe mainly as threat and rather prefer national protection over growing transnationalization. Fligstein's analysis inspired a whole range of research that studied the disparities in European identification and the growing polarization of political attitudes (Kuhn 2015; Fernández et al. 2016). To some extent, Fligstein's (2008) thesis of a growing "clash" of EU-related attitudes and identifications was proven as well by the close Brexit vote in 2016 and the rise of new anti-EU sentiments since 2010.

Apart from primary sociological studies, the question of how much EU citizens identify with Europe is also regularly queried in Eurobarometer surveys for decades. The data on the question of European identification are usually published in the Standard Eurobarometer Reports on *EU citizenship* (European Commission 2020). The data shows clearly that a vast majority of EU citizens identify somewhat with the EU, and that only a minority declares to have a sole national or sole European identity. Most striking, the numbers are very stable over time (European Commission 2014); however, we can find significant differences between different member states (for example, citizens of the founding member states show a consistently higher level of identification with the EU than do Scandinavian citizens) and along different socio-demographic factors (e.g., the higher the educational level, the higher the individual level of EU identification) (Fernández & Eigmüller 2018).

Debates over European Memory and European Cultural Politics

Scholarly studies and debates about European identity are also intricately linked to reflections on European memory and explorations of major features, characteristics, and aims of European cultural politics. Although there is a strong awareness of common European experiences and a common European heritage, scholarly discussions of **collective memory** in the pan-European context began to emerge in sociology and relating disciplines only in the early 2000s (Eder & Spohn 2005; Leggewie 2008; Pakier & Stråth 2010; Assmann 2012)

Collective memory still represents a central element of national memory cultures and national cultural politics. Eder & Spohn (2005) were among the first sociologists, who studied European collective memory against the backdrop of EU enlargement in 2004. Claus Leggewie (2008) examined the conditions of supra- and transnational memory and proposed a concentric model of pan-European memory, with the holocaust as a negative founding myth in the center of his model and six further elements and pan-European *problematiques* that could also serve as "anchor points" of European collective memory. Gerhards et al. (2017), moreover, have analyzed collective memory in Europe in comparative perspective, asking whether and to what extent an emerging European culture of remembrance influences national collective memories within Europe. They acertain a strong persistence of national myths and narratives of remembrance in EU member states. Other scholars have explored the major elements, cultural foundations, and larger institutional context of European memory politics that are, in part, also highly contested in European politics (Sierp & Wüstenberg 2015; Kaiser 2015; Büttner & Delius 2015; Sierp 2020). This research attempts to shed light on the overarching question of the significance of a European identity for collective memory processes (and vice-versa).

The focus of European cultural politics, however, is by far not only limited to the promotion of remembrance, historical narratives, and historical education. European institutions proactively promote the development of the arts, music, cinema, sports, education, cultural sectors and creative industries, as well as the European continent's so-called 'cultural heritage' (Shore 2000; Calligaro 2014).[3] Initially lead by the *Council of Europe*, this policy area is now headed by the European Commission, which pro-actively defends and promotes European culture. The importance that EU policymakers attach to cultural policy is reflected in its culture budget: the EU spent 400 million euros on its cultural program from 2007 to 2013, 1.801 billion euros from 2014 to 2020, and a budget of 1.85 billion euros for 2021–2027 is assigned to funding numerous initiatives such as the European cultural capitals, European cultural heritage, or digital culture (Patel 2013).

---

3 See the Web portal of the DG EAC of European Commission: https://ec.europa.eu/info/de partments/education-youth-sport-and-culture_en (accessed June 21, 2021).

It is striking to see that the EU's cultural politics closely resemble the political strategies used by 19th century European nation states to establish and consolidate common cultural perceptions, understandings, and practices. As Kathy McNamara (2015: 66) has pointed out: "[T]he cultural arena is one rife with the underlying dynamics at work in the effort to construct the EU as a legitimate political authority." In addition to its function as a potentially legitimizing force, cultural policy also serves the top-down process of creating symbols – a common currency or flag, an anthem, or even a contested capital city, to name just a few – that can strengthen collective identity (Shore 2000). One of the strongest markers of collective identity, however, a common European language, has neither been invented nor successfully established (even though the idea of Esperanto as common European language was promoted for some time). In line with what we have presented as concepts two and three, therefore, the main motto of European cultural policy continues to be 'unity in diversity'.

Concluding Remarks

As we have shown, culture and cultural issues are central themes in the sociology of Europeanization. Important social, political, and fundamental ethical issues are intricately linked with cultural questions. However, studies and reflections on culture are never apolitical, and they are all but free from normative considerations. Scholarship on the cultural history of Europe always carries certain political expectations, and always implicitly feeds into political quarrels over the 'correct' and 'appropriate' way to narrate Europe's past, thereby indirectly shaping what and who will be highlighted or neglected, acknowledged, or forgotten and excluded. Similar things can be said about explorations of *European values* and *identity*, Europe's common *cultural heritage*, and of a common European *collective memory*. In all these areas of European cultural studies, as we have shown, normative, ethical, and political issues play a central role. While analyzing European culture, it is paramount that we should be aware of these inherent normative tensions. If we are to understand how cultural forces are shaping the Europe of today, we must find a way to navigate through them by being reflective and transparent about the aims, objectives, and normative implications of our own work, and by being as clear as possible about our conceptions and methodologies.

Didactical Section

Key Learning Points

- Culture is a vague and ambivalent notion that also conveys normative implications; however, it is also an important interpretative framework that helps us to analyse both historical and current social transformations.
- It is a major challenge for a sociology of Europeanization to reflect on culture without presupposing a single dominant understanding of European culture or reifying static notions of regional, national, or European culture.
- There is not one major notion of European culture, but rather many different ones. We can identify at least five different meanings of European culture.
- Sociological analyses of European culture are linked to debates in neighboring disciplines, such as cultural studies, history, philosophy, and ethnology. These analyses and debates mainly centre around five major topics: values, public sphere, European identity, explorations of European memory and European Cultural Politics.

Glossary

Ball model of culture ("Kugelmodell"): The so-called 'ball model of cultures' was proposed by the German poet and philosopher Johann Gottfried Herder (1744–1803) in his writings about nations and national culture in Europe. In his model, Herder conceptualized (national) culture(s) as closed and homogenous social entities resting – as balls – on relatively stable gravitational centres comprising distinctive cultural features (such as the language, customs, or traditions of a certain ethnicity, for instance). It represents a prime example of traditional conceptions of national culture(s) that were prevalent during the 19th and 20th century nation-building era conceiving of culture in highly deterministic and essentialist ways (see also *Essentialism*). Herder's ball model also carried strong normative assumptions, since it considered the "blurring" of cultural distinctions or even the "mixing" of cultures to be problematic, something that "weakens" the "strength and cohesion of a nation or an ethnic group" (Welsch 1999: 194f.). Even today, political groups and movements that propagate strong and exclusionary conceptions of a stable and distinctive 'cultural identity' rest on similar conceptions of culture.

Civilization(s): This term originates from the Latin word *civis* ("citizen", inhabitant of a city). It is typically used to designate larger and more complex 'societies' (in contrast to smaller and less complex collectives). Hence, the concept of civilization is often used synonymously to those of 'society' or larger 'empires' and 'cultural areas'. However, the term can also have strong normative connotations, especially in the German and French contexts. The French term *civilité* was used to distinguish certain aristocratic cultural standards and practices from the 'primitive' or even 'barbarous' cultural standards of ordinary people and folk traditions (Elias [1939] 1994). Similarly, the concept was also immensely popular during the colonialist and imperialist periods to distinguish 'civilized' Western societies from 'primitive' and 'less developed' societies, areas, and regions.

Collective identity: In sociology and related disciplines, *collective identity* refers to prevalence of a sense of belonging or a sense of commonness within groups and collectives. In other words, it denotes the prevalence of certain *we-feelings* or a certain *we-identity*. Collective identities are typically based on assumptions of common characteristics (e.g., ideas, values, virtues, or other qualities) that distinguish one collective from other collectives. The notion of collective identities refers to different forms of collective belonging: e.g., ethnic, religious, or class identities, for instance, but also national identities. Conceptualizations of collective identity in sociology date back to Émile Durkheim's classical reflections on the structural changes of *conscience collective* ('collective consciousness') between smaller and larger collectives. Contemporary studies on collective identities mainly assume that collective identities do not exist per se (essentialism) but are socially constructed (Eisenstadt & Giesen 1995). Consequently, Brubaker and Cooper (2000) suggest that sociology should go "beyond identity" and mainly focus on processes of identification and identity-building and on the frames and strategies of actors and groups propagating collective identities.

Collective memory: As with studies of collective identity, reflections on collective memory have also been influenced by Durkheim's concept of collective consciousness, with collective memory mainly being viewed as a socially constructed phenomenon. Memory, like identity, is not just considered to be a quality of individuals (i.e., an activity taking place in the brain), but rather a highly social and cultural phenomenon that can be attributed to all sorts of collectives (families, groups, organizations, associations, nation states etc.). Hence, collective memory means that memory is strongly shared in collectives – and collectives, in turn, share a common history, common historical narratives, and narrations. These histories, stories and narratives are communicated face-by-face on different occasions (e.g., in families, in school and through exhibitions, on official days of remembrance, etc.) and through variety of different media (pictures, books, songs, movies, and the like). Accordingly, the concept of *"cultural memory"* is central in this research field (Assmann 2012). For much of modern history, nation states dominated memory politics and the definition of major historical narratives.

Constructivism (social): A fundamental epistemological position in philosophy, humanities, and the social sciences. Constructivism denotes the fundamental epistemological assumption that the meaning, conception, and characteristics of an object are not inherent to this object itself, but rather dependent on the perception, views, and conceptions of human observers. Since meanings and conceptions are socially shared, communicated, and negotiated, there is a strong link between fundamental constructivist conceptions in philosophy and the idea of a "social construction of reality" in sociology (Berger & Luckmann 1966). Consequently, the terms (social) *constructivism* and *constructionism* are often used interchangeably. But there is a slight difference between them: While constructivism derives from general discourses about truth, meaning, objectivity, and perception in epistemology, constructionism is more specifically associated with theories and conceptions of human agency and certain traditions of social thought, above all the phenomenological tradition and relating theories.

Cultural rationalization: A conception that was mainly coined by Max Weber to denote long-term historical processes during which cultural systems and practices were strongly cultivated and systematized. With his concept of cultural rationalization, Weber mainly aimed to describe the rise of (Western) modernity and an unprecedented rationalization of social and cultural life that led to the rise of capitalism and industrialization, to the emergence of modern states order and modern bureaucracy, and an all-encompassing 'disenchantment' ['*Entzauberung*'] and 'methodical rationalization' of social life.

Cultural turn: This phrase describes a larger interdisciplinary conceptual shift in the humanities and social sciences and the rise of new cultural understandings during the second half of the 20th century. The so-called 'cultural turn' represents neither a uniform movement nor a unitary theoretical shift. A multi-faceted concept, it has developed quite differently in various disciplines (Bachmann-Medick 2016). Nonetheless, generally it can be said that the *cultural turn* spurred broader and more extensive reflections on and conceptions of culture, dissolving the classical distinctions and dichotomies, such as culture *vs.* nature, high culture *vs.* folk culture, power *vs.* culture, or economics *vs.* culture, that had predominated until then. In sociology, it is often associated with a renaissance of cultural sociology and the emergence of new methodologies and theoretical approaches, such as practice theory, ethnomethodology, linguistic and discourse theories, or postcolonial theories (Alexander 1988; Reckwitz 2000).

Essentialism: A major epistemological approach emphasizing that objects have certain characteristics defining their 'nature' or 'essence', and the identity of these objects. Essentialist positions generally claim that these characteristics can be perceived, measured, and identified objectively. Hence, essentialism is seen as a counter-position to constructivism (see above).

Institutions/Institutionalism: Institutions are defined in sociology and relating disciplines as relatively stable, supra-individual, and objectified patterns of social behavior. Institutions usually convey certain values and normative expectations. In this way, they exert a certain social pressure on individuals and groups to behave in a certain way, or structuring social conduct in standardized or scripted ways. Institutions can be formally structured and explicitly formulated. At the same time, they can be less formalized and convey implicit expectations. Accordingly, there is strong connection between conceptions of culture and institutions in sociology (Berger & Luckmann 1966; Meyer 2010). *Institutionalism* is a theoretical approach in sociology and relating disciplines that mainly focuses on the conception, analysis, and exploration of institutions as well as institutional elements, patterns, and effects.

Path dependency: This term was initially brought up by institutional economists and economic historians to account for differences in economic performance and enforcements of innovations, such as the establishment of the ubiquitous QUERTY keyboard design (Thelen 1999: 384–401). The major argument is the assumption that social developments proceed in different stages and that fundamental change is only possible during an uncertain and contingent initial phase, when different alternatives are possible. Once a certain path is selected and followed for some time, it is more likely that this path will be continued and that fundamental changes become unlikely – even if it later turns out that an alternative path would have been better or superior (institutional *lock-in*).

Permissive consensus: In European studies, this term refers to EU citizens' 'tacit consent' to the project of European integration and EU politics – an attitude that prevailed for a certain period during the history of European integration, even though this project hardly served their interests, or even opposed them (Lindberg & Scheingold 1970). *Permissive consensus* means that it was not given consciously, but simply allowed European integration without paying much attention to the phenomenon, due to its complexity and geographic distance. With increasing economic problems and stagnating growth in the European economic community, however, this permissive consensus shifted into a 'constraining dissensus' (Hooghe & Marks 2009), describing citizens' increasing tendency to question and even fight against the EU and the European integration process.

Symbol/symbolic: Derives from the Greek term *sýmbolon* meaning 'identification' or 'distinctive mark'. Is usually understood as a sign or a certain expressive form/object that carries meaning (such as, for instance, traffic signs or letters, but also more complex scripts, images, or gestures). Symbols are central features of what is usually considered as 'culture' or 'cultural'. Therefore, symbols and the multiple symbolic forms and dimensions of social life are central to cultural sociology and relating cultural sciences (Eco 1976; Lévi-Strauss 1983).

Further Readings

Beck, U. & E. Grande, 2007: *Cosmopolitan Europe*. London: Polity Press.
Berting, J., 2006: *Europe: A Heritage, a Challenge, a Promise*. Utrecht: Eburon Academic Publishers.
Delanty, G., 2019: *Formations of European Modernity: A Historical and Political Sociology of Europe*. Basingstoke and London: Palgrave Macmillan.
Foret, F. & O. Calligaro (eds.), 2018: *European Values: Challenges and Opportunities for EU Governance*. London and New York: Routledge.
Joas, H. & K. Wiegandt, 2005: *Die kulturellen Werte Europas*. Frankfurt a.M.: Fischer.
Pan, C., Pfeil, B. S. & P. Videsott (eds.), 2018: *National Minorities in Europe. Handbook of European National Minorities*, Volume 1. Vienna and Berlin: Verlag Österreich & Berliner Wissenschaftsverlag, 2nd edition.
Rietbergen, P., 1998: *Europe: A Cultural History*. London and New York: Routledge.

Additional Web-Sources

Official information of the European Union on 'Culture': *https://europa.eu/european-union /topics/culture_en*
Web portal of the DG EAC 'Education, Youth, Sport, and Culture' of the European Commission: *https://ec.europa.eu/info/departments/education-youth-sport-and-culture_en*
Web portal of the Council of Europe on Culture and Cultural Heritage: *https://www.coe.int/en/ web/culture-and-heritage/home*
Official information of the UNESCO on issues and activities in the area of 'culture': *https://en. unesco.org/themes/protecting-our-heritage-and-fostering-creativity*
Web portal of the Eurobarometer survey:*https://ec.europa.eu/commfrontoffice/publicopinion/ index.cfm*
The World Value Survey: *https://www.worldvaluessurvey.org/wvs.jsp*
The European Values Study: *https://europeanvaluesstudy.eu/*

Questions for Discussion

- Try to define culture in your own words based on what you have read in this chapter! What is the element of culture that you find most important?
- What is European culture? Do the five concepts suffice, or can you think of other ideas and distinctions not mentioned here?
- Please go through the major research areas on culture (values, identity, public sphere, memory, cultural policy). Can you link the topics and themes addressed there with the discussion of the five concepts of European culture from before?
- Please got to the official website of the Eurobarometer and look up various "Standard Eurobarometers" and look for tables with the variable *identity* (you usually find them in Standard Eurobarometer reports on 'EU citizenship'). What do you find? How is *identity* measured? Please interpret these in terms of a) country differences b) time differences.

References

Alcock, A., 2000: *A History of the Protection of Regional Cultural Minorities in Europe: From the Edict of Nantes to the Present Day*. Basingstoke and London: Palgrave Macmillan.

Adloff, F., S. M. Büttner, S. Moebius & R. Schützeichel (eds.), 2014: *Kultursoziologie. Klassische Texte – Aktuelle Debatten*. Frankfurt a.M. and New York: Campus.

Aldrin, P., 2013: The World of European Information: The Institutional and Relational Genesis of the EU Public Sphere. In: Georgakakis, D. & J. Rowell (eds.), *The Field of Eurocracy: Mapping EU Actors and Professionals*, pp. 105–136. Basingstoke and London: Palgrave Macmillan.

Alexander, J., 1988: The New Theoretical Movement. In: Smelser, N. J. (ed.), *Handbook of Sociology*, pp. 77–101. Beverly Hills, CA: Sage Publications.

Alexander, J., 2003: *The Meanings of Social Life: A Cultural Sociology*. Oxford: Oxford University Press.

Anderson, B., 1983: *Imagined Communities. Reflections on the Origin and Spread of Nationalism*. London: Verso.

Assmann, A., 2012: *Auf dem Weg zu einer europäischen Gedächtniskultur?* Vienna: Picus Verlag.

Bach, M., 2008: *Europa ohne Gesellschaft*. Wiesbaden: VS Verlag für Sozialwissenschaften.

Bachmann-Medick, D., 2016: *Cultural Turns: New Orientations In The Study Of Culture*. Berlin and Boston: De Gruyter.

Beck, U., 1999: *World Risk Society*. London: Polity Press.

Beck, U. & E. Grande, 2007: *Cosmopolitan Europe*. London: Polity Press.

Berger, P. L. & T. Luckmann, 1966: *The Social Construction of Reality: A Treatise in the Sociology of Knowledge*. Garden City, NY: Anchor Books.

Berting, J., 2006: *Europe: A Heritage, a Challenge, a Promise*. Utrecht: Eburon Academic Publishers.

Bhambra, G. K., 2016: Whither Europe? Postcolonial versus Neocolonial Cosmopolitanism. *Interventions: International Journal of Postcolonial Studies* 18(2):187–202.

Bhambra, G. K., 2017: The current crisis of Europe: Refugees, colonialism, and the limits of cosmopolitanism. *European Law Journal* 23(5):395–405.

Bourdieu, P., 1985: *Distinction: A Social Critique of the Judgement of Taste*. Boston: Harvard University Press.

Bourdieu, P., 1990: *In Other Words: Essays Toward a Reflexive Sociology*. Stanford: Stanford University Press.

Bourdieu, P., 2013: *Algerian Sketches*. London: Polity Press.

Braudel, F., 1981: *Civilization and Capitalism, 15th-18th century*, 3 Vols. London: Collins.

Braudel, F., [1949] 2002: *The Mediterranean in the Ancient World*. London and New York: Penguin Books.

Brubaker, R., 1996: *Nationalism Reframed. Nationhood and the National Question in the New Europe*. Cambridge: Cambridge University Press.

Brubaker, R., 2002: Ethnicity without groups. *European Journal of Sociology* 43 (2): 163–189.Brubaker, R. & F. Cooper, 2000: Beyond 'identity'. *Theory and Society* 29(1): 1–47.

Büttner, S. M., 2012: *Mobilizing Regions, Mobilizing Europe: Expert Knowledge and Scientific Planning in European Regional Development*. London; New York: Routledge.

Büttner, S. M. & A. Delius, 2015: World Culture in European Memory Politics? New European Memory Agents Between Epistemic Framing and Political Agenda Setting. *Journal of Contemporary European Studies* 23(3):391–404.

Calligaro, O., 2014: From 'European Cultural Heritage' to 'Cultural Diversity'? The changing core values of European cultural policy. *Politique Europénne* 45(3):60–85.

Castells, M., 2009: *The Rise of the Network Society*, 3 Vols. Malden, MA and Oxford, UK: Blackwell-Wiley.

Cole, J. E., (ed.), 2011: *Ethnic Groups of Europe. An Encyclopaedia*. Santa Barbara: ABC-CLIO.

Council of Europe, 2018: *European Cultural Heritage Strategy for the 21st century. Recommendation of the Committee of Ministers to Member States*. https://rm.coe.int/eu ropean-heritage-strategy-for-the-21st-century-strategy-21-full-text/16808ae270 (accessed February 9, 2021).

Davies, N., 1996: *Europe: A History*. Oxford: Oxford University Press.

Delanty, G., 2019: *Formations of European Modernity: A Historical and Political Sociology of Europe*. Basingstoke and London: Palgrave Macmillan.

Delanty, G. & C. Rumford, 2005: *Rethinking Europe: Social Theory and the Implications of Europeanization*. London and New York: Routledge.

Deutsch, K. W., Burrell, S. A., Kann, R. A., Lee, M., Lichterman, M., Lindgren, R. E., Loewenheim, F. L. & R. W. van Wagenen, 1957. *Political Community and the North American Area*. Princeton: Princeton University Press.

Diez Medrano, F., 2003: *Framing Europe: Attitudes to European Integration in Germany, Spain, and the United Kingdom*. Princeton: Princeton University Press.

Durkheim, É., [1893] 1997: *The division of labour in society*. New York: The Free Press.

Eco, U., 1976: *A Theory of Semiotics*. Indianapolis: Indiana University Press.

Eder, K., 2000: Zur Transformation nationalstaatlicher Öffentlichkeit in Europa. *Berliner Journal für Soziologie* 10:167–184.

Eder, K. & W. Spohn, 2005: *Collective Memory and European Identity: The Effects of Integration and Enlargement*. Burlington: Ashgate Publishing Company.

Eigmüller, M. & H. J. Trenz, 2020: Werte und Wertekonflikte in einer differenzierten EU. In: Grimmel, A. (ed.), *Die neue Europäische Union*, pp. 31–56. Baden-Baden: Nomos.

Eisenstadt, S. & B. Giesen, 1995: The construction of collective identity. *European Journal of Sociology* 36(1):72–102.

Elias, N., [1939] 1994: *The Civilizing Process: The History of Manners and State Formation and Civilization*. Reprint Edition. London: Blackwell Publishers.

EPRS, 2018: Briefing: Cultural heritage in EU policies. Members' Research Service, PE 621.876, June 2018.

European Commission, 2014: *Eurobarometer – 40 years*. Brussels. https://ec.europa.eu/commfrontoffice/publicopinion/topics/forty_en.htm (accessed March 5, 2021).

European Commission, 2017: *Data collection in the field of ethnicity*. Directorate-General for Justice and Consumers. Brussels: Publications Office.

European Commission, 2019: Report from the Commission to the European Parliament, the Council, the European Economic and Social Committee and the Committee of the Regions on the implementation, results and overall assessment of the European Year of Cultural Heritage 2018. COM(2019) 548 Final. https://ec.europa.eu/transparency/regdoc/rep/1/2019/EN/COM-2019-548-F1-EN-MAIN-PART-1.PDF (accessed February 25, 2021).

European Commission, 2020: Standard Eurobarometer Report on European Citizenship (EB 93). https://ec.europa.eu/commfrontoffice/publicopinion/topics/fs5_citizen_40_en.pdf (accessed March 05, 2021).

Fernández, J. J. & M. Eigmüller, 2018: Societal education and the education divide in European identity, 1992–2015. *European Sociological Review* 34(6):612–628.

Fernández, J. J., M. Eigmüller & S. Börner, 2016: Domestic transnationalism and the formation of pro-European sentiments. *European Union Politics* 17(3):457–481.

Fligstein, N., 2008: *Euroclash: The EU, European identity, and the future of Europe*. Oxford: Oxford University Press.

Foret, F. & O. Calligaro (eds.), 2018: *European Values: Challenges and Opportunities for EU Governance*. London and New York: Routledge.

Gellner, E., 1983: *Nations and Nationalism*. Oxford: Blackwell Publishing.

Gerhards, J., 2001: Missing a European public sphere. In: Kohli, M. & M. Novak (eds.), *Will Europe Work? Integration, Employment and the Social Order*, pp. 145–158. Oxfordshire: Taylor and Francis.

Gerhards, J., 2007: *Cultural overstretch? Differences between old and new member states of the EU and Turkey*. London and New York: Routledge.

Gerhards, J., 2010: Culture. In: Immerfall, S., & G. Therborn (eds.), *Handbook of European Societies. Social Transformations in the 21st Century*, pp. 157–215. New York, Dodrecht, Heidelberg and London: Springer.

Gerhards, J., L. Breuer & A. Delius, 2017: *Kollektive Erinnerungen der europäischen Bürger im Kontext von Transnationalisierungsprozessen. Deutschland, Großbritannien, Polen und Spanien im Vergleich*. Berlin: Springer VS.

Haarmann, H., 2011: *Europe's Mosaic of Languages*. European History Online. http://ieg-ego.eu/en/threads/crossroads/mosaic-of-languages (accessed February 25, 2021).

Habermas, J., 2009: *Europe: the faltering project*. London: Polity.

Hann, C., 2016: A concept of Eurasia. *Current Anthropology* 57(1):1–10.

Harris, O., 2004: Braudel: Historical Time and the Horror of Discontinuity. *History Workshop Journal* 57:161–174.

Heidenreich, M. (ed.), 2019: *Horizontal Europeanisation: The Transnationalisation of Daily Life and Social Fields in Europe*. London and New York: Routledge.

Hjerm, M., 1998: National identities, national pride and xenophobia: A comparison of four Western countries. *Acta sociologica* 41(4):335–347.

Hobsbawm, E., 1990: *Nations and Nationalism since 1780. Programme, myth, reality*. Cambridge: Cambridge University Press.

Hobsbawm, E. & T. Ranger, 1983: *The Invention of Traditions*. Cambridge: Cambridge University Press.

Hooghe, L. & G. Marks, 2009: A postfunctionalist theory of European integration: From permissive consensus to constraining dissensus. *British Journal of Political Science* 39(1):1–23.

Immerfall, S. & G. Therborn (eds.), 2010: *Handbook of European Societies. Social Transformations in the 21st Century*. New York, Dodrecht, Heidelberg and London: Springer.

Inglehart, R., 1971: The silent revolution in Europe: Intergenerational change in post-industrial societies. *The American Political Science Review* 65(4):991–1017.

Inglehart, R., 2006: Mapping Global Values. *Comparative Sociology* 5(2–3):115–136.

Inglehart, R. & C. Welzel, 2005: Liberalism, postmaterialism, and the growth of freedom. *International Review of Sociology* 15(1):81–108.

Jacobs, M. & L. Spillman, 2005: Cultural sociology at the crossroads of the discipline. *Poetics* 33(1):1–14.

Joas, H. & K. Wiegandt, 2005: *Die kulturellen Werte Europas*. Frankfurt a.M.: Fischer.

Kaiser, W., 2015: Clash of Cultures: Two Milieus in the European Union's 'A New Narrative for Europe' Project. *Journal of Contemporary European Studies* 23(3):364–377.

Kohli, M., 2000: The Battleground of European Identity. *European Societies* 2(2):113–137.

Koopmans, R. & P. Statham (eds.), 2010: *The making of a European public sphere: Media discourse and political contention*. Cambridge: Cambridge University Press.

König, M., 2002: Cultural diversity and language policy. *International Social Science Journal* 51 (161):401–408.

Krastev, I., 2017: *After Europe*. Philadelphia: University of Pennsylvania Press.

Kroeber, A. L. & T. Parsons, 1958: The concept of culture and of social system. *The American Sociological Review* 23:582–3.

Krücken, G. & G. S. Drori (eds.), 2010: *World Society: The Writings of John W. Meyer*. Oxford: Oxford University Press.

Kuhn, T., 2015: *Experiencing European integration: Transnational lives and European identity*. OUP Oxford.

Leggewie, C., 2008: A Tour of the Battleground: The Seven Circles of Pan-European Memory. *Social Research* 75(1):217–234.

Lepsius, M. R., 1999: Bildet sich eine kulturelle Identität in der Europäischen Union? In: Reese-Schäfer, W. (ed.), *Identität und Interesse: Der Diskurs der Identitätsforschung*, pp. 91–99. Wiesbaden: VS Verlag für Sozialwissenschaften.

Lévi-Strauss, C., 1983: *The Raw and the Cooked. Mythologiques*, Vol. 1. Chicago: University of Chicago Press.

Lindberg, L. & S. Scheingold, 1970: *Europe's Would-be Polity*. Englewood Cliffs, NJ: Prentice-Hall.

Luhmann, N., 1995: Kultur als historischer Begriff. In: Luhmann, N., *Gesellschaftsstruktur und Semantik, Studien zur Wissenssoziologie der modernen Gesellschaft Band. 4*, pp. 31–54. Frankfurt a.M.: Suhrkamp.

Luhmann, N., 1997: *Die Gesellschaft der Gesellschaft*, 2 Vols. Frankfurt a.M.: Suhrkamp.

McNamara, K. R., 2015: *The politics of everyday Europe: Constructing authority in the European Union*. Oxford: Oxford University Press.

Meyer, J. W., 2010: World Society, Institutional Theories, and the Actor. *Annual Review of Sociology* 36:1–20.

Mishkova D. & B. Trencsényi (eds.), 2017: *European Regions and Boundaries. A Conceptual History*. New York and Oxford: Berghahn Books.

Murphy, A. B., T. G. Jordan-Bychkov & B. Bychkova Jordan, 2020: *The European Culture Area: A Systematic Geography*. Lanham: Rowman & Littlefield, 7th edition.

Müller, H. P., 2010: Die europäische Gesellschaft als Ausdruck einer Fortentwicklung der Moderne? In: Eigmüller, M. & S. Mau (eds.), *Gesellschaftstheorie und Europapolitik: Sozialwissenschaftliche Ansätze zur Europaforschung*, pp. 109–129. Berlin: Springer VS.

Münch, R., 1994: *Das Projekt Europa – Zwischen Nationalstaat, regionaler Autonomie und Weltgesellschaft*. Frankfurt a.M.: Suhrkamp.

Münch, R., 2010: *European Governmentality. The Liberal Drift of Multilevel Governance*. London and New York: Routledge.

Norris, P. & R. Inglehart, 2019: *Cultural backlash: Trump, Brexit, and authoritarian populism*. Cambridge: Cambridge University Press.

Ostergren, R. C. & M. Le Bossé, 2011: *The Europeans: A Geography of People, Culture, and Environment*. New York: The Guilford Press, 2nd edition.

Osterhammel, J., 2005: *Colonialism. A theoretical overview*. Princeton: Wiener Publishers.

Outhwaite, W. (ed.), 2017: *Brexit: Sociological Responses*. London and New York: Anthem Press.

Pakier, M. & B. Stråth (eds.), 2010: *A European memory? Contested histories and politics of remembrance*. New York: Berghahn.

Pan, C. & B. S. Pfeil, 2018: Introduction. In: Pan, C., B. S. Pfeil & P. Videsott (eds.), *National Minorities in Europe. Handbook of European National Minorities*, Vol. 1, pp. 1–27. Vienna and Berlin: Verlag Österreich & Berliner Wissenschaftsverlag, 2nd edition.

Pan, C., B. S. Pfeil & P. Videsott (eds.), 2018a: *National Minorities in Europe. Handbook of European National Minorities*, Vol. 1. Vienna and Berlin: Verlag Österreich & Berliner Wissenschaftsverlag, 2nd edition.

Pan, C., B. S. Pfeil & P. Videsott (eds.), 2018b: General: The Peoples, States, Languages, and National Minorities of Europe. In: Pan, C., B. S. Pfeil & P. Videsott (eds.), *National Minorities in Europe. Handbook of European National Minorities*, Vol. 1, pp. 29–70. Vienna and Berlin: Verlag Österreich & Berliner Wissenschaftsverlag, 2nd edition.

Panayi, P., 1999: *An Ethnic History of Europe Since 1945: Nations, States and Minorities*. London and New York: Routledge.

Panther, S., 1997: Cultural Factors in the Transition Process. Latin Center, Orthodox Periphery? In: Backhaus, J. G. & G. Krause (eds.), *Issues in Transformation Theory*, pp. 95–122. Marburg: Metropolis.

Patel, K. K., 2013: *The Cultural Politics of Europe: European Capitals of Culture and European Union since the 1980s*. London and New York: Routledge.

Reckwitz, A., 2000: *Die Transformation der Kulturtheorien. Zur Entwicklung eines Theorieprogramms*. Weilerswist: Velbrück.

Rietbergen, P., 1998: *Europe: A Cultural History*. London and New York: Routledge.

Risse, T., 2015: *A community of Europeans? Transnational identities and public spheres*. Ithaca and London: Cornell University Press.

Ritzer, G., 2010: *Globalization. The Essentials*. Wiley Blackwell.

Rumford, C. & D. Buhari-Gulmez (eds.), 2018: *Europe and World Society*. London and New York: Routledge.

Said, E. W., 1985: *Orientalism*. London: Penguin Books.

Said, E. W., 1993: *Culture & Imperialism*. London: Random House.

Shore, C., 2000: *Building Europe: The cultural politics of European integration*. London and New York: Routledge.

Sierp, A., 2020: EU Memory Politics and Europe's Forgotten Colonial Past. *Interventions* 22(6): 686–702.

Sierp, A. & J. Wüstenberg, 2015: Linking the Local and the Transnational: Rethinking Memory Politics in Europe. *Journal of Contemporary European Studies* 23(3):321–329.

Strath, B. & P. Wagner, 2017: *European modernity: a global approach*. London: Bloomsbury.

Thelen, K., 1999: Historical Institutionalism in Comparative Politics. *Annual Review of Political Science* 2(1):369–404.

Therborn, G., 1995: *European Modernity and Beyond: The Trajectory of European Societies, 1945–2000*. London and New York: Sage.

Tomlinson, J., 1999: *Globalization and Culture*. Chicago: Chicago University Press.

Trenz, H. J., 2004: Media coverage on European governance: Exploring the European public sphere in national quality newspapers. *European Journal of Communication* 19(3): 291–319.

Trenz, H. J., 2008: Understanding media impact on European integration: Enhancing or restricting the scope of legitimacy of the EU? *European Integration* 30(2):291–309.

van Deth, J. W. & E. Scarbrough (eds.), 1998: *The impact of values*, Vol. 4. New York: Oxford University Press.

Wagner, P., 2017: The end of European modernity? *Changing Societies & Personalities* 1(2): 128–135. https://core.ac.uk/download/pdf/204260118.pdf (accessed February 25, 2021).

Weber, M., 1920: *Gesammelte Aufsätze zur Religionssoziologie*, 3 Vols. Tübingen: Mohr (Paul Siebeck) Verlag.

Weber, M., 1991: *From Max Weber: Essays in Sociology*. Edited by H.H. Gerth and C. Wright Mills. Milton Park: Routledge.

Weber, M., [1904] 2002: *The Protestant ethic and the "spirit" of capitalism and other writings*. New York and London: Penguin.

Welsch, W., 1999: Transculturality – the Puzzling Form of Cultures Today. In: Featherstone, M. & S. Lash (eds.), *Spaces of Culture: City, Nation, World*, pp. 194–213. London: Sage.

Zürn, M., & P. de Wilde, 2016: Debating globalization: cosmopolitanism and communitarianism as political ideologies. *Journal of Political Ideologies* 21(3):280–301.

Fabio Santos & Manuela Boatcă

5 Europeanization as Global Entanglement

Europeanization is mainly used as a label for a specific and relatively new set of processes. The term aims to capture the economic and political integration and collective identity formation expected of member states and associate countries of the European Union in the context of their accession to some or all EU structures such as the single market, EU legislation, or the monetary union. Yet, Europeanization had already encompassed widely differing processes for various geopolitical actors long before the creation of the European Union or its predecessors, the European Coal and Steel Community (ECSC), the European Atomic Energy Community (EAEC), and the European Economic Community (EEC). This chapter draws attention to the fact that sociological research on Europeanization is bound to remain at least incomplete and self-referential, and at times downright self-congratulatory, as long as it does not situate Europe and Europeanization in a global and historical context. Drawing on critical scholarship on Europeanization and on post- and decolonial approaches, the following account connects some of the ties cut by dominant political and academic discourse by asking a series of provocative questions: How does the fact that four of the six founding members of the EEC held substantial colonies across the world at the time of its creation in 1957 factor into Europeanization? How has the ongoing control exercised by the EU and its member states over territories in Africa and across the world shaped discourses of Europeanness? And how is this extra-European history related to questioning the Europeanness of non-Western, (semi-)peripheral European spaces like 'the Balkans' or to denying it to EU overseas territories in the Caribbean altogether?

We address these and other questions by placing Europeanization in the *longue durée* and tracing it back to global structures rarely considered in prevailing research: the 'inconvenient' histories and legacies of colonialism, including the European prosecution, extermination, enslavement, and evangelization of people in and between Africa and the Americas. We focus on how the political project commonly referred to as 'European integration' was planned from its outset, and has been partially realized, as one that both incorporated and exploited colonized and occupied territories, in particular the African continent, its people, and its natural resources. In four consecutive steps, we reframe and expand Europeanization as a set of processes emerged in the context of the historically entangled projects of colonization, Eurafrican integration, **Eastern enlargement**, and global statehoods. In doing so, we not only offer correctives for long-held

https://doi.org/10.1515/9783110673630-005

historical narratives bound to national and continental 'containers', but also provide concrete examples of how Europeanization as a centuries-old – rather than
decades-old – process continues to unfold globally. We argue that it is this larger
historical process and its manifold **entanglements**, rather than the latest installments of the European Union project, that should constitute the object of study
of a critical sociology of Europeanization.

Any attempt to define Europe has to confront the controversial question of
its external and internal borders, implicitly tied to its status as a continent (Balibar 2002, 2009). Although geographers and world historians have long criticized the textbook classification of Europe as a full-fledged continent separate
from Asia and distortedly inflated on standard Mercator world maps (Hodgson
1963: 227–231), Europe is repeatedly presented as the norm, or "archetypal continent" (Lewis & Wigen 1997: 36). The elevation to norm status comes with momentous political, economic, and cultural consequences, as Lewis and Wigen
(1997: 36) have noted in their critique of meta-geography:

> Viewing Europe and Asia as parts of a single continent would have been far more geo-
> graphically accurate, but it would also have failed to grant Europe the priority that Euro-
> peans and their descendants overseas believed it deserved. By positing a continental
> division between Europe and Asia, Western scholars were able to reinforce the notion of a
> cultural dichotomy between these two areas – a dichotomy that was essential to modern
> Europe's identity as a civilization.

The meta-geographical East-West division has also served as the most common
and long-standing internal differentiation within Europe, periodically transfer-
ring geopolitical, economic, and cultural divides into an ahistorical distinction
between Eastern and Western Europe. The European East thereby sanctions
Western Europe's position as the norm, while partly acquiring attributes of a
larger East in being portrayed as Oriental or "somehow Asian" (Bakić-Hayden
1995; Lewis & Wigen 1997: 7).

Historically, the concept of Europe has never had a mere geographic reference but has instead always mirrored the geopolitics and epistemology of the
various epochs and global power relations that characterized them. However, political maps that represent distinct continents naturalize them as common-sense
entities. In the case of Europe in particular, such naturalization has the absurd
effect of generating anomalies from the definition of a continent that is itself
anomalous. Thus, the territory of several European states is partially or completely
outside continental Europe; Cyprus is, strictly speaking, located in West Asia, on
the Anatolian Plate, while Malta and Sicily are on the African continental plate.

If, however, geographical incongruities result in a few exceptions to the
rule, it is colonial history that reveals exceptions as systematic and the rule

itself as a function of the political economy of global capitalism. The fact that Europe cannot be easily pinpointed to any one location means that neither its place on a territorial surface nor the processes of integration and identity formation it initiated are mere regional phenomena. Rather, they are the result of complex transregional entanglements in the context of worldwide colonial domination. To do justice to the global historical depth of a process the standard literature commonly traces to the post-World War II era (at best), we therefore consider Europeanization in the very long-term. We contend that its *multiple temporalities* – in other words, the various answers to the question: *when* was Europeanization? – open the possibility to both provincialize Europe and historicize globalization. In line with arguments made by global sociologies, including world-systems analysis, post- and decolonial approaches (Conrad et al. 2013; Gutiérrez Rodríguez et al. 2010), we then explore the ways in which the different temporalities inform the meanings and histories of successive and partly overlapping processes of Europeanization.

Europeanization as Colonization

From a decolonial perspective, apparently disconnected events such as the conquest of Muslim Granada by the Catholic Monarchs in 1492, the expulsion of the Jews from Spain, and Columbus' arrival in the Americas that same year all signal the growing self-assertion of Europe as Christian and Western in the 'long' sixteenth century (Mignolo 2006). As such, they represent a turning point with momentous geopolitical consequences. As Janet Abu-Lughod (1989) has shown, up until the mid-fourteenth century Europe was peripheral to the Afro-Eurasian division of labor and partly dependent on eastern Mediterranean trade for access to Asian markets (Figure 5.1). Economic and technological innovations came primarily from Asia and the Middle East (e.g., shipbuilding and navigational techniques, see Frank 1998: 185–204), as did civilizational notions such as democracy and freedom, later claimed by and increasingly associated with Western Europe alone (Goody 2006: 50–56).

The incorporation of the Americas into the emerging capitalist world-economy after 1492 allows for a dramatic shift in both the terms of trade and the self-understanding of Europe as a coherent entity. Recourse to precious metals, especially silver, through the colonization of the Americas, the genocide of the indigenous population and the trade in enslaved Africans granted Europe access to intra-Asian trade (Frank 1998: 282). The category '*European*' gradually became a self-designation, replacing local and regional allegiances and identities on the

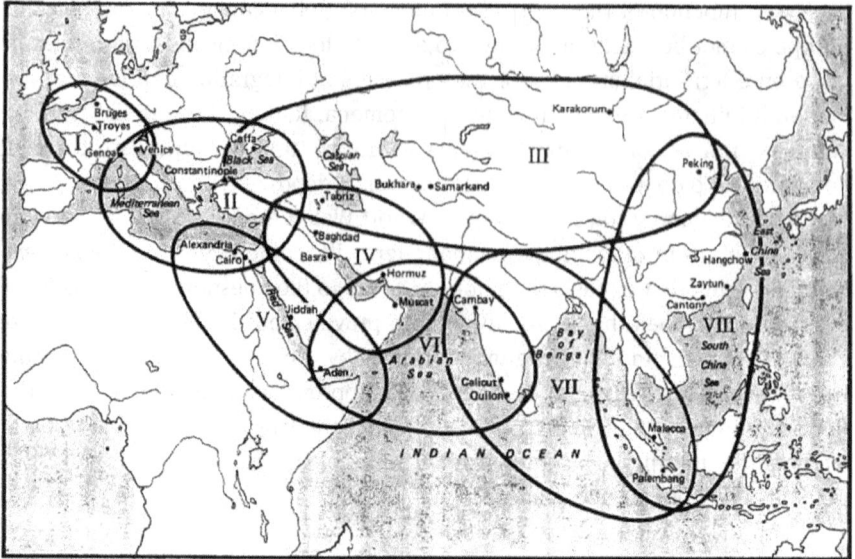

Figure 5.1: The eight trade circuits of the thirteenth century, with Europe at the margin.
Source: Abu-Lughod 1989: 34. Reproduced with permission of the Licensor through PLSclear.

continent (Quijano & Wallerstein 1992: 550), thus translating the colonial enterprise overseas into a collective self-identification at home, or colonization into Europeanization. As poignantly summarized by André Gunder Frank (1998: 277): "the Europeans bought themselves a seat, and then even a whole railway car, on the Asian train. How were any-literally-poor Europeans able to afford the price of even a third-class ticket to board the Asian economic train? Well, the Europeans somehow found and/or stole, extorted, or earned the money to do so."

If we remember that Columbus was looking for a sea route to Japan, China, and India in order to improve Europe's position within the Afro-Eurasian trade system, we view his "accidental discovery" of the Americas as marking "the opening of the era of European expansion – the process of exploration, conquest and colonization by which virtually the whole globe was harnessed in one way or another to Europe" (Hall 1991: 18). What we call *Europeanization-as-colonization* thus became a global process. The ensuing colonialism in the Americas was successfully challenged for the first time in 1804, as the Haitian Revolution turned France's most lucrative colony of St. Domingue into the region's first independent nation (Trouillot 1995). Yet, colonialism is still ongoing in several non-sovereign territories to this day (Adler-Nissen & Gad 2013; Connell & Aldrich 2020; Murdoch 2021).

More than five hundred years of colonial rule were only possible due the inhumane and centuries-long exploitation of over 12 million African captives who were shipped to the Americas in the context of the **European trade in enslaved people** (Figure 5.2). The term "European slave trade", deliberately chosen by Guyanese historian Walter Rodney over the abstract label of "transatlantic slave trade", is meant to "call attention to the fact that the shipments were all by Europeans to markets controlled by Europeans, and this was in the interest of European capitalism and nothing else" (Rodney 1982: 95). From a European and capitalist perspective, the life-threatening, and certainly life-shortening enslavement and transportation of Africans to the Americas was especially urgent in light of the decimation of indigenous people in the Americas: an estimated 90 per cent of the indigenous population, that is 55 million people, died in the process of Europeanization-as-colonialization due to significantly higher morbidity and mortality rates from influenza, smallpox, and other infectious diseases brought by Europeans (Koch et al. 2019).

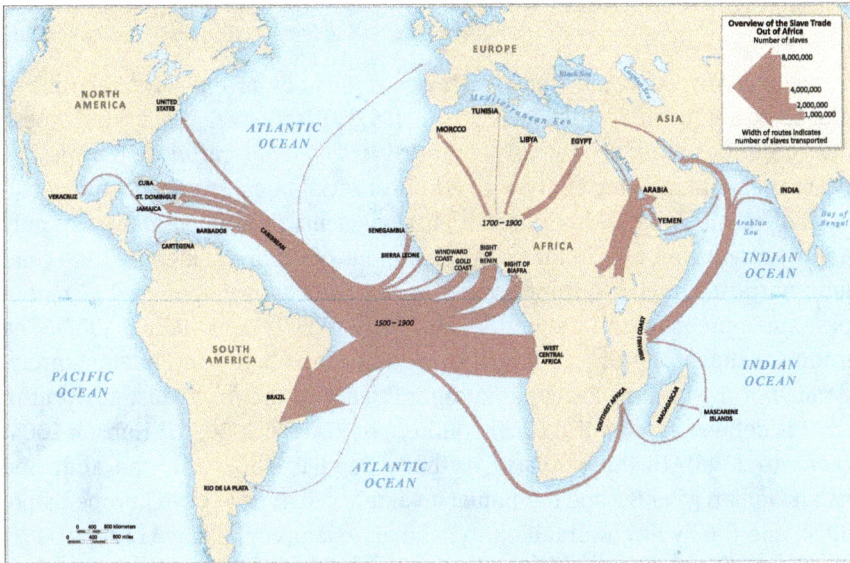

Figure 5.2: European trade in enslaved people.
Source: *Atlas of the Transatlantic Slave Trade* (Eltis & Richardson 2010), reproduced on slavevoyages.org and here with permission of the Licensor through PLSclear.

This highly unequal entanglement of world regions is illustratively encapsulated in the engraving "Europe supported by Africa and America" by abolitionist William Blake (Figure 5.3). Depicted as female figures, the three continents are interconnected through their arms and the braid, most likely representing the tobacco processed by enslaved Black and indigenous people on colonial plantations. Commodities such as coffee, sugar, and tobacco, previously unknown in Europe, became central both to the surplus appropriation of the European *bourgeoisie* and the productivity and diet of industrial workers in Europe, thus strongly stimulating global capitalism (Mintz 1985). In Blake's engraving, we see Africa and America adorned by golden armbands that symbolize enslavement and the plundering of precious minerals. Quite literally, then, Africa and America support the central figure: white Europe, the only one of the three female figures whose hair partially masks her nudity, implying a higher degree of civilization than that of her non-European, non-white counterparts. The following quote from the 18th century further illustrates these unequal entanglements:

> I do not know if coffee and sugar are essential to the happiness of Europe, but I know well that these two products have accounted for the unhappiness of two great regions of the world: America has been depopulated so as to have land on which to plant them; Africa has been depopulated so as to have the people to cultivate them.
>
> (J. H. Bernardin de St. Pierre 1773, quoted in Mintz 1985: iii)

Europe, and by extension "the West", would thus not have risen to the rank of global power without "the Rest" (Hall 1992). Discursively separated, these macro entities cannot be neatly delinked in any clear-cut way: Europe has never been a monolithic entity with ethnic or racial homogeneity, let alone cultural or religious. The Afro-Eurasian entanglements mentioned above not only apply to trade, but also to the very foundations of Europe's 'identity': the common narrative tracing Europe's roots back to a Graeco-Roman and Christian past omits pre-modern Europe's Semitic and Arabic origins (Bernal 1987). The unilinear diachrony Greece-Rome-Europe obscures both the Phoenician mythology of the birth of Europe and the influence of the Arab Muslim world in what is defined as 'classical Greek' philosophy (Dussel 2000: 41; Hobson 2004; Dainotto 2006). In the words of Anthony Pagden (2002: 35), "an abducted Asian woman gave Europe her name; a vagrant Asian exile gave Europe its political and finally its cultural identity; and an Asian prophet gave Europe its religion". Clearly, there is no such thing as a homogeneous Christian and white cultural identity developed in a hermetically sealed Europe. Rather, Europe, and hence people defining themselves or defined as Europeans, have complex, Afro-Eurasian roots and entangled transregional histories (Whitmarsh 2018; Otele 2020). Describing these histories simply as 'shared', as done in recent political and academic discourses, euphemizes interactions made under blatantly unequal conditions, flattens enduring hierarchies, and minimizes lasting traumas and ongoing structural inequalities (Owuor 2020).

Figure 5.3: *Europe Supported by Africa and America*, engraving of William Blake.

Europe's historical and current identity politics is therefore based on wrongful claims to have single-handedly pioneered modernity and exported it to the rest of the world. Against this background, Boatcă (2010, 2013) has suggested replacing the notion of a single Europe by one of "multiple Europes" with different and unequal roles in shaping the hegemonic definition of modernity and in ensuring its propagation. This differentiation helps account for the varying and contested degrees of Europeanness attributed to and claimed by regions, states, and peoples. While the European status of today's Germany and most of its citizens, for example, is never contested, this is not the case for Romania and most Romanians. These national examples, however, stand for a larger East-West divide on the continent. The European East, an economically semi-peripheral and predominantly agrarian region with a pluriconfessional and multiethnic history at the crossroads of the Habsburg, Ottoman, and Russian empires, has been systematically constructed as Europe's "incomplete self" (Todorova 1997: 18; see also Wolff 1994). The remaining non-EU countries in the Balkans are accordingly portrayed as the EU's shrinking "immediate outside" (Jansen 2009). As such, the European (South-)East, often conflated with the Balkans, has been conventionally depicted as "lagging behind" and never quite fulfilling the (economic, cultural, or political) standards as defined in Western European terms. Negotiations of Europeanness thus take place under unequal conditions and at the expense of Europe's multiethnic, multiracial, and pluriconfessional history and present reality. The European status of territories and individuals subject to ongoing colonial relations with European countries is questioned even more in the case of the EU's 'outermost regions', 'overseas countries and territories', and most of their inhabitants (Boatcă & Santos 2022). Forceful arguments on the long-term consequences of the globally entangled developments outlined above have been made by intersectional analyses in and of today's Europe, ravaged by structural racism in interdependence with other forms of exclusion (e.g., El-Tayeb 2016; Krivonos & Diatlova 2020; Mazouz 2017).

Nevertheless, the multifaceted colonial dimensions of Europeanization would not be complete without a consideration of the history of Europe's colonization of African territories and of how the long-term interests in prolonging or reframing that project decisively shaped the process known as 'European integration'.

Europeanization as Eurafrican Integration

On its homepage, the European Union (2021) presents itself as "set up with the aim of ending the frequent and bloody wars between neighbors, which culminated in the Second World War. As of 1950, the European Coal and Steel Community begins to unite European countries economically and politically in order to secure lasting peace". In addition, the integration efforts of the six founding countries (Belgium, France, Germany, Italy, Luxembourg, and the Netherlands) are mainly situated in a Cold War context, with the EEC (or Common Market, created in 1957) becoming a necessary buffer in an allegedly bipolar world order. Yet, as an increasing number of works impressively demonstrate, the political impetus behind the creation of the European Economic Community was significantly fuelled by the loss of colonial empires after World War II and by the strong desire to mobilize the remaining colonies for the common market (Muller 2001; Hansen & Jonsson 2014). In this section, we thus frame Europeanization as Eurafrican integration.

In their book-length analysis of this neglected topic, Peo Hansen and Stefan Jonsson (2014) provide compelling historical evidence for re-thinking European integration as a political project underpinned by a colonial complementarity between Europe and Africa. The project of a 'coordinated' European exploitation of Africa's raw materials, resources, and people can be dated back to the 'scramble for Africa' formalized by fourteen imperial powers invited to the Berlin Conference (also known as Congo Conference) in 1884/85 by Germany's chancellor Otto von Bismarck (Wirz & Eckert 2004). Yet, events in the interwar period ultimately set the stage for Eurafrican integration: with the intellectual and political Pan-European movement flourishing, influential politicians, and thinkers such as Richard Coudenhove-Kalergi envisioned 'European unity' by way of a united colonial effort in Africa. "In their view, Africa was seen as a natural and necessary part of Europe's geopolitical sphere, a part that needed to be more strongly connected to Europe, and to be exploited by united European forces in order to turn its resources to full advantage" (Hansen & Jonsson 2014: 28).[1] The proponents of inter-European cooperation in colonial Africa claimed that, besides providing raw materials and nutrition, Africa offered enough space and labor for the impoverished and unemployed in an overpopulated Europe. The political and infrastructural proposals drafted between the two world wars to unequally 'unite' Europe and Africa had clear utopian overtones. They nevertheless served as blueprints that cleared the way for Eurafrica's transformation from utopia to political reality in the 1950s.

In the aftermath of World War II, Europe was renegotiating its role in a world marked by the Cold War division. However, the EU's self-presentation omits that, in finding its place in a world dominated by the USSR and the US, Europe was dependent on Africa. European politicians began to map out strategies establishing

---

[1] A world map of the Pan-European movement is provided in the online supplement to this book.

Eurafrica as a 'third force' in world politics alongside Euramerica and Eurasia. As Hansen and Jonsson (2014: 73) show, these strategies were also made "to prevent the push for decolonization in Asia from gaining a foothold on the African continent". Eurafrican ideas were partially realized in institutional settings such as the OEEC (today's OECD), NATO, the Council of Europe, and the ECSC (Hansen & Jonsson 2014: 71–146), while Eurafrica became a political reality with the Treaty of Rome: In 1957, French Algeria became a fully integrated member of the Common Market, and most of Europe's other colonies, including vast territories such as the Belgian Congo and French West and Equatorial Africa, were associated with the EEC (Figure 5.4).

Hansen and Jonsson (2014: 13) emphasize that the EU "would not have come into existence at this point in time had it not been conceived as a Eurafrican enterprise in which colonialism was Europeanized". Rather than regarding Eurafrica as a short-lived project, they reveal that the unequal Eurafrican complementarity conceived and exploited by Europeans was more than a rarely considered footnote in the early process commonly labeled 'European integration'. In addition to its political and discursive precursors (in the Pan-European movement, among others), Eurafrican integration served as a mediator that would ensure the long-term continuation of power relations and inequalities inherited from colonialism. This was not only implemented through official integration and association in the 1950s, but also in the form of continued political and economic dependency structures long after most African states gained independence on unfavorable terms in the 1960s. The title of Hansen and Jonsson's book *Eurafrica. The Untold History of European Integration and Colonialism*, and the amount of historical evidence they uncover, point to the imperative need to *unlearn* the one-sided trajectory delineated by the EU and the bulk of EU research, while placing a critical focus on the temporal and geopolitical entanglements of European integration and colonialism, especially on the African continent.

Today we can still observe the manifold legacies of lasting Eurafrican interdependencies in the guise of development aid, military force, and the outsourcing and offshoring of migration control to North Africa (Bialasiewicz 2012). We can clearly see the long shadow cast by Eurafrica as a political institution in North Africa: the barbed-wire fences around the Spanish and EU exclaves of Ceuta and Melilla, both bordering Morocco (by whom these territories are still claimed), have become the epitome of Europe's deadly border regime (Bahl 2021; Kobelinsky 2017; Schindel 2018). Less visible is the violence unfolding in other Eurafrican borderlands, especially the Spanish autonomous community of the Canary Islands west of the Moroccan coast and the French overseas department of Mayotte off the Southeastern African coast. Together with the

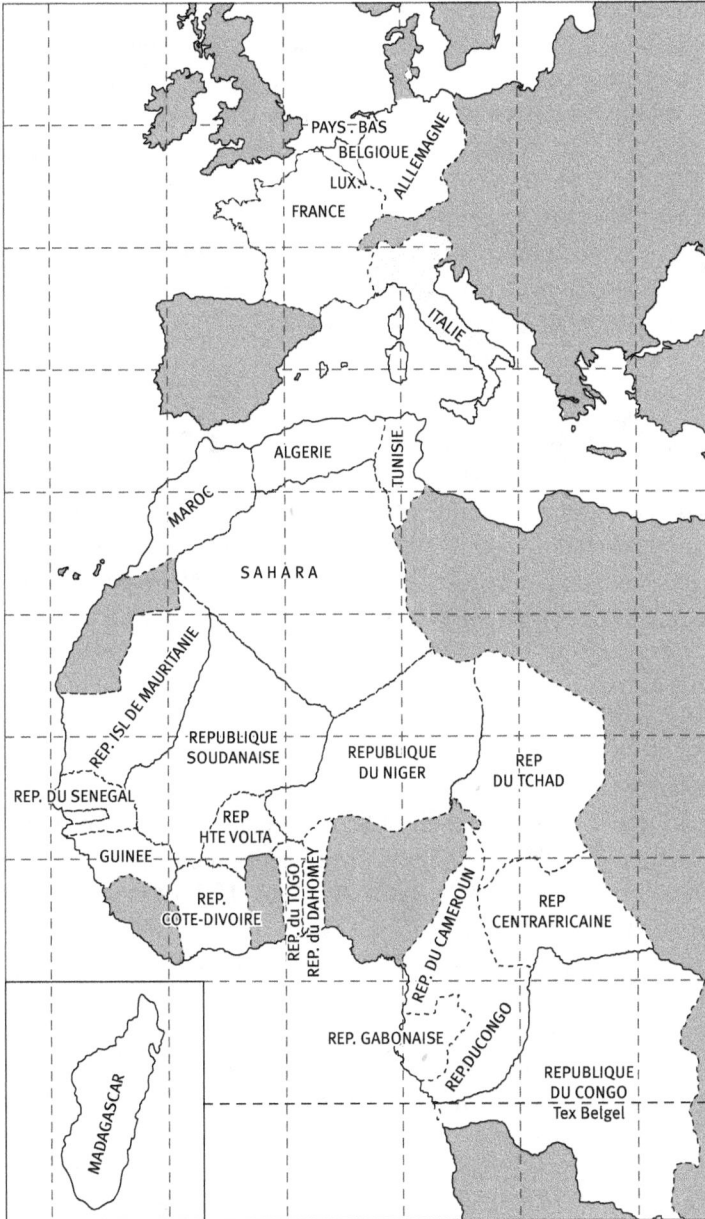

Figure 5.4: Map of Eurafrica, with the Sahara region inserted at its center, as perceived from a French–Algerian perspective.
Source: *Cahiers économiques et de liaison des Comités Eurafrique*, Nos 5–7, 1960 (see also Hansen & Jonsson 2014: 219).

Portuguese autonomous region of Madeira and the French overseas department of Réunion, they are full-fledged parts of the European Union, yet geographically located on or near the African continent. With their fences raised and their shores increasingly controlled, these Eurafrican territories have become perilous borderlands for tens of thousands of people seeking a life of safety and dignity (Santos 2020, 2021). Through the lens of global entanglements applied in this chapter, we show that these unequal mobilities are not unique to the process termed here Europeanization-as-Eurafrican-integration, for they also shape past and present 'Europeanizations' in other parts of the world, especially in Eastern and Southeastern Europe and in the Caribbean.

Europeanization as Eastern Enlargement

The constructed and ahistorical notion of a Europe ultimately coherent in its main features is apparent in the economic and political project of the European Union, which has been gradually monopolizing the label of '*Europe*'. As a result, only current member states of the European Union, or those about to become members, are considered 'European' and consequently included in the term. This attests to the above-mentioned geopolitical rather than geographical foundation of the notion of Europe, which used to denote Western, Northern and (parts of) Southern Europe throughout the nineteenth and the twentieth centuries. Today, references to Europe and the European Union are used interchangeably, while the Eastern parts of the continent have been recast as a region whose political, socio-cultural, or religious institutions are seen as proof of questionable Europeanness and lacking in economic and juridical standards. It is thus telling that the EU's latest expansion process in the East has been framed both as 'Europeanization' (implying that these countries had to 'become' fully European) and 'Eastern enlargement' (perpetuating the Western cognitive map on which Eastern and Southeastern European countries occupy intermediate positions between Europe and Asia). Although it is one of the more recent installments of Europeanization, the EU's Eastern enlargement has hence tended to be conflated with the term, thus obscuring the plural character of Europeanization described in this chapter. In this section, we therefore situate Europeanization-as-Eastern-enlargement in the longer history and larger context of previous and parallel global Europeanizations.

Europeanization-as-Eastern-enlargement is the process of asymmetric negotiation of EU membership and all ensuing rights to Eastern European countries historically defined in and out of Europeanness. As Boatcă (2010, 2013) has argued, the exclusionary logic underlying the discourse of 'Europeanization' applied to countries with a century-old European cultural and social tradition (from Poland and the Czech Republic to Hungary and Romania) is twofold. On the one hand, the discourse and practice of Europeanization instrumentalize an Orientalist imagery to imply that distance from Asia (*'the Orient'*) represents the underlying yardstick by which standards of an allegedly unique and exemplary European modernity and civilization are measured. On the other hand, discursively framing these countries and their citizens as perpetually 'catching up' pays off in geopolitical terms: soon after 9/11, as the 'Islamic threat' replaced the Communist one in the hegemonic Occidental imaginary, Eastern Europe exchanged its political and economic Second World status for that of a culturally and racially Second (Hand) World, and thus remained within the framework of a lesser Europe condemned to mere imitation of its 'proper' counterpart, Western Europe. Imagined as 'white, but not quite', Christian, and geographically European, yet also backward, traditional, and still largely agrarian, the European East thus reassumes the identity of Western Europe's "incomplete Self" (Todorova 1997). In other words, it is cast as heroic, modern Europe's lesser version: 'epigonal', backward Europe (Boatcă 2010, 2013).

That the theory and practice of the European Union's 'Eastern enlargement' act as a repudiation of Easternness and the Orient (Böröcz 2001: 6) becomes apparent in the fact that the last countries to join the EU were Romania, Bulgaria (2007), and Croatia (2014), while those currently negotiating accession are North Macedonia, Serbia, Montenegro, and Albania. The membership negotiations with Turkey, whose application for accession dates back more than thirty years, have effectively been at a standstill since 2016. Yet, even before the outspoken critiques of rising political authoritarianism in the country, Turkey's EU membership bid had faced strong opposition, especially from France and Germany, whose governments have also repeatedly opposed Romania and Bulgaria joining the Schengen Area. Thus, the sequence of the incorporation of new countries into the European Union and its common agreements matches the degree of their connection to or overlap with the Ottoman (and therefore Oriental) legacy, constructed as the opposite of politically desirable Europeanness (Boatcă 2010, 2013).[2]

The criteria according to which the performance of the Eastern candidates is evaluated poignantly reflect this Orientalist prism: corruption, human trafficking (especially in the form of forced prostitution) and the insufficient rule of

---

2 The European Commission provides a map of Eastern Enlargement: https://audiovisual.ec. europa.eu/en/photo/P-009412~2F00-2 (accessed April 02 2021). The map, also available in the online supplement to this book, is color-coded for existing (yellow), joining (blue), and candidate states (purple) before 2004.

law, responsible for the belated accession of both Romania and Bulgaria during the fifth enlargement round (European Commission 2006a), for stalling negotiations with Croatia until 2010 and currently with Turkey (European Commission 2006b: 5–7), clearly belong to the repertoire of Orientalism now being reproduced in relation to the European East. By singling them out as critical issues in candidate countries of the European East, such characteristics were placed within a past that the EU member states had supposedly overcome. The official rhetoric of accession negotiations was accordingly underpinned by pedagogical overtones: "This fifth enlargement of the EU had a political and moral dimension. It enabled countries – Cyprus, the Czech Republic, Estonia, Hungary, Latvia, Lithuania, Malta, Poland, Slovakia and Slovenia – *which are as European as the others, not just geographically but also in terms of culture, history and aspirations*, to join the democratic European family" (emphasis added). The same official document from 2006[3] cryptically stated that the entry process for Bulgaria and Romania merely "took longer". While these formulations were removed in later editions, the statement on the reasons for the belated opening of Turkey's application procedure is still accessible: "Given Turkey's geographical location and political history, the EU hesitated for a long time before accepting its application" (European Union 2017: 22).

The EU accession rhetoric at play in such statements is in line with the logic of the discursive framework of "Balkanism", a term proposed by Milica Bakić-Hayden (1995): if the Balkan peninsula has been viewed for centuries as Europe's "incomplete Self" (Todorova), the discursive strategy employed by national elites has often been to distance themselves from an Oriental past, while instead stressing their contribution to European civilization and mapping their integration into the European Union as a "return to Europe" (Bakić-Hayden 1995; Lindstrom 2003). The framings of historical reparation have dominated identity rhetoric across Eastern Europe as long as the hope of EU accession looms. While in the Western Balkans, Europeanization as Eastern enlargement remains a distant prospect, it serves to reproduce the imaginary of an epigonal, backward, and ultimately lesser Europe, always displaced onto an Other within the region: In Bosnia-Herzegovina and Serbia, many people see the EU membership of other former state socialist countries and the strict visa regime as "the inversion of European geopolitical hierarchies, including a sense of shamefully having to *catch up* with those Eastern Europeans who until recently were not even considered to be in the same league" (Jansen 2009: 828; italics in original).

---

3 The 2006 version of the document is no longer available on the EU website but is still online as a flipbook under https://issuu.com/espee7/docs/eu_12_lessons (accessed April 02, 2021).

Staple arguments in negotiating Europeanization as Eastern enlargement have involved emphatic re-assertions of Eastern European countries' European-ness and recurrent demands of 'returning to Europe' as 'bulwarks of Christian-ity' who have historically staved off the Ottoman threat. More recent Eastern European claims of safeguarding Christianity have resulted in policies and po-licing aimed at hindering the influx of Muslim refugees into Western Europe.[4] In the process, such arguments not only reinforced claims of historical belong-ing to Central Europe (rather than Eastern Europe or the Balkans) – but, more importantly, undeniable whiteness (Bakić-Hayden 1995: 924; Böröcz 2001: 32; Lindstrom 2003: 324). At the same time, claims of 'returning to Europe' made by citizens and non-citizens whose Europeanness is mainly questioned on grounds of religion and race, are frequently repudiated; their widespread slo-gan 'We are here because you were there' has failed to result in noteworthy structural changes thus far.

Exclusionary politics as attempts to 'return to Europe', which required un-conditional adaptation to Western European expectations, were met with criti-cism from several EU member states as well as from candidate countries: Serbia's Prime Minister Aleksandar Vučić reacted to Hungary's border closure in 2015 by invoking European values of tolerance. Milica Trakilović (2020: 55) aptly disentangles how differently positioned countries and their governments can choose diverging strategies while claiming to build on values deemed European:

> Hungary could permit to close its borders and express anti-migrant sentiment because it is part of the official European framework, as represented by the EU and the Schengen zone. On the other hand, Serbia and similar non-EU countries could not permit to express anti-migrant sentiment because of their precarious position in the official European polit-ical structures, and therefore they performed an openness to difference in accordance with supposed core European values as well. What should be kept in mind here is that both responses may have a remarkably similar discursive effect: namely, reinstating the idea of Europe as a unique and privileged place, a civilizational model. While their rheto-ric differs, both Hungary and Serbia are performing Europeanness to come closer to Eu-rope proper, which is always already located elsewhere, namely in the West.

As these examples show, Europeanization-as-Eastern-enlargement is central to several connected fields. Among them, unequal mobilities serve as a magnify-ing glass that in turn renders Europe's global entanglements visible: in the

---

4 Note that we reject the established categories of *forced* and *voluntary* migration, often in-voked in language and imagery of migrants 'undeserving' and refugees 'deserving' of protec-tion. Regularly perpetuated in media (Holmes & Castañeda 2016; Holzberg et al. 2018), this dichotomy rarely mirrors the complex lived experiences of people on the move (Crawley & Skleparis 2018).

Eurafrican borderlands, in epigonal Europe, and in the EU overseas territories omitted in the official discourse, which therefore comprise a politically and rhetorically "forgotten Europe" (Boatcă 2019).

Europeanization as Overseas Statehoods

The premise that nation states hold territorially bounded authority which emerged with the Peace of Westphalia in 1648 and which was consolidated after the 1789 French Revolution is central to sociological Europeanization research. The widespread definition of the EU as an organization characterized by "sharing and pooling of the member states' sovereignty", and therefore operating as a "meta-state" (Böröcz & Sarkar 2005: 156), prompts the notion that European nation states with clearly defined borders pool their sovereignty for the sake of greater European integration. Yet, notions such as sovereignty, citizenship, the nation state, and borders are immediately upended when we consider the historical inclusion and association of African territories into the EU discussed above. Today, the relatively visible and disputed Eurafrican territories of Ceuta and Melilla are often viewed as 'anomalies' that fail to seriously trouble either the geographic referent claimed by and as Europe, or the idea of a modern world constituted of sovereign nation states.

However, Ceuta and Melilla are but the tip of an iceberg of territories colonially entangled – not only, but especially – with Europe. While this 'iceberg' is spread out across the globe (e.g., New Caledonia in the South Pacific, the Falkland Islands in the South Atlantic, Greenland in the North Atlantic and Arctic, and Réunion in the Indian Ocean), most of the territories still administered by European states today are located in the Greater Caribbean: Anguilla, Aruba, Bermuda, Bonaire, the British Virgin Islands, the Cayman Islands, Curaçao, French Guiana, Guadeloupe, Martinique, Montserrat, Réunion, Saba, Saint-Barthélemy, Saint Helena, Saint-Martin, Sint Eustatius, Sint Maarten, and the Turks and Caicos Islands.[5]

How can the Caribbean territories, 'belonging' to the EU and/or a European nation state (as in the case of the UK, whose EU membership ended in 2020) be conceptually understood without dismissing them as negligible exceptions from the assumed historical transition from empire to nation and as anomalies in a modern world of sovereign nation states? A growing literature tries to capture the paradoxical logic behind the functioning of state structures in the non-

---

5 Maps of the of overseas countries and territories and outermost regions are provided in the online supplement to this book.

independent Caribbean by denouncing "the myth of sovereignty" (Lewis 2013) and instead making use of concepts such as "extended statehood" (De Jong & Kruijt 2005), "postcolonial sovereignty games" (Adler-Nissen & Gad 2013), or "non-sovereign futures" (Bonilla 2015) to denote these territories' administratively and politically dependent status. In previous works, we have proposed the interrelated concepts of "Overseas Europe" (Santos 2017), "Caribbean Europe" (Boatcă 2018) and "European elsewheres" (Boatcă & Santos 2022) in order to provide spatial referents and visibility to political and administrative entanglements that continue to be structurally silenced. Scholars of global history have provided ample evidence for the coexistence of imperial and national state structures in the nineteenth and most of the twentieth centuries. Yet the dominant view is that they no longer coexist in the twenty-first. In a detailed analysis of the transformations undergone by the French state in the aftermath of the French Revolution and the Napoleonic era, Frederick Cooper argues that France remained an empire-state for most of its modern history. According to Cooper, the moment that marked France's transition from empire to nation state was Algeria's independence: "If one wants to rethink France from its colonies, one might argue that France only became a nation state in 1962, when it gave up its attempt to keep Algeria French and tried for a time to define itself as a singular citizenry in a single territory" (Cooper 2005: 22). Cooper is well aware of the existence of the French overseas departments in the Caribbean, and even considers them decisive for this argument. Yet in addressing the need to rethink France from its colonial borders, he disregards these territories' ongoing colonial status.

Thus, even a radically critical view of empire in the European context once again manages to obscure the Caribbean component of European statehood today and to conclude that "the most important fact about empires is that they are gone" (Cooper 2005: 203). However, when taking the French outermost regions into account, the very definition of 'empire' becomes a more apt characterization of post-1962 France than any available definition of a unitary nation state, for which France has been seen as paradigmatic. Here, it is telling that France began to discursively define its territorial outlines in the 1960s as a 'hexagon', that is, a territory roughly shaped by six lines delimiting 'metropolitan' France. As historian Todd Shepard (2016: 53) has explained, the coining of this imagery coincided with Algeria's independence in 1962, a date that reminds us "that the territorial boundaries of modern France were never just European, although in 1962 the percentage of its territory outside of Europe shrunk from more than 50 per cent to far less than 20 per cent (with almost all of that in sparsely populated French Guiana" (Shepard 2016: 53).

Roughly the same size as Austria, Guyane (the official and locally preferred shorthand for French Guiana) was one of the so-called Old Colonies (together with Réunion, Martinique, and Guadeloupe) to become an 'overseas department' of France in 1946, hoping to achieve equality vis-à-vis the 'metropole' under the French flag. Yet, as feminist political scientist Françoise Vergès (1999: 74; italics in original) reminds us,

> 1946 was *not* a decolonization. In the second half of our century, decolonization has sig-
> nified rupture with the *metropole*, construction of a nation state, access to sovereignty.
> There was no rupture, no construction of a nation state, no access to sovereignty in the
> Old Colonies. The majority of their populations called for a greater integration within
> French democracy. Their demand focused on social equality between the inhabitants of
> the Old Colonies and those of metropolitan France.

Accordingly, not only does the term 'overseas' (*outre-mer*) locate these territories 'elsewhere' and render them invisible, but it also masks the appropriate term: 'colonial' (Vergès 2017: 166). The argument made by Vergès about the ongoing yet reframed colonial relations in the French overseas departments can be extended to all lands in European possession: the traces of the colonial past "are to be found today in fragile economies, weak industry and high rates of unemployment, as well as rampant inequality" (Vergès 2017: 165).

However, these features are rendered invisible by official EU maps, as becomes obvious upon closer inspection of the figure (un)veiling the regional at-risk-of-poverty rates (see Chapter 3 in this volume): while the Canary Islands and Madeira are at high or very high risk of poverty, it is indicated that there are 'no data' available for the other entities termed 'outermost regions' by the EU. As far as the French 'overseas departments' are concerned, poverty rates are disproportionately high in comparison to 'metropolitan' France, where 14 per cent of the population lives below the national poverty line. This number is up to five times higher 'overseas': 34 per cent in the case of Guadeloupe, 33 per cent in Martinique, 53 per cent in Guyane, 42 per cent in Réunion, and 77 per cent in Mayotte (INSEE 2020). In Guyane (Figure 5.5), the inequalities at the crossroads of various variables are especially glaring.

Bordering Suriname and Brazil at the juncture of Amazonia and the Caribbean, Guyane has struggled with several interrelated issues such as unemployment and precarious housing and sanitary conditions. Recent ethnographic research has shown the racialization at play in the context of access to housing for non-white, especially Maroon communities in Guyane's racially stratified society, in particular near the border with Suriname, a Dutch colony until 1975 (Léobal 2018). In 2017, this racial injustice was one of interconnected reasons that sparked mass protests and a general strike calling for social transformation

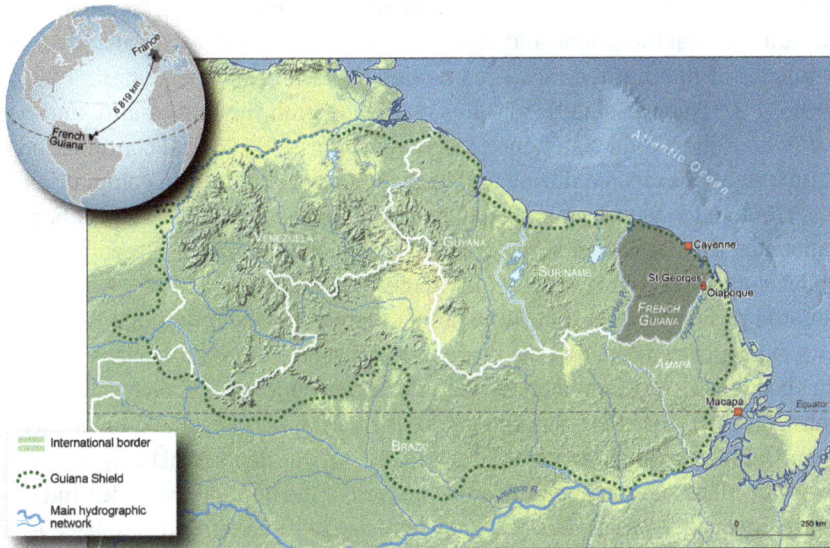

Figure 5.5: French Guiana within its regional and global context.
Source: Map created by Matthieu Noucher and Olivier Pissoat (CNRS, UMR Passages).
Reproduced by kind permission.

(Mam Lam Fouck & Moomou 2017). Notwithstanding the inequalities within Guyane as well as between Guyane and the 'metropole', the EU territory has also become an "€udorado" (Police 2010) – a pun combining French Guiana's official currency (euro) with the mythical *El dorado* – prompting the influx of many migrants, especially from Haiti, Suriname, and Brazil. These migrants, in turn, are especially vulnerable in Guyane's underfunded health sector (Jolivet et al. 2012). Critical migration research has provided evidence that in recent years Guyane has been turned into an extension of '*Fortress Europe*' with several legal provisions set up to prevent mobilities and illegalize people of different nationalities and "stateless natives" (Benoît 2020: 225). With this term, anthropologist Catherine Benoît describes non-white people, especially individuals identifying as Amerindians and Maroons, who were born on French and EU soil yet are turned into 'undocumented migrants' in the absence of administrative facilities documenting their place of birth in 'remote' regions of the French Republic. The entangled inequalities reproduced and contested in this 'forgotten' part of the European Union and its South American borderlands are not isolated phenomena (Santos 2022). Rather, they (should) alert us to the exclusionary patterns systematically reproduced by Europeanization-as-overseas-statehoods. As anthropologist Ann Laura Stoler has pointed out, "temporary exclusions, partial inclusions and legal exemptions are not occasional and ad hoc strategies of rule but the racialized modus operandi of imperial states" (Stoler 2016: 177). Overseas statehoods thus challenge both the universality and normativity of the nation state, once it is understood as the logical continuation of state formations created during and in the interests of European colonial rule.

Through the lens of global entanglements applied in this chapter, Europeanization can thus be placed in its forgotten global and Caribbean 'elsewheres'. The political and legal frameworks set up in these territories, as well as the differently situated positionings of their inhabitants, defy textbook definitions of borders, sovereignty, citizenship, and the modern nation state. Europeanization-as-overseas-statehoods reveals – even more so than the aforementioned re-framings of Europeanization – the "overlaps between the formerly colonized world and today's European Union" (Randeria & Römhild 2013: 22; our translation). Actively forgetting these "overlaps" results in an undertheorization of the unequal mobilities and existential inequalities that have come to characterize these territories (Boatcă et al. 2022). Rather than regarding them as negligible and remote relics of a past supposedly overcome, we must acknowledge their global relevance, not only because of their spatial dispersion across several of the world's oceans, but even more due to the structural similarities their histories and non-sovereign presents exhibit despite their distinct – and distant – locations (Boatcă & Santos 2022). They therefore signal the need to address Europe's structural links to its "last colonies" (Connell & Aldrich 2020) through a sociology of systematic colonial continuities, rather than viewing them as sociologically irrelevant anomalies in a world of sovereign nation states for which European nations have long served as models to be imitated.

Conclusion

In this chapter, we have proposed to read standard depictions of Europeanization against their grain: rather than presuming an ahistorical and geographically inaccurate understanding of Europe, our presentation and discussion of the works highlighted in this chapter argues for a placing of Europe – and hence Europeanization – in the *longue durée* of global entanglements. We have reframed the process commonly known as Europeanization in the context of and as colonization, Eurafrican integration, Eastern enlargement, and overseas statehoods. In all these instances, power relations that have emerged globally and historically were shown to be central to current asymmetric negotiations of what Europe, Europeanness, and Europeanization might mean.

Manifold legacies of European entanglements persist to this day. While more attention has been paid to geopolitical and economic power asymmetries, recent examples also focus on cultural politics: should objects 'acquired' under unequal conditions by Europeans in Africa and currently on display or, more often, gathering dust in the basements of European museums, be restituted to their places and communities of origin? Commissioned by French President Emanuel Macron, a restitution report by social scientist Felwine Sarr and art historian Bénédicte Savoy (Sarr & Savoy 2018) makes a clear plea for returning African art and artefacts as a start for a "new relational ethics" between Europe, Africa, and other parts of the world. As Savoy's latest research shows, the debates sparked by their scientific report are not the first ones to be held, as claims for restitution had already been made, yet usually opposed, immediately after Eurafrica's institutional heyday, that is, with formal independence gained by African states in the 1960s (Savoy 2021: 11–20).

As we have briefly shown with respect to unequal mobilities in different temporal and spatial contexts, and as poignantly emphasized by other critical scholars, conflicts over the hegemonic definition of Europe are encapsulated in current debates of racist migrant scapegoating and anti-immigration policies: "The question of and about Europe, therefore, is ever increasingly fashioned against the postcolonial specter of a mob of mobile (nonwhite) non-Europeans. This requires the ideological projection of a singular, unified Europe, which is after all a central project of the European Union itself" (De Genova 2016: 89). A stringently critical sociological perspective of Europeanization thus needs to unpack this singular Europe, shifting focus instead onto *multiple* and *unequal Europes* whose normative and geopolitical weight has shifted in time and space: Europe's Afro-Eurasian roots, the European trade in enslaved persons, Algeria's EU membership, the Balkans as Europe's 'incomplete Self', and the inequality-ridden overseas territories across the globe, and especially in the Caribbean, are poignant yet rarely addressed examples multiplying the singular and methodologically flawed notion of Europe that currently dominates political and academic discourse.

Didactical Section

Key Learning Points

- Global sociological perspectives, often informed by post- and decolonial approaches, situate Europeanization in the *longue durée*, tracing it back to global structures and 'inconvenient' histories rarely considered in prevailing research.
- Although it is now widely accepted, Europe's status as a full-fledged continent, separate from Asia and distortedly inflated on standard Mercator world maps, has long been criticized by geographers and world historians.
- With its Afro-Eurasian roots, Europe has never been a monolithic entity with ethnic, racial, let alone cultural or religious homogeneity.
- The Treaty of Rome 'Europeanized' colonialism in Africa and stands in the tradition of Eurafrican ideas presuming an unequal complementarity between Europe and Africa.
- The project and discourse of 'Eastern enlargement' perpetuates images of the European East as Western Europe's 'incomplete Self', with new EU member states and candidate countries from Eastern Europe outperforming desirable Europeanness (e.g., by invoking Christian heritage).
- EU, national and imperial state structures reveal a complex overlap across the globe, in particular in the Caribbean, where a number of entities that are commonly considered European 'nation states' (e.g., France) have ongoing colonial relations with non-sovereign territories (e.g., Guyane), which in turn are actively rendered invisible and at a systematic economic disadvantage.

Glossary

Eastern enlargement: The process of asymmetric negotiation of EU membership and all ensuing rights to Eastern European countries historically defined in and out of Europeanness. In dominant political and academic discourse, the term often perpetuates the Western cognitive map on which Eastern and Southeastern European countries occupy intermediate positions between Europe and Asia.

Entanglements: Another term for interconnections; used here to point to the common origin and mutual influences between structures that developed and should therefore be analyzed jointly.

Eurafrica: A political project targeting a 'coordinated' European exploitation of Africa's raw materials, resources, and people. Realized with the full integration of French Algeria into the Common Market and the association of most of Europe's other colonies, including vast territories such as the Belgian Congo and French West and Equatorial Africa (1957), Eurafrica can be dated back to the 'scramble for Africa' (Berlin conference) and the Pan-European movement, among others. Its legacies are visible today in various forms, including development aid, military force, and remaining EU territories on and near the African continent.

European trade in enslaved people: An adapted version of the term 'European slave trade' coined by Walter Rodney (1982) to highlight the European dominance glossed over in the label 'transatlantic slave trade'. More than five hundred years of colonial rule were only possible due the inhumane and centuries-long enslavement and transportation of more than 12 million Africans to the Americas following the genocide of the latter's indigenous population.

Overseas countries and territories (OCTs) and **outermost regions (ORs)**: The European Union counts nine so-called 'outermost regions' located outside the European continent. Outermost regions are an integral part of the EU and its single market and are part of the member states to which they are constitutionally linked – France, Portugal, and Spain. Additionally, there are 13 OCTs linked to Denmark, France, and the Netherlands. OCTs are not part of the single market and must comply with the obligations imposed on third countries in terms of trade, health and plant health standards, and safeguard measures.

Further Readings

Adler-Nissen, R. & U. P. Gad (eds.), 2013: *European Integration and Postcolonial Sovereignty Games: The EU Overseas Countries and Territories*. London: Routledge.

Conrad, S., S. Randeria & R. Römhild (eds.), 2013: *Jenseits des Eurozentrismus. Postkoloniale Perspektiven in den Geschichts- und Kulturwissenschaften*. Frankfurt am Main: Campus.

De Genova, N., 2016: The European Question: Migration, Race, and Postcoloniality in Europe. *Social Text* 34(3(128)):75–102.

Hansen, P. & S. Jonsson, 2014: *Eurafrica: The Untold History of European Integration and Colonialism*. London: Bloomsbury.

Gutiérrez Rodríguez, E., M. Boatcă & S. Costa (eds.), 2010: *Decolonizing European Sociology: Transdisciplinary Approaches*. Farnham: Ashgate.

Additional Web-Sources

The website http://slavevoyages.org offers an overview of the European trade in enslaved people in a series of maps and digital resources on the topic.

The cross-European research project ECHOES ("European Colonial Heritage Modalities in Entangled Cities") explores engagements with colonialism in different European and non-European cities. The project's website also contains a keywords section: http://projectechoes.eu

The international conference "Colonialism as Shared History. Past, Present, Future" was opened with a keynote lecture by Yvonne Adhiambo Owuor, entitled "Derelict Shards: The Roamings of Colonial Phantoms". Her lecture offers critical reflections on the disputed concept of 'shared history': https://lisa.gerda-henkel-stiftung.de/sharedhistory_keynote_owuor

The video entitled "Why is my curriculum white?" will make you (further) question the normalized whiteness of university curricula, teaching, and research, as unpacked by students of University College London: https://www.youtube.com/watch?v=Dscx4h2l-Pk

The website "Global Social Theory" serves as a resource to be used and amplified by students, academics, and others interested in concepts, thinkers, and topics relevant to social theory beyond Eurocentrism: https://globalsocialtheory.org/

The video "Visualizing Sovereignty" by Yarimar Bonilla and Max Hantel provides you with a 'temporal map' illustrating the constant re-structuring of the Caribbean as a prime example defying standard notions of sovereignty: https://vimeo.com/169690419. Reflections on the video and other (counter-)mappings are given in a joint article (Bonilla & Hantel 2016).

The online tool provided on https://www.thetruesize.com allows users to move the outlines of countries, thus exploring how much the Mercator map distorts land mass.

References

Abu-Lughod, J. L., 1989: *Before European Hegemony: The World System A. D. 1250–1350.* Oxford: Oxford University Press.

Adler-Nissen, R. & U. P. Gad (eds.), 2013: *European Integration and Postcolonial Sovereignty Games: The EU Overseas Countries and Territories.* London: Routledge.

Bahl, E., 2021: *Verflochtene Geschichten im postkolonialen Grenzraum. Biographien, Zugehörigkeiten und Erinnerungspraktiken in Ceuta und Melilla.* Göttingen: Göttingen University Press.

Bakić-Hayden, M., 1995: Nesting orientalisms: The case of former Yugoslavia. *Slavic Review* 54(4): 917–931.

Balibar, É., 2002: The Borders of Europe. In: Balibar, E., *Politics and the Other Scene*, pp. 87–103. London: Verso.

Balibar, É., 2009: Europe as Borderland. *Environment and Planning D: Society and Space* 27(2): 190–215.

Benoît, C., 2020: Fortress Europe's Far-Flung Borderlands: 'Illegality' and the 'Deportation Regime' in France's Caribbean and Indian Ocean Territories. *Mobilities* 15(2):220–240.

Bernal, M., 1987: *Black Athena: Afroasiatic Roots of Classical Civilization, Volume I: The Fabrication of Ancient Greece, 1785–1985*. New Brunswick: Rutgers University Press.

Bialasiewicz, L., 2012: Off-Shoring and Out-Sourcing the Borders of EUrope: Libya and EU Border Work in the Mediterranean. *Geopolitics* 17(4):843–866.

Boatcă, M., 2010: Multiple Europes and the Politics of Difference Within. In: Brunkhorst, H. & G. Grözinger (eds.), *The Study of Europe*, pp. 51–66. Baden-Baden: Nomos.

Boatcă, M., 2013: Multiple Europes and the Politics of Difference Within. *Worlds and Knowledges Otherwise* 3 (3). https://globalstudies.trinity.duke.edu/sites/globalstudies. trinity.duke.edu/files/file-attachments/v3d3_Boatca2.pdf (accessed April 14, 2021).

Boatcă, M., 2018: Caribbean Europe: Out of Sight, out of Mind? In: Reiter, B. (ed.), *Constructing the Pluriverse: The Geopolitics of Knowledge*, pp. 197–218. Durham: Duke University Press.

Boatcă, M., 2019: Forgotten Europes. Rethinking Regional Entanglements from the Caribbean. In: Bringel, B. & H. Cairo (eds.), *Critical Geopolitics and Regional (Re)Configurations: Interregionalism and Transnationalism between Latin America and Europe*, pp. 96–116. London: Routledge.

Boatcă, M. & F. Santos, 2022: Europe's Place in the World. Towards Decolonizing Sociologies of European Space. In: Bartmanski, D., H. Füller, J. Hoerning & G. Weidenhaus (eds.), *Considering Space. The Spatial Refiguration of the Social*. London: Routledge.

Boatcă, M., C. Di Stefano & F. Santos, 2022: Marginalizing Europe: Unequal Mobilities and Existential Inequalities in Caribbean Europe. In: Loftsdóttir, K., B. Hipfl & S. Ponzanesi (eds.), *Creating Europe from the Margins*. London: Routledge.

Bonilla, Y., 2015: *Non-Sovereign Futures: French Caribbean Politics in the Wake of Disenchantment*. Chicago: The University of Chicago Press.

Bonilla, Y. & M. Hantel, 2016: Visualizing Sovereignty: Cartographic Queries for the Digital Age. *Sx Archipelagos* 1 (1). http://smallaxe.net/sxarchipelagos/issue01/bonilla-visualizing.html (accessed April 14, 2021).

Böröcz, J., 2001: Introduction: Empire and Coloniality in the 'Eastern Enlargement' of the European Union. In: Böröcz, J. & M. Kovács, *Empire's New Clothes. Unveiling EU Enlargement*, pp. 4–50. Holly Cottage: Central European Review.

Böröcz, J. & M. Sarkar, 2005: What Is the EU? *International Sociology* 20(2):153–173.

Connell, J. & R. Aldrich, 2020: *The Ends of Empire: The Last Colonies Revisited*. London: Palgrave Macmillan.

Conrad, S., S. Randeria & R. Römhild (eds.), 2013: *Jenseits des Eurozentrismus. Postkoloniale Perspektiven in den Geschichts- und Kulturwissenschaften*. Frankfurt am Main: Campus.

Cooper, F., 2005: *Colonialism in Question. Theory, Knowledge, History*. Berkeley: University of California Press.

Crawley, H. & D. Skleparis, 2018: Refugees, Migrants, Neither, Both: Categorical Fetishism and the Politics of Bounding in Europe's 'Migration Crisis'. *Journal of Ethnic and Migration Studies* 44(1):48–64.

Dainotto, R., 2006: *Europe (in Theory)*. Durham: Duke University Press.

De Genova, N., 2016: The European Question: Migration, Race, and Post-Coloniality in Europe. *Social Text* 34(3(128)):75–102.

De Jong, L. & D. Kruijt (eds.), 2005: *Extended Statehood in the Caribbean: Paradoxes of Quasi Colonialism, Local Autonomy, and Extended Statehood in the USA, French, Dutch, and British Caribbean*. Amsterdam: Rozenberg Publishers.

Dussel, E., 2000: Europa, Modernidad y eurocentrismo. In: Lander, E. (ed.), *La colonialidad del saber: eurocentrismoy cienciassociales. Perspectivaslatinoamericanas*, pp. 41–52. Buenos Aires: CLACSO.

El-Tayeb, F., 2016: *Undeutsch: Die Konstruktion des Anderen in der postmigrantischen Gesellschaft*. Bielefeld: transcript.

Eltis, D. & D. Richardson, 2010: *Atlas of the Transatlantic Slave Trade*. New Haven: Yale University Press.

European Commission, 2006a: *Monitoring report on the state of preparedness for EU membership of Bulgaria and Romania*. https://ec.europa.eu/neighbourhood-enlargement/sites/near/files/pdf/key_documents/2006/sept/report_bg_ro_2006_en. pdf (accessed April 14, 2021).

European Commission, 2006b: *Enlargement Strategy and Main Challenges 2006–2007 Including annexed special report on the EU's capacity to integrate new members*. https://ec.europa.eu/neighbourhood-enlargement/sites/near/files/pdf/key_documents/2006/nov/com_649_strategy_paper_en.pdf (accessed April 14, 2021).

European Union, 2017: *Europe in 12 lessons*. Luxembourg: Publications Office of the European Union. http://data.europa.eu/doi/10.2775/12586 (accessed April 14, 2021).

European Union, 2021: *The history of the European Union*. https://europa.eu/european-union/about-eu/history_en (accessed April 14, 2021).

Frank, A. G., 1998: *ReOrient: Global Economy in the Asian Age*. Berkeley: University of California Press.

Gutiérrez Rodríguez, E., M. Boatcă & S. Costa (eds.), 2010: *Decolonizing European Sociology: Transdisciplinary Approaches*. Farnham: Ashgate.

Goody, J., 2006: *The Theft of History*. Cambridge: Cambridge University Press.

Hodgson, M. G. S., 1963: The Interrelations of Societies in History. *Comparative Studies in Society and History* 5(2):227–250.

Hall, S., 1991: Europe's Other Self. *Marxism Today* 35(8):18–19.

Hall, S., 1992: The West and the Rest. Discourse and Power. In: Hall, S. & B. Gieben (eds.), *Formations of Modernity*, pp. 275–332. Cambridge: Polity Press.

Hansen, P. & S. Jonsson, 2014: *Eurafrica: The Untold History of European Integration and Colonialism*. London: Bloomsbury.

Hobson, J., 2004: *The Eastern Origins of European Civilisation*. Cambridge: Cambridge University Press.

Holmes, S. M. & H. Castañeda, 2016: Representing the "European Refugee Crisis" in Germany and beyond: Deservingness and Difference, Life and Death. *American Ethnologist* 43(1): 12–24.

Holzberg, B., K. Kolbe & R. Zaborowski, 2018: Figures of Crisis: The Delineation of (Un)Deserving Refugees in the German Media. *Sociology* 52(3):534–550.

INSEE, 2020: Une pauvreté marquée dans les DOM, notamment en Guyane et à Mayotte. *INSEE Première* 1804. https://www.insee.fr/fr/statistiques/4622377 (accessed April 14, 2021).

Jansen, S., 2009: After the Red Passport: Towards an Anthropology of the Everyday Geopolitics of Entrapment in the EU's "Immediate Outside". *Journal of the Royal Anthropological Institute* 15(4):815–832.

Jolivet, A, E. Cadot, S. Florence, S. Lesieur, J. Lebas & P. Chauvin, 2012: Migrant Health in French Guiana: Are Undocumented Immigrants More Vulnerable? *BMC Public Health* 12(1).

Kobelinsky, C., 2017: Exister au risque de disparaître. Récits sur la mort pendant la traverse vers l'Europe. *Revue Européennedes Migrations Internationales* 33(2–3):115–131.

Koch, A., C. Brierley, M. M. Maslin & S. L. Lewis, 2019: Earth System Impacts of the European Arrival and Great Dying in the Americas after 1492. *Quaternary Science Reviews* 207 (March):13–36.

Krivonos, D. & A. Diatlova, 2020: What to wear for whiteness? The 'whore stigma' and the East/West politics of race, sexuality and gender. *Intersections: Journal of East European Society and Politics* 6(3):116–132.

Léobal, C., 2018: La blancheur bakaa, une majorité bien spécifique. Race, classe et ethnicité dans les situations de démolition à Saint-Laurent-du-Maroni, Guyane. *REVUE Asylon(s)* 15. http://www.reseau-terra.eu/article1412.html (accessed April 14, 2021).

Lewis, L., 2013: *Caribbean Sovereignty. Development and Democracy in an Age of Globalization*. Abingdon: Routledge.

Lewis, M. W. & K. Wigen, 1997: *The Myth of Continents: A Critique of Metageography*. Berkeley: University of California Press.

Lindstrom, N., 2003: Between Europe and the Balkans: Mapping Slovenia and Croatia's "Return to Europe" in the 1990s. *Dialectical Anthropology* 27:313–329.

Mam Lam Fouck, S. & J. Moomou, 2017: Les racines de la 'mobilisation' de mars/avril 2017 en Guyane. *Amerika* 16 (July).

Mazouz, S., 2017: *La République et ses autres. Politiques de l'altérité dans la France des années 2000*. Lyon: ENS Éditions.

Mignolo, W., 2006: Islamophobia/Hispanophobia. The (Re)Configuration of the Racial/Imperial/Colonial Matrix. *Human Architecture: Journal of the Sociology of Self-Knowledge* 1:13–28.

Mintz, S., 1985: *Sweetness and Power. The Place of Sugar in Modern History*. New York: Penguin.

Muller, K., 2001: Shadows of Empire in the European Union. *The European Legacy* 6(4): 439–451.

Murdoch, H. A. (ed.), 2021: *The Struggle of Non-Sovereign Caribbean Territories: Neoliberalism since the French Antillean Uprisings of 2009*. New Brunswick: Rutgers University Press.

Otele, O., 2020: *African Europeans: An Untold History*. London: Hurst.

Owuor, Y. A., 2020: Derelict Shards: The Roaming of Colonial Phantoms. *CODESRIA Bulletin Online* 10: 1–10. https://www.codesria.org/IMG/pdf/10-_y_owuor_codbul_online_1_.pdf (accessed April 14, 2021).

Pagden, A. 2002: Europe: Conceptualizing a Continent. In Pagden, A. (ed.), *The Idea of Europe*, pp. 33–54. Cambridge: Cambridge University Press.

Police, G., 2010: *€udorado: le discours brésilien sur la Guyane française*. Matoury: Ibis Rouge Éditions.

Quijano, A. & I. Wallerstein, 1992: Americanity as a Concept, or the Americas in the Modern World-System. *International Journal of the Social Sciences* 134:549–57.

Randeria, S. & R. Römhild, 2013: Das Postkoloniale Europa: Verflochtene Genealogien der Gegenwart – Einleitung zur erweiterten Auflage (2013). In: Conrad, S., S. Randeria & R. Römhild (eds.), *Jenseits des Eurozentrismus. Postkoloniale Perspektiven in den Geschichts- und Kulturwissenschaften*, pp. 9–31. Frankfurt am Main: Campus.

Rodney, W. 1982: *How Europe Underdeveloped Africa*. Washington D.C.: Howard University Press.

Santos, F., 2017: Re-mapping Europe. Field notes from the French-Brazilian borderland. *InterDisciplines. Journal of History and Sociology*, 8(2): 173–201.

Santos, F., 2020: Von Zentralafrika nach Brasilien und Französisch-Guyana: Transnationale Migration, globale Ungleichheit und das Streben nach Hoffnung. In: Bahl, E. & J. Becker (eds.), *Global Processes of Flight and Migration. The Explanatory Power of Case Studies*.

Globale Flucht- und Migrationsprozesse. Die Erklärungskraft von Fallstudien, pp. 63–82. Göttingen: Göttingen University Press.

Santos, F., 2021: Migration und Gewalt an den vergessenen Rändern der Europäischen Union. In: Ehlers, S., S. Frenking, S. Kleinmann, N. Régis Scholz & V. Triesethau (eds.), *Begrenzungen, Überschreitungen – Limiter, franchir. Interdisziplinäre Perspektiven auf Grenzen und Körper – Approches interdisciplinaires sur les frontières et les corps*, pp. 275–296. Göttingen: V&R unipress.

Santos, F., 2022: *Bridging Fluid Borders. Entanglements in the French-Brazilian Borderland*. London: Routledge.

Sarr, F. & B. Savoy, 2018: *The Restitution of African Cultural Heritage. Toward a New Relational Ethics*. http://restitutionreport2018.com/sarr_savoy_en.pdf (accessed April 14, 2021).

Savoy, B., 2021: *Afrikas Kampf um seine Kunst. Geschichte einer postkolonialen Niederlage*. München: C. H. Beck.

Schindel, E., 2018: Violent Borders. The Melilla fence and the injuries of the Schengen regime. In: Tyner, J. (ed.), *The Idea of Violence*, pp. 117–132. Rome: Viella.

Shepard, T., 2016: The Birth of the Hexagon: 1962 and the Erasure of France's Supranational History. In: Borutta, M. & J. C. Jansen (eds.), *Vertriebene and Pieds-Noirs in Postwar Germany and France: Comparative Perspectives*, pp. 53–69. London: Palgrave Macmillan.

Stoler, L. A., 2016: *Duress: Imperial Durabilities in Our Times*. Durham, NC: Duke University Press.

Todorova, M., 1997: *Imagining the Balkans*. New York and Oxford: Oxford University Press.

Trakilović, M., 2020: "On this path to Europe" – the symbolic role of the "Balkan corridor" in the European migration debate. In: Buikema, R., A. Buyse & A. C. G. M. Robben (eds.), *Cultures, Citizenship and Human Rights*, pp. 49–63. London: Routledge.

Trouillot, M. R., 1995: *Silencing the Past: Power and the Production of History*. Boston, MA: Beacon Press.

Vergès, F., 1999: *Monsters and Revolutionaries: Colonial Family Romance and Métissage*. Durham: Duke University Press.

Vergès, F., 2017: Overseas France: A Vestige of the Republican Colonial Utopia? In: Bancel, N., P. Blanchard & D. Thomas (eds.), *The Colonial Legacy in France: Fracture, Rupture, and Apartheid*, pp. 165–171. Bloomington: Indiana University Press.

Whitmarsh, T., 2018: Black Achilles. Aeon. https://aeon.co/essays/when-homer-envisioned-achilles-did-he-see-a-black-man (accessed April 14, 2021).

Wirz, A. & A. Eckert, 2004: The Scramble for Africa. Icon and Idiom of Modernity. In: Pétré-Grenouilleau, O. (ed.), *From Slave Trade to Empire: European Colonisation of Black Africa, 1780s–1880s*, pp. 133–153. London: Routledge.

Wolff, L., 1994: *Inventing Eastern Europe: The Map of Civilization on the Mind of the Enlightenment*. Stanford: Stanford University Press.

Timm Beichelt & Susann Worschech
6 Transformation and Post-Transformation

In the social sciences, the notion of transformation is used in a wide range of meanings. It sometimes enjoys the status of a theoretic paradigm and is frequently furnished with normative connotations while often being employed in empiric description. Consequently, if used as a concept, transformation is sometimes located in the sphere of societal theories; it can also appear in public or political debates, and also plays a role in social analysis.

Transformation unfolds in different layers of the social sphere: political transformation concerns the character of political regimes, economic transformation is related to economic systems, and societal transformation runs through various segments of society. Against these different meanings, any definition of transformation carries both an epistemic and disciplinary bias: its use by political scientists usually refers to the political sphere (see, for example, Linz 1990), economists focus on the economic sphere (Kolev & Zweynert 2015), and so on. Furthermore, the way the term is employed is connected to various imaginations on the purpose of social science and objects of scientific scholarship. A first approximate definition outlines transformation as a particular case of deep social change that applies to larger entities such as systems or regimes. Contrastingly, social change also includes dynamism in social behavior or social relations; these dimensions are not covered by the concept of transformation.

If we look at the economic, political, and social tides in Europe in the last thirty years, it immediately becomes clear that many developments bear a transformative character. In several Central, South-East, and East European countries, the fall of the iron curtain brought about a transformative path of autocratic socialist to democratic pluralist political systems. A planned economic system was then replaced by a capitalist market economy. These two developments, which will be discussed in more detail below, mark the origin of the emergence of the concept of transformation in European Studies. Other arenas of transformative social change should not be overlooked, however. Globalization and European integration have softened internal European borders and initiated social transformation in the fields of labor, education, and several other areas affected by migration. In any case, the concept of transformation was initially developed with a global perspective, with Latin America and Southeast Asia as further regions of transformation studies.

The publication which developed this global perspective and can be seen as the first landmark of transformation studies with a focus on political regime change was written by Guillermo O'Donnell, Phillipe Schmitter, and Laurence

https://doi.org/10.1515/9783110673630-006

Whitehead (1986) and bore the title *Transitions from authoritarian rule*. In fact, the term used by the authors was not transformation, but 'transition'. Despite their focus on authoritarian rule in the four-volume series, the idea was based on an analysis of two vectors: transition from authoritarian rule, and transition to democracy. While the terms transition and transformation were later used interchangeably, it became clear that both authoritarianism and democracy could exist in varying forms, which later led to different paths of transformation and to a phenomenon that is sometimes called 'post-transformation' – a constellation in which transformation has led to specific social balances and institutional settings that need to be categorized beyond existing regime models (Holtmann & Wiesenthal 2009).

The high point of transformation and transformation studies coincided with *The Third Wave* (Huntington 1991) of democratization, a term introduced by Samuel Huntington to group countries that had begun to democratize their regimes from the 1970s onwards. The initial third wave in Europe took place in the south, where crisis engulfed military regimes that were eventually overthrown in Greece (1974), Portugal, and Spain (both 1981). Even more attention was drawn to the fall of the iron curtain, the seeds of which originated in Central Europe in the late 1980s before extending to the Balkans and culminating in the permanent lowering of the red flag of the Soviet Union on December 31, 1991. The new year of 1992 began with more than ten countries on the map of Europe which had either never previously existed as independent states or had only briefly done so. In a strict sense, newly founded states did not witness a transformation, but a design of national political, economic, and social institutions from scratch. The term transformation was employed for these new states as well, however, as the dynamics here were like those in established states such as Hungary, Poland, Romania, and Russia.

Transformation is a core concept in sociology of Europeanization because the whole process of the emergence of society, values, culture, politics, economy, and institutions in Europe is itself a conglomeration of multiple processes of transformation. Europeanization consists of a multitude of transformative processes, ranging across local, regional, national, and transnational levels. The transition of political structures and regimes, value systems, narratives and beliefs, cooperation, and action patterns from the individual to the collective level in Europe's past and present – that is, the transition of institutions, interpretations, and interaction – can be characterized as a core element of Europeanization (Worschech 2018a).

Info-Box 6.1: The different notions of transformation in the social sciences

In the social sciences, transformation has been a relevant issue since the very outset of the discipline. Although sociology originated from a fascination with the stability of social structures, bureaucracies, and the phenomenon of 'how society is possible' (Simmel 1910), early scholars such as Emile Durkheim or Karl Marx focused on non-stable, transitional aspects. Durkheim ([1988] 2019) described the path from anomic pre-modern society to a differentiated society as the result of the social reorganization of solidarity; pre-modern societies are tied together by *mechanical solidarity* – that is, a concept of direct solidarity based on integration into a community of shared traditions, norms, customs, and sanctions. In contrast, differentiated societies are composed of collaborative and contractual structures, allowing for more dynamism and variance, and providing *organic solidarity* as a network of interdependencies. The opposite of this evolutionary societal change is marked by the intended, encompassing, and revolutionary system change that was initiated by Marx, a social philosopher. Finally, a first integrative conflict perspective of societal transformation – neither evolution nor revolution – was emphasized by Georg Simmel, who argued that conflict and dispute are core aspects of societal development.

The term *transformation* itself became more popular in sociology in the mid-20th century, when Karl Polanyi ([1944] 2007) outlined the genesis of the modern capitalist market system and its respective political and social implications in his book *The Great Transformation*. Although Polanyi was not responsible for conceptualizing the term transformation itself, his study sheds light on the processes that led to the breakdown of 19th century social order and paved the way for modern as well as totalitarian systems in 20th century Europe. Polanyi's argument was based on an assertion that these developments were rooted in the politically supported establishment of a liberal market system based on the commodification of 'fictional goods' such as work and land, resulting in the subsequent 'disembedding' of economy and society. Consequently, the increasing independence of economic development from state intervention, the circle of 'market liberalization – tempted intervention – more liberalization' initiated a profound process of structural change that was labeled by Polanyi as *The Great Transformation*. Today, the book can be viewed as one of the first comprehensive attempts to combine political, social, and economic perspectives on large change processes and their manifold societal results since the 19th century.

Therefore, transformation is a process that can be located between evolutionary and revolutionary change. It is often initiated or catalyzed by revolutions – in the case of political transformation, the 'Monday Demonstrations' in Leipzig and other cities in the GDR in the autumn of 1989, for example – yet the entire process encompasses a combination of short-term mechanisms and mid- to long-term processes. Charles Tilly (2004) uses the word 'contentious' to describe political transformation processes that involve public claims, changing state capacity and consultation. He points out that, particularly in European transformation history, we find a variety of trajectories followed by contention, and that (only) one rare, contingent outcome of contentious politics is democracy (Tilly 2004: 6). Furthermore, contention as a central concept in transformation studies underlines the opaque, non-teleological, non-linear, and open-ended nature of these processes, although in politics and social sciences alike, there is a tendency to find or formulate a 'script' of the phenomenon as a planned process of 'transformation into something'. Teleology, however, as recent, or ex-post-characteristic, denies contingency and ambivalence as core aspects of any transformation.

Transformation in Europe: Historical Overview & Description

With reference to the broad definition provided above, it seems plausible to place the beginning of transformative processes in Europe in the late 18th century, during which two differing dynamics occurred. On the one hand, democracy developed beyond a select few parliamentary chambers into broader political regimes that deserved to be regarded as democracies in coherent territorial spaces ('Large-Scale Democracy', Dahl 1998). On the other, industrialization and various forms of role differentiation led to deep-rooted social change (Rokkan 2000). This simultaneous transformation, in both the political and social spheres, was later theorized as modernization. One of the main ideas of modernization theory focused on the dependency of political reforms geared towards democracy on specific forms of societal organization. In particular, schooling, and higher education, as well as societal division of labor, gave rise to citizens who – other than peasants – had both the time and individual interest to engage in political participation (Lerner 1958; Lipset 1959; Rostow 1960).

Beginnings of Democratization and Regime Change in Europe from the 18th Century

Before the 20th century, democracy developed gradually und inconsistently in geographic terms. It seems more appropriate to speak of the emergence of certain institutions in certain regions than to think of Europe as a continent undergoing a process of continuous democratization. English parliamentarism dates back to the 13th century, yet it had not developed universal franchise before 1918. In many Nordic states, assemblies were known as an arena for political decision-making with remarkable degrees of freedom from the monarchy. The French Revolution of 1789 introduced civic rights and the Republic, but the new elites soon turned to terror and paved the way for the imperial politics of the ancient régime. Poland established a constitution that included the separation of powers in 1791, but this was annulled with the division of Poland in 1795. The first of its kind in Europe, the Polish constitution of 1791 granted rights of participation to the gentry and the clergy, but not to peasants. Prussia was renowned for its constitutional state in which citizens were able to claim their rights from the state. While Prussia and the German Reich (after 1871) indeed established the rule of law, the lack of political participation made it all but impossible for it to be classified as a democracy.

While democratization presents a core object of transition, the precondition of nation building as a foundational principle of democracy is sometimes overlooked (Linz & Stepan 1996: 16–37). Without a consolidated nation within clearly defined geographic borders, the formation of a demos is impossible. From the moment of the founding of political nations – in the cases of Germany and Italy, this only took place in the late 19th century –, we should again regard democratization in layers rather than as one seismic shift that converts autocracies into democracies. In particular, the building of democracies was accompanied by societal conflicts. Their moderation was anything but an easy accomplishment, and many of the resulting conflicts remain unsolved to this day. The institutionalization of these conflicts, and the growing tendency to integrate conflict resolution into parliaments, can be seen as a major motive for the gradual development of democracy in Europe (Tilly 2004).

However, political institutions such as parliaments and constitutions were but one aspect of democracy building. Another was the capacity of many European societies to find a mix of formal and informal arrangements that fostered economic growth and societal integration. The most famous of these was the establishment of societal cleavages that translated into political parties (Lipset & Rokkan 1967; Rokkan 1970). Even in non- or half-democratic regimes, this meant conflict moderation between center and agrarian parties, and socialist and liberal parties – parties that would later turn into the core of civic representation against the state. Of course, these processes should not be idealized in hindsight. Power, domination, suppression, and hegemony were elements of European political regimes, not least as many of them were closely linked to (or were dependent on) actors from the economic sphere who were less interested in political or social equality. There is no frictionless path to modernity and/or democracy in Europe, even if – in comparison with other regions on a global scale – major goals of transformation such as democracy or social market economy have been accomplished relatively successfully.

The European history of nation-building and democratization reached a first terminus at the end of World War I. The Austrian, Ottoman, and Russian empires fell apart and left behind a good number of new nation states that had previously existed as *Kulturnationen ('Cultural Nations')* with no political sovereignty. The Baltic States or Hungary would be pertinent examples. Most of these new political systems were characterized by parliamentarism, universal franchise, the division of powers, and the rule of law. Many existing democracies also included active and passive suffrage into their constitutions after 1918. Democracy therefore became the dominating regime form in Europe during the 1920s, with the notable exception of the Soviet Union, which was formed in the years after the Russian Revolution of 1917, while remaining an autocratic entity. Most of the new and many of the older democracies were neither able to moderate the huge conflicts between centers and peripheries nor between political camps. By the middle of the 1930s, Southern and Central Europe had returned to authoritarianism. The rule of General Franco in Spain had begun in 1936. The German (and later Soviet) occupation of many European countries led to the founding of further authoritarian regimes – not only in Central and Eastern Europe, but also in France with the Régime de Vichy.

After the return of democracy in Western and parts of Southern Europe after 1945, the tumultuous first half of the twentieth century had laid the ground for the use of the metaphor of 'waves' of democratization. The first long rise from the late 18th century to 1918 had been followed by a fall in the 1920s and 1930s, followed by huge swell after 1945, when many countries re-democratized, and Germany and Italy were provided with assistance to become functioning democracies. While the first wave had been initiated by the end of imperial rule in combination with national self-determination, the second rested on the remnants of the coalition against Hitler's Germany that had ended World War II. Especially with the outbreak of the Cold War in the late 1940s, democratization and modernization were intricately linked to the most important protector of Western Europe from the Soviet Union – the United States of America. Especially in Germany, but also in Italy and several other countries, the mixture of societal modernization, a moderately capitalist economy and political competition was interpreted as 'Americanization' (Rupieper 1993; Fluck 1999).

Although these elements were coherently theorized much later, the consolidation of democracies in Germany, Italy, and beyond rested on a relatively clear set of variables (Merkel 1996b). In order to remain stable and to strengthen their resilience, democracies needed a solid constitutional system which all politically relevant actors would adhere to; Juan Linz and Alfred Stepan coined this constellation as democracy being "the only game in town" (Linz & Stepan 1996: 5).

Furthermore, democracies needed a stable party system in which all relevant societal forces were able to voice and – at least to some degree – achieve their particular interests; and, last but not least, citizens who respect the values of democracy and thus form a civic culture (Almond & Verba 1963).

Of course, these elements were hardly present in all European countries after 1945 (Patel 2018). France required a new constitution in 1958, Italian party politics were instable and partly linked to organized crime, and Germans were somewhat reluctant to develop affirmative attitudes towards democracy. However, democracy was able to take root throughout Western Europe. When Greece, Portugal, and Spain became members of the European Union in the 1980s, there was a clear dichotomy between Western and Eastern Europe regarding their respective economic, political, and social regimes. This was the constellation that would enable transformation (and transformation studies) to become one of the most seminal developments by the end of the 20th century.

Post-Socialist Transformations of 1989/91: The Peak of the Third Wave

After the fall of the socialist regimes in Eastern Europe, the new regime form was tagged by different terms. The new regimes were named post-communist, post-socialist, or post-Leninist. The differences were not always clear and coherent. Leninism was mostly used with reference to the revolutionary moment of transition and was employed when ideas of Marxism were explicitly involved (Jowitt 1992a). The term post-communism was often rooted in studies that were interested in ideological and utopian aspects but was also conveniently used whenever party politics and/or party politicians were the object of analysis (Holmes 1997). After all, it was the Communist Party that had steered the Soviet Union for more than seven decades. Contrastingly, post-socialism was the term of choice when regimes or systems were the object of analysis. This often included a comparative perspective and contained a certain focus on the state and its functions (Stark & Bruszt 1998; Higley & Lengyel 2000).

Unlike the examples of Southern Europe, the post-socialist constellation presented a multiple transformation. Not only the political regime (as in Latin America or South-East Asia in the 1970s), but virtually every aspect of society had to undergo deep and thorough change. The difficulty for societies and elites not only consisted of managing the complexity of multi-layered transition. It soon became evident that the need to transform the spheres simultaneously had created dilemmas that could not be easily ignored. In particular, the main quandary involved keeping pace in meeting long-term challenges in economic and social transformation while newly introduced democratic institutions gave room to groups and parties, which in turn orchestrated social and political protest. Rapid democratization led to a slowdown of economic transformation, while rapid economic transformation risked presenting populist or ancient regime forces with the opportunity to turn the clock back to authoritarianism. This constellation was characterized as the "dilemma of simultaneity" (Offe 1991).

Interestingly, the talk of dilemmas contrasted with the contention that transformation studies were teleological at their core. This criticism rested on the fact that many transition scholars – explicitly or implicitly – rooted their thinking in modernization theory, which links the emergence of democracy to market capitalist forms of the socio-economic regime. Historically, it seems adequate to trace several reference regimes – in particular, England – to a simultaneous emergence of economic liberty, civil society (with a strong economic component), and democratic institutions. This historic emergence was sometimes confused with variable oriented explanations. Especially in the early stages of transition, a range of authors advocated for privatization and the ease of capital restrictions as the silver bullet that would lead to fully functioning democracies in Central and Eastern Europe (most prominently Sachs 1989). It is hard to trace the extent to which teleological thinking was present in the minds of transformation scholars. The authors have the impression that transition scholarship was more intrinsically characterized by a critical discussion of potential teleology than by obviously teleological studies – which is, of course, based on anecdotal memory.

Nevertheless, the interplay of economic and political transition deserves greater attention. While comparatively few examinations may have been teleological, many were certainly based on linear thinking. The potentially constructive elements of economic and political freedom, civil society, and organic national communities were far more appealing than their possible dangers. Normative assumptions on an inbuilt societal equilibrium in social market economies were contrasted with elements of the less effective planning system, but not weighed against the huge inequalities present in certain market economies. With its limited number of variables, modernization theory led to rather naïve conclusions regarding the effectiveness of the combination of market economy and democracy, painting an over-idealized picture of Western democracy. This idealization was heavily criticized, not least because it stood in contrast with the non-linear processes of transformation that had taken place in reality.

These contradictions may not have carried much weight had they been limited to their academic field; yet this was not the case. Transition scholarship evolved in an inverse relationship to the practice of regime transition. In practical terms, the pace was set by economists, who followed a program later known as the Washington Consensus. The program was founded on the conviction that economic recovery can be reached by measures such as macroeconomic stabilization, allowing for entrepreneurial freedom, the end of price restrictions, and opening states to foreign trade and investment.

In hindsight, these recommendations rather adhere to programs of good governance in connection to excessive national debt and/or state default. However, the above-mentioned dilemma of simultaneity was – intuitively or explicitly – known to theorists and practitioners of economic reform. If economic hardship proved too painful or lengthy, voters might vote for politicians who promised to end economic transformation, or at least slow it down. This led to a strong preference for fast and radical reform regardless of the social frictions such a course might cause (Aslund 2001). It should be underlined, however, that the program of rapid reform was not only propagated by radical market economists, but also by transformation scholars who were more sensitive to social hardship and were in favor of coherent programs of economic recovery (Offe 1994; Pickel & Wiesenthal 1997).

Regime Change, System Change, Transition: Standard Theories & Definitions in Transformation Research

In the linear model of transformation based on modernization theory, the world appears to follow a well-arranged path of development (Kollmorgen 2015b). Education and economic wealth are seen as major factors that enable people to overcome autocratic power as well as economic and social domination. In that framework, leading a self-fulfilled life is made possible by open societies that are characterized by democratic regimes, economic freedom, and a (liberal) state that protects its corresponding norms, values, and institutions. During the 1990s, Francis Fukuyama's (1992) famous book *The End of History and the Last Man* likely represented the best expression of this sentiment. His book rested on a late interpretation of Hegel's philosophy of history, yet there were several theories that shared core elements of modernization theory. In particular, the core model of liberalism was seen as a major normative reference for newly formed democracies (Popper [1945] 2003; Dahl 1989).

Against this backdrop a small number of popular and widely read books inspired the early phase of classical transformation research. Among them were the already mentioned four volumes on *Transitions from Authoritarian Rule* (O'Donnell et al. 1986) and Samuel Huntington's (1991) *The Third Wave*. Further monographs or edited volumes to receive increased attention were those of Adam Przeworski (1991), John Higley and Richard Gunther (1992), as well as Dietrich Rueschemeyer, Evelyne Huber-Stephens, and John Stephens (1992). These authors embodied epistemological perspectives that would accompany transition research in the decade to come. Adam Przeworski adopted a critical actor-oriented perspective that sought to highlight the interplay of specific groups in the imminent transition phase; he was one of the most prominent figures of a school that combined post-Marxist theories of society with rational choice methodology (see below). Higley and Gunther also focused on actors but placed greater emphasis on the embeddedness of elites in specific contexts of regimes and regime change – thus basing their work on a foundation of historical and/or sociological institutionalism (Thelen et al. 1992). Contrastingly, Rueschemeyer, Huber-Stephens, and Stephens belonged to the school of historically oriented Marxism that focused on the unequal distribution of wealth and welfare in young democracies on the path to capitalism.

The above-mentioned books were heavily inspired by transitions that did not belong to examples of post-socialism; their main cases were democracies in Latin America and Southern Europe that had succeeded military dictatorships. This early ABC of transition research (Argentina, Brazil, and Chile) explains the relatively pessimistic outlook on the development of democracy in a post-transition environment. Empirical developments in Latin America have shown – and do show until today – that democratic development is heavily impeded if (political or non-political) elites depend on third forces. In particular, young democracies in Latin America and Southern Europe had to face two disruptive factors: the military, which had backed the ancient regime, was still present and often enjoyed the reputation of being a stabilizing anchor in times of crisis, and economic elites, comprised of business magnates, particularly in industry, leading business representatives, great landowners, actors in international finance, and, in some cases, trade union leaders. All these groups were needed for the development of the domestic economy; they all had access to considerable resources but were undoubtedly representatives of partial interests. Whether viewed from a Marxist, historical institutionalist or rational choice perspective, a similar argument can be formed: if collective actors with non-democratic sentiments and/or an agenda beyond the common good are able to wield too much power, democratization or consolidation are in danger, both from an empirical and theoretical perspective.

From these founding contributions to transformation studies, several aspects continued into the early 1990s, as post-socialist transition increased in importance, and, at least from the perspective of European-oriented sociology, took precedence over the knowledge which had been gathered on non-European cases. A second wave of transition studies began to focus on the fourth wave of transition, as post-socialist transformation was sometimes called. This second wave of transition studies rested on two pillars: the previously mentioned theoretical insights of O'Donnell and Przeworski, among others, and numerous empirical studies of transition by country and/or area experts that focused on dynamism in countries they knew well.

The scholars of these two competing fields cooperated on occasion, but they were also made up of two camps. On the one hand, post-socialist transformations were studied with an explicitly comparative intention; Dieter Nohlen even named this pertinent approach the "comparative method" (Nohlen 1994; for an overview see Jahn 2013). This research was usually based on qualitative methods – there were simply not enough cases of European transition to delve into large-N studies – and focused on variables that were to be identified within the cases under study. On the other hand, several scholars insisted that the comparative approach resulted in superficial findings. Instead, they propagated a case-oriented perspective and suggested methods such as regime description, event analysis, or process tracing. Obviously, this approach would lead to deeper empirical knowledge of the cases in question. Studies of this kind could have an exclusively descriptive focus, while others combined case orientation with advanced methodology (one example would be Alexander 2000; for a methodological overview see Gerring 2007).

While most empirical knowledge in the transition scholarship of the 1990s originated in area studies, the basic terminology of transformation was developed by scholars of comparative politics, comparative political economy, and to a lesser degree comparative sociologists. This took place in several research groups and locations. In the German context, Klaus von Beyme's (1996) *Systemwechsel in Osteuropa* [*Transition to Democracy in Eastern Europe*] presented a summary of knowledge on the transition phase which ranged from historical institutionalism to comparative politics. In the international sphere, Juan Linz and Alfred Stepan continued to cooperate with scholars of the *Transitions from authoritarian rule*-project and later published their seminal book *Problems of Democratic Transition and Consolidation* (Linz & Stepan 1996). This work represented a landmark publication in the focus on the stage that followed democratization, namely consolidation. Linz and Stepan looked at cases in several transition areas across the globe and offered an in-depth insight into elites, regime constellations, statehood, and civil society to carve out regularities which led some of the new regimes to democratic stability.

The books of von Beyme, Linz, and Stepan were important milestones for Wolfgang Merkel's (1999b) *Systemtransformation*, a book which is even more systematic, yet has had a lesser impact on international transformation studies as it is written in German. Merkel was able to base his approach on the multi-annual work of the working group *Systemwechsel* ('*system change*') of the German Association for Political Science [*Deutsche Vereinigung für Politikwissenschaft*]. For a period of almost ten years, this working group published edited volumes on various aspects of political transformation; the single volumes covered theories and concepts (Merkel 1994b), institutions (Merkel et al. 1996), political parties (Merkel & Sandschneider 1997), interest groups (Merkel & Sandschneider 1999), and civil society (Merkel 2000). Even if this set-up appears a bit static and omits important strands of the social sciences, the panorama established in these workshops has set certain standards that remain relevant today. They are laid down in the *Handbook Transformation Studies* that appeared in German in 2015 (Kollmorgen et al. 2015) and in an English translation in 2019 (Merkel et al. 2019). Of course, a handbook of almost 700 pages (in the English version) cannot be summarized in a few short paragraphs, but these aspects seem to be the most central:

– In order to understand processes of economic, political, and social transformation, focusing on actors, institutions, or systems alone does not suffice. Either can be done in studies with a limited focus, but transformation as a whole needs inspiration from a *macro-sociological perspective* in combination with a focus on actors, their strategies, and their embeddedness in institutional regimes (Merkel 1994a).

– Beyond actors and specific institutions (such as parliament), the macro level can be taken into consideration in different guises. Polity, constitution, and constitutionalism are terms that refer to basic legal configurations; they are used in judicial contexts and in environments in which there is a tradition of following formal rules. In contrast, scholars speak of regimes when both formal and informal norms (including institutions) are accounted for. The notion of regime is also suited to include the economic and/or political and/or social sphere – the key area is the sector of society that must be guided by regular norms on a routine basis. In that sense, the regime constitutes an entity that differs from the state (Fishman 1990).

– While uncertain in many respects, the process of transformation can be distinguished by different phases: *the breakdown of authoritarianism, democratization, institutionalization,* and *consolidation* (Przeworski 1992). On occasion, the terms transition/transformation have been reserved for the nexus of breakdown, regime opening, and the first stages of democratization. By and large, however, both notions are used for processes that range beyond the very first years of democracy.

– The *phase of breakdown* in the fourth wave was accompanied by a limited number of relevant actors and constellations, even if they differed from country to country. In many countries, especially in the Soviet Union, the first steps of opening the regime were initiated from within the elite apparatus. These were often in the form of rifts within the ancient regime that had already been theorized by Adam Przeworski in the 1980s (Przeworski 1986). In Hungary and Poland, shuffles in the socialist elite had brought up forces that were ready to negotiate with so-called 'soft liners' from within the ranks of the regime opposition. Here, reformers within the old elite undertook decisive steps to open the public sphere, restructuring the economy and tearing down border regimes. In contrast, socialist elites in Bulgaria and Romania (and in Yugoslavia) hesitated to reach out to those opposed to the regime.

Ironically, the old socialist elites were able to stay within the political game in Bulgaria, Romania, and Yugoslavia, even if they lost the founding elections that took place everywhere between 1989 and 1991 (Klingemann 2015). In Hungary and Poland, in the so-called founding elections of 1989, and in Spain in 1986 – the classical cases of negotiated revolutions –, the parties of the ancient regime had to undergo far deeper changes to be able to re-enter the political stage. In general, negotiated regime changes were able to keep the masses off the streets. This scenario unfolded in Czechoslovakia, the GDR, Romania, and (after the August coup of 1993) Russia.

For more than a decade, transformation scholars believed that the negotiation mode of regime change had offered better opportunities for a kickstart to democracy. Elites of the socialist regime remained in state structures and were able to bring their expertise to the new regime. In addition, Poland and Hungary were clear frontrunners in attracting foreign investment and thus stimulating economic growth during the 1990s. Only approximately twenty years after 1989 did it become clear that disclaiming a thorough break with the communist regime had severe long-term consequences (see below).

– The *phase of consolidation* received particular attention and was again inspired by scholarship on Latin America and Southern Europe (Mainwaring et al. 1992; Gunther et al. 1995). With ongoing transition research, two models of consolidation evolved. The first, developed by Andreas Schedler (1998), brought clarity regarding the periods of transition the term consolidation was used for, even if Schedler's suggestion was somewhat complex. We can talk of consolidation in three circumstances: a) if consolidation is explicitly demarcated from imminent regime change, b) if democratic institutions become more solidified and stabilize a young democracy, and c) if a 'minimal' democracy – a democracy that is mainly characterized by free and competitive elections – develops into a democracy with broadened forms of participation.

The *second model of consolidation*, again developed by Wolfgang Merkel (1996a; 1998), has been mentioned above. It concentrates on consecutive levels regarding temporal development and the quality of democracy. The core institutions of democracy come first, followed by the consolidation of further groups of participation such as political parties and interest groups. The consolidation of democratic behavior then occurs, particularly involving potential veto players such as the military and business elite. The fourth layers consist of civic culture and/or the attitudes of the population towards democracy. Merkel essentially argues that the overall stability and legitimacy of a democracy can only be regarded as assured if all four layers of the regime are consolidated.

Most of these core findings of transformation studies can be classified as *structural* in the sense that (political) institutions serve as major orientation points to understand or explain processes and outcomes of transformation. However, not all transition researchers share a bias towards narrow institutional explanation. Further approaches concentrate on elites or culture. Most notably John Higley has gathered a group of researchers who judge the behavior of elites as decisive for the success of regime change, democratization, and consolidation. In these works, relational elite constellations and the attitudes/ideologies of elites are core variables (Higley & Gunther 1992; Higley & Lengyel 2000; Higley & Pakulski 2000).

Another set of approaches focuses on *culture*, though their notions of culture may differ from one another. The prominent theory of neo-institutionalism (North 1990) distinguished between 'formal' and 'informal' institutions. The latter consisted of social rules and norms that were sometimes referred to as 'culture' by transformation scholars (Harrison & Huntington 2000; in particular Sachs 2000). Within transformation research, the occupation with informal institutions inspired the concept of neopatrimonialism, which explained illiberal forms of democracy and hybrid regimes with cultural patterns of traditional power that co-existed with legal democratic rules (Erdmann & Engel 2007). In 2015, Henry Hale (2015) drew together major ideas of neopatrimonialism and established both an empirical and theoretical model of *Patronal politics*. Culture also played a major role in transition-oriented anthropology. Many works from this field failed to reach a wide audience due to their often limited regional or even local focus. In summary, the anthropology of transformation was clearly able to present a very instructive mosaic of the economic, political, and social dynamics in post-socialist Europe (Burawoy & Verdery 1999, see also Chapter 4 of this volume).

In hindsight, the classic phase of transformation research was combined with the previous decade in which both the intellectual and public discourses broadly accepted the idea that democracy and (social) market capitalism were superior to other forms of economic and political regimes. This in turn raised the *concept of external democratization*; the effort of institutions, elites and civil society in democratic regimes to foster regime change in countries with autocratic or hybrid regime forms in an international context (Pridham 1995). As with the first years of the fourth wave, the literature in this field was heavily inspired by figures who at least spent a portion of their time as actors in democracy promotion or were paid by institutions that were active in democracy assistance (Carothers 1999; Grabbe 2003; Leininger 2015). Research focused on a range of democracy promoting actors such as states, international institutions, or civil society organizations (Hahn-Fuhr & Worschech 2014). Different modes of democracy aid such as conditionality or socialization were also highlighted

(Whitehead 2001). As research continued, the focus shifted from promoting and receiving actors to networks of external governance, especially within an EU context (Lavenex & Schimmelfennig 2009). By and large, the main body of research on external democratization came to the conclusion that real incentives, in particular the credible prospect of EU and/or NATO membership, may even play a decisive role in the consolidation of democracy. One of the main factors consists of the division of elites who are skeptical of democracy into a diminished regime opposition, and a second group that is ready to form coalitions with Western and democracy-oriented actors and parties (Schimmelfennig 2005; 2007).

Info-Box 6.2: Forced transformation? External democracy promotion in post-socialist Europe

Can democratization and transformation from the outside-in work (Pevehouse 2002)? This question has occupied many social scientists and political practitioners alike since external democracy promotion became a core feature of Western countries' foreign policies towards post-socialist, and in particular post-Soviet, states. International organizations, embassies, development agencies and public political foundations, NGOs and culture diplomacy institutes such as the British Council remain active promoters of societal and political transition in many post-socialist countries. The European Union itself is one of the most active promoters of democracy in these societies, with multilateral cooperation (for example, with the Council of Europe) and bilateral support projects in the framework of the European Neighborhood Program (ENP) and here in particular, with the Eastern Partnership program. By far the largest and most successful democracy promotion conducted by the EU was the enlargement of 2004 and 2007, when the transformation of whole state systems to comply with the EU's *acquis communautaire* was the necessary condition for accession to the EU. In contrast, democracy support within the ENP can be seen as the EU's approach to secure peace and stability within its immediate vicinity, and to define an endpoint of European enlargement and provide a political offer to neighboring countries (Sasse 2007). Most EU member states have programs that support democracy, community building, government transparency and other initiatives in post-Soviet countries.

External democracy promotion can be characterized as "a set of actions by non-domestic actors who intentionally try to overcome authoritarian power by supporting domestic actors who share the same objective" (Beichelt 2012). As evident in the case of the ENP, intentions of democracy promoters are rooted in the *Kantian* idea of democratic peace (democratic countries do not attack each other) and the hypothesis that political and economic prosperity, including good governance, in neighboring countries contribute to international peace and security. Conflicting goals between different approaches of democracy promotion (for example, towards the government on one hand and civil society on the other) and between different strategies of foreign policy (for example, democratization and stabilization as contrary processes) are a problematic feature of democracy promotion and illustrate the ambivalence of the approach (Spanger & Wolff 2007).

Parallel to this range of intentions, the recipients and measures of external democracy promotion differ significantly. While a large part of external democracy promotion addresses state institutions, where democratization can be initiated through leverage and coercion or the transfer of procedures, values and 'best practice' among administrative units, a smaller but politically relevant part of external democracy promotion focuses on civil society. In processes of democratization, civil society is considered either as a 'watchdog' of political and civil rights, or a 'school of democracy' where negotiation, communication, and building social capital are relevant effects [see also chapter 14 in this book]. External democracy promotion in civil society can be distinguished into three different strategies: the strategy of professionalization mainly addresses organized civil society actors, when projects are assigned through calls for proposals, NGOs compete for support and resources, and donors usually support those NGOs who can already show a certain level of professional structures and working procedures. This strategy usually fails to support small or innovative organizations, grassroots initiatives, and volunteer groups. The latter are more likely to be supported by donors following a second scheme of democracy promotion that can be called 'external culture support'. Most culture diplomacy agencies, some embassies, political foundations, and several development agencies follow this scheme by deliberately supporting small or new initiatives, thereby supporting civic innovation and volunteer activism. A third strategy is public diplomacy as 'democracy promotion en passant', when embassies or other agencies include democracy support in their activities to increase their impact and broaden networks in their target society, thereby supporting their actual activities (Worschech 2018b).

The effects of external democracy promotion have been criticized as 'engineering civil society' and building an 'artificial' civil society (Ishkanian 2007). Furthermore, in many post-Soviet countries, a divided civil society emerged. A divided civil society consists of 'political service providers' who on the one hand were supported by professionalization strategies, and grassroots initiatives and new forms of civic activism on the other. The latter risk becoming marginalized due to a lack of support and a lack of compliance with donors' norms. Because of this divide, external democracy promotion towards civil society might undermine trust in civic organization within society, thereby counteracting social capital and contributing to the alienation of civic actors from their target society (Hahn-Fuhr & Worschech 2014: 32ff.).

Post-Transformation: The Long Bumpy Road After Transition

Throughout the 1990s, the modernist and/or liberal expectation that authoritarian states would – under the right circumstances – disintegrate, only to reform as democracies with social market economies, was met with criticism. In fact, some of the most prominent authors of classical transformation theory held relatively skeptical views of capitalist democracy. Adam Przeworski, Dietrich Rueschemeyer and many others suspected that the economies of newly formed regimes might be taken over by actors with little interest in participatory democracy and a developed welfare state. Others such as Lawrence Whitehead hinted at the ambivalence of a unipolar international order and expressed early and sustained concern at the possibility that domestic forces of self-determination would not win out everywhere (Whitehead 1986).

The Empirical Perspective: Transformation Troubles in the 20th Century

The most significant doubts on linear transformation, however, were inspired by real-world developments in post-authoritarian regimes. Of course, many countries had undergone thorough transformations that enabled them to fulfil the Copenhagen criteria as formulated by the European Union as conditions for EU accession. Amongst others, these concerned democratic institutions, the rule of law and developed market economies. However, the accession of countries in Central and Southeast Europe proved to be a rare occurrence, and it soon became obvious that major elements of democratic consolidation – for example, a stable party system or a rooted civic culture – had not successfully formed during the ten to fifteen years following the breakdown of the socialist regimes. Additionally, the fact that the vast territory of post-socialism was still dominated by non-democratic rule could not be overlooked. Russia had fallen back into authoritarianism by 2004 (the first re-election of Vladimir Putin) at the latest. Armenia, Azerbaijan, and Belarus as well as the states of Central Asia were not characterized by the most minimal criterion of democracy, namely free elections.

At least in European Studies, these real-world developments strongly lowered the number of cases in which a transformation in the broad sense of the word seemed possible. Another small wave of authoritarian breakdown took place in form of the so-called color revolutions in Serbia (2000), Georgia (2003), and Ukraine (2004). None of them, however, led to a consolidated democracy. Consequently, a famous article published in 2002 referred to the *End of the transition paradigm* (Carothers 2002). Researchers in this constellation had to make a decision. They could either stay with the object of transformation, and thus limit the number of cases in which transition could be studied, or they could continue to use their previously accumulated conceptual and empirical knowledge and apply it to countries that had either become democratic or (re)developed non-democratic regimes. All options were employed in post-transformation research, but they led to a diversification of the field as a whole. Today, researchers who study regime dynamics in formerly authoritarian regimes do not all belong to the same epistemic community.

Subtypes of Democracy: Towards Differentiation

In order to understand the development of the field, we must go back to the regime typologies that existed prior to the rise of transformation studies. Based on Max Weber's famous typology of legitimate power (rational vs. traditional vs. charismatic, see Weber 1980), Juan Linz argued that authoritarian regimes should not simply be seen as traditional and/or parochial, but instead investigated various roots of legitimation (Linz 1975). The major approach in his handbook entry of 240 pages consisted of drawing a line between totalitarian and authoritarian regimes. According to Linz, totalitarian rule is monistic in its approach to power and refers to an all-encompassing ideology. In contrast, authoritarianism allows for some pluralism and participation in alluding to "mentalities" (see also Linz 1989). While Linz used his concept of authoritarianism to explain the character and persistence of nationalist, bureaucratic-militaristic or post-totalitarian regimes, post-transformation research went on to more systematic categorizations of autocratic rule (Merkel 2010: 40–54).

The first issue to appear on the agenda of post-transformation studies was the classification of countries that were neither clearly democratic nor autocratic. The term *hybrid regime* was introduced with reference to regime cases in Latin America (Karl 1995) but was soon reflected at the theoretic level (Diamond 2002; Bendel et al. 2002). Two competing conceptions were discussed (Krennerich 2002; Beichelt 2011).

– One approach brought together elements that were, taken as such, typical for different regime types. For example, Russia conducted competitive elections in the late Yeltsin and early Putin years, which rendered plausible the classification as a democracy. However, the regime also allowed for non-elected elites to run a part of the system (under Yeltsin) or fought against independent media (under Putin) – both clear elements of authoritarian rule (Shevtsova 2001).

– The other approach consisted of introducing sub-categories to the two anchoring concepts of democracy and authoritarianism. Pertinent articles talked of *Democracy with Adjectives* (Collier & Levitsky 1997) or highlighted notions like competitive, bureaucratic, electoral or many other forms of authoritarianism (Levitsky & Way 2002; Shevtsova 2004; Schedler 2006).

By and large, the fate of the two conceptual paths was decided along the lines of empirical/area studies and comparative politics. In studies that concentrated on certain regions, countries, or sub-regional units, authors had little fear of working with the concept of hybridity (see, for example, Knobloch 2006). The combination of contradictory elements in political or social constellations was not seen as damaging to a coherent analysis in such studies. Quite on the contrary, the amalgam of inconsistent elements formed part of a general trend in cultural studies – where many area experts were situated – that saw hybridity as a general trend of late-modern societies and political regimes (for example, see Ackermann 2011; Hale 2015).

Studies that focused on typologies, in contrast, worked on the specificities of the respective core regimes. From many adjectives to democracy – delegative (O'Donnell 1994), illiberal (Zakaria 1997) or other forms of democracy – typologies of regimes soon emerged that were able to integrate 'defects' or 'sub-types'. Again, Wolfgang Merkel presented the most coherent description with a model he sometimes called *defective democracy* or *embedded democracy* (Merkel 1999a; Merkel et al. 2003; Merkel et al. 2006). Here, the idea is to divide democracy into differing partial regimes. The core of democracy, namely a free and fair regime of competitive elections, is embedded into further partial regimes, namely the regimes of political freedoms, civic rights, horizontal accountability, and effective state power. Each of these regimes may have 'defects' that lead to exclusion (from elections), to enclaves in which veto powers such as the military have their say, to illiberalism in the case of violated political or civic rights, and to delegation if no horizontal control can be exerted.

Subtypes of Autocracy: Resilience of Authoritarianism

At the other end of the spectrum, the research on authoritarianism concentrated on different types as well. The most important of these concerned, as already mentioned, *competitive authoritarianism* (Levitsky & Way 2002; 2010) or *electoral authoritarianism* (Schedler 2006). Both concentrated on a similar phenomenon, namely the partial openness of elections for contenders to incumbent presidents or governing parties. Empirically, this concerns a wide range of competitors. Sometimes, especially if an incumbent president cannot run for re-election due to illness or for constitutional reasons, the field is relatively open, and even forces from the former opposition camp may win elections. In this case, regime outsiders subsequently must co-exist with previously established elites of the authoritarian regime (for example in the administrative branches or the security forces). More commonly, however, competitors are faced with an "uneven playing field" (Levitsky & Way 2002) – as if they had to play football in a headwind while the favorites of the regime play with a tailwind at their backs. The instruments of authoritarian regimes in holding down competitors from the opposition are manifold, as can be shown by a wide array of works on Putin's Russia (Fish 2005; Gelman 2015; Schmid 2016). They range from manipulating the electoral system, pressurizing local political elites, manipulating discursive frameworks, and the use of outward repression on modest opposition parties.

Beyond these specific types, another layer of research on authoritarianism concentrated on identifying basic characteristics of autocracies. This research concentrated less on European cases, where geographical proximity to democracies and the EU regime induced an element of electoral process in all post-socialist states. With regard to other regions of the world, post-transition research took another twist in categorizing authoritarian regimes (Geddes 1999). Several scholars discussed whether to uncouple the types established by Juan Linz from historical cases and establish criteria by which authoritarian regimes could be identified. A loose set of prominent articles focused on the circumstances in which autocratic regimes can survive despite their de-legitimizing properties such as repression and (often) inferior socio-economic development. Greater attention was paid to elite practices; in particular, the cooptation of non-political elites was introduced as a major variable that secures authoritarian power (Gandhi & Przeworski 2007; Gerschewski 2010; 2013). Here, the main idea is that cultural and economic elites are paid off with (material or non-material) resources in order not to challenge the regime or its leading representatives.

Each of these conceptions of post-transformation research are still of importance for the sociology of Europe because they are relevant in a description of real-world developments. Eastern European countries such as Belarus or Russia remain firmly autocratic in the third decade of the 2000s – thus the tools of authoritarianism remain relevant for European Studies. Furthermore, the pushbacks in democratic consolidation that took place in Hungary, Poland, and other new EU member states have not always been judged within the defective democracy framework. Bálint Magyar, for example, located the weakening of Hungarian democracy in the context of mafia-like practices in Hungary's private and public economy (Magyar 2016). The development in Poland has typically been judged as being within a democratic framework, but some authors have seen the country as being more on the brink of majoritarian authoritarianism (Sapper & Weichsel 2016; 2018).

Eastern Germany: The Neglected Transitional Society?

Amidst these debates, the case of Eastern Germany plays an interesting role. Although much research focused on institution-building processes, the inclusion and exclusion of East Germans into the labor market, and the demographic and economic aspects of Germany's re-unification (Wollmann 2001; Kollmorgen 2015a; Böick 2018), East Germany has rarely been considered a 'real' transitional society (for an exception, see Howard 2003). This is astonishing, as regional disparities still matter to this day (Kawka 2007), and an increasing sentiment of non-recognition and subalternization can still be witnessed among many contemporary Eastern Germans (Kollmorgen 2011; Mau 2019).

On the one hand, empirical studies demonstrate that Eastern Germany has far stronger indicators of economic and social wealth than other post-socialist countries: democratic stability, the effectiveness of public administration and the rule of law as well as the economy and general living conditions are at a high level compared to other European countries (Croissant 2015). On the other hand, however, mistrust in institutions, political discontent and democratic illiteracy have increased in some regions and social realms, and feelings of relative deprivation, disdain and being politically ignored have gained a foothold in particular segments of society, opening new social cleavages and a broad basis for populist and authoritarian movements. Mau (2019) argues that facing the hardships or chances of transformation after 1989 is inherently linked to a generational belonging, as people were confronted with the breakdown of an old regime at various stages of life; to a certain degree, the establishment of a new order determined whether people could make use of new freedoms, experienced an erosion of certainties, or were lost in a literally borderless and limitless world. However, the particular situation of authoritarian breakdown and the immediate 'import' of democratic institutions, norms and rules have encouraged a broader conceptual debate on Eastern Germany's hybrid transformation path. Yet, in doing so, this left the case to a very particular type of 'area studies'.

Legacies, Interdependencies, and Culture: Contextualizing Transition

In this context, the actual state of politics and societies in post-socialist Europe can be interpreted along another rift that divided transformation studies from its outset. On the one hand, comparative and/or theoretic transition research concentrates on the prospects of regime types. While research in the 1990s was linear in its expectations of post-transition development, the conceptual framework of the 2010s developed the concept of populism, which again classifies cases into certain strata of relations between elites and electorates. Although it may be correct to categorize certain regimes at certain times as populist or 'defective', such notions often overshadow the nuances in political regimes, which are linked to historic and/or social contexts.

This position, on the other hand, is maintained by scholarship that provides in-depth analyses of given regime constellations from a sociological, historical, or institutional perspective. One of the key texts in this respect is Ken Jowitt's (1992b) article on *The Leninist legacy*, which ascribed the development of post-socialist regimes to the trajectories implied by the socialist order, such as a certain type of state bureaucracy, a certain structure of the economy, or a certain attitudinal culture. The legacy approach has received much attention in approaches from scholars who regard analyses of cases rather than variables as essential to understand post-socialism (Kubik 2003).

The same credo persists in the sociology of Central and Eastern Europe to this day. Russian and Central European (semi-)authoritarianism may be classified as such, yet its character is maybe better understood if its roots in conservative thinking are highlighted (Bluhm & Varga 2019). The conflict between Russia and the Ukraine can be contextualized in the framework of geopolitics, but the everyday occurrences along the 'borders' of the Donbass also speak of lasting interdependencies in a zone of intermingled cultural heritage (Dubasevych & Schwartz 2020).

These last two publications form part of an ongoing strand of post-transition research that favors an accurate view of events and situations over typological considerations. In more recent years, research on the problems of institutionalization and consolidation of democracy and social market economy has increasingly highlighted the inner contradictions of modernity itself. Beyond transition studies, modernity and modernization have been judged in multi-faceted ways. Zygmunt Bauman (1991) has discussed *Modernity and Ambivalence*, Samuel Eisenstadt (1992) wrote on *multiple modernities*, and Trüper, Chakrabarty, and Subrahmanyam (2015) on *teleological modernity*. With this shift, the unevenness of post-socialism is being projected away from dynamics to the telos of transformation. Beyond these explicit conceptions of modernity, post-colonial studies have criticized the negligence in shunning the victims of the West European path of modernity and have subsequently transferred that criticism to the study of Central and Eastern Europe (Boatcă & Spohn 2010). If we follow this train of thought, a coherent transformation to capitalist democracy and the adaptation of the principles of European integration can no longer be viewed as problem-solvers to post-socialist societies (Beichelt et al. 2019). Instead, scholars such as Ivan Krastev and Stephen Holmes (2019) argue that post-socialist societies have lived through three decades of 'imitating the West', which in turn has blocked the formation of genuine socio-political structures, norms, and processes.

The perspective from the 'peripheries' of Europe offers a further insight that helps broaden und update the concept of transformation as processes that are shifting in scope more than ever before (Krastev 2017). Profound societal changes are still ongoing in post-socialist Europe at great speed, as characterized by European disintegration, criticism of the liberal democratic system and growing populism. The former 'transition countries' have now become post-transformation countries, leading a process of re-structuring of national institutions and narratives towards more reactionary and less cosmopolitan attitudes. Post-transformation seems to be the unintended result of small-scale political and social shifts, rather than large revolutionary events. Post-transformation and European disintegration are societal dynamics that first took root in Central and Eastern Europe amidst the process that was still considered to be democratic consolidation – in fact, European integration and disintegration have co-existed for more than a decade since Poland, Hungary, The Czech Republic, Slovakia, Slovenia, and other post-socialist countries joined the EU. It would be naive to assume that Western European countries will not join the path of disintegration in the near future. From this perspective, the catch-up-transformation in post-socialist Europe has turned into anteceding transformation, eventually hinting at many Western European countries' future paths and conflicts. Europeanization research has only recently taken up this insight on a conceptual basis by formulating Europeanization as a fundamentally ambivalent, conflictual, contingent and critical process of transnational transformation (Beichelt et al. 2021).The crisis of democratic liberalism in Central and Eastern Europe mirrors the fractures, inconsistencies and contradictions of transformation processes and helps to conceptualize transformation as a conflictual, ambivalent and fragile set of social mechanisms.

Outlook: The Ongoing Transformation

Around thirty years ago, many European societies were faced with rapid change in their institutions at almost every layer of their lives. While often complicated and painful, these processes have led to diverging results and quite different forms of economic, political, and social regimes. Market capitalism has been introduced everywhere, and its problematic consequences, such as income inequality and rifts between economic centers and peripheries have arguably hit Eastern Europe even harder than Central or Southern Europe (Milanović 2018). The more successful economies in Central Europe have often moved into the managerial hands of external actors, be they in lending institutions such as the European Bank for Reconstruction and Development or the agents of international corporations and shareholder considerations (Halpern 2015).

In terms of political regimes, it still makes sense to distinguish between European sub-regions (Beichelt 2013). Eastern Europe – in particular Belarus and Russia – seems to be locked into ever more repressive security states. While this seems broadly in line with the Stalinist legacy of both countries, contemporary populations in Eastern Europe (including Ukraine) are characterized by a will for selective protest if their respective political elites go too far in their corrupt and often dishonest practices. In that sense, liberal and reformist attitudes in parts of the population stand in contrast with repressive-minded political elites, which in turn leaves the whole post-Soviet space in a peculiar imbalance with a long-term outlook of instability. In Central Europe, a first phase of economic stabilization and democratic consolidation has been replaced by a slowing down in the deepening of democracy. Populist thought and voluntarist leadership have appeared in many places, horizontal accountability, and at times political rights, have remained limited. In the Western Balkans, transformation still seems to be heavily influenced by ongoing processes of nation building and ethnic demarcation. In Southern Europe, democracy has been rooted but is characterized by deep polarization between political camps, especially in times of economic and social crisis.

In summary, therefore, transformation processes in Europe are ongoing. They reflect deep changes in the economic, political, and social spheres that are also tangent to Western and Northern Europe, such as in the context of Europeanization and globalization. In that sense, both real developments and theoretical views on transformation have indeed lost their telos, as social market economies and democracy have now entered transformative waters themselves.

Didactical Section

Key Learning Points

- Transformation is defined as a substantial and systemic process of social, political, economic, and cultural change that is initiated by identifiable actors in a purposeful manner. It often bears a quasi-revolutionary character. The term transformation is a special case of social change which includes any a long-term dynamic process that profoundly affects multiple dimensions of a society at the same time, being more disruptive and extensive than social change.
- Transformation is a multi-faceted and multi-layered process and concerns a range of sub-systems such as the economy, norms and value systems, civil society, the political system, and all realms of societal life. In recent years, ecological or digital transformation and the impact of technical or environmental developments on social issues are increasingly moving into the foreground of transformation research.
- Transformation research was the 'other side of the coin' of early sociological research, in contrast to the initially more visible research on societal stability. Later, transformation research was strongly influenced and advanced by empirical 'waves of democratization', in particular the third wave of democratization that included the democratizations in Southern Europe and Latin America in the 1970s and 1980s, as well as the breakdown of socialist regimes in 1989/1991.
- Transition can be systematized and split up in three different phases for analytical purposes: (1) transition starts with *liberalization* as the breakdown of the authoritarian system; (2) it continues with *institutionalization* as the implementation of democratic processes on all political levels, starting with founding elections; (3) and it merges into a full-fledged democracy in the *consolidation* when societal acceptance of democratic processes and rules as well as internalization of democratic values increase. Although processes in all three dimensions and phases overlap empirically and this systematization is regarded much too static today, it points the attention to the different levels of 'technical functioning' and the (more difficult) societal appreciation of democracy, thereby helping to discern different steps and processes.
- Post-transformation concerns social and political developments in former transition countries that cannot be linked to the initial transition itself. Typically, such developments mirror dynamics that can be found in long-

established democracies as well, such as the decline of trust in political elites. Post-transformation research therefore focuses on inner contradictions and ambivalences of modernity and European integration. Consequently, a conflict perspective on cleavages, ruptures and disputes within Europeanization pays attention to processes such as re-authocratization, social voids and anomy.

Further Readings

Krastev, I. & S. Holmes, 2019: *The Light That Failed: A Reckoning*. London: Penguin Books.
Levitsky, S. & L. A. Way, 2010: *Competitive Authoritarianism. Hybrid Regimes After the Cold War*. New York: Cambridge University Press.
Levitsky, S. & D. Ziblatt, 2018: *How democracies die*. New York: Crown.
Merkel, W., R. Kollmorgen & H. J. Wagener (eds.), 2019: *The handbook of political, social, and economic transformation*. Oxford: Oxford University Press.
Polanyi, K., [1944] 2007: *The Great Transformation: The Political and Economic Origins of Our Time*. Boston: Beacon Press, 2nd Beacon paperback ed., 8th printing.
Tilly, C., 2007: *Democracy*. Cambridge, NY: Cambridge University Press.

Additional Web-Sources

Varieties of Democracy provides comparative and country-based data on multidimensional democracy evaluation, hosted by the V-Dem Institute: https://www.v-dem.net/en/
The Bertelsmann Transformation Index reports on transformation processes towards democracy and market economy, with a particular focus on 'nations in transit': https://bti-project.org/en/
Freedom House reports on freedom & democracy in the world, freedom of the press, based on in-depth and score-based country analyses: https://freedomhouse.org/

References

Ackermann, A., 2011: Das Eigene und das Fremde: Hybridität, Vielfalt und Kulturtransfers. In: Jaeger, F. & J. Ruesen (eds.), *Handbuch der Kulturwissenschaften. Vol. 3. Themen und Tendenzen*, pp. 139–154. Stuttgart: Metzler.
Alexander, J., 2000: *Political Culture in Post-communist Russia. Formlessness and Recreation in a Traumatic Transition*. Houndsmills: MacMillan Press.
Almond, G. & S. Verba, 1963: *The Civic Culture*. Newsbury Park: Sage.
Aslund, A., 2001: The Advantages of Radical Reform. *Journal of Democracy* 12(4):42–48.

Bauman, Z., 1991: *Modernity and ambivalence*. Cambridge: Polity.

Beichelt, T., 2011: Forms of Rule in the Post-Soviet Space. Hybrid Regimes. In: Stewart, S., M. Klein, A. Schmitz & H. H. Schröder (eds.), *President, Oligarchs and Bureaucrats: Forms of Rule in the Post-Soviet Space*, pp. 15–28. London: Ashgate.

Beichelt, T., 2012: The research field of democracy promotion. *Living Reviews in Democracy* 3. https://www.ethz.ch/content/dam/ethz/special-interest/gess/cis/cis-dam/CIS_DAM_2015/WorkingPapers/Living_Reviews_Democracy/Beichelt.pdf.

Beichelt, T., 2013: Verkannte Parallelen. Transformationsforschung und Europastudien. *Osteuropa* 63(2/3):277–294.

Beichelt, T., C. M. Frysztacka, C. Weber & S. Worschech, 2019: Ambivalences of Europeanisation. Modernity and Europe in Perspective. *IFES Working Paper* 1, 2019.

Beichelt, T., C. M. Frysztacka, C. Weber & S. Worschech (eds.), 2021: *Ambivalenzen der Europäisierung*. Stuttgart: Franz Steiner Verlag.

Bendel, P., A. Croissant & F. Rüb (eds.), 2002: *Hybride Regime. Zur Konzeption und Empirie demokratischer Grauzonen*. Opladen: Leske + Budrich.

Bluhm, K. & M. Varga (eds.), 2019: *New conservatives in Russia and East Central Europe*. London: Routledge.

Boatcă, M. & W. Spohn (eds.), 2010: *Globale, multiple und postkoloniale Modernen*. München: Hampp.

Böick, M., 2018: *Die Treuhand: Idee – Praxis – Erfahrung 1990–1994*. Göttingen: Wallstein Verlag.

Burawoy, M. & K. Verdery (eds.), 1999: *Uncertain Transition. Ethnographies of Change in the Postsocialist World*. Lanham: Rowman & Littlefield.

Carothers, T., 1999: *Aiding Democracy Abroad. The Learning Curve*. Washington: Carnegie.

Carothers, T., 2002: The End of the Transition Paradigm. *Journal of Democracy* 13(1):5–21.

Collier, D. & S. Levitsky, 1997: Democracy with Adjectives. Conceptual Innovation in Comparative Research. *World Politics* 49(3):430–451.

Croissant, A., 2015: Demokratische Transformation seit 1989: Der „Fall Ostdeutschland" aus Perspektive der politikwissenschaftlich-vergleichenden Transformationsforschung. *Zeitschrift für Politikwissenschaft* 25(3):367–376.

Dahl, R. A., 1989: *Democracy and its Critics*. New Haven: Yale University Press.

Dahl, R., 1998: *On Democracy*. New Haven and London: Yale University Press.

Diamond, L., 2002: Thinking About Hybrid Regimes. *Journal of Democracy* 13(2):21–35.

Dubasevych, R. & M. Schwartz (eds.), 2020: *Sirenen des Krieges. Diskursive und affektive Dimensionen des Ukraine-Konflikts*. Berlin: Kulturverlag Kadmos Berlin.

Durkheim, É., [1988] 2019: *Ueber soziale Arbeitsteilung: Studie über die Organisation höherer Gesellschaften*. Edited by Mueller. H. P. & M. Schmid. Suhrkamp Taschenbuch Wissenschaft 1005. Frankfurt am Main: Suhrkamp, 8th edition.

Eisenstadt, S. N., 1992: *Democracy and Modernity*. Leiden.

Erdmann, G. & U. Engel, 2007: Neopatrimonialism Reconsidered: Critical Review and Elaboration of an Elusive Concept. *Commonwealth & Comparative Politics* 45(1):95–119.

Fish, M. S., 2005: *Democracy Derailed in Russia. The Failure of Open Politics*. Cambridge: Cambridge University Press.

Fishman, R., 1990: Rethinking State and Regime. Southern Europe's Transition to Democracy. *World Politics* 42(3):422–440.

Fluck, W., 1999: Amerikanisierung und Modernisierung. *Transit* 17:55–71.

Fukuyama, F., 1992: *The end of history and the last man*. New York: Free Press.

Gandhi, J. & A. Przeworski, 2007: Authoritarian Institutions and the Survival of Autocrats. *Comparative Political Studies* 40(11):1279–1301.

Geddes, B., 1999: What Do We Know about Democratization after Twenty Years? *Annual Review of Political Science* 2(1):115–144.

Gelman, V., 2015: *Authoritarian Russia. Analyzing post-Soviet regime changes.* Pittsburgh: University of Pittsburgh Press.

Gerring, J., 2007: *Case Study Research. Principles and Methods.* Cambridge: Cambridge University Press.

Gerschewski, J., 2010: Zur Persistenz von Autokratien. Ein Literaturüberblick. *Berliner Debatte* 21(3):42–53.

Gerschewski, J., 2013: The three pillars of stability. Legitimation, repression, and co-optation in autocratic regimes. *Democratization* 20(1):13–38.

Grabbe, H., 2003: *The EU's Transformative Power. Europeanization Through Conditionality in Central and Eastern Europe.* Basingstoke: Palgrave.

Gunther, R., N. Diamandouros & H. J. Puhle (eds.), 1995: *The Politics of Democratic Consolidation. Southern Europe in Comparative Perspective.* Baltimore and London: Johns Hopkins University Press.

Hahn-Fuhr, I. & S. Worschech, 2014: External Democracy Promotion and Divided Civil Society – Conceptualizing the Link. In: Beichelt, T., I. Hahn-Fuhr, F. Schimmelfennig & S. Worschech (eds.), *Civil Society and Democracy Promotion*, pp. 11–41. Houndsmills: Palgrave.

Hale, H., 2015: *Patronal Politics. Eurasian Regime Dynamics in Comparative Perspective.* New York: Cambridge University Press.

Halpern, L., 2015: Internationalisierung der Wirtschaft. In: Kollmorgen, R., W. Merkel & H. J. Wagener (eds.), *Handbuch Transformationsforschung*, pp. 575–580. Wiesbaden: Springer VS.

Harrison, L. E. & S. P. Huntington (eds.), 2000: *Culture Matters. How Values Shape Human Progress.* New York: Basic Books.

Higley, J. & R. Gunther (eds.), 1992: *Elites and Democratic Consolidation in Latin America and Southern Europe.* Cambridge: Cambridge University Press.

Higley, J. & G. Lengyel (eds.), 2000: *Elites after State Socialism.* Oxford Lanham: Rowman & Littlefield.

Higley, J. & J. Pakulski, 2000: Jeux de pouvoir des élites et consolidation de la démocratie en europe centrale et orientale. *Revue française de science politique* 50(4/5):657–678.

Holmes, L., 1997: *Post-Communism. An Introduction.* Oxford: Polity Press.

Holtmann, E. & H. Wiesenthal, 2009: *Transition – Transformation – Posttransformation* (SFB 580 Mitteilungen; 31), Jena & Halle.

Howard, M. M., 2003: *The Weakness of Civil Society in Post-Communist Europe.* Cambridge, MA: Cambridge University Press.

Huntington, S. P., 1991: *The Third Wave. Democratization in the Late Twentieth Century.* Norman: University of Oklahoma Press.

Ishkanian, A., 2007: Democracy Promotion and Civil Society. In: Anheier, A, M. Glasius &M. Kaldor (eds.), *Global Civil Society: Communicative Power and Democracy*, pp. 58–85. London: Sage Publications.

Jahn, D., 2013: *Einführung in die vergleichende Politikwissenschaft.* Wiesbaden: VS Verlag für Sozialwissenschaft, 2nd ed.

Jowitt, K. (ed.), 1992a: *New World Disorder: The Leninist Distinction*. Berkeley: University of California Press.

Jowitt, K., 1992b: The Leninist Legacy. In: Jowitt, K. (ed.), *New World Disorder: The Leninist Distinction*, pp. 284–305. Berkeley: University of California Press.

Karl, T. L., 1995: The Hybrid Regimes of Central America. *Journal of Democracy* 6(3):72–86.

Kawka, R., 2007: Regional Disparities in the GDR – Do They Still Matter? In: Lenz, S. (ed.), *Restructuring Eastern Germany*, pp. 41–55. Berlin: Springer.

Klingemann, H., 2015: Gründungswahlen. In: Kollmorgen, R., W. Merkel & H. J. Wagener (eds.), *Handbuch Transformationsforschung*, pp. 553–560. Wiesbaden: Springer VS.

Knobloch, J., 2006: *Hybride Systeme. Politische Praxis und Theorie am Beispiel Rußlands*. Münster: Lit.

Kolev, S. & J. Zweynert, 2015: Transformationsökonomische Ansätze. In: Kollmorgen, R., W. Merkel & H. J. Wagener (eds.), *Handbuch Transformationsforschung*, pp. 151–160. Wiesbaden: Springer VS.

Kollmorgen, R., 2011: Subalternisierung: Formen und Mechanismen der Misachtung Ostdeutscher nach der Vereinigung. In: Kollmorgen, R, F. T. Koch & H. L. Dienel (eds.), *Diskurse der deutschen Einheit: Kritik und Alternativen*, pp. 301–359. Wiesbaden: VS, Verlag für Sozialwissenschaften.

Kollmorgen, R., 2015a: Aus dem Osten an die Spitze? Ostdeutsche in den bundesdeutschen Eliten. In: Busch, U. & R. Kollmorgen (eds.), *25 Jahre Deutsche Einheit: Ostdeutschlands fragmentierte Integration*. Potsdam: WeltTrends.

Kollmorgen, R., 2015b: Modernisierungstheoretische Ansätze. In: Kollmorgen, R., W. Merkel & H. J. Wagener (eds.), *Handbuch Transformationsforschung*, pp. 77–88. Wiesbaden: Springer VS.

Kollmorgen, R., W. Merkel & H. J. Wagener (eds.), 2015: *Handbuch Transformationsforschung*. Wiesbaden: Springer VS.

Krastev, I., 2017: *After Europe*. Philadelphia: University of Pennsylvania Press.

Krastev, I. & S. Holmes, 2019: *The Light That Failed: A Reckoning*. London: Penguin Books.

Krennerich, M., 2002: Weder Fisch noch Fleisch? Klassifikationsprobleme zwischen Diktatur und Demokratie. In: Bendel, P., A. Croissant & F. Rüb (eds.), *Hybride Regime. Zur Konzeption und Empirie demokratischer Grauzonen*, pp. 55–70. Opladen: Leske + Budrich.

Kubik, J., 2003: Cultural Legacies of State Socialism. History Making and Cultural-Political Entrepreneurship in Postcommunist Poland and Russia. In: Ekiert, G. & S. E. Hanson (eds.), *Capitalism and Democracy in Central and Eastern Europe*, pp. 317–352. Cambridge: Cambridge University Press.

Lavenex, S. & F. Schimmelfennig, 2009: EU rules beyond EU borders. theorizing external governance in European politics. *Journal of European Public Policy* 16(6):791–812.

Leininger, J., 2015: Demokratieförderung. In: Kollmorgen, R., W. Merkel & H. J. Wagener (eds.), *Handbuch Transformationsforschung*, pp. 509–516. Wiesbaden: Springer VS.

Lerner, D., 1958: *The Passing of Traditional Society*. Glencoe.

Levitsky, S. & L. A. Way, 2002: The Rise of Competitive Authoritarianism. *Journal of Democracy* 13(2):51–65.

Levitsky, S. & L. A. Way, 2010: *Competitive Authoritarianism. Hybrid Regimes After the Cold War*. New York: Cambridge University Press.

Linz, J., 1975: Totalitarian and Authoritarian Regimes. In: Greenstein, F. & N. Polsby (eds.), *Handbook of Political Science*, pp. 175–412. Reading.

Linz, J., 1989: Autoritäre Regime. In: Nohlen, D. (ed.), *Politikwissenschaft 1. Pipers Wörterbuch zur Politik*, pp. 62–65. München: Piper.

Linz, J., 1990: Transitions to Democracy. *Washington Quarterly* 13(3):143–164.

Linz, J. & A. Stepan, 1996: *Problems of Democratic Transition and Consolidation*. Baltimore and London: Johns Hopkins University Press.

Lipset, S. M., 1959: Some Social Requisites of Democracy. Economic Development and Political Legitimacy. *American Political Science Review* 53(1):69–105.

Lipset, S. M. & S. Rokkan, 1967: *Party Systems and Voter Alignments. Cross-National Perspectives*. New York: The Free Press.

Magyar, B., 2016: *Post-communist mafia state. The case of Hungary*. Budapest: Central European University Press.

Mainwaring, S., G. O'Donnell & J. S. Valenzuela (eds.), 1992: *Issues in Democratic Consolidation. The New South American Democracies in Comparative Perspective*. Notre Dame: University of Notre Dame Press.

Mau, S., 2019: *Lütten Klein. Leben in der ostdeutschen Transformationsgesellschaft*. Frankfurt: Suhrkamp Verlag.

Merkel, W., 1994a: Struktur oder Akteur, System oder Handlung. Gibt es einen Königsweg in der sozialwissenschaftlichen Transformationsforschung? In: Merkel, W. (ed.), *Systemwechsel 1. Theorien, Ansätze und Konzeptionen*, pp. 303–333. Opladen: Leske + Budrich.

Merkel, W. (ed.), 1994b: *Systemwechsel 1*. Opladen: Leske + Budrich.

Merkel, W., 1996a: Institutionalisierung und Konsolidierung der Demokratien in Ostmitteleuropa. In: Merkel, W., E. Sandschneider & D. Segert (eds.), *Systemwechsel 2. Die Institutionalisierung der Demokratie*, pp. 73–112. Opladen: Leske + Budrich.

Merkel, W., 1996b: Theorien der Transformation. Die demokratische Konsolidierung postautoritärer Gesellschaften. In: von Beyme, K. & C. Offe (eds.), *Politische Theorien in der Ära der Transformation*, pp. 30–58. Opladen: Westdeutscher Verlag.

Merkel, W., 1998: The Consolidation of Post-Autocratic Democracies. A Multi-level Model. *Democratization* 5(3):33–67.

Merkel, W., 1999a: Defekte Demokratien. In: Merkel, W. & A. Busch (eds.), *Demokratie in Ost und West*, pp. 361–381. Frankfurt am Main: Suhrkamp.

Merkel, W., 1999b: *Systemtransformation*. Opladen: Leske+Budrich.

Merkel, W. (ed.), 2000: *Systemwechsel 5. Zivilgesellschaft und Transformation*. Opladen: Leske + Budrich.

Merkel, W., 2010: *Systemtransformation. Eine Einführung in die Theorie und Empirie der Transformationsforschung*. Wiesbaden: VS Verlag für Sozialwissenschaften, 2nd edition.

Merkel, W. & E. Sandschneider (eds.), 1997: *Systemwechsel 3. Parteien im Transformationsprozeß*. Opladen: Leske + Budrich.

Merkel, W. & E. Sandschneider (eds.), 1999: *Systemwechsel 4. Die Rolle von Verbänden im Transformationsprozeß*. Opladen: Leske + Budrich.

Merkel, W., R. Kollmorgen & H. J. Wagner (eds.), 2019: *The handbook of political, social, and economic transformation*. Oxford: Oxford University Press.

Merkel, W., E. Sandschneider & D. Segert (eds.), 1996: *Systemwechsel 2. Die Institutionalisierung der Demokratie*. Opladen: Leske + Budrich.

Merkel, W., H. J. Puhle, A. Croissant & P. Thiery (eds.), 2006: *Defekte Demokratien. Vol. 2. Regionalanalysen*. Wiesbaden: VS Verlag für Sozialwissenschaften.

Merkel, W., H. J. Puhle, A. Croissant, C. Eicher & P. Thiery, 2003: *Defekte Demokratie. Vol. 1. Theorie.* Opladen: Leske + Budrich.

Milanović, B., 2018: *Global inequality. A new approach for the age of globalization.* Cambridge, MA: The Belknap Press of Harvard University Press.

Nohlen, D., 1994: Vergleichende Methode. In: Nohlen, D. (ed.), *Lexikon der Politik. Band 2,* pp. 507–517. München: C.H. Beck.

North, D. C., 1990: *Institutions, Institutional Change and Economic Performance.* Cambridge: Cambridge University Press.

O'Donnell, G. A., 1994: Delegative Democracy. *Journal of Democracy* 5(1):55–69.

O'Donnell, G. A., P. C. Schmitter & L. Whitehead (eds.), 1986: *Transitions from Authoritarian Rule. Prospects for Democracy (4 volumes).* Baltimore: Johns Hopkins University Press.

Offe, C., 1991: Das Dilemma der Gleichzeitigkeit. Demokratisierung und Marktwirtschaft in Osteuropa. *Merkur* 505:279–292.

Offe, C., (ed.), 1994: *Der Tunnel am Ende des Lichts. Erkundungen der politischen Transformation im Neuen Osten.* Frankfurt and New York: Campus Verlag.

Patel, K. K., 2018: *Projekt Europa. Eine kritische Geschichte.* München: C.H. Beck.

Pevehouse, J. C., 2002: Democracy from the Outside-In? International Organizations and Democratization. *International Organization* 56(3):515–549.

Pickel, A. & H. Wiesenthal (eds.), 1997: *The Grand Experiment. Debating Shock Therapy, Transition Theory, and the East German Experience.* Colorado, Oxford: Westview Press.

Polanyi, K., [1944] 2007: *The Great Transformation: The Political and Economic Origins of Our Time.* Boston: Beacon Press, 2nd Beacon paperback ed., 8th printing.

Popper, K. R., [1945] 2003: *Die offene Gesellschaft und ihre Feinde.* Tübingen: J.C.B. Mohr (Paul Siebeck).

Pridham, G., 1995: The International Context of Democratic Consolidation. Southern Europe in Comparative Perspective. In: Gunther, R., P. N. Diamandouros & H. J. Puhle (eds.), *The Politics of Democratic Consolidation. Southern Europe in Comparative* Perspective, pp. 166–203. Baltimore: Johns Hopkins University Press.

Przeworski, A., 1986: Some Problems in the Study of the Transition to Democracy. In: O'Donnell, G., P. Schmitter & L. Whitehead (eds.), *Transitions from Authoritarian Rule, vol. 2,* pp. 47–63. Baltimore: Johns Hopkins University Press.

Przeworski, A., 1991: *Democracy and the Market. Political and Economic Reforms in Eastern Europe and Latin America.* Cambridge: Cambridge University Press.

Przeworski, A., 1992: The Games of Transition. In: Mainwaring, S, G. O'Donnell & J. S. Valenzuela (eds.), *Issues in Democratic Consolidation. The New South American Democracies in Comparative* Perspective, pp. 105–152. Notre Dame: University of Notre Dame Press.

Rokkan, S., 1970: *Citizens, Elections, Parties. Approaches to the Comparative Study of the Processes of Development.* Oslo: Universitetsforlaget.

Rokkan, S., 2000: *Staat, Nation und Demokratie in Europa. Die Theorie Stein Rokkans aus seinen gesammelten Werken rekonstruiert und eingeleitet von Peter Flora.* Frankfurt: Suhrkamp.

Rostow, W. W., 1960: *The Stages of Economic Growth. A Non-Communist Manifesto.* Cambridge: Cambridge University Press.

Rueschemeyer, D., E. Huber-Stephens & J. Stephens, 1992: *Capitalist Development & Democracy.* Cambridge: Cambridge University Press.

Rupieper, H. J., 1993: *Die Wurzeln der westdeutschen Nachkriegsdemokratie. Der amerikanische Beitrag 1945–1952*. Opladen: Westdeutscher Verlag.

Sachs, J., 1989: My Plan for Poland. *The International Economy* 24–29.

Sachs, J., 2000: Notes on a New Sociology of Economic Development. In: Harrison, L. E. & S. P. Huntington (eds.), *Culture Matters. How Values Shape Human* Progress, pp. 29–43. New York: Basic Books.

Sapper, M. & V. Weichsel (eds.), 2016: *Gegen die Wand. Konservative Revolution in Polen*. Berlin: Berliner Wissenschaftsverlag (also as Osteuropa 1-2/2016).

Sapper, M. & V. Weichsel (eds.), 2018: *Unterm Messer. Der illiberale Staat in Ungarn und Polen*. Berlin: Berliner Wissenschaftsverlag (also as Osteuropa 3-5/2018).

Sasse, G., 2007: 'Conditionality-lite': The European Neighbourhood Policy and the EU's Eastern Neighbours. In: Casarini, N. & C. Musu (eds.), *European foreign policy in an evolving international system. The road towards* convergence, pp. 163–180. Basingstoke: Palgrave Macmillan.

Schedler, A., 1998: What is Democratic Consolidation? *Journal of Democracy* 9(2):91–107.

Schedler, A. (ed.), 2006: *Electoral Authoritarianism. The Dynamics of Unfree Competition*. Boulder: Lynne Rienner Publishers.

Schimmelfennig, F., 2005: Strategic Calculation and International Socialization. Membership Incentives, Party Constellations, and Sustained Compliance in Central and Eastern Europe. *International Organization* 59(4):827–860.

Schimmelfennig, F., 2007: European Regional Organizations, Political Conditionality, and Democratic Transformation in Eastern Europe. *East European Politics and Society* 21(1): 126–141.

Schmid, U., 2016: *Technologien der Seele. Vom Verfertigen der Wahrheit in der russischen Gegenwartskultur*. Berlin: Suhrkamp.

Shevtsova, L., 2001: Russia's Hybrid Regime. *Journal of Democracy* 12(4):65–70.

Shevtsova, L., 2004: The Limits of Bureaucratic Authoritarianism. *Journal of Democracy* 15(4): 67–77.

Simmel, G., 1910: How Is Society Possible? *American Journal of Sociology* 16(3):372–391.

Spanger, H.-J. & J. Wolff, 2007: Why promote democratization? Reflections on the instrumental value of democracy. In: van Doorn, M. & R. von Meijenfeldt (eds.): *Democracy, Europe's Core Value?: On the European Profile in World-wide Democracy Assistance*, pp. 33–49. Delft: Eburon.

Stark, D. & L. Bruszt (eds.), 1998: *Postsocialist Pathways. Transforming Politics and Property in East Central Europe*. Cambridge: Cambridge University Press.

Thelen, K., S. Steinmo & F. Longstreth (eds.), 1992: *Structuring Politics. Historical Institutionalism in Comparative Analysis*. Cambridge: Cambridge University Press.

Tilly, C., 2004: *Contention and Democracy in Europe, 1650–2000*. Cambridge: Cambridge University Press.

Trüper, H., D. Chakrabarty & S. Subrahmanyam (eds.), 2015: *Historical teleologies in the modern world*. London: Bloomsbury Academic, an imprint of Bloomsbury Publishing Plc.

von Beyme, K., 1994: *Systemwechsel in Osteuropa*. Frankfurt: Suhrkamp.

Weber, M., 1980: *Wirtschaft und Gesellschaft*. Tübingen: J.C.B. Mohr.

Whitehead, L., 1986: International Aspects of Democratization. In: O'Donnell, G. A., P. C. Schmitter & L. Whitehead (eds.), *Transitions from Authoritarian Rule. Comparative Perspectives*, pp. 3–47. Baltimore: Johns Hopkins University Press.

Whitehead, L. (ed.), 2001: *The International Dimension of Democratization. Europe and the Americas*. Oxford: Oxford University Press.

Wollmann, H., 2001: Die Transformation der politischen und administrativen Strukturen in Ostdeutschland – zwischen „Schöpferischer Zerstörung", Umbau und Neubau. In: Bertram, H. & R. Kollmorgen (eds.), *Die Transformation Ostdeutschlands: Berichte zum sozialen und politischen Wandel in den neuen Bundesländern*, pp. 33–52. Wiesbaden: VS Verlag für Sozialwissenschaften.

Worschech, S., 2018a: The 'Making' of Europe in the Peripheries: Europeanization Through Conflicts and Ambivalences. *Culture, Practice, and Europeanization* 3(3):56–76. https://www.uni-flensburg.de/fileadmin/content/seminare/soziologie/dokumente/culture-practice-and-europeanization/cpe-vol.3-no.3-2018/worschech-2018.pdf (accessed June 23, 2021).

Worschech, S., 2018b: *Die Herstellung von Zivilgesellschaft. Strategien und Netzwerke der externen Demokratieförderung in der Ukraine*. Wiesbaden: VS Verlag.

Zakaria, F., 1997: The Rise of Illiberal Democracy. *Foreign Affairs* 76(6):22–43.

Part III: **Dynamics of Europeanization: Core Dimensions of Institution-Building**

Susanne Pernicka & Günter Hefler

7 The Europeanization of Economy and Society

Economic integration is commonly understood as an 'expansion of markets', engendered by the removal of barriers to trade and the imposition of regulations facilitating economic exchange. Within the European Union (EU) economic cooperation and market expansion across national borders form the bedrock of the European integration project. The policies and politics of market making, with the four freedoms of movement – for goods, capital, services, and labor – at its heart, set in motion an engine of social change within Europe, however, with various intended and unintended outcomes, winners and losers, supporters, and opponents. From a sociological point of view, the economy and its markets are not a-historic, ideal-type entities as conceived by economics, but socially embedded entities and societal spheres that have their own rules, norms, and practices. The creation of a common European market therefore presupposes at least to some degree the 'transnational sociation' (in the sense of the German term '*Vergesellschaftung*') and 'social embeddedness' of people within Europe (Münch & Büttner 2006). The sociologist Emile Durkheim wrote already in 1893 that

> [. . .] a function, whether of an economic or any other kind, can only be divided up between societies if these share in some respects in the same common life and, consequently, belong to the same society. [. . .] For a people to allow itself to be penetrated by another, it must have ceased to shut itself up in an exclusive form of patriotism, and must have learned another that is more all-embracing.   (Durkheim [1902] 2013: 219)

The opening up of societies in the wake of European economic integration, however, creates new contradictions and conflicts that cannot be easily resolved. On this point, the sociologist Neil Fligstein accurately pointed out that

> [. . .] in spite of the creation of both a European economy and a nascent European society and polity, there are some crucial problems that create the possibility of a clash between those citizens of member states who have not been the beneficiaries of the economic project of the EU and those who have.   (Fligstein 2008: vii)

Processes of European integration and disintegration are not only guided by economic competition, political cleavages, conflicts and bargains between EU member states, key stakeholders, and corporate actors. These Europeanization and (re)nationalization processes also have a strong societal component because

https://doi.org/10.1515/9783110673630-007

citizens throughout Europe also attribute their economic and social living conditions and prospects to the EU's merits and failures (Pernicka & Lahusen 2018).

Does Economic Integration Drive Social Integration?

The grand narrative of the European integration project as peacekeeping mission from its very beginning has been underpinned by a strong belief that transnational *economic* integration will eventually lead to *societal* integration across national borders. The devastating experiences of two world wars fueled the conviction that conflicts between nation states can only be overcome by tying national economies closer together. In his proposal to place French and West German production of coal and steel under one common High Authority (which later merged into the European Commission), the French foreign minister Robert Schuman laid the foundation of what became the European Steel and Coal Community (ESCC) in 1952.

> The pooling of coal and steel production should immediately provide for the setting up of common foundations for economic development as a first step in the federation of Europe, and will change the destinies of those regions which have long been devoted to the manufacture of munitions of war, of which they have been the most constant victims. The solidarity in production thus established will make it plain that any war between France and Germany becomes not merely unthinkable, but materially impossible.
>
> (Schuman Declaration [1950] 2011)

The integrative effects of deliberate transnational community building by independent nation states also lie at the heart of the book *The Uniting of Europe* by Ernst B. Haas, published in 1958; the same year, when the European Economic Community (EEC) came into being. Haas, a sociologically minded International Relations Scholar, has been widely considered as one of the founders of European integration studies. He was praised (and criticized) for his invention of the idea of **spill-over**, i.e., the notion that integration in one functional area would almost certainly lead to integration in others. Haas laid the groundwork for what later became one of the most influential theorical frameworks in European Union (EU) studies, neo-functionalism. **Neo-functionalism** is a theory of regional integration that singles out three interacting causal factors for regional integration: (1) growing economic interdependence between nations, (2) supranational market rules that replace national regulatory regimes, and (3) the organizational capacity to resolve international disputes.

The neo-functional concept of spill-over does not derive from economic determinism or a belief in a mechanism that automatically converts functional needs into institutional outcomes. Instead, the concept of spill-over is built on the assumption that the attitudes, interests, and behavior of agents matter in defining the rules and boundaries of transnational markets. Haas especially suggested that "[. . .] group pressure will spill over into the federal sphere and thereby add to the integrative impulse" (Haas 1958: xxxiii). International institutions are viewed as having socialized bureaucrats and policy actors in a way that they engage in building cooperation and policy instruments across an ever-expanding range of policy areas beyond the nation state (Favell & Guiraudon 2011: 5). More recent institutionalist accounts of neo-functionalism, in comparison to earlier neo-functional concepts, deal with the question of how much leeway European actors have in a highly institutionalized EU setting. Fligstein points out that European rules, norms, and practices imply constraints and opportunities not available in earlier stages of international politics (Sandholtz & Stone Sweet 1998; Fligstein 2008). Thus, the institutionalized 'European space' has bound member governments, interest groups, bureaucracies, and politicians in ever-tighter interdependencies.

The European integration process has faced many critical challenges. The Great Recession from 2008 onwards, the strong inflow of refugees in 2015/2016, the Brexit referendum 2016 and Britain's subsequent exit from the European Union as well as the Covid-19 pandemic in 2020 compose some of the major European challenges. The still largely lacking social dimension of the European Union that has contributed to an ever-larger incongruence of economic and social integration (Bach 2015), however, might pose the greatest future challenge for the European project. This development can also be traced to the familiar contrast between 'negative' and 'positive integration' (Scharpf 1996: 91), i.e., between measures increasing market integration by eliminating national restraints on trade and distortions on competition, on the one hand, and common European policies to shape the economic, political, and social conditions under which markets operate, on the other hand. **Negative integration** has advanced, sometimes behind the back of political processes, by the European Court of Justice and the European Commission, whereas **positive integration** is much harder to accomplish (Scharpf 1996). Social rights, such as pensions, healthcare, unemployment benefits, collective wage bargaining and many other basic labor and social rights continue to be nationally based whereas companies, capital, goods, services, and workers can freely move across national borders (Pernicka et al. 2019). Different groups (especially, business and labor as well as rich and poor people) in different geographies (e.g., Northern, Eastern and Southern European countries) are unevenly affected by European economic integration. In his widely received book

Euroclash. The EU, European Identity, and the Future of Europe Fligstein (2008) goes even so far as to argue that the winners and losers of European integration are likely to clash over whether a deepening of integration will bring them (further) benefits or disadvantages and – one might add – over the European project as such. Over the long history of European integration, however, reluctant politician leaders as well as Eurosceptical movements and debates repeatedly called into question the future of the European project which nevertheless continue to provide promising responses towards international and global economic, political, societal, and environmental challenges.

Studying EU Economic Integration – A Multidisciplinary Project

The study of European integration is a multidisciplinary project in which economists, political scientists, law, and public-administrative scholars, as well as sociologists participate. Social scientists largely reject the position of neoclassical economists who view market expansion as primarily pushed forward by the 'natural forces' of supply and demand between market actors (Lindert & Williamson 2003). One of the founders of liberal economic thought, Adam Smith ([1776] 1989) pointed out that corporations that maximize their own gain serve the benefit of further market integration, promoting an "end which was no part of their intention" (cit. in Berend 2016: 146). Social scientists, by contrast, emphasize the deliberate contributions of governments, supranational actors, large corporations, interest groups and other societal actors to market building processes. National governments contributed to the reintegration of Western European countries into the world economy after 1945 and created a common set of rules that shaped European patterns of production, trade, corporate finance, and consumption.

Among social scientists in EU studies however, there is less consensus over how, to what extent and at which spatial level, or scale, such as the local, regional, national, or global, actors and institutions have contributed to the creation of the Single Market with – for the larger part of EU member states – its own currency, the Euro. Political scientists were among the first EU scholars who have convincingly argued that the European Union has established a complex intergovernmental and supranational multi-level system (Kohler-Koch & Eising 1999). This system has spurred processes of 'vertical Europeanization' that presses for institutional convergences by uploading and downloading policy agendas, policy ideas, and legal regulations (Börzel & Risse 2009). The shift of competences in monetary policy making from the national to the supranational level in 1999 is a case in point. The Treaty on the Functioning of the European Union (TFEU, now Article 127) gives the EU and the European Central Bank exclusive competence for monetary policy for member states whose currency is the Euro. Economic and social welfare policies, by comparison, have remained within the realm of each individual member state, at least as long as there is no excessive deficit. There is, however, multilateral coordination in economic policies and, to a smaller extent, in social policies, between EU countries.

EU studies, however, used to pay less attention to the societal processes within the Europeanized social space and the diversity of **social fields** within it, such as economic fields, political-administrative fields, associational fields or fields of education and research, to name just a few. Sociologists, who joined the group of European integration scholars comparatively late, have emphasized these social underpinnings of European integration. They argue that European integration has not only increased the political, economic, and social interactions and interdependencies across national borders. It has also opened and restructured national social space and social fields, and thereby led to the emergence of a social entity between national and global scales. The processes of creating such a European social entity, which has been more recently referred to as 'horizontal Europeanization' (Beck & Grande 2004; Heidenreich et al. 2012; Mau & Verwiebe 2010; Heidenreich 2019) helped establish or extend social fields in many areas based on horizontal relations of cooperation, competition and conflict.

Despite their importance for the European project, however, the economy and markets have rarely been studied by sociologists of Europeanization. The field of economic sociology – with a few notable exceptions – has also largely neglected European economic integration. While the sociology of market making moved into the center of their interest from the 1980s onwards (Fligstein & Dauter 2007; Aspers & Beckert 2017), the creation of the *Single European Market* received comparatively little attention by economic sociologists. Understanding markets as historically constructed 'social fields', potentially spanning different spatial scales, go beyond the notion of social embeddedness (Swedberg 2011). In drawing on Bourdieu's social theory, we can say that in modern differentiated societies social space is made up of a large variety of historically evolved, interdependent and hierarchically structured, but relatively autonomous social fields (Bourdieu 2005). With Pierre Bourdieu's work on economic fields as a starting point, Neil Fligstein (2008) has so far suggested the most promising sociological approach to study the Europeanization of economy and society (see section 4).

The Creation of the European Single Market

The creation of the European Single Market together with the enlargement of the European Economic Community (EEC, renamed in 1993 as European Community, EC/EU) from six to 28 countries clearly left its traces in European economic history as well as in the overall societal organizations of its member states (Eichengreen & Boltho 2010). The emergence of a European transnational economic and social space within which goods, services, capital, and labor can freely circulate was, however, by no means a smooth or automatic process. In the following subsection we identify the global social forces, i.e., the objective and subjective relations of power between social groups operating in the economy, the state, and the wider society, that gave rise to cooperation and conflict around the European free market building project.

The Start of a European Free-Trade Project

The foundation of the European integration project after 1945 came after a centuries-long 'great transformation' of society towards a market society (Polanyi [1944] 2002), two devastating world wars and one of the deepest global economic crises, capitalist societies had experienced so far. Besides many other initiatives to create political and societal bridges between former enemies, the foundation of a European economic community was one of the longest-lasting, international community building projects not only in Europe but worldwide.

The early stages of European community building after 1945 were overshadowed by the so-called 'German Question' of how any future German aggression against neighbors in Europe could be prevented. However, the intend to tame extreme forms of (economic) nationalism, shared by the World War II Allies, the United States, Britain, France, and the Soviet Union, was quickly accompanied and partly replaced by an anti-communist hysteria (Berend 2016: 8, 21). The United States took the lead in providing financial means including grants, loans, food, and other kinds of shipments to Europe, leading up to the *Marshall Plan* (1948), named after the US Secretary of State, General George C. Marshall, to finance European recovery. In hindsight, the Marshall Plan contributed to both, to restore stability and peace between European WWII enemies and to fend off communism as a political-military and economic force by facilitating the emergence of a European free trade project.

From the beginning, the US pushed for Britain taking on a more active role in the European integration process, however, with no avail. Under French leadership, in 1952, the *European Steel and Coal Community* was created, followed by the *European Economic Community* (EEC) in 1958 (Berend 2016). The EEC consisted of France, West Germany, Italy and the three Benelux countries. While more ambitious plans for a political and military cooperation failed, the EEC member states gradually abolished tariffs and other restrictions to trade. Britain found the *European Free Trade Area* as a 'counter organization' to the EEC with Austria, Denmark, Sweden, Norway, Switzerland, and Portugal as additional members. The economic integration process, however, lost momentum when the French government under General de Gaulle largely withdrew from supranational coordination (so called 'empty chair crisis') and instead attempted to strengthen France's position via intergovernmental cooperation (Berend 2016) (For an overview on key events and phases of the history of integration see Figure 7.1).

The 1970s – Fighting Stagflation

Although Denmark, Ireland and the United Kingdom joined the EEC in 1973, the economic integration process was widely perceived as entering a stage of stagnation in the early 1970s which lasted until 1984. In the 1970s, however, the *European Court of Justice* (ECJ) found a much more active and increasingly powerful role, with "[. . .] jurists increasingly compared the EC with a nascent federal state" (Griffiths 2014: 167). European case law became a major driver of economic integration. The *Rewe-Zentral v. Bundesmonopolverwaltung für Branntwein* (1979) Case 120/78, popularly known as *Cassis de Dijon* ruling after its subject matter demonstrated the supremacy of European law over national legislation and jurisdiction (Stone Sweet 2004). In terms of its economic and regulatory impact, the Cassis de Dijon ruling created the precedent for all future rulings that enforce the mutual recognition of rules and norms pertaining to goods, services, and workers in one member state by all others instead of their harmonization. As the main thrust of the ECJ's judicial action is to extend the reach of 'negative integration' (Scharpf 1999) this ruling has in fact weakened the possibility of the Europeanization of a common social welfare system.

The political stalemate at the European level stood in stark contrast to upheavals across Europe, including the global student movement, the Prague Spring (1968) and the breakdown of authoritarian regimes in Portugal, Greece (1974) and Spain (1975). The Oil crisis (1973) and the breakdown of the monetary and financial order (**Bretton Woods system**) brought the post-war phase of economic progress to an end.

End World War II	Bretton Woods agreement and Foundation of IMF and World Bank (1944)	1945
	General Agreement on Tariffs and Trade, GATT (1948)	
	Start Marshall Plan, ERP (1948)	
Cold War culminates in Korean War (1950-53)		1950

Bretton Woods agreement and
Foundation of IMF and World Bank (1944)
General Agreement on Tariffs and Trade, GATT (1948)
Start Marshall Plan, ERP (1948)

End World War II

Cold War culminates in Korean War (1950-53)

1945

1950

ECSC, EC6 EUROPEAN COAL AND STEEL COMMUNITY, ECSC (1952)
(FR, DE, IT, BE, NL, LU)

Hungarian uprising (1956)   1955

EUROPEAN ECONOMIC COMMUNITY, EEC (1958)

Foundation of the European
Peak year of 'Decolonialisation' Free Trade Area, EFTA (1960) 1960
('African Year')

1965   "EMPTY CHAIR CRISIS" (1965)

Prague Spring (1968)

1970

Collapse of the Bretton Woods System (1971)

Oil crises (1973, and 1979–80)

1973: EC9
(+ UK, IE, DK)

Break down of fascist regimes in PT, ES, EL (1974/75)   1975

1980   1981: EC10
(+GR)

1985   SCHENGEN (1985)
1986:   SINGLE EUROPEAN ACT (1986)
EU12
(+ES, PT)

Regime changes in 'Communist Bloc' (1989)
German Unification (1990)
Post-Soviet States emerge (1990-)   1990

COMPLETION OF EUROPEAN SINGLE MARKET (1993)

Wars in Ex-Yugoslavia (1995-2001)   1995   1995: EU15
(+AT, FI, SE)

STABILITY AND GROWTH PACT, SGP (1998, 1999)
Dot-com bubble (2000-2002) 2000   INTRODUCTION OF SINGLE CURRENCY EURO (1999)

2005   2004: EU25
(+ CZ, CY, EE, HU, LV, MT, PL, LT, SL, SK)

Onset of Global financial crisis (2008)   2007: EU27
(+ BG, RO)   EU MEASU RES RESPONDING TO SOVEREIGN DEBT CRISES OF
Arab Spring (2010/11) and Syrian war (2011-)   2010   GR, PT, IRE, ESP, CY (2009-)
Krim-Crisis and Donbas war (2014 -)

2013: EU28
(+ HR)   BANKING UNION (2014)
Great Refugee Crisis (2015)   2015
BREXIT (2016-2020)
Donald Trump 45st US president (2017-21)

2020   2020: EU27-   EU AND MS RESPONSE TO THE COVID-19
(-UK)   PANDEMIC (2020-

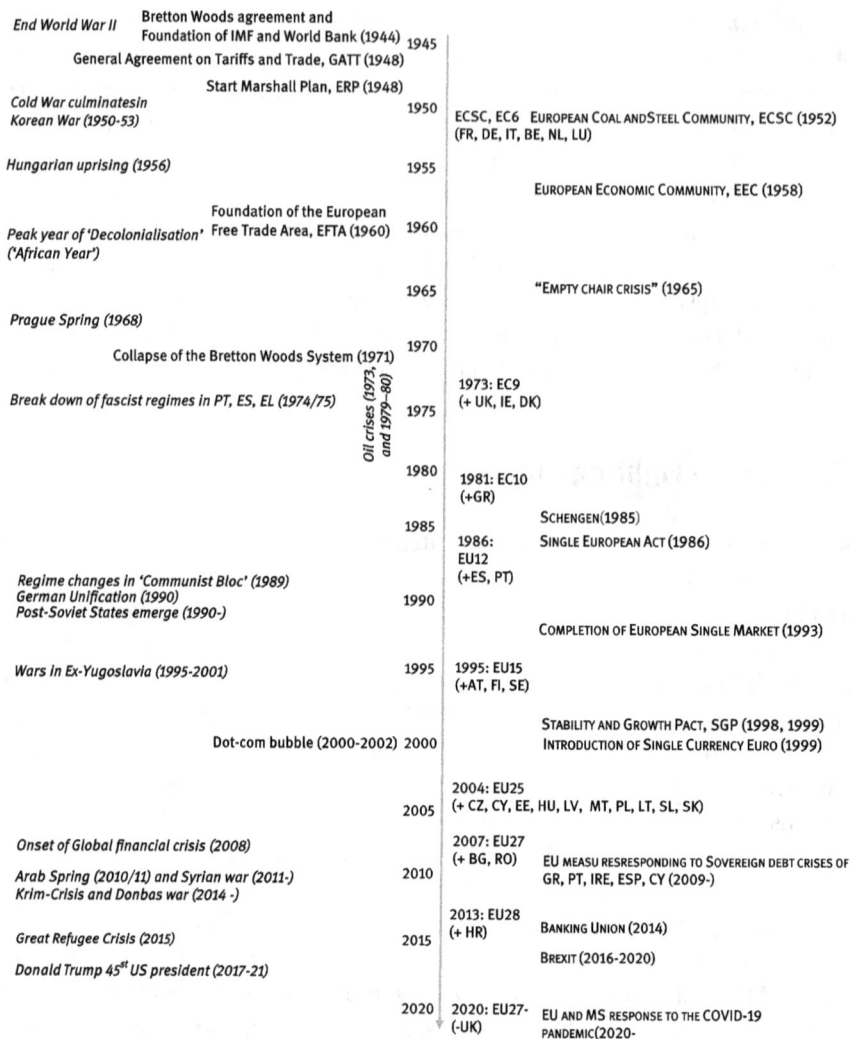

Figure 7.1: Timeline of European economic (dis-)integration in global context.

The 1980s – 'Neoliberal Turn' Targeting Economic Stalemate

The return of global recession staring in the early 1980s helped to establish what was later called the 'neoliberal turn' or the 'Washington consensus'. Policy preferences turned from a state-centered Keynesian approach of economic policy towards globalized neoliberalism and free-market ideology ('Reaganomics', 'Thatcherism'), which also shaped the European common market building project (Hermann 2007). Japan and the Asian Tiger States became model cases for how to increase productivity, with European companies both lagging behind its Asian and US rivals and therefore losing ground in the unfolding global economic competition. Notably, in 1984 the EU also launched its Framework Programs for Research and Technological Development that have become one of the chief instruments in research funding at European level (Büttner & Leopold 2016).

Post-authoritarian Greece (in 1981), Spain and Portugal (in 1986) were allowed to join the EEC after undergoing painful reforms and curbing left-leaning political ambitions which had dominated the years after the change to liberal democracies. Further economic integration, however, was largely opposed by the Council of Ministers where the veto of a single member state was enough to block the implementation of any change (Scharpf 2010). The turning point in the history of European integration was the appointment of Jacque Delors as the European Commission's president in 1985. The European Commission under Delors played a leading role in establishing a system of multilevel industrial relations that gave trade unions and employers' associations influential voices at European level. The so-called *European Social Dialogue* received formal recognition in 1986 and paved the way for several Framework Agreements between European business and labor. They led to EU directives on part-time work, fixed-term work, and parental leave during the 1990s when trade unions were strong enough to trade off their consent to the upcoming European Single Market for business associations' acceptance of social protection legislation (Keller 2008, Falkner 1998). The formation of the European Round Table of Industrialists consisting of the twelve largest information technology companies in the early 1980s was another strong sign of departure from **Eurosclerosis** towards transnational cooperation and a deepening of European economic integration (Green Cowles 1995).

The 1990s – End of the Post-War Order and the Completion of the European Single Market

With the breakdown of communist rule in the Soviet Union and Germany's reunification a unique situation arose propelling both the expansion of the European Community and the creation of the European Single Market. The completion of the Single Market in 1993 and the subsequent rounds of enlargement appeared to provide the most promising response to tackle both, the competitiveness crisis, and the end of the regime competition between East and West. Eastern European states, including the newly founded Baltic states, underwent 'shock therapies' in exchange for entering the accession process, leading to the enlargement rounds of 2004 and 2007. The wars in former Yugoslavia (1995–2001) reemphasized the EU's peace keeping mission. The supply-side orientation of the EU's economic policies found manifold expressions. It imprinted the European Employment Strategy (1998), accompanied waves of down-sizing in corporate Europe and promoted the privatization of state-owned companies and the 'liberalization' of economic sectors formerly reserved for the public sector, such as telecom and postal services, media, or energy (Clifton et al. 2006).

The 2000s – From Triumphant to Crisis Mode

With the Euro implemented (1999, 2002), the biggest enlargement round (2004) under way and an economic upswing, the new millennium saw EU optimism unleashed with the Lisbon Strategy launched in March 2000 as its most vivid expression. EU heads of state declared their intention to make Europe "[. . .] the most competitive and dynamic knowledge-based economy in the world, capable of sustainable economic growth with more and better jobs and greater social cohesion" (European Council 2000). The aim of social cohesion within the EU, however, was challenged by the shrinking yet still huge wage and social welfare gaps between old and new members states. Moreover, the global financial crisis that began in the United States in 2008 (collapse of Lehman Brothers) and spill over to Europe in 2009, shed light on the structural weaknesses of the single currency's architecture that contributed to the Euro and sovereign debt crises in which the countries affected (Portugal, Ireland, Greece, and Spain) were not able to repay their debt. As the countries of the Eurozone were deprived of the exchange rate instrument to adapt to weaknesses in international competitiveness, labor markets, institutions of collective bargaining and wages came under severe pressure, especially in those countries that have not institutionalized collective wage moderation practices (Pernicka & Glassner 2019).

The 2010s – Between Recovery and More Trouble

The second decade of the new European Single Market millennium saw a phase of economic consolidation turning into an economic boom from 2015 onwards in many member states. Better economic fundamentals helped to establish new mechanisms of policy coordination (e.g., the European Semester from 2011 onwards) and projects aiming at increasing the EU's resilience to crises (e.g., the introduction of the Banking Union in 2014). In stark contrast to the economic upswing, EU politics were absorbed by an infinite series of challenges, ranging from major foreign policy crises requiring firm responses (e.g., the Crimea crisis), internal conflicts with illiberal governments of EU member states, the 2015/16 Refugee Crisis, or the fallout of Islamic terror attacks in European capitals, including Brussels (2016). The attempt to develop shared policies in the face of external threats and challenges required a European political integration that went beyond economic rationales. With Donald Trump entering the White House in 2017, the EU policy makers (again) lost US support for the European integration project. The EU crisis measures to overcome the crisis of the previous decade had spurred the support for both left and right-leaning euro-sceptic movements and political parties. Yet, the outcome of the 2016 Brexit referendum came as an unexpected setback to the European economic integration project.

European Economic and Social Integration from a Sociological Perspective

The sociology of the Europeanization of economy and society offers a wide range of theoretical conceptions, some of which are more concerned with the social (dis)embeddedness of European markets (Münch & Büttner 2006) while others put more emphasis on the contentious character of market expansion and the foundation of a common currency within the EU (Streeck 2015). Still others attempt to grasp both dynamics, the opening-up of national borders and horizontal integration of European markets, on the one hand, and the contested nature of the processes of European political, economic, and socio-cultural integration on the other hand (Heidenreich 2019). Neil Fligstein's (2008) pioneering sociological approach to the Europeanization of the economy and society, meanwhile, offers insights into what he terms 'European society' and which will determine the future of the European polity. Fligstein derived his approach mainly from economic sociology and organization studies, as well as Pierre Bourdieu's (2005) social theory. Fligstein argues that in modern societies the material production, exchange, and consumption, i.e., the economy, are mainly organized within social fields.

Fligstein (2008: 217) considers European integration to be a process that is primarily social in nature, driven by the interests, identities and shifting demands of businesspeople, educational elites, tourists, etc. rather than an outcome of interaction between political-economic and social processes (for a critical assessment, see also Streeck 2009). As people experience the benefits of free trade, tourism, and education, Fligstein (2008: 218) assumes, they will become more European in outlook and support the creation of more European Union rules and hence, more free market fields. Economic losers, by contrast, are assumed to share a national rather than a European identity and thus, oppose more European coordination. The abovementioned lack of social rights at European level is consequently attributed to the interests, identities and voting behavior of economic losers who decide in favor of keeping competencies in social policy at national level. Neil Fligstein derived his field-theoretical perspective on European integration from two main strands of literature. First, from economic sociology Fligstein takes the basic insight that markets are socially constructed orders of social interaction. Institutions (rules, norms, beliefs) and governments play a fundamental role in shaping markets for the production, exchange, and consumption in capitalist economies (Weber [1922] 1978; Polanyi [1944] 2002). All the processes of material life can best be understood as fundamentally social processes (Granovetter 1985). Second, by drawing from organization studies and social movement theory, Fligstein devised his strategic action field approach that views social fields as arenas of social interaction; and strategic action as the attempt by social actors to create and maintain stable social fields by securing the cooperation of others (Fligstein & McAdam 2011). In applying his theoretical framework to the EU, Fligstein focusses on the horizontal linkages and interactions of individual and collective actors across national borders that have evolved into several European-wide fields. Markets are viewed as Europeanized fields in which business firms have transformed from being predominately participants in national markets to being involved in European-wide markets (Fligstein 2008).

Fligstein suggests particular social mechanisms that have contributed to the creation and spatial expansion of markets and societies. Following the foundation of the EEC and the subsequent increase in economic and social interdependence, Fligstein observed people across Europe who began to trade with one another more regularly, which fueled demand for more political cooperation and thus the creation of new market opening projects. Like Ernst Haas (see above), Fligstein (2008) argues that positive feedback loops push steadily for deeper integration. The transnational interactions of people who get to know one another through their participation in politics or business, and their knowledge of and interest in what each other is doing increased in many ways. Not unlike early neo-functional theories, Fligstein perceives processes of European integration as results of socialization and institutionalization processes which are not likely to be easily reversed.

Fligstein decisively breaks with the a-sociological assumptions of neo-classical economics that views market processes as fundamentally about supply and demand and the formation of prices. While neo-classical economists view governments mainly as bad for market processes and national borders as limiting the effectiveness of potentially global markets, Fligstein underscores the important role of governments in creating and sustaining modern markets. These theoretical arguments are convincingly demonstrated by his study of economic integration across national borders from the late 1940 until the 1990s. Fligstein and Merand (2002) attempt to disentangle the effects of globalization and Europeanization and put the effects of the European market integration project to a quantitative test. For the period under investigation, they show that European governments and supranational actors – by the time being – created the largest trading zone in the world. It accounted for nearly half of world trade by the end of the 1990s. Astoundingly, almost 70 per cent of that total originated and ended up in the EU (15) in the late 1990s (Fligstein & Merand 2002: 14), and even in 2018 the large majority of EU (28) member countries' exports went to other EU countries (see Figure 7.2).

As of 1992, Eurostat, the agency in charge of collecting statistics for the EU, started to describe this trade (i.e., exports to EU28) as internal trade, while only trade outside the EU was considered as foreign trade (Fligstein & Merand 2002: 20). The EU's role in global trade was also impressive. In 1999, more than 40 per cent of all world merchandise exports came from Western Europe, clearly outperforming the North American region that accounted for 17 per cent (see Table 7.1).

Against the increasingly important part played by the emerging economies including especially China and India in contemporary world trade, however, Europe lost its leading role (see Figure 7.2). The EU, the United States and China accounted for 45 per cent of world trade in goods in 2018. It is important to note, however, that the transformation from an industrial towards a service economy has repercussions on the composition of international trade. US American digital platforms such as Amazon, Google, or Uber, for instance, provide their services to almost the entire world population, yet their services 'exports' are barely captured by official statistics (Gröning et al. 2020).

Business firms responded strategically to European market integration. Fligstein (2008) points to the important part played by multinational corporations and their foreign direct investments, transnational mergers and acquisitions which boosted international social and economic relations and interdependencies. His analysis provides an indispensable contribution to our understanding of the transforming economic and social landscapes within the European Union. Fligstein shows how the political project of the EU has deliberately constructed a particular version of the liberal market economy – with a distinctive range of property rights, governance structures, rules of exchange and conceptions of corporate control – that both distinguishes Europe from its American and Asian rivals (Fligstein 2008).

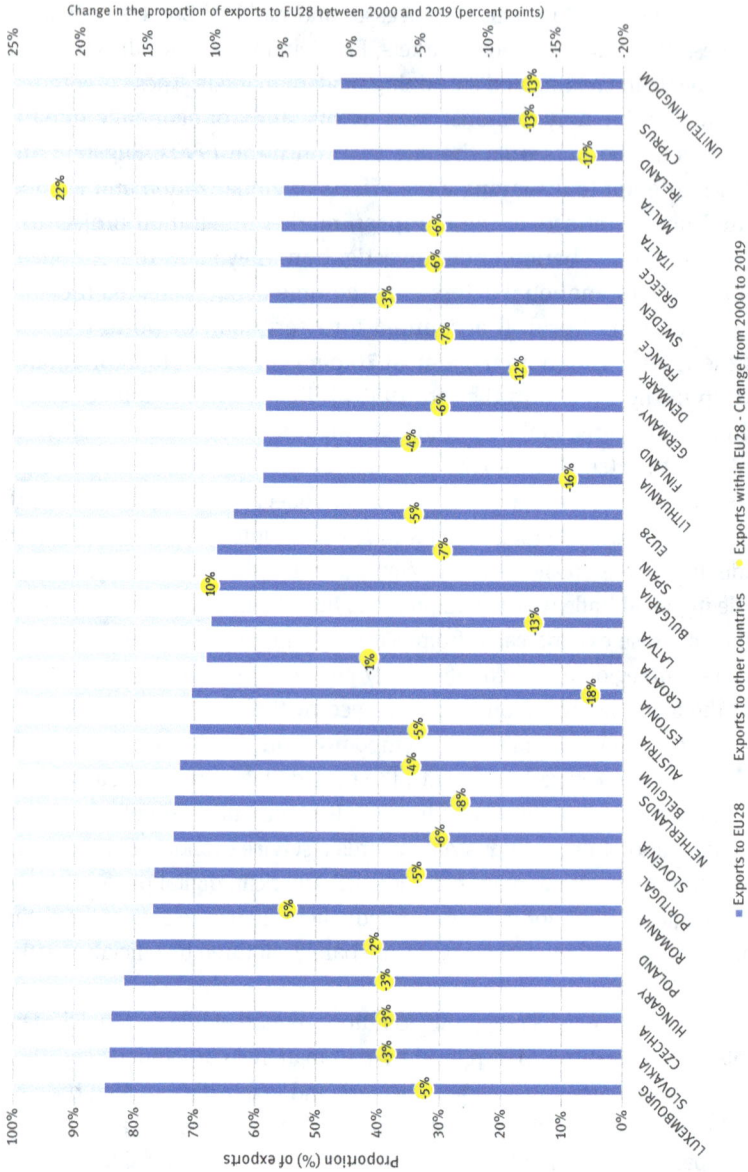

Figure 7.2: Comparison of the proportion of Intra-EU exports of goods and extra-EU exports of goods by member state, 2019.
Source: Eurostat, EU trade since 1988 by SITC [DS-018995], [data extraction: 22.03.2020], own calculation.

Table 7.1: Historic long-term trends: Percentage of world merchandise imports and exports by region, 1948–1999.

	1948	1953	1963	1973	1983	1993	1999
North America							
Exports	27.5	24.6	19.4	17.2	15.4	16.8	17.1
Imports	19.8	19.7	15.5	16.7	17.8	19.8	22.3
Western Europe							
Exports	31.0	34.9	41.0	44.8	39.0	43.7	43.0
Imports	40.4	39.4	45.4	47.4	40.0	42.9	42.2
Asia							
Exports	13.8	13.2	12.6	15.0	19.1	26.3	25.5
Imports	14.2	15.1	14.2	15.1	18.5	23.4	20.9

Source: World Trade Organization, Selected long term trends, Table II.2 [Asia includes Japan, China, Australia, New Zealand, Six East Asian Traders, Other Asia], https://www.wto.org/en glish/res_e/statis_e/its2000/section2/ii02.xls (accessed, January 24, 2020).

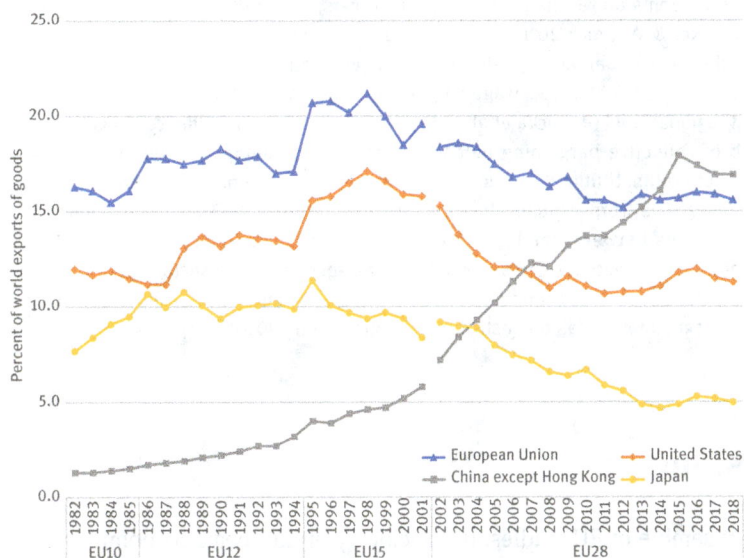

Figure 7.3: Share of EU28 in the world trade (all goods) – EU28 comparted to United States of America, China and Japan.
Source: Eurostat – Share of EU in the World Trade [ext_lt_introle], Version of March 18, 2020. https://ec.europa.eu/eurostat/statistics-explained/index.php?title=World_trade_in_goods_ and_services_-_an_overview&oldid=542750 (accessed, October 20, 2020)

Info-Box 7.1: Critical Appraisal of Fligstein's approach

Fligstein's approach can be praised as an original sociological account of European integration that goes beyond a main controversy in EU studies. The question about what drives European integration has been addressed either by emphasizing spill-over effects of integration (neo-functionalism) or by pointing to negotiations and bargaining between EU main actors such as individual member states (liberal inter-governmentalism). Fligstein, instead, considers citizens' cross-border interactions and experiences, European identity formation and identification, as key for explaining political, economic, and social integration beyond national borders. In his overemphasis on the transnational cooperation among people and organizations, however, Fligstein largely deviates from his original inspiration derived from Bourdieu who sees social fields as arenas of struggle where the unequal endowment of economic, cultural, and social capital create enduring conflict.

In addition, a Bourdieusian perspective also emphasizes the contested political nature of the boundaries and practices of social fields. An example refers to the relationship between economic fields and collective bargaining fields. In collective bargaining fields, collective conflicts and negotiations take place between employers' associations and trade unions over the setting of wages and working conditions. Collective bargaining fields and market fields are strongly interrelated and interdependent, however, they largely differ from each other in terms of their specific power relations, rules, beliefs, and practices, as well as their spatial extension. The European Court of Justice (ECJ) has in many instances placed international market freedoms above the basic rights of workers, including autonomous collective bargaining (Bücker & Warneck 2010). Despite European attempts to coordinate more effectively national collective bargaining fields within the Eurozone, especially during the latest financial and sovereign debt crises, wage bargaining coordination still mainly takes place at national and regional level (Pernicka et al. 2019). However, empirical evidence suggests that the strength of collective bargaining fields and their agents alongside supportive legal-political and cultural institutions can outweigh the economic dominance of transnationally operating transnational corporations. The relatively stable state of Austrian trade unions and protracted struggles between employer and employees' associations, for instance, were found to condition multinational firms' behavior in the social services sector because these for-profit firms have been brought under the same regulations and norms – including collective bargaining agreements – as domestic firms (Pernicka et al. 2018).

Conclusion

Within the ensemble of EU studies, the Sociology of European economic and social integration is a relatively young discipline. In comparison to political, legal, and administrative EU studies, it draws more attention to the wider societal underpinnings of European integration, which makes is particularly prone to draw a more holistic picture of Europeanization processes and its merits, crises, and drawbacks. Grand theories such as Durkheimian functionalism (Münch & Büttner 2006), Weber's institutionalism (Bach 2015) or Gramscian Marxist conflict theory (Hermann 2007) provide indispensable sociological frames of reference for our understanding of the Europeanization of the economy and society. To grasp the full complexity of European integration and disintegration, however, it is necessary to conceive of Europeanization as two intertwined processes: First, the reconfiguring of the European space with its distinct rules, norms, and values, and second, agents' struggles over the definition and enforcement of the means and ends of Europeanization. Such a theoretical framework is still lacking; Fligstein's (2008) and Bourdieu's (2005) accounts of the Europeanization and globalization of economic markets provide a promising starting point.

Didactical Section

Key Learning Points

- The sociology of European economic and social integration draws attention to the wider societal underpinnings of European integration.
- Economic markets are not a-historic, ideal-type entities as conceived by economics, but socially embedded entities and societal spheres that have their own rules, norms, and practices.
- Besides sociological grand theories and conventional theorizing in EU studies, social field theories have become important explanatory frameworks in the sociology of European integration.

Glossary

Bretton Woods System: The Bretton Woods System was the first, fully negotiated, monetary order intended to govern monetary relations among independent states.

Eurosclerosis: The term refers to economic stagnation that can result from excessive regulation, labor market rigidities, and overly generous welfare policies.

Negative integration: Measures increasing market integration by eliminating national restraints on trade and distortions of competition.

Neo-functionalism: The theory holds in the widest sense that regional integration is the result of past integration.

Positive integration: The establishment of common European policies to shape the conditions under which markets operate.

Social field: An arena of social interaction where organized individuals and groups routinely interact under a set of shared understandings about the nature of the goals of the field, the rules governing social interaction, who has power and why, and how actors make sense of one another's actions.

Spill-over: The concept of spill-over is built on the assumption that the integration in one policy-area spills over into others.

Further Readings

Bourdieu, P., 2015: *The social structures of the economy*. Cambridge: Polity.

Fligstein, N., 2008: *Euroclash: the EU, European identity, and the future of Europe*. Oxford: Oxford University Press.

Fligstein, N. & F. Merand, 2002: Globalization or Europeanization? Evidence on the European economy since 1980. *Acta Sociologica* 45(1):7–22.

Münch, R. & S. Büttner, 2006: Die europäische Teilung der Arbeit. Was können wir von Emile Durkheim lernen? In: Heidenreich, M. (ed.), *Die Europäisierung sozialer Ungleichheit: zur transnationalen Klassen- und Sozialstrukturanalyse*, pp. 65–107. Frankfurt: Campus Verlag.

Pernicka, S., V. Glassner, N. Dittmar & K. Neundlinger, 2019: The contested Europeanisation of collective bargaining fields. In: Heidenreich, M. (ed.), *Horizontal Europeanisation. The transnationalization of daily life and social fields in Europe*, pp. 119–128. London: Routledge.

Streeck, W., 2017: *Buying time. The delayed crisis of democratic capitalism*. New York: Verso, 2nd edition.

Additional Web-Sources

European Commission, Economic and Financial Affairs: https://ec.europa.eu/economy_fi nance/publications/european_economy/index_en.htm

European Foundation for the Improvement of Living and Working Conditions: https://www. eurofound.europa.eu/

Round Table of Industrialists: https://ert.eu/

The European Trade Union Institute: https://www.etui.org/

References

Aspers, P., & J. Beckert, 2017: Märkte. In: Maurer, A. (ed.), *Handbuch der Wirtschaftssoziologie*, pp. 215–240. Wiesbaden: Springer.

Bach, M., 2015: *Europa ohne Gesellschaft Politische Soziologie der Europäischen Integration*. Wiesbaden: Springer, 2nd edition.

Beck, U. & E. Grande, 2004: *Das kosmopolitische Europa Gesellschaft und Politik in der zweiten Moderne*. Frankfurt a.M.: Suhrkamp.

Berend, I. T., 2016: *The history of European integration: a new perspective*. London and New York: Routledge.

Bourdieu, P., 2005: *The social structures of the economy*. Cambridge: Polity.

Börzel, T. A. & T. Risse, 2009: The transformative power of Europe: The European Union and the diffusion of ideas. *KFG Working Paper* No. 1. Berlin: FU Berlin.

Bücker, A. & W. Warneck (eds.), 2010: *Viking-Laval-Rüffert: consequences and policy perspectives*. Bruxelles: ETUI.

Büttner, S. M. & L. M. Leopold, 2016: A 'new spirit' of public policy? The project world of EU funding. *European Journal of Cultural and Political Sociology* 3(1):41–71.

Clifton, J., F. Comín, & D. Díaz Fuentes, 2006: Privatizing public enterprises in the European Union 1960–2002: ideological, pragmatic, inevitable? *Journal of European Public Policy* 13(5):736–756.

Durkheim, É., [1902] 2013: *The division of labour in society*. Houndmills: Palgrave, 2nd edition.

Eichengreen, B. & A. Boltho, 2010: The economic impact of European integration. In: Broadberry, S. & K. H. O'Rourke (eds.), *Cambridge Economic History of Modern Europe – Volume 2: 1870 to the Present*, pp. 267–295. Cambridge: Cambridge University Press.

European Council, 2000: Lisabon European Council 23 and 24 March 2000. Presidency Conclusions. https://www.europarl.europa.eu/summits/lis1_en.htm (accessed February 11, 2021).

Falkner, G., 1998: *EU social policy in the 1990s: towards a corporatist policy community, Routledge research in European public policy*. London and New York: Routledge.

Favell, A. & V. Guiraudon, 2011: Sociology of the European Union: An Introduction. In: Favell, A. & V. Guiraudon (eds.), *Sociology of the European Union*, pp. 1–24. Houndmills: Palgrave.

Fligstein, N., 2008: *Euroclash: the EU, European identity, and the future of Europe*. Oxford: Oxford University Press.

Fligstein, N. & L. Dauter, 2007: The Sociology of Markets. *Annual Review of Sociology* 33:105–28.

Fligstein, N. & D. McAdam, 2011: Toward a General Theory of Strategic Action Fields. *Sociological Theory* 29(1):1–26.

Fligstein, N. & F. Merand, 2002: Globalization or Europeanization? Evidence on the European economy since 1980. *Acta Sociologica* 45(1):7–22.

Granovetter, M., 1985: Economic action and social structure: The problem of embeddedness. *American Journal of Sociology* 91(3):481–510.

Green Cowles, M., 1995: Setting the agenda for a new Europe: The ERT and EC 1992. *Journal of Common Market Studies* 33(4):501–526.

Griffiths, R. T. (ed.), 2014: *Under the shadow of stagflation-European integration in the 1970s*. Oxford: Oxford University Press.

Gröning, S., C. de la Rubia & T. Straubhaar, 2020: On the Remeasurement of International Trade in the Age of Digital Globalisation. In: Klasen, A. (ed.), *The Handbook of Global Trade Policy*, pp. 47–78. Hoboken, NJ: John Wiley & Sons.

Haas, E. B., 1958: *The uniting of Europe political, social and economical forces, 1950–1957*. Notre Dame, Indiana: University of Notre Dame Press.

Heidenreich, M. (ed.), 2019: *Horizontal Europeanisation: the transnationalisation of daily life and social fields in Europe*. Abingdon, Oxon, New York, NY: Routledge.

Heidenreich, M., J. Delhey, C. Lahusen, J. Gerhards, S. Mau, R. Münch & S. Pernicka, 2012: Europäische Vergesellschaftungsprozesse. Horizontale Europäisierung zwischen nationalstaatlicher und globaler Vergesellschaftung. WorkingPaper 1 of the DFG Research Unit 'Horizontal Europeanisation: An emerging social entity between national and global scales'.

Hermann, C., 2007: Neoliberalism in the European Union. *Studies in Political Economy*, 79(1): 61–90.

Keller, B., 2008: *Einführung in die Arbeitspolitik* Arbeitsbeziehungen *und Arbeitsmarkt in sozialwissenschaftlicher Perspektive*. München: Oldenbourg, 7th edition.

Kohler-Koch, B. & R. Eising (eds.), 1999: *The transformation of governance in the European Union, Routledge/ECPR studies in European political science*. London and New York: Routledge.

Lindert, P. H. & J. G. Williamson, 2003: Does globalization make the world more unequal? In: Bordo, M. D., A. M. Taylor & J. G. Williamson (eds.), *Globalization in historical perspective*, pp. 227–276. Chicago: University of Chicago Press.

Mau, S. & R. Verwiebe: 2010. *European societies: mapping structure and change*. Bristol U.K. and Portland OR: Policy Press.

Münch, R. & S. Büttner, 2006: Die europäische Teilung der Arbeit. Was können wir von Emile Durkheim lernen? In: Heidenreich, M. (ed.), *Die Europäisierung sozialer Ungleichheit: zur transnationalen Klassen- und Sozialstrukturanalyse*, pp. 65–107. Frankfurt am Main: Campus.

Pernicka, S., V. Glassner & N. Dittmar, 2018: The restructuring of employment relations in social services between transnational competition and coordination. *Österreichische Zeitschrift für Soziologie* Sonderheft, 43(1. Suppl.):93–116.

Pernicka, S. & C. Lahusen, 2018: Editorial. Power and counter-power in the transnational restructuring of social spaces and social fields in Europe. *Österreichische Zeitschrift für Soziologie* Sonderheft, 43(1. Suppl.):1–11.

Pernicka, S. & V. Glassner, 2019: The Europeanisation of wage bargaining coordination. In: Kiess, J. M. & M. Seeliger (eds.), *Trade Unions and European Integration: A Question of Optimism and Pessimism?* London and New York: Routledge.

Pernicka, S., V. Glassner, N. Dittmar & K. Neundlinger, 2019: The contested Europeanization of collective bargaining fields. In: Heidenreich, M. (ed.), *Horizontale Europeanization. The Transnationalisation of Daily Life and Social Fields in Europe*, pp. 119–128. London: Routledge.

Polanyi, K., [1944] 2002: *The Great Transformation – The Political and Economic Origins of Our Time*. Boston: Beacon Press.

Sandholtz, W. & A. Stone Sweet (eds.), 1998: *European integration and supranational governance*. Oxford and New York: Oxford University Press.

Scharpf, F. W., 1996: Negative and Positive Integration in the Political Economy of European Welfare States. In: Marks G., F. W. Scharpf, P. C. Schmitter & W. Streeck (eds.), *Governance in the European Union*, pp. 15–39. London and Thousand Oaks.: SAGE.

Scharpf, F. W., 1999: *Governing in Europe: effective and democratic?* Oxford: Oxford University Press.

Scharpf, F. W., 2010: The asymmetry of European integration, or why the EU cannot be a 'social market economy'. *Socio-Economic Review* 8(2):211–250.

Schuman Declaration, [1950] 2011: Declaration of 9th may 1950 delivered by R. Schuman. In: Foundation Robert Schuman (ed.), *European Issue no.204 10th may 2011*.

Smith, A., [1776] 1989: *An inquiry into the nature and causes of the wealth of nations*. Chicago: University of Chicago Press.

Stone Sweet, A., 2004: *The judicial construction of Europe*. Oxford: Oxford University Press.

Streeck, W., 2009: Review symposium on N. Fligstein Euroclash: The EU, European identity and the future of Europe. *Socio-Economic Review* 7:545–552.

Streeck, W., 2015: Why the Euro divides Europe. *New Left Review* 95. https://newleftreview.org/issues/ii95/articles/wolfgang-streeck-why-the-euro-divides-europe (accessed February 09, 2021).

Swedberg, R., 2011: The economic sociologies of Pierre Bourdieu. *Cultural sociology* 5(1):67–82.

Weber, M., [1922] 1978: *Economy and society: an outline of interpretive sociology.* G. Roth and C. Wittich (eds.). 2 vols. Berkeley: University of California Press.

Sabine Frerichs & Fernando Losada

8 Europeanization and Law: Integration through Law and its Limits

European integration is a political and economic process, which can be depicted in different terms. From a political point of view, the integration process consists in "the voluntary creation and maintenance of [shared] regional institutions" by national governments in different policy areas (Bickerton & Zielonka 2011: 842). From an economic point of view, integration is about "the gradual elimination of economic frontiers" between member states, that is, market integration and, by extension, monetary integration (Molle 2006: 4). The creation of a European polity and economy has been promoted by law, in particular by legislation and adjudication in supranational decision-making bodies. The concept of 'integration through law' highlights the role of law as a means of economic and political integration, and of legal action as a driving force.

To understand the critical role played by law in European integration, it is necessary to know about some of the basic features of the European Union (EU/Union). First, to promote shared policy goals the EU member states conferred concrete powers (competences) on the Union by signing international treaties. Second, EU institutions make use of these limited competences to adopt decisions and legislate, creating European law. And third, the member states apply and implement European law in their territories by way of national institutions and procedures. Therefore, law works as an interface between the member states' abstract policy goals and their collective specification at EU level, and subsequently between stipulated European policies and their actual national implementation.

The political, economic, and legal process of European integration is also sociologically relevant. This is not only the case because the integration process involves a social dimension in terms of how it affects the lifeworld of the people, their relations to each other, and their wellbeing. Rather, the European process of market- and polity-building also entails a more comprehensive process of society-building, or a re-ordering of societies on a transnational scale. Even though sociology has from the outset been concerned with phenomena of integration and disintegration, the field of European integration studies has long been dominated by economic, political, and legal theories. A key contribution of the sociology of Europeanization is to (re)interpret the integration process in terms of transnational social interaction and society-building. Integration through law forms part of this.

https://doi.org/10.1515/9783110673630-008

Law and Policymaking in the EU: Four Modes of Integration Compared

Law and policymaking in the European Union involve different institutions. At the core of the European polity stand the European Commission (an administrative organ of the EU with the right of legislative initiative), the Council of Ministers (a decision-making body comprising national ministers responsible for their respective departments) and the European Parliament (a decision-making body elected by EU citizens in pan-European elections). These institutions represent the general European interest, the interest of the member states and the interest of the European people, respectively. In one way or the other, these institutions are involved in the adoption of decisions in the hugely different substantive areas that the EU deals with, from competition law to judicial cooperation in criminal matters, from citizenship to foreign policy – to name but a few. The decision-making procedures differ between policy fields, with institutional setup and voting rules representing the particular mix of interests relevant to each field (Majone 2005). Based on these features, it is possible to distinguish four modes, or 'methods', of integration: the *Community method*, the *intergovernmental method*, the *monetary method*, and the *coordinative method* (see Table 8.1).

Historically, the **Community method** comes first. This describes the way in which the European institutions interact in matters of the internal market. The Commission has the right of legislative initiative, the Council and European Parliament co-decide, while interpretation of what is promulgated as European law rests with the **Court of Justice of the EU (CJEU)**, which has come to play a pro-integrative role. This mode of decision-making prevailed during the formative stages of the EU, or European Community as it was originally called. It reached its zenith in the Single European Act (1986), which aimed at completion of the internal market encompassing free movement of goods, services, persons, and capital.

Since then, the integration project has become more diverse. The Maastricht Treaty (1992) broadened the focus of integration beyond the internal market project into areas where core state powers are involved, such as military force, police power, border control, public revenue, and administrative power (Genschel & Jachtenfuchs 2014). Important markers of this new layer of integration are the establishment of European citizenship, a common currency (the Euro), and shared foreign policy. Adding these policy areas increased not only the number of competences but also gave rise to the other three decision-making methods.

Most prominently, the Maastricht Treaty introduced the *intergovernmental method* in some of the new policy fields. This decision-making method is led by the Council of Ministers and the European Council (a distinct decision-making

Table 8.1: The four modes of integration and their features.

	Institutional setup	Field	Competences	Outcome
Community method	Commission, European Parliament, Council of Ministers	Internal market	Shared (EU law acts have priority)	Law
Intergovernmental method	European Council, Council of Ministers	Common Foreign and Security Policy	National (loose EU framework for policy alignment)	Political decisions
Monetary method	European System of Central Banks (European Central Bank and National Central Banks)	Monetary policy	Exclusively European	Monetary policy decisions
Coordinative method	Member States, coordinated at Eurogroup (informal meeting of national Economy and Finance Ministers), Commission	Fiscal policy	National (strict EU framework for policy coordination)	Recommendations

body consisting of national heads of government or state), with the remaining institutions having a much more limited role. The intergovernmental mode of decision-making reflects the intricate link between the new policy areas and core national competences – for instance, common foreign, security and defense policy (Puetter 2014).

Moreover, the Maastricht Treaty also established the legal foundations for Economic and Monetary Union (EMU), which came to rest on the other two decision-making methods mentioned. On the one hand, the ***monetary method*** (Losada Fraga 2009: Ch. 5) describes decision-making on monetary policy by the European System of Central Banks. The particular institutional setting for this policy is specifically aimed at ensuring price stability. On the other hand, the ***coordinative method*** (Dawson 2015: 50–53) gives shape to the coordination of economic policies, which became crucial once a single currency was established. Since fiscal policymaking remains a national competence, this decision-making method came into being as a soft-law approach – the so-called open method of coordination – with moral rather than legal, and discretional rather than automatic sanctions. In response to the European sovereign debt crisis (or Eurozone crisis) in the 2010s, this regime was 'hardened', reflecting a need for more efficient means of supranational coordination and intervention to bring national economic policies into line with the financial stability requirements of the common currency.

Hence, in its early decades, when the integration project focused on **market integration**, the Community method reigned as a law-making procedure. This decision-making method remains central for the governance of the internal market. However, in the EU of today, foreign relations and **monetary integration** have become important policy areas, which bring other modes of decision-making to the fore. Moreover, whereas legal interpretation by the CJEU exerted great influence in the context of market integration, its role is less accentuated regarding foreign relations and monetary integration.

This qualification is relevant for the narrative dealt with in this chapter: that European integration proceeded as 'integration through law'. Accordingly, 'judicial knowledge' (*jurisprudence*), 'authority' (*jurisdiction*), and 'legal argumentation' (*justification*) were key elements, or ingredients, of Europeanization. The fact that the CJEU acted as a driving force in central areas and stages of the integration process left a strong imprint on the understanding of the European polity. In this regard, some scholars even speak of the "judicial construction of Europe" (Stone Sweet 2004).

Integration through Law as Political Strategy and Theoretical Approach

What is implied by referring to the process of European integration as 'integration through law'? On the one hand, this label seeks to capture the observable reality of European integration; on the other hand, it refers to a normative project advanced by legal practitioners and scholars. Avbelj (2011: 29) speaks of the "double nature" of integration through law as a "policy conception" and an "academic project".

Integration through Law as a Political Strategy

As a policy conception, integration through law describes a specific strategy of European integration. Accordingly, it is characteristic of the European project that it proceeds through the medium of law, is endowed with the rational authority of law, and linked with practices of adjudication. Law, as it is understood in this context, is backed by the enforcement powers of the state. Private law structures relations between private actors, provides economic transactions with stability, and makes business life more predictable. Public law regulates relations between legal subjects and the sovereign; it stipulates the rights of individuals, including economic and political freedoms, and their duties towards the state, such as to comply with the law and the liability to pay taxes.

In the European context, the law of the nation state is superimposed by EU law, which adds an extra layer of jurisdiction. This was a novelty at the time: instead of solving legal conflicts by means of retaliation or externalizing them to the International Court of Justice, the foundational Treaties of what later became the EU established an internal court. Access to the CJEU was granted by several legal remedies, which from the outset included the so-called 'preliminary ruling' procedure. This procedure allowed ordinary national courts to address questions about the validity and interpretation of EU law directly to the CJEU.

Located at the intersection between national legal orders and the provisions of the European Treaties, preliminary ruling came to play a prominent role in the integration process. It forms the basis of landmark decisions by the CJEU, which established certain legal principles, or doctrines, which, in turn, furthered integration through law (see Table 8.2). This includes, first and foremost, the doctrines of *supremacy* and *direct effect*, which helped to establish an effective supranational legal order: in crucial judgments the CJEU clarified the ability of EU law to endow private actors with rights that they could directly enforce through ordinary courts ('direct effect') and the formal superiority of EU law in the case of conflicts with national law ('supremacy'). Accordingly, national courts are granted the power to disregard national law if necessary to guarantee the 'full effectiveness' of EU law.

The innovative legal setup of the Treaties effectively created a triangular relation between national courts, private economic actors and the CJEU. This allowed economic actors and national courts to become active in promoting the development of European case law. That is, economic actors were entitled by EU law to free movement and could claim these rights in ordinary courts; and for their part, national judges could turn to the CJEU in the preliminary ruling procedure to clarify the validity and interpretation of EU law in concrete cases. Access by economic actors to the CJEU through ordinary courts proved to be an effective (private) enforcement mechanism of European law, which complements the Commission's task of monitoring legal compliance by the member states.

Over time CJEU decisions in specific cases became general doctrines. Acceptance of these doctrines by national courts opened the way to their application to a much wider range of substantive questions of European law. This was premised on acquiescence by the member states. When national political representatives gained awareness of the scope and implications of the new legal order, they

Table 8.2: Milestones of integration through law in CJEU case law.

Principle	Case	Explanation
Direct effect	26/62 – *Van Gend en Loos* (5 February 1963)	Ability of EU law to entitle private actors with rights that they could directly enforce through ordinary courts.
Supremacy (or primacy)	6/64 – *Flaminio Costa vs. ENEL* (15 July 1964)	Formal superiority of European law in case of conflicts with national law.
Full effectiveness	106/77 – *Simmenthal* (9 March 1978)	When applying European law national courts are entitled to disregard contradicting national provisions.
Mutual recognition	C-120/78 – *Cassis de Dijon* (20 February 1979)	In the absence of European legislation, products lawfully marketed in one Member State can be sold in other member states.
Rule of law	C-294/83 – *Les Verts vs European Parliament* (23 April 1983)	Foundational character of the rule of law for the integration project. The CJEU explicitly recognizes that "the [EU] is a Community based on the rule of law".
Member State liability	C-6/90 and C-9/90 – *Francovich and Bonifaci* (19 November 1991)	A State must be liable for loss and damage caused to individuals resulting from breaches of European law for which the State can be held responsible.
	C-46/93 and C-48-93 – *Brasserie du Pêcheur* (5 March 1996)	Conditions under which the State may incur liability for acts and omissions of the national legislature contrary to EU law.
	C-224/01 – *Köbler vs Austria* (30 September 2003)	Judicial power can be liable under *Francovich* principles, but only "in the exceptional case where the court has manifestly infringed the applicable law". A deliberate refusal to follow EU law would result in liability.

could not overrule the respective judgments without questioning their own legal systems, which had become intertwined with European law (Alter 2001).

As final interpreter of European rights, the CJEU was able to "reveal" and gradually develop the meaning of EU law (Chalmers & Barroso 2014: 109). Instead of relying on European legislation promoting harmonization of national laws (positive integration), the doctrines of supremacy and direct effect allowed national courts to implement market freedoms and competition law in the member states based on the Treaties only (negative integration) (Scharpf

1996). European integration through law proceeded as "integration through courts" (Sciarra 2001).

This became particularly striking in the case law advancing the free movement of goods in the 1970s (Maduro 1998). In this area, the Court established the doctrine of *mutual recognition*. Accordingly, in the absence of EU legislation, products lawfully marketed in one Member State can be sold in other member states – even if they do not comply with the national technical rules in force in those member states. Given its largely pro-integrative effects, adjudication by the CJEU offered an alternative to political bargaining in EU legislative bodies to promote integration.

A premise for this strategy to work is the observance of EU law in all member states, despite occasional national disagreement with specific outcomes. For this reason, the Treaties require member states' compliance with EU law by way of the principle of loyalty (Klamert 2014). Additionally, the CJEU adopted several measures to further guarantee compliance. First, it explicitly declared that the EU is based on the rule of law, ensuring that once a measure of EU law is enacted political disagreements must be articulated through legal remedies and according to the rationale of law (the *rule of law* principle). To further increase enforceability, the CJEU established the principle of *Member State liability* for damage caused to individuals resulting from breaches of EU law. Accordingly, the member states are considered responsible even when a violation is caused by the legislative branch (lack of implementation) or the judicial branch (non-effective application). With this doctrine, the CJEU created the ultimate legal mechanism to make enforcement of European law via private claimants effective.

Integration through Law as a Theoretical Approach

Integration through law also describes a paradigm in the academic field of European studies, which goes back to the 'Florence Integration Project' launched at the European University Institute in 1981. Scholars in this project shared a supranational vision of Europe, which could be promoted by means of law (Cappelletti et al. 1986). Building on this line of scholarship, Dehousse & Weiler (1990: 243) famously described law as "both the object and agent of integration". When national law is Europeanized, law is the object of integration; but it is also the agent of integration in that this is largely a "law-making exercise" (Dehousse & Weiler 1990: 243). Based on this distinction, it has been argued that law is not only a dependent variable of political and economic integration, implying "integration *of* law", but also an independent variable shaping the integration process, which is "integration *through* law" properly understood (de Búrca 2005: 313–314, original emphasis).

The perspective became notable beyond the 'Florence project' and has been taken up in different strands of scholarship within the field of European studies. The classic distinction is between 'intergovernmentalist' and 'neofunctionalist' approaches to European integration. These labels refer to two different ways of interpreting the integration project: as one negotiated between governments, with Member State interests playing a major role, or as one which develops a life of its own, beyond what the member states could foresee. Hence, intergovernmentalist approaches to European integration focus on the gate-keeping function of Member State governments as "Masters of the Treaties", who follow their own self-interest (Moravcsik 1998). In contrast, neofunctionalist approaches assume that a new social system is emerging, in which functional interdependencies between different social spheres lead to 'spillover effects', for example from one economic sector or policy area to the next (Haas [1958] 2004). This idea of complex social systems, in which the different parts are interconnected, has a sociological pedigree (Favell & Guiraudon 2011: 4–5). The 'integration through law' paradigm builds on the legacy of the neofunctionalist approach. Emphasis is laid on how the dynamic of legal integration could unfold in the interplay of sub- and supranational actors and institutions – to a certain extent bypassing political decision-making on the member states' level.

This perspective is further developed in approaches that consider the integration process from an 'institutionalist' point of view. The idea that 'institutions matter' for an understanding of social action and interaction is inherent to the sociological discipline but also used beyond. The institutionalist perspective has been applied to the relationship between the member states and the CJEU to explain why the latter might have been able to go beyond what was initially intended by the member states. According to one interpretation, the member states delegated limited tasks to the CJEU, namely to ensure that the European Treaties and the legislation are interpreted uniformly. However, given its position in the institutional system of the EU, the Court developed a preference for greater integration, which turned it into an 'engine of integration' alongside other supranational actors (Pollack 2003). In another interpretation, the institutionalist perspective is applied to the whole system of relations between sub- and supranational actors in the EU. Integration is depicted "as a dynamic, self-sustaining, causal system", which involves "firms engaged in cross-border trade", "litigants", "national judges", "the [CJEU]", "lobbying groups", and "[EU] officials in Brussels" (Fligstein & Stone Sweet 2002: 1209–1216). Interaction of these actors in an institutional and legal context supportive of integration explains how integration could proceed.

The Concept of Law in 'Integration through Law'

The strategy of integration through law is based on an image of "law's *neutrality* in the face of rival political and moral preferences" (Mac Amhlaigh 2011: 75, original emphasis). As an instrument of integration, law appears to be more of a technical than a political nature. This is, in part, the effect of using legal discourse: to matter before the courts, political interests must be translated into legal arguments. Moreover, a "politics of de-politicization" stands behind using law as a means of promoting European integration (Augenstein & Dawson 2011: 2). The fact that integration through law could avoid impasses between the member states does not make it less political in its outcomes. The gist of this strategy has been condensed as follows: "[L]aw functions both as mask and shield. It hides and protects the promotion of one particular set of political objectives against contending objectives in the purely political sphere." (Burley & Mattli 1993: 72)

This instrumentalist account of the role of law in European integration is linked with a concept of law that draws a line between the validity of the law as such and its legitimacy on moral or political grounds. This conception is known as legal positivism, according to which whatever is enacted and enforced as law is valid as such, and not what is deemed legitimate according to certain ideals or ideologies. While such an understanding of law may have helped to establish the European polity "as an autonomous legal system in its own right" (Augenstein 2011: 103), it is by no means uncontested. Indeed, law's quality as an agent of integration could also be interpreted in terms of its ability "to translate norm into fact and fact into norm" (Everson & Eisner 2007: 98). This view emphasizes law's inherent link with questions of legitimacy and justice, which to some extent, are downplayed in the legal-positivist approach.

In recent decades, a growing number of critics have opposed using European law as a 'mask and shield' for certain political objectives. Instead, they are interested in the potential of law to provide the European polity with legitimacy, and to promote a shared identity between the European people (Augenstein 2011). This links them with social-constructivist accounts of European integration, which have been on the rise in the field of European studies and international relations more generally (Favell & Guiraudon 2011: 8). Focusing on the role of norms, values, symbols, and identities in explaining behavior, including by collective actors such as the member states, they emphasize law's cultural qualities over its technical effects in promoting integration.

Sociological Approaches to Studying the Role of Law in European Integration

Sociology can contribute in several ways to an understanding of the role of law in the process of European integration and in the constitution of the European polity. What was early on depicted as a 'community of law' (*Rechtsgemeinschaft*) can also be interpreted in sociological terms (Frerichs 2008). Basically, this can be achieved in two ways. One way is to build on and enrich socio-legal approaches that emphasize the social context of European law, which is usually neglected in doctrinal legal scholarship. This includes enquiries into the social validity of the law in force. The other way is to consider European integration from the viewpoint of theories of societal integration, which originally aimed at understanding modern national societies and also considered the role of law in this respect. By expanding these theories to the European level, European integration can be depicted as a project of society-building on a transnational scale, which uses law as its means.

Considering Law's Normative and Empirical Validity

The field of European studies largely reflects a division of labor in the social sciences, which credits lawyers with the normative study of law's content and puts other social scientists – economists, political scientists, historians, and sociologists – in charge of the empirical study of law's context. In legal scholarship, law's content is clearly key and interpreted in its own right. In this regard, one can speak of law as doctrine, or legal dogmatics. In other social sciences, an evaluation of law's content is often subordinated to analysis of its political, economic, historical, and social context. Law as such may be regarded as a dependent variable only.

This state of the field has been criticized as "the detachment of legal reasoning from empirical causalities, on the one hand, and the normative complacency of social sciences, on the other" (Joerges & Kreuder-Sonnen 2017: 138). Accordingly, legal scholars could not, or should not, leave aside the social forces behind the law, and other social scientists could not, or should not, hide behind the apparent neutrality of their observations. The concern behind this position is that the hidden politics of the law which served the integration process may also undermine the legitimacy of the European polity. In contrast, scholars who adopt a law-in-context approach to European law (Snyder 1995) often combine normative and empirical perspectives.

This debate is informed by the distinction of 'Is' and 'Ought', a frequent reference in the philosophy of science. Based on this, Kelsen (2002), a jurist and legal philosopher, drew a line between legal and sociological method. Similarly, Weber (1978), one of the founding figures of the sociological discipline, separated the normative validity of legal propositions, which is the subject of legal dogmatics, from their empirical validity, which would be the subject of sociological analysis. Accordingly, law's empirical validity can be found in the degree to which legal norms are accepted, acted upon, and enforced. This includes actors' motivations to follow the law: be it by the threat of sanctions (instrumental rationality) or a belief in the legitimacy of the legal order in place (value rationality). Following Weber, it is not only the effectiveness of enforcement powers that makes law empirically valid but also the prevalence of beliefs in its legitimacy.

A related distinction is between *internal* and *external* points of view. For Hart (1961: 88–89), a legal philosopher, the internal point of view was prerequisite to understanding the legal rules and "the normative structure of society", whereas the external point of view would ultimately account for rule-following behavior "in terms of observable regularities" only. While the observer perspective is clearly important for the empirical study of law, sociology is also an interpretive discipline, which is interested in the meaning of law from the perspective of legal professionals or laypersons. In Hart's terms, "the observer may, without accepting the rules himself, assert that the group accepts the rules, and thus may from outside refer to the way in which *they* are concerned with them from the internal point of view" (1961: 89, original emphasis).

Hence, a sociological understanding of law is not left with the outsider perspective only but can also make sense of the law from the inside: the perspective of the legal community. In the present context, this is the European community of law. It has been argued that "at least in the long run, integration *through* law in the European Union will only be effective if positive legal rules connect with a socio-cultural environment that can bolster their claim to social validity" (Augenstein 2011: 102, original emphasis). Put differently, a community of law is, at best, also a community of shared values and beliefs pertaining to the law in force.

In keeping with this perspective, social-constructivist approaches in European studies are concerned with the "socialization effects" (Risse 2009: 149) which EU membership and, by implication, European law, entail. Accordingly, European citizens and the member states would not evaluate the effects of European law and policies based on their predefined interests and material outcomes only. Instead, socialization into the European community of law goes hand in hand with internalization of its formal and informal norms, and successive adaptation of individual interests and collective identities towards norm conformity. This perspective may explain how the European community of law turned from a political objective into societal practice.

However, recent scholarship warns against the opposite effect: a legitimacy crisis of European law (Joerges 2016). This may be observed in increasing reservations by the member states and even popular resistance against the enforcement of EU law, such as in the context of the Eurozone crisis. A reason can be seen in the overburdening of legal structures created for market integration with policy questions relevant to monetary integration. A widening gap between the law that is positively enforced and the law that is accepted as legitimate puts the European polity at risk. Applying Weber's perspective, legal subjects will become more instrumentally rational and less value-rational in orientation. Voluntary compliance diminishes and law's validity increasingly depends on actual enforcement.

Applying Theories of Societal Integration to Europe

While socio-legal research is primarily concerned with the quality of law in the European context, as well as its social conditions and effects, sociologists take a more comprehensive approach to European integration as a process of association and society-building on the transnational scale. Law is recognized as a relevant factor in promoting integration. Substantively, the European project is seen as an extension of building the modern nation state and creating national societies in its wake. Theories once developed to understanding the foundations and functioning of modern societies are applied and adapted to a European society in the making and transnational processes more generally.

From the outset, questions of social order and societal integration have stood at the forefront of sociological theorizing. Classical sociologists like Marx, Durkheim, and Weber responded to massive transformations in the demographic, political and economic structure of their surrounding societies and sought to come to grips with processes of differentiation, rationalization, and individualization, which characterize modern societies. A common assumption in theories of modernization is that there has been a shift in prevailing modes of integration, which distinguishes modern societies from more traditional ones. This is captured by contrasting ideal types of 'community' (*Gemeinschaft*) and 'association' (*Gesellschaft*), concrete and abstract forms of solidarity, religious and secular sources of authority, and other distinctions. Even though reality does not easily fit such dichotomies, they help to bring out differences between societies in different times and places. The relevant element here is that modern societies are characterized by an accentuated role of law as a means of integration.

Sociological theories of integration may focus on *systems integration* or *social integration*. As defined by Lockwood, systems integration refers to the "orderly or conflictual relationships between the *parts* [. . .] of a social system" and social integration to the "orderly or conflictual relationships between the *actors*" (1992: 400, original emphasis). Scholars concerned with systems integration typically consider society from a macro-analytical point of view, and often on a high level of abstraction. A key question is how societies operate under conditions of functional differentiation, in which different social spheres or subsystems are specialized in different tasks. In contrast, scholars studying social integration are more microanalytical in orientation and take the perspective of concrete or average individuals into account. What matters to them is actors' moral orientation towards others, which may vary considerably between different social contexts.

Moreover, Lockwood (1992: 402, fn. 10) also pointed to the "interrelationships of 'normative' and 'realistic' elements of social systems". Analysis of complex social phenomena, which not only work behind our backs but also through our minds, requires combining inside and outside perspectives. An example of this is the social validity of law, which can only be accurately assessed if the internal point of view is taken as seriously as the external point of view. Generally speaking, processes of social ordering and integration – whether national or transnational – can be approached from both their material or objective side and their symbolic or (inter)subjective side.

More comprehensive sociological theories speak to all these dimensions: macro and micro, objective and subjective (see Chapter 2 in this volume). With this complexity, they also enrich the field of European studies and provide an alternative to rational-choice theory. The rational-choice approach, which focuses on individual decision-making and utility calculations by private and public actors, is still standard in much of economics and political science, also featuring prominently in the field of international relations and European studies. This leads to an understanding of regional cooperation and/or integration as proceeding based on self-interest and instrumental rationality, which downplays the structural and normative context of European integration, as well as integration through law in particular.

To illustrate somewhat richer understandings of European integration, one can draw on different sociological traditions, which are relevant also outside the field of European studies (Frerichs 2008, 2018). This includes structural functionalism, discourse theory, and field theory, which relate to the names of Talcott Parsons, Jürgen Habermas, and Pierre Bourdieu, respectively. All three approaches, combining the levels of systems integration and social integration, have been applied to European integration, and shed light on the role of law in this context. All of them also acknowledge that as a medium of integration law must be studied both from without and within.

Sociological Approaches Emphasizing the Role of Law

The first approach reflects the tradition of *structural functionalism*, or the 'normative paradigm' in sociology, which emphasizes the integrative effect of shared norms and values. In modern society, this normative core is also expressed in the rules and principles of the legal system. This yields a macro-sociological account of integration through law, which can be summarized as follows: "[T]he integration of society would, first of all, be the result of shared values and norms, especially legal norms, which are internalized and thus ensure conformity of action" (Rottleuthner 1999: 408, translation by authors). In Parsons' (2007) work, the integrative function was seen in the subsystem of the 'societal community', which can be equated with 'civil society', or a 'legal community', broadly understood as a community not of legal professionals but of all citizens. At the core is legal solidarity, an abstract form of solidarity that works on the level of nation states and beyond.

Münch (2008) argues that law also acts as an integrative force on the European level, and offers a sociological response to the 'integration through law' paradigm. His account of European integration is informed by Parsons' work and draws on Durkheim's (1964) famous study *The Division of Labor in Society*. Accordingly, the division of labor promotes a new form of ('organic') solidarity, which distinguishes modern societies from more traditional ones. Münch applies this idea to how market integration on the European scale furthers solidarity across national boundary lines. More specifically, he explores how the case law of the CJEU indicates a change in solidarity which is associated with, and expressed in, moving from national legal communities to the European community of law. The shift is illustrated by consolidation of the principle of non-discrimination in European law, which underpins market integration and can be regarded as an important premise for creating a societal community on the European scale: "Non-discrimination of non-nationals has become the cornerstone of the emerging European society, which acknowledges equal rights of nationals and non-nationals across national borders." (Münch 2008: 531)

The second approach is Habermas' *discourse theory of law*, which has its roots in critical theory: a school of thought that exposes the negative effects of capitalist society on human freedom and reason, and makes questions of truth, morality, and justice amenable to sociological analysis by turning to their social conditions. Advancing this approach, Habermas focuses on the communicative rationality embodied in language, which can develop a binding force without resorting to external means of power. The condition is that people address each other on equal terms, consider all relevant arguments, and eventually arrive at a consensus. Such 'deliberation' is at the roots of democratic society – or at least is an ideal to strive for. Social integration would then not be premised on shared norms and values only but could also emerge from communicative action. Importantly, "[m]odern societies are integrated not only socially through values, norms, and mutual understanding, but also systemically through markets and the administrative use of power" (Habermas 1996: 39).

For Habermas, law plays an essential role: it connects the instrumental rationality of states and markets with the communicative rationality of the lifeworld, thus linking systems integration with social integration. The discourse-theoretical perspective combines internal and external points of view. On the one hand, it emphasizes the democratic ideals from which law derives its legitimacy; on the other hand, it also specifies the factual preconditions of deliberative practices in social reality. Law is understood as "a social category of mediation between facts and norms" (Habermas 1996: 1).

This approach is critical of the 'integration through law' paradigm since law is presented as a quasi-neutral technique applied by experts. Discourse theory aims to enhance the deliberative quality of European law by giving (more) space to processes of reasoning in law-making fora and the public sphere more generally: "The integration through law project – or law-mediated legitimacy in the EU – can only be secured through an alternative, albeit radical, proceduralization of the category of law" (Everson & Joerges 2012: 662–663). The normative premise is that the 'addressees' of law should also be able to perceive themselves as its 'authors', be it on the national or the European level. Only then would (formal) legality and legitimacy converge.

The third approach is inspired by Bourdieu's *theory of social fields*. Similar to systems-theoretical approaches, field theory is concerned with the macro-sociological level of systems integration, that is, the dynamics and interrelations of different social spheres. However, the concept of social fields is more flexible than that of systems. Moreover, field theory does not picture society as a normatively integrated whole. Instead, it links with the conflict-theoretical tradition, which highlights the conflicts and tensions inherent to society and brings phenomena of power and inequality to the fore. On the micro-sociological level, field theory works with the concept of 'habitus', which describes the interpretive schemes that individuals use to orient themselves in the world and to act in accordance with their social positions.

Regarding law, the question is how the juridical field is structured and how it relates to other social fields (including bureaucratic, political, economic), which likewise form part of the overarching field of power. Bourdieuhighlights that the juridical field has its own rules but also reflects principles of stratification which link it with neighboring fields. Hence, law and jurisprudence are neither as autonomous as assumed by legal formalists, who think of law in doctrinal terms only, nor as dependent on social forces as claimed by instrumentalist approaches, which ultimately reduce law to a means in power battles (Bourdieu 1987: 814–815).

Studies of the European legal field have focused on 'Euro-lawyering' (Vauchez & de Witte 2013). Accordingly, the state and development of European law is contested between lawyers of different origins and with different allegiances. However, in the heyday of integration through law the European legal community, which here consists of legal professionals only and not of ordinary citizens, appeared to be rather united by a certain esprit de corps: "While building a legal theory of Europe, the otherwise segmented and often antagonistic ensemble of Euro-implicated lawyers was [. . .] constituting itself *as a specific EC elite*" (Vauchez 2010: 27, original emphasis). In other words, EU-oriented legal scholars and practitioners formed a relatively cohesive social group, which shared the normative project to advance European integration by means of law. Over time, 'Euro-lawyering' has become more differentiated, and the normative consensus has waned.

The Limits of Integration through Law: The EU post-Maastricht until Today

Law is a means of economic and political integration. In the context of the Community method, supranational institutions were driving forces of the integration process: the European Commission with its monopoly of legislative initiative and the CJEU with its monopoly of legal interpretation. However, classic accounts of European integration, which center around integration through law, fall short of explaining the state of the Union today.

While successful in promoting market integration, integration through law is a success story that has become increasingly contested over time. Already with the Maastricht Treaty this strategy of integration became more contained. Member states did not want to allow the same dynamic of integration to unfold in other, more sensitive policy fields. Therefore, new competences conferred on the Union, specifically those dealing with core state powers, came under different decision-making procedures of a more intergovernmental character (Bickerton et al. 2015). In common foreign and security policy, judicial control is limited to procedural matters only (see Table 8.3). This leaves out any substantive questions which the CJEU could resolve by relying on mobilization of private actors and preliminary references by national courts.

Integration through law is also less effective in terms of monetary integration. The classic Community method is not the method of choice in this context. Decision-making in the EMU, even more so after the Eurozone crisis, can better be described as a combination of the monetary and 'hardened' coordinative method. The monetary method is the preserve of the European System of Central Banks, with the European Central Bank (ECB) at its core. The ECB enjoys considerable independence in pursuing monetary objectives but is also subject to the provisions of the Treaties. Thus, formally the CJEU can review the ECB's monetary policy. However, the substantive expertise of judges is much more debatable when controversial macroeconomic issues are involved than in purely legal conflicts. In turn, the coordinative method "combines highly centralized supranational intervention, particularly in budgetary policy, with intergovernmental control of key political decisions" (Dawson 2015: 43). This institutional setup reflects the heightened need for fiscal and economic policy coordination in the EMU, but it does not give much influence to the CJEU. The latter is constrained to procedural control, making it less powerful as a force for integration.

Table 8.3: Modes of decision-making and the role of the CJEU.

	Political decision-making (EU)		Judicial control (CJEU)	
	Supranational	**Intergovernmental**	**Substantive**	**Procedural**
Community method	Commission, European Parliament, Council of Ministers	–	Yes	Yes
Intergovernmental method	–	European Council, Council of Ministers	No	Yes
Monetary method	European System of Central Banks	–	Formally yes, but practically contested	Yes
Coordinative method	(Commission)	Member States, coordinated at Eurogroup	No	Yes

Altogether, the role of the CJEU is much more contained in the policy areas added with the Maastricht Treaty. This means that integration through law cannot unfold in the same way as in the realm of market integration, where the Court acted as a pacemaker. Moreover, integration through law is premised on masking the political dimension of law behind the appearance of its technicalities. However, growing politicization of the European integration project because of different crises (economic, migration, rule of law, pandemic) has led to a 'constraining consensus' among European citizens and the member states (Blauberger & Martinsen 2020). Under these circumstances, a 'politics of depoliticization' that leaves controversial political decision to the CJEU is much more likely to backfire, that is, to undermine the legitimacy of the European polity and increase non-compliance with its law (Börzel 2021).

Recent events illustrate that the CJEU's capacity to resort to integration through law is met with countervailing forces. On the one hand, different understandings of how monetary policy, crucial in the reaction to the Eurozone crisis, should be conceived and assessed led to a conflict between the CJEU and Germany's Federal Constitutional Court. In this context, the latter openly challenged the principle of supremacy (or primacy) of EU law. On the other hand, it is not only the CJEU which is under observation but also its interlocutors in the member states. In Poland, judicial independence has been challenged by national legislation, leading to a rule of law crisis that also concerns the EU. If judicial independence can no longer be taken for granted in the member states, the whole legal construction on which European integration rests would be compromised. Not only the legitimacy but also the legality of the EU thus remains topical in political and scholarly discussions.

Didactical Section

Key Learning Points

- Sociologically speaking, law is an abstract form of solidarity that helps to integrate modern societies, typically on the level of nation states.
- The European integration process can be conceived as a project of society-building on a transnational scale, in which law likewise plays a prominent role.
- Integration through law refers to the strategy of using law as a relatively neutral or 'depoliticized' means of promoting European integration.
- This strategy was particularly prominent in the context of the internal market, but it is less effective in the context of monetary union.
- Sociological approaches bring out the specific social conditions on which the European community of law rests as the kernel of a transnational society in the making.

Glossary

Community method: Mode of decision-making in the context of the internal market, which involves the European Commission, the Council of Ministers, and Parliament, and results in the adoption of EU legislation.

Coordinative method: Mode of decision-making in the context of monetary union which rests on a combination of intergovernmental control by the Council of Ministers or the European Council and supranational intervention by the European Commission in matters of economic and fiscal policy coordination.

Court of Justice of the European Union (CJEU): EU institution in charge of ensuring uniform interpretation of EU law across the member states.

Market integration: Measures to establish and complete the European internal market, that is, to promote free movement of goods, services, persons, and capital as well as freedom of establishment between the member states.

Monetary integration: Measures and policies to promote and safeguard European monetary union, which rests on a common currency, a common monetary policy, and mechanisms of economic and fiscal policy coordination.

Monetary method: Mode of decision-making in the context of monetary union which rests on independent decision-making by the European System of Central Banks in matters of monetary policy.

Further Readings

Blauberger, M. & D. S. Martinsen, 2020: The Court of Justice in times of politicisation: 'law as a mask and shield' revisited. *Journal of European Public Policy* 27(3):382–399.

Lenaerts, K., 2020: No Member State is More Equal than Others: The Primacy of EU law and the Principle of the Equality of the Member States before the Treaties. *Verfassungsblog* (VerfBlog) (blog). 2020/10/08. https://verfassungsblog.de/no-member-state-is-more-equal-than-others/ (accessed October 18, 2021).

Nicola, F. G. & B. Davies (eds.), 2017: *EU law stories: contextual and critical histories of European jurisprudence*. Cambridge, New York, NY, Port Melbourne, Delhi, Singapore: Cambridge University Press.

Přibáň, J. (ed.), 2020: *Research Handbook on the Sociology of Law*. Cheltenham: Edward Elgar.

Rosas, A., 2019: The European Court of Justice: Do all roads lead to Luxembourg? CEPS Policy Insights (No. 2019/03, February 2019).

Vauchez, A., 2015: *Brokering Europe: Euro-Lawyers and the Making of a Transnational Polity*. Cambridge: Cambridge University Press.

Additional Web-Sources

Developments in EU law (I). The official websites of the European Commission and the Court of Justice of the European Union are essential data sources for any research on EU law and policy: https://ec.europa.eu and https://curia.europa.eu/

Developments in EU law (II). Ongoing debates relevant to EU law are covered by different news websites specialized on Europe, such as *EUobserver* and *Politico* as well as blogs focusing on legal developments, such as *Verfassungsblog*. As search terms, try any combination of 'EU', 'law', 'court' and/or 'case' with keywords describing the specific subject you are interested in: https://euobserver.com, https://www.politico.eu and https://verfassungs blog.de

Questions for Discussion

– What role do the enforcement powers of the state have in promoting integration through law? And what is the relevance of the people's belief in the legitimacy of the law? Consider these aspects for both the national and the European level.

– Find out about how the principle of 'gender equality' evolved in the European context (Burri 2018). How does this illustrate the dynamic of integration through law and its interplay with legislative activities on the European level?

- Get further information on the 'rule of law' crisis in the EU. How has it been dealt with? Has it been solved in the meantime? Check the above-mentioned news sites and go to the European Commission's website for updates.

References

Alter, K., 2001: *Establishing the Supremacy of European Law: The Making of an International Rule of Law in Europe*. Oxford: Oxford University Press.

Augenstein, D., 2011: Identifying the European Union: Legal Integration and European Communities. In: Augenstein, D. (ed.), *'Integration through Law' Revisited: The Making of the European Polity*, pp. 99–112. Farnham: Ashgate.

Augenstein, D. & M. Dawson, 2011: Introduction: What Law for What Polity? 'Integration through Law' in the European Union Revisited. In: Augenstein, D. (ed.), *'Integration through Law' Revisited: The Making of the European Polity*, pp. 1–8. Farnham: Ashgate.

Avbelj, M., 2011: The Legal Viability of European Integration in the Absence of Constitutional Hierarchy. In: Augenstein, D. (ed.), *'Integration through Law' Revisited: The Making of the European Polity*, pp. 29–46. Farnham: Ashgate.

Bickerton, C. J., D. Hodson & U. Puetter (eds.) 2015: *The new intergovernmentalism: states and supranational actors in the post-Maastricht era*. Oxford: Oxford University Press.

Bickerton, C. J., & J. Zielonka, 2011: European Integration. In: Badie, B., D. Berg-Schlosser & L. Morlino (eds.), *International Encyclopedia of Political Science*, pp. 842–848. London: Sage.

Blauberger, M. & D. S. Martinsen, 2020: The Court of Justice in times of politicisation: 'law as a mask and shield' revisited. *Journal of European Public Policy* 27(3):382–399.

Bourdieu, P., 1987: The Force of Law: Toward a Sociology of the Juridical Field. *Hastings Law Journal* 38(5):805–853.

Börzel, T. A., 2021: *Why Noncompliance? The Politics of Law in the European Union*. Ithaca, NY: Cornell University Press.

Burley, A. M. & W. Mattli, 1993: Europe Before the Court: A Political Theory of Legal Integration. *International Organization* 47(1):41–76.

Burri, S., 2018: EU gender equality law – update 2018. (Luxembourg: 2018 Publications Office of the European Union). https://www.equalitylaw.eu/downloads/4767-eu-gender-equality-law-update-2018-pdf-444-kb (accessed October 18, 2021).

Cappelletti, M., M. Seccombe & J. H. Weiler (eds.), 1986: *Integration Through Law: Europe and the American Federal Experience. Volume 1: Methods, Tools and Institutions. Book 1: A Political, Legal and Economic Overview*. Berlin: Walter de Gruyter.

Chalmers, D. & L. Barroso, 2014: What *Van Gend en Loos* Stands For. *International Journal of Constitutional Law* 12(1):105–134.

Dawson, M., 2015: The Euro Crisis and Its Transformation of EU Law and Politics. In: Hertie School of Governance (ed.), *The Governance Report 2015*, pp. 41–68. Oxford: Oxford University Press.

de Búrca, G., 2005: Rethinking Law in Neofunctionalist Theory. *Journal of European Public Policy* 12(2):310–326.

Dehousse, R. & J. H. H. Weiler, 1990: The Legal Dimension. In: Wallace, W. (ed.), *The Dynamics of European Integration*, pp. 242–260. London: Pinter Publishers.

Durkheim, É., 1964: *The Division of Labour in Society*. London: Free Press of Glencoe.

Everson, M. & J. Eisner, 2007: *The Making of a European Constitution: Judges and Law Beyond Constitutive Power*. Abingdon: Routledge.

Everson, M. & C. Joerges, 2012: Reconfiguring the Politics-Law Relationship in the Integration through Conflicts-Law Constitutionalism. *European Law Journal* 18(5):644–666.

Favell, A. & V. Guiraudon, 2011: Sociology of the European Union: An Introduction. In: Favell, A. & V. Guiraudon (eds.), *Sociology of the European Union*, pp. 1–24. Basingstoke: Palgrave Macmillan.

Fligstein, N. & A. Stone Sweet, 2002: Constructing Polities and Markets: An Institutionalist Account of European Integration. *American Journal of Sociology* 107(5):1206–1243.

Frerichs, S., 2008: *Judicial Governance in der europäischen Rechtsgemeinschaft: Integration durch Recht jenseits des Staates*. Baden-Baden: Nomos.

Frerichs, S., 2018: Integration durch Recht. In: Bach, M. & B. Hönig (eds.), *Europasoziologie: Handbuch für Wissenschaft und Studium*, pp. 151–161. Baden-Baden: Nomos.

Genschel, P. & M. Jachtenfuchs (eds.), 2014: *Beyond the Regulatory Polity? The European Integration of Core State Powers*. Oxford: Oxford University Press.

Haas, E. B., [1958] 2004: *The Uniting of Europe: Political, Social and Economic Forces, 1950–1957*. Notre Dame: University of Notre Dame Press.

Habermas, J., 1996: *Between Facts and Norms: Contributions to a Discourse Theory of Law and Democracy*. Cambridge: MIT Press.

Hart, H. L. A., 1961: *The Concept of Law*. Clarendon Press.

Joerges, C., 2016: Integration Through Law and the Crisis of Law in Europe's Emergency. In: Chalmers, D., M. Jachtenfuchs & C. Joerges (eds.), *The End of the Eurocrats' Dream: Adjusting to European Diversity*, pp. 299–338. Cambridge: Cambridge University Press.

Joerges, C. & C. Kreuder-Sonner, 2017: European Studies and the European Crisis: Legal and Political Science between Critique and Complacency. *European Law Journal* 23 (1–2):118–139.

Kelsen, H., 2002: On the Borders Between Legal and Sociological Method. In: Jacobsen, A. & B. Schlink (eds.), *Weimar: A Jurisprudence of Crisis*, pp. 57–63. Berkeley: University of California Press.

Klamert, M., 2014: *The Principle of Loyalty in EU Law*. Oxford: Oxford University Press.

Lockwood, D., 1992: Appendix: Social Integration and System Integration. In: Lockwood, D. (ed.), *Solidarity and Schism: 'The Problem of Disorder' in Durkheimian and Marxist Sociology*. Oxford: Clarendon Press.

Losada Fraga, F., 2009: *Gobernanza y legitimidad democrática: Modelos téoricos aplicados a la Unión Europea*. University of Madrid, Doctoral Dissertation.

Mac Amhlaigh, C., 2011: Concepts of Law in Integration through Law. In: Augenstein, D. (ed.), *'Integration through Law' Revisited: The Making of the European Polity*, pp. 69–84. Farnham: Ashgate.

Maduro, M. P., 1998: *We The Court – The European Court of Justice and the European Economic Constitution: A Critical Reading of Article 30 of the EC Treaty*. Oxford: Hart Publishing.

Majone, G., 2005: *Dilemmas of European Integration: The Ambiguities and Pitfalls of Integration by Stealth*. Oxford: Oxford University Press.

Molle, W., 2006: *The Economics of European Integration: Theory, Practice, Policy*. Aldershot: Ashgate, 5th edition.

Moravcsik, A., 1998: *The Choice for Europe: Social Purpose and State Power from Messina to Maastricht*. Ithaca, NY: Cornell University Press.

Münch, R., 2008: Constructing a European Society by Jurisdiction. *European Law Journal* 14(5): 519–541.

Parsons, T., 2007: *American Society: A Theory of the Societal Community*. Boulder, CO: Paradigm Publishers.

Pollack, M. A., 2003: *The Engines of European Integration: Delegation, Agency, and Agenda Setting in the EU*. Oxford and New York: Oxford University Press.

Puetter, U., 2014: *The European Council and the Council: New Intergovernmentalism and institutional change*. Oxford: Oxford University Press.

Risse, T., 2009: Social Constructivism and European Integration. In: Wiener, A. & T. Diez (eds.), *European Integration Theory*, pp. 144–166. Oxford: Oxford University Press.

Rottleuthner, H., 1999: Recht und soziale Integration. In: Friedrichs, J. & W. Jagodzinski (eds.), *Soziale Integration*, pp. 398–415. Opladen: Westdeutscher Verlag.

Scharpf, F. W., 1996: Negative and Positive Integration in the Political Economy of European Welfare States. In: Marks, G., F. W. Scharpf, P. C. Schmitter & W. Streeck (eds.), *Governance in the European Union*, pp. 15–39. London: Sage.

Sciarra, S., 2001: Integration Through Courts: Article 177 as a Pre-Federal Device. In: Sciarra, S. (ed.), *Labour Law in the Courts: National Judges and the European Court of Justice*, pp. 1–30. Oxford: Hart Publishing.

Snyder, F., 1995: Editorial. *European Law Journal* 1(1):1–4.

Stone Sweet, A., 2004: *The Judicial Construction of Europe*. Oxford: Oxford University Press.

Vauchez, A., 2010: The transnational politics of judicialization. Van Gend en Loos and the making of EU polity. *European Law Journal* 16(1):1–28.

Vauchez, A. & B. de Witte, 2013: *Lawyering Europe: European Law as a Transnational Social Field*. Oxford: Hart Publishing.

Weber, M., 1978: *Economy and Society: An Outline of Interpretive Sociology*. Ed. by G. Roth & C. Wittich. Berkeley, CA: University of California Press.

Niilo Kauppi

9 The Political Field of the European Union

The political field of the European Union constitutes a *dynamic topography* (Kauppi 2005), an evolving and uneven multileveled space of action. With time, social differentiation and the development of the division of political labor have made the three subfields of the multi-level political field of the European Union, namely the local/regional, the national, and the European, more distinct. Institutions such as the European Parliament and its representatives, the MEPs (Members of the European Parliament), who like to present themselves as the true representatives of European citizens, have become more autonomous in comparison with national parliamentarians and the national political field. Even after nearly 70 years of European integration, the national political arena remains the dominant subfield in this configuration. In terms of their sociological profiles, MEPs are more European compared to national parliamentarians, and are more likely to be feminine with greater cultural capital. However, they have less national political capital. European Commissioners, the 'ministers' of the European 'government' (Smith 2004), have similar social profiles to MEPs, yet have even more European and national political capital. They are key players in the executive political networks linking national and European political subfields that still dominate the political field of the European Union.

Expanding upon this train of thought, in this chapter *Europeanization* refers to the institutionalization and differentiation of groups and discourses through political struggles and negotiations that aim to define and reproduce legitimate principles (idea(l)s and practices) of social domination. Principles can range from relatively specific political interests, such as preferences in the political agenda or a more powerful European Parliament, to more abstract goals such as universal moral values like human rights and a responsibility to future generations. The dialectical interaction between consensus and conflict as a key dimension of Europeanization has largely been insufficiently analyzed until this juncture. Conflict scholars have concentrated on political competition, overlooking analyses on a key topic in EU policy making, consensus, as a condition of possibility for socially organized political conflict.

https://doi.org/10.1515/9783110673630-009

EU Politics from a Sociological Perspective

The sociological approach challenges established political science perspectives by taking the complexities of social action as its starting point. A sociological perspective provides us with a more realistic and critical picture of Europeanization and democratic politics as a non-violent socially organized form of conflict and cooperation. Full-time politicians compete for power and cooperate in institutionalized political fields. These specialized areas of activity have historically evolved from being relatively unspecified to a currently more specific framework. In the Middle Ages, politics and social life were generally inseparable (Gaxie 2003). Specialized institutions and agents first came into existence in the 19th century (Offerlé 1999). Nation states developed a host of institutions and practices that were aimed at democratization (Elias 1983; Giddens 2017). In the latter part of the 20th century, European integration began, adding a European level to what is known in some circles as democratic politics. This has led to further specialization in terms of political and bureaucratic careers (Büttner et al. 2015; Michel 2006).

In contrast to national settings, several highly structured national and regional/local political spaces are partly united into a *European space* that is unevenly structured (Fligstein 2009). More specifically, it forms an unevenly evolving dynamic topography in which different types of power evolve. European studies literature has unduly separated European, national, and regional/ local dimensions from one another. One of the main advantages of a sociological perspective is its analysis of phenomena in a relational fashion. Any social entity derives its value from the relevant evolving social context in which it is embedded; this context can include various scalar levels such as regional, national, European, and global levels. In this sense, agency is always embedded.

The institutionalization of a European level of power has been the key feature of European integration since the 1950s, shaping national and local/regional politics. Thus, before Finland's integration into the European Union in 1995, European institutions were not on the radar of Finnish politicians. Yet after Finland's entry into the European Union, they began to play a more significant role in their political strategies. The European Parliament and Commission appeared as potential sources of alternative political capital. When evaluating the relative value of these institutions after 1995, one must consider their existence as sources of political capital that enable a politician to diversify his or her capital portfolio. No politician was previously able to combine local and regional/national/European careers.

Political sociologist Daniel Gaxie (2003: 16) has divided the area of what he calls democratic competition into two political fields: the central and the peripheral political fields. The first includes positions of power in nation states, while the second concerns political power at regional and local levels. Gaxie describes the latter as specific spaces of democratic competition that are integrated into the central political field. Since the publication of Gaxie's study, the political game has changed, with the increasing power of the EU as a site of political competition. It is then necessary to add a third political field, the European field, as political authority has shifted from national and subnational levels to supranational institutions (Hooghe & Marks 2001). These three subfields overlap to varying degrees and are in an interactive relationship with one another. It would therefore be a mistake to separate them from one another. For instance, MEPs are in constant interaction with agents at national and regional/local levels. It is impossible to understand the political strategies applied by political parties in one subfield without situating them in their appropriate context and relation to rationales in other subfields. However, the logic of political competition in the European Parliament differs from that in the national political field; it takes the form of accumulating a specific kind of political capital, European political capital that can be contrasted with national political capital or regional/local forms of political capital. This is because European institutions were not originally conceived as political but as bureaucratic institutions. European integration was presented by politicians and scholars alike as an essentially non-political process.

The Field-Approach to EU Politics

While sensitive to the materiality of political reality, the *symbolic character* of political action is another key element of a sociological approach. Institutions are not only objective but also subjective entities (Berger & Luckmann 1966). Known as 'symbolic structuration', the meanings individuals and groups assign to a political process is crucial in understanding political integration and international relations. European Parliament research has shown that its status varies from member state to member state and political party to political party. European Parliament elections are a lifesaver for the parties and movements that are unsuccessful in their electoral system and in the structure of political competition in winning seats in national elections, but whose candidates are elected to the European Parliament (Landorff 2019; Shemer-Kunz 2017). For these parties, the European Parliament allows for continued political action. Without a consideration of these 'positive' uses of the European Parliament, certain key elements of contemporary domestic European politics cannot be understood, especially the rise of populist and extreme-rightist political parties since the 1980s and the bankruptcy of center-left and center-right parties.

For a sociological study of Europeanization, analyzing the link between individual, group and institution is crucial. Individuals are always members of various social groups. Informal and formal groups are embedded in various institutions that are discursive and non-discursive. From an individual's viewpoint, Europeanization takes the form of an interactive relationship with various groups (in-groups and out-groups). Individuals will adopt certain ideas, values, and roles, such as being a European and not a national parliamentarian. Europeanization is neither a top-down process nor one of pure and simple imposition of certain values or institutions from the supranational to the national level, for instance. It mainly exhibits what Bourdieu calls 'symbolic violence'. It concerns the formation of groups, institutions, and policies. At the most basic sociological and socio-psychological level, individuals appropriate certain values, such as habits of thinking and patterns of behavior, once they encounter European institutions as trainees, parliamentary assistants, MEPs, lobbyists or some other capacity. Adaptation can be observed even at the most trivial level, in the clothing style of politicians, their way of talking, and so on, which is because they must adapt to the dominant codes and conventions of their new in-groups. Politicians are improvisers or *bricoleurs*, to use anthropologist Lévi-Strauss's term (Lévi-Strauss 2009). They solve the problems they are faced with, improvising as they go along, using whatever means are available to them in a specific power constellation.

> **Info-Box 9.1: The Political field of the European Union**
> The political field of the European Union is a political space of competition comprising three subfields: European, national, and regional/local, each endowed to a certain extent with its own autonomous institutions, norms, conventions, and political practices/logics.

This broader unit of social interaction, *a multi-leveled political field of the European Union*, includes three political subfields: the *European*, the *national* and the *regional/local* (Kauppi 1996a). They all have their own logic of political competition and cooperation, as well as rules of specific political capital accumulation. The dynamics between these fields are centered on the uses of this specific capital in other subfields: at the institutional level, at the level of policy, and the level of political agents, parties, and individuals. Institutions and policies involve analyses of the relationships between the European political field and other fields such as the European administrative field; I will not explore this issue in detail here (see for specifics: Page 1996). Instead, I will focus on positions of political power in the emerging political field of the European Union.

The relatively rapid structuration of a European level of political action has changed the horizon of political action for individual politicians and political groups such as parties, but also for NGOs. It offers numerous material and immaterial resources or capital. For nationally established cartel parties (Katz & Mair 1995), which are so-called as they use state resources to maintain their position within the national political system and that dominate the three subfields, the European Parliament has been an extension of national politics. It is part of the political reward system. For politicians who have become marginalized in their own parties, or for members of small or new political parties that do not have access to the national capital and its networks, the European Parliament is a means to continue their political activities at all subfield levels (Hix & Lord 1997: 90). Removed from the everyday concerns of voters and detached from the electorate, the European Parliament and its representatives are faced with an uphill battle. Since 1979, European Parliament elections have been characterized by low levels of participation. However, in 2019 over 50 per cent of EU citizens eligible to vote took part in the election for the first time since 1979.

From a sociological perspective, individuals always operate in a largely goal-oriented manner in mostly structured institutional and social environments (Kauppi 2010). States and institutions are not just 'out there', and they do nothing by themselves. In fact, individuals and groups represent states and political organizations of all kinds, including supranational institutions, which act in their name. Political positions clearly differ when a high civil servant from the EU's Directorate General for Competition presents the EU's position on climate change, in comparison to a high civil servant from the Directorate General for Environment doing so.

Field Analysis and Politics – Basic Theoretical Orientations

One prominent sociological approach is based on the tools developed by Pierre Bourdieu and colleagues (Bourdieu 1986; Bourdieu et al. 1968; Zimmermann & Favell 2011; Swartz 2013). Bourdieu based his field perspective on an interpretation of Weber's contextual analysis of social action (Weber 1991, for discussion see: Kauppi 2000), in which social action is meaningful and necessarily involves others. Weber distinguished contrasting spheres of social action, such as the economy of religious activity, arguing that each sphere had its own goal, values, and logic. Bourdieu developed this perspective, multiplying the number of social fields to include, among others, the cultural, literary, and political fields (Bourdieu 1985) while adding a binary logic such as dominant-dominated. In other works, he combined other concepts to this interpretation of Weber, such as capital, as a form of social resource and practice as the logic of social action.

These studies on French education, culture and elites have become standard references. As for Weber, the field was a tool of analysis for Bourdieu, not reality but a model of reality. While Bourdieu studied the French national context, some of his former students and other scholars (Gaxie & Godmer 2007; Gaxie & Hubé 2013; Kauppi 1996b, 2005, 2018; Beauvallet et al. 2016; Georgakakis & Rowell 2013; Landorff 2019; Schmidt-Wellenburg & Bernhard 2020) have applied and developed elements of his tools to the analysis of European integration.

Info-Box 9.2: The definition of the term 'field'
A field can be defined as a dynamic, socially structured space of action, in which individuals, groups and organizations with an interest in the same issue cooperate and compete. It is a structured space that can be expansive or contractive. To varying degrees, it is both autonomous and heteronomous, that is consisting of values and practices that are specific to it, and values and practices that it shares with other fields.

At its foundation, a phenomenon makes sense in this context only in relation to other phenomena. Social value stems from this interaction. Nothing is valuable in itself but only in relation to other elements. The key scholarly operation is to decide the relational space or reference category in which a phenomenon is to be studied. Compared to established normative political science concepts such as the nation state or sovereignty, this approach provides the scholar with the flexibility to combine elements within a space of action that are not usually analyzed together. For instance, the nation state may not be the only relevant framework for an analysis of EU integration, major technological revolutions, or global policy issues such as climate change. There are heuristic advantages to analyzing the EU as a field of political competition that takes both member states and supranational institutions as an interactive whole, from which new forms of power or capital are generated. The actions of one element are thus best understood in relation to the actions of other elements in the same space. This approach will depend on available information. It will be more difficult to study certain objects than others. In the EU, many sectors of the political field of the European Union, such as the meetings of the Council of the European Union or those of the governors of the European Central Bank, are sealed off from scholarly analysis. Certain policy areas such as military and security issues will also be particularly difficult to study. However, this does not mean that these spaces of social action would be labeled as weak fields. There may be significant field effects, but these could be out of reach for scholarly research. We are now touching upon the limits of field analysis (Kauppi 2020). There is no field if the scholar cannot demonstrate the existence of field effects – in other words, social interactions, forms of dependencies and social value.

Sociology is sensitive to the links between society and politics. Individuals operate in several roles in society that include family, the workplace, political parties, to name but a few. To analyze this complex social dynamic, sociological tools are necessary to take types of action into account and to delimit their areas of activity.

Info-Box 9.3
The more specific sociological perspective engaged in this article is structural constructivist, an approach pioneered by Pierre Bourdieu and developed by his colleagues and students. This approach is concerned with the practical logic of social action in terms of power resources or capital, in more or less structured areas of activity or fields.

Epistemological vigilance, or the reflexivity concerning the scholar's perspective, tools and their impact on the objects studied, is a key feature of the structural constructivist approach (Bourdieu et al. 1968). In terms of European integration and Europeanization, one clear objectified political field of the EU, or one reality that corresponds to that concept, does not exist. It is a scholarly construct and must be related to the perspective of the scholar, to the research tools used and to the available information and data. It is a tool that enables the scholar to explore certain aspects of social reality that she deems relevant for the questions she has raised.

Politics is a dynamic, future-oriented activity. Political agents constantly create new fields or domains of specialized competition. For instance, climate change has become a new field of political competition in which a variety of agents compete to define the political value of emissions and their carbon footprint. Agents compete and cooperate for the specific value or the questions that interest them and in turn lead them to invest their capital, time, and energy. It is a dynamic space of action that can be expansive or contractive, both formally, when centrifugal social forces attract more and more agents with an interest in the issue in question, in turn leading to a numerical increase in players, or substantially, when the prized value becomes more and more central to society (Kauppi 2020). An issue such as human rights is an expansive field in which the values and resources linked to human rights are fought over. A field can also be contractive when the key value is devalued. For instance, forms of fossil fuels have become negative political capital. These values gain or decrease in power and influence, shaping the opportunities and probabilities for certain types of political action and capital accumulation.

'Capital' is a value or power share that is considered significant in society. As a social resource, asset, or form of legitimacy, it is not restricted to economic activity (Bourdieu 1986; Gaxie 2003; Kauppi 1996b; Svendsen & Svendsen 2003). It can include cultural, intellectual, and technological value, among others. As an advantage or asset, it can be instrumentally used in view of a certain goal or purpose (Merriam-Webster 2021). Political capital refers to trust and legitimacy accumulated in a political field. It is commonly objectified following success or failure in elections. The winners receive credit that they can use to follow up on their promises and pursue their political goals while taking political responsibility for their actions. Capital can be positive or negative. Positive capital leads to the accumulation of more capital or to possibilities of conversion into other types of capital such as economic capital. Negative capital leads to decreasing returns and the inability to convert it into other types of capital.

The Development of European Capital

Transnational capital, or more precisely European capital defined as social resources developed in European institutions, was a negative capital for many political agents for an extended period. It was simply a bad investment, to be avoided if possible (Reif & Schmitt 1980). The political field of the European Union has evolved from a bureaucratic space into a more political space. The tension between the two is constant in the history of European integration. Political capital at European level equated to executive capital linked with the European Commission and Council for several years. With increases in the power of the European Parliament it became more political, involving a specific form of legislative capital and new groups of politicians such as MEPs. With the introduction of the Euro and economic integration, it also became more economic, with the establishment of institutions like the European Central Bank. The institutionalization of the European Union has thus not been linear and even, and the definition of European political capital itself has evolved.

A speculative dimension is vital when assessing the value of capital. Current negative or positive value depends on anticipated future value, on future confirmability. The future impacts the present 'retro causally' through embodied beliefs, ideals, hopes and anticipations for the future that have an impact on present action. These can include political goals such as a more democratic Europe. For instance, after the signing of the Lisbon Treaty of Lisbon (2009), the power of the European Parliament has formally increased in relation to other European institutions, the European Commission, a supranational bureaucracy, and the Council of the EU, composed of the ministers of the bloc's member states. It has been surmised by some researchers that the European Parliament's influence will continue to expand in the future. However, there is neither political consensus nor shared anticipative knowledge on this, and therefore the value of a political position in the European Parliament has not increased as much as its past and present formal powers had implied. However, research has shown that after the Lisbon Treaty the European Parliament has become more autonomous in relation to other institutions in the EU's institutional triangle, the European Commission, and the Council of the EU.

Formally, the European Parliament is a source of institutional political and legislative capital. This capital is legislative, not executive, involving an election, not an appointment. In this sense it depends fundamentally on the electorate and the awareness and knowledge of voters concerning European politics, and on the trust and credit they are willing to give to a party and its representative. It is political, involving political power and influence, in contrast to bureaucratic power in discussing EU institutions such as the European Commission and its permanent personnel. In other words, political capital concerns competition that is political and not bureaucratic, involving political stakes and power shares. In practice, these analytical categories are of course intertwined in complicated ways, to which I refer to again later. It is European, in contrast to national or regional/local, and the capital in question is institutional in that it is accumulated in a specific institution, the European Parliament. Individual politicians and collective political enterprises such as political parties and NGOs in turn have access to a variety of capital.

The European Commission and the Council are sources of legislative and executive capital (Kauppi 2011). The EU's policies are areas of social action that involve various agents such as lobbyists and experts, aside from European bureaucrats (Kauppi & Madsen 2013; Michel 2006). Given the small size and budget of European bureaucracy and its expanding outputs, these agents have a real impact on European public policies.

Apart from political capital, the assets available to a political agent can include cultural capital, economic capital, and social capital, among others. The uses of this capital portfolio depend on the reflexivity of the agent (Bourdieu & Wacquant 1992; Kauppi 2018), and her capacity to learn and creatively adapt to changing circumstances that may suddenly provide opportunities for the use of actual or potential assets. For instance, if a politician is not re-elected to the European Parliament or re-appointed to the European Commission, social capital in other quarters of society such as NGOs or businesses can help to save a suddenly fragile political career. One key site of conversion for high-level European executive politicians is the banking sector, a key sector in neoliberal economies.

Resources and their value are not conclusively defined, but are capable of change, while being the object of political competition. In certain circumstances and from a longer historical perspective, the 'weak' can defeat the 'strong'.

Though they may be dominated, the powerless do not remain permanently so. Fields evolve, as do social dynamics. If dominated in one political subfield such as the national political field, social mobility into another field such as the European political field can enable individuals and parties to reuse their assets to better their situation. The case of the French *Front/Rassemblement national* (F/RN) is particularly illustrative of this possibility. Unable to gain an electoral foothold either in the French national parliament or at regional levels, the F/RN had already succeeded in obtaining positions in the European Parliament with Jean-Marie Le Pen's election in 1984. The party has succeeded in capitalizing on this opportunity. Nearly forty years later, it is the second largest political party in France. The dynamic between local/regional, national, and European levels is key to gaining a greater understanding of this major political development, namely the rise of right-wing populism and extremism. Furthermore, powerlessness can become capital in changing technological, economic, and political circumstances. The struggle to prevent the use of nuclear power undertaken by social movements from the 1970s onwards was originally viewed as an endeavor that engaged overly negative political capital; today, however, anti-nuclear stances are definitely regarded as positive political capital.

Dynamics within Subfields

The result of the integration of the European subfield with the national and regional/local political fields, and the structuration of this space, has been a more pluralistic structure of political competition for political parties and individual political agents. In national politics, cartel parties now face increasing challenges in controlling political competition, as we have seen with the crashes of socialist and conservative cartel parties in France, Italy, Germany, and other EU member states. This is partly due to the interaction between the three political subfields and the loosening of control of cartel parties in the political arena.

The European Parliament (EP): A Key Entry Point to Electoral Politics

In the European Parliament, political socialization is of a different kind from national parliaments. MEPs must specialize in specific areas such as human rights, or the environment, among other. This diversity can be seen in the educational background of MEPs, ranging from law and economics to the humanities and science and technology. However, compared to the broader spectrum of public action in national settings, the scope of their involvement and the institution's political impact is narrower. To succeed, MEPs must access positions of power in the assembly, in the party, or in the committees (Landorff 2019). In member states with list elections, MEPs are not only dependent on national party leaders to renew their position but are also physically removed from the national political centers. There are fewer MEPs combining the European mandate with a local/ regional mandate, at around 15 per cent in the 2010s (Beauvallet et al. 2016: 108), testifying to an institutional differentiation. Furthermore, while European politics now has more visibility in the national media than previously, the European Parliament is still occupying a marginal role in the national and regional/local media. For small and marginal parties that are not cartel parties, it is vital not to sever the link to national and local/regional poles to enable the conversion of European legislative political capital into national political capital. This requires a sustained presence in the intra-European subfields and media, especially in view of local/regional and national elections. The example of the *Front/Rassemblement National* is particularly illustrative of the dynamics between the subfields of the political field of the European Union and the political problems created as a result.

MEPs share a distinct political profile compared to national politicians. The European Parliament has been relatively stable in terms of renewal, with the share of new entrants ranging from 50 per cent in 1989 to 61.8 per cent in 1999 (Beauvallet et al. 2016). Significantly, for 37 per cent of MEPs since 1979 the post in the European parliament has been their first elected mandate. In other words, for a large group of MEPs the European Parliament is a place of access to electoral politics that can continue into national politics. A particularly instructive example of this are the candidates elected from Emmanuel Macron's party *La République en marche* in 2019. They were all newcomers to the European Parliament.

Which previous positions have gained most in importance since the first direct elections to the European Parliament in 1979? In terms of prior political experience, the local level has grown in importance by 12 per cent. For 24 per cent of MEPs, a local mandate preceded access to the European Parliament. This figure indicates that the link between local/regional and European is vital in terms of social dynamics. However, the most important change in political value since 1979 has been that of political aid or collaborator, including working as an assistant to an MEP, which has increased by 16 per cent. These figures indicate the importance of regional/local political capital as well as that of political capital accumulated in non-electoral positions, such as for an aid to a politician or in ministerial cabinets, in gaining access to the European Parliament. In certain national political fields, such as in France, non-elected positions are of great significance, especially those in ministerial cabinets.

The percentage of female MEPs is another factor that highlights the dynamics in the political field of the European Union. While in many national political fields female politicians have struggled to access any political positions at all, European institutions present an altogether different picture (Kauppi 1999). Female representation rose from 15.2 per cent in 1979 to 40.4 per cent in 2019 (European Parliament 2019). In 2019, 57 per cent of all vice-presidents of the European Parliament and 54.5 per cent of committee chairs were female. In the European Commission, 42.8 per cent of Commissioners were female in 2019.

The Social Dynamics of Commissioners

The social profiles of MEPs and European Commissioners, holders of European legislative and executive capital, are remarkably similar. In both groups, about 25 per cent hold PhDs. While 8 in 10 MEPs have higher education degrees (BA, MA, or PhD), all commissioners have tertiary degrees. This extremely high level of educational capital is also visible in the electorate that mobilizes to vote in European elections. These homophilic relationships testify to structural similarities in terms of educational and European capital, resources that bring these social groups together. Differences emerge in terms of educational background. In the European Commission, economics, social sciences, and law are most significant, whereas in the EP the humanities, and science and technology are more prominent (Kauppi 2014).

Other differences between European Commissioners and MEPs exist. Commissioners enjoy more European political and cultural capital than MEPs. While 60.7 per cent of commissioners had ministerial experience, between 14 and 17 per cent of MEPs could say the same, a significantly lower figure. The type of capital is also relevant as ministers are executive politicians, whereas MEPS or parliamentarians are legislative actors. While MEPs are less dependent on national political experience than before, it remains an important part of their portfolio. For as many as 39 per cent of all MEPs since 1979, the position in the European hemicycle has followed a national mandate. Just under a third have held previously local/regional positions, and approximately a third have had no local/regional or national experience whatsoever. In the Finnish national political field, direct access to the EP plays an even more important role, amounting to nearly 80 per cent of MEPs between 1979 and 2014.

In 2019, nearly half of European Commissioners had studied in a European country other than their own, mostly in the UK and France. 20 per cent of MEPs had studied in a European country other than their own (Beauvallet et al. 2016). In terms of mobility in the European political subfield, clear differences between MEPs and Commissioners can be noted. While 1 in 10 MEPs had held a position at the European level before integrating into the EP, for commissioners the figure is a staggering 7 in 10, testifying to the centrality of this institution in the European political subfield. In 2019, 1/3 of commissioners were former MEPs, confirming the direction of social mobility between the EP and the College of Commissioners from a lower to a higher-level political position. 4 out of 10 commissioners had previous experience in other European institutions, in the Commission's Directorate Generals or as members of cabinets (7 out of 10 commissioners), in the European Court of Auditors, and in the Council of Europe. Social age partly explains this, as commissioners are older than MEPs on average. However, it also clearly shows that the College of Commissioners is a key destination for ascending social mobility in the European political subfield. Other supranational destinations of upwardly mobile careers include the European Central Bank (ECB), the European Investment Bank (EIB), as well as major investment banks such as Goldman Sachs, an employer of former head of the ECB Mario Draghi, and former president of the European Commission Jose Manuel Barroso.

Given the form European integration has taken, emphasizing eliminating obstacles to mobility of people and capital, these banking institutions wield considerable power and do so by furthering a modality of European integration that has been presented as being 'non-political' and 'technical' (economic or legal) (Lebaron 2006; Vauchez 2015). The reality is markedly different, of course, as decisions on the economy are always eminently political. More fundamentally, the initial decision to create supranational institutions in the 1950s was a major political move that both politicians and scholars have presented to citizens as a non-political, purely technical decision (for analysis of (de)politicization, see for instance: Kauppi & Wiesner 2018; Wiesner 2018). In so doing, a group of high-level executive politicians succeeded in monopolizing the modalities and directions of European integration and Europeanization, making these their *domaine réservé*. The consensus on the economy that has developed in more than 60 years of integration, favoring capital over labor and the liberalization of the financial sector, has led to the constitution of a European political and economic establishment that upholds a specific neoliberal economic doctrine very closely (Varoufakis 2018). This doctrine is being increasingly contested by politicians and economists alike.

The European Bureaucratic Field

Given the centrality of European public policies in an analysis of the EU, it is not possible to scrutinize political power and power shares without regarding the European Commission as the EU's executive arm, including the European Central Bank and the lobbyists that shape European public policies. European public policies emphasize the key role of European bureaucracy. As a field, European bureaucracy is both autonomous and heterogeneous. On the one hand, it is autonomous, with a dominant and specific kind of European bureaucratic capital, while on the other, it is linked in multiple ways to other European and national fields. These intra-field relationships form a variety of political, economic, and social dependencies. While the European Commission wields considerable power as the initiator of European legislation and the promoter of European interests, however they may be defined, it is still a relatively small bureaucracy, comparatively speaking. It is therefore dependent on exterior expertise of various kinds in its ever-expanding activities. This is provided by lobbyists, non-partisan national civil servants, and trainees, among others. Knowledge of developments in Brussels and in other European institutions, as well as access to these centers and their agents, is crucial for these agents and for all those dependent on EU funding such as structural funds. This knowledge has become extremely valuable. This specific form of bureaucratic capital is at stake in what some scholars have called "the field of Eurocracy" (Georgakakis & Rowell 2013) or "EU affairs" (Büttner et al. 2015). While the Eurocracy refers to the main agents in the European Commission and other key institutions in the capitals of the EU (Brussels, Luxembourg, Strasbourg), it should be emphasized that tens of thousands of agents in various parts of the EU follow events in European capitals on a professional basis. Scattered in member states and beyond, these often neglected 'small hands' of European integration are in fact central to the political dynamics between the many levels in the political field of the European Union. While certain specialists in European affairs are permanent employees, most are part-time or project employees (Büttner & Leopold 2016).

European political capital as a source of influence and legitimacy, rooted in electoral process, has developed alongside another form of transnational capital; European bureaucratic capital. At higher levels, these two forms of capital overlap. Many top-level national politicians have spent time in Brussels as European commissioners. Many high-level civil servants in the European Commission are 'parachuted' political appointees that are tasked with promoting European interests, but who have, for understandable reasons, links with their member states of origin while maintaining their own economic interests. European executive capital is thus a mixture of political and bureaucratic capital. While certain highly positioned agents have more political than bureaucratic capital, European bureaucratic capital is more prevalent at lower levels.

Since the beginnings of European integration in the 1940s, the tension between these forms of capital and political legitimacy, the political and the non-political or technical, has been constant. An elite consensus existed from the outset, according to which European integration and the transfers of power to supranational institutions were to be presented as purely technical, non-political operations. This formatting enabled European integration to proceed smoothly until 1966, when French president Charles de Gaulle put a stop to it. De Gaulle saw European integration as a national government-controlled process. Since then, the tug of war between supranational and government-led integration has taken other forms. In 1979, a move towards a more political direction took place, with direct elections to the European Parliament. Similarly, the *Spitzenkandidaten* process, by which the EP controls the nomination of commissioners, is a move towards more political and less technocratic procedures (Kauppi & Trenz 2021).

In European bureaucracy, more political Directorate Generals are often contrasted with more technical DGs. In reality, European integration has been a highly political affair from its outset. Nonetheless, an elite consensus has preserved it as a monopoly of national, executive political leaders, represented at the European level by the Council of the EU. This has enabled integration to advance in a certain direction.

Conclusions

The sociological approach developed in this chapter in terms of capital and fields enables an empirically focused analysis of European institutional dynamics. This holistic approach focuses on the evolving relationships between agents, resources, strategies, and action fields. The EU as a *dynamic topography* refers to the complex, evolving interactions between three subfields: the local/regional, national, and European. The latter has grown in autonomy. While Europeanization has led to the development of new European institutions and power resources, at this juncture it has not led to the social differentiation of a permanent and separate European political class living from European politics in the manner of permanent European bureaucrats in the European Commission, the Council of the EU, and other European institutions. This is largely since the elective process, the key source of political capital, is not a permanent source, but must rather be renewed at regular intervals. European integration has meant that an increasing number of professional politicians have held temporary positions in the European Parliament or in other European institutions, mostly the Commission, either as commissioners or civil servants, or as national ministers in the Council of the EU, without constituting a separate social group. As a result of this Europeanization of political personnel, experience in the European field has become a normal asset in a more diverse national politician's capital portfolio. Therefore, to gain a foothold in both national and European politics, it has become increasingly important to understand the evolving dynamics between the subfields of the political field of the European Union, the European, the national and the regional/local, and European political and bureaucratic capital.

These social dynamics include upward social mobility from local/regional to European subfields in terms of a first electoral mandate in the European Parliament, from a role as a political assistant of a parliamentarian or minister to the European Parliament or the European Commission, European Parliament, and national ministerial positions, to the college of the European Commission. The European subfield has also promoted female politicians in important ways. Nevertheless, it is clear that in terms of their social characteristics, politicians occupying positions in the European Commission, the European Parliament and in institutions such as the European Central Bank represent a European cultural and political elite in the making. Politically and economically, they form a European establishment that is globally linked to powerful neoliberal interests (Kauppi & Madsen 2017; Varoufakis 2018).

Didactical Section

Key Learning Points

- A field is a dynamic, socially structured space of action in which individuals, groups, and organizations with an interest in the same issue cooperate and compete.
- The political field of the European Union is a political space of competition composed of three subfields: European, national, and regional/local, each endowed with its own institutions, norms, conventions, and political practices/logics functioning at varying levels of autonomy.
- Capital is a value or power share that is considered important in society.
- The European Parliament is a key entry point to European and national electoral politics.
- European political capital has become a standard requirement for ambitious politicians.

Further Readings

Büttner, S. M., L. Leopold, S. Mau & M. Posvic, 2015: Professionalization in EU Policy-Making? The Topology of the Transnational Field of EU Affairs. *European Societies* 17(4):569–592.

Favell, A. & V. Guiraudon (eds.), 2011: *Sociology of the European Union*. Cham: Palgrave.

Georgakakis, D. & J. Rowell (eds.), 2013: *The Field of Eurocracy: Mapping EU Actors and Professionals*. Cham: Palgrave.

Kauppi, N., 2005: *Democracy, Social Resources and Political Power in the European Union*. Manchester: Manchester University Press.

Kauppi, N., 2018: *Toward a Reflexive Political Sociology of the European Union*. Cham: Palgrave.

Kauppi, N. & M. R. Madsen (eds.), 2013: *Transnational Power Elites: The New Professionals of Governance, Law and Security*. London: Routledge.

Trenz, H. J., 2016: *Narrating European Society: Toward a Sociology of European Integration*. London: Lexington Books.

Additional Web-Sources

Corporate Europe Observatory. https://corporateeurope.org/en

Euractiv. https://www.euractiv.com/

European institutions. https://europa.eu/european-union/about-eu/institutions-bodies_en

VoteWatch. https://www.votewatch.eu/

References

Beauvallet, W., S. Michon, V. Lepaux & C. Monicolle, 2016: The Changing Composition of the European Parliament: MEPs from 1979 to 2014. *French Politics* 14(1):101–125.

Berger, P. & T. Luckmann, 1966: *The Social Construction of Reality*. Garden City, NJ: Anchor Books.

Bourdieu, P., 1985: *Sosiologian kysymyksiä*. Tampere: Vastapaino.

Bourdieu, P., 1986: The Forms of Capital. In: Richardson, J. (ed.), *Handbook of Theory and Research for the Sociology of Education*, pp.241–258. New York, NY: Greenwood.

Bourdieu, P. & L. Wacquant, 1992: *Invitation to Reflexive Sociology*. Chicago, IL: University of Chicago Press.

Bourdieu, P., J. C. Chamboredon & J. C. Passeron, 1968. *Le métier de sociologue*. Paris: Mouton de Gruyter.

Büttner, S. M. & L. Leopold, 2016: A 'new spirit' of public policy? The project world of EU funding. *European Journal of Cultural and Political Sociology* 3(1):41–71. DOI: 10.1080/23254823.2016.1183503.

Büttner, S. M., L. Leopold, S. Mau & M. Posvic, 2015: Professionalization in EU Policy-Making? The Topology of the Transnational Field of EU Affairs. *European Societies* 17(4):569–592.

Elias, N., 1983: *The Civilizing Process I*. Oxford: Wiley-Blackwell.

European Parliament, 2019: Women in the European Parliament (infographics). https://www.europarl.europa.eu/news/en/headlines/society/20190226STO28804/women-in-the-european-parliament-infographics (accessed February 2, 2021).

Fligstein, N., 2009: *Euroclash*. Oxford: Oxford University Press.

Gaxie, D., 2003: *La démocratie représentative*. Paris: Montchretien.

Gaxie, D. & L. Godmer, 2007: Cultural Capital and Political Selection. In: Cotta, M. & H. Best (eds.), *Democratic Representation in Europe. Diversity, Change and Convergence*, pp.106–135. Oxford: Oxford University Press.

Gaxie, D. & N. Hubé, 2013: On the National and Ideological Backgrounds of Elites' Attitudes Toward European Institutions. In: Kauppi, N. (ed.), *A Political Sociology of Transnational Europe*, pp. 165–190. Colchester: ECPR Press.

Georgakakis, D. & J. Rowell (eds.), 2013: *The Field of Eurocracy: Mapping EU Actors and Professionals*. Cham: Palgrave.

Giddens, A., 2017: *Sociology*. Cambridge: Polity.

Hix, S. & C. Lord, 1997: *Political Parties in the European Union*. Cham: Palgrave Macmillan.

Hooghe, L. & G. Marks, 2001: *Multi-level Governance and European Integration*. Boulder, CO: Rowman & Littlefield.

Katz, R., & P. Mair, 1995: Changing Models of Party Organization and Party Democracy. The Emergence of the Cartel Party. *Party Politics* (1):5–28.

Kauppi, N., 1996a: European Union Institutions and French Political Careers. *Scandinavian Political Studies* 19(1):1–24.

Kauppi, N., 1996b: *French Intellectual Nobility: Institutional and Symbolic Transformations in the Post-Sartrian Era*. Albany, NY: SUNY Press.

Kauppi, N., 1999: Power or Subjection? French Women Politicians in the European Parliament. *The European Journal of Women's Studies* 6(3):331–342.

Kauppi, N., 2000: *The Politics of Embodiment: Habits, Power and Pierre Bourdieu's Theory*. Frankfurt: Peter Lang.

Kauppi, N., 2005: *Democracy, Social Resources and Political Power in the European Union.* Manchester: Manchester University Press.

Kauppi, N., 2010: The Political Ontology of European Integration, *Comparative European Politics* 8(1):19–36.

Kauppi, N., 2011: EU Politics. In: Favell, A. & V. Guiraudon (eds.), *Sociology of the EU,* pp.150–171. Cham: Palgrave.

Kauppi, N., 2014: Knowledge Warfare: Social Scientists as Operators of Global Governance. *International Political Sociology* 8(3):330–332.

Kauppi, N., 2018: *Toward a Reflexive Political Sociology of the European Union.* Cham: Palgrave.

Kauppi, N., 2020: How Many Fields Can Stand on the Point of a Pin? Methodological Notes on Reflexivity, the Sociological Craft and Field Analysis. In: Schmidt-Wellenburg, C. & S. Bernhard (eds.), *Charting Transnational Fields: Methodology for a Political Sociology of Knowledge,* pp.37–54. London: Routledge.

Kauppi, N. & M. R. Madsen (eds.), 2013: *Transnational Power Elites: The New Professionals of Governance, Law and Security.* London: Routledge.

Kauppi, N. & M. R. Madsen, 2017: Global Elites. In: Guillaume, X. & P. Bilgin (eds.), *Routledge Handbook of International Political Sociology,* pp.166–174. London: Routledge.

Kauppi, N. & H. J. Trenz, 2021: *Notes on the 'Politics' of EU Politicization.* University of Oslo. Arena EU3D Research Papers No. 5.

Kauppi, N. & C. Wiesner, 2018: Exit Politics, Enter Politicisation. *Journal of European Integration* 40(2):227–233. https://papers.ssrn.com/sol3/papers.cfm?abstract_id= 3772901 (accessed January 27, 2021).

Landorff, L., 2019: *Inside European Parliament Politics.* Cham: Palgrave.

Lebaron, F., 2006: *Ordre monétaire ou chaos social? La BCE et la révolution néolibérale.* Paris: Croquant.

Lévi-Strauss, C., 2009: *Oeuvres.* Paris: La Pléiade.

Merriam-Webster, 2021: Capital. Merriam-Webster.com.https://www.merriam-webster.com/ dictionary/capital (accessed February 16, 2021).

Michel, H. (ed.), 2006: *Lobbyistes et lobbying de l'Union Européenne.* Strasbourg: Presses Universitaires de Strasbourg.

Offerlé, M. (ed.), 1999: *La profession politique, XIXè-XXè siècles.* Paris: Belin.

Page, E. C., 1996: *People Who Run Europe.* Oxford: Clarendon Press.

Reif, K. & H. Schmitt, 1980: Nine Second-order National Elections: A Conceptual Framework for the Analysis of European Elections Results. *European Journal of Political Research* 8(1): 3–44.

Schmidt-Wellenburg, C. & S. Bernhard (eds.), 2020: *Charting Transnational Fields. Methodology for a Political Sociology of Knowledge.* London: Routledge.

Shemer-Kunz, Y., 2017: *Parties' Transnational Coordination in the EU after Lisbon: The Greens and Beyond.* PhD Dissertation. Universities of Amsterdam and Strasbourg.

Smith, A., 2004: *Le gouvernement de l'Union européenne.* Paris: LGDJ.

Svendsen, G. L. H. & G. T. Svendsen, 2003: On the Wealth of Nations: Bourdieuconomics and Social Capital. *Theory and Society* 32:607–631.

Swartz, D., 2013: *Symbolic Power, Politics, and Intellectuals: The Political Sociology of Pierre Bourdieu.* Chicago: Chicago University Press.

Varoufakis, Y., 2018: *Adults in the Room.* London: Vintage.

Vauchez, A., 2015: *Brokering Europe: Euro-Lawyers and the Making of a Transnational Polity*. Cambridge: Cambridge University Press.

Weber, M. 1991: *From Max Weber*. Eds. by H. H. Gerth & C. W. Mills. London: Routledge.

Wiesner, C., 2018: *Inventing the EU as a Democratic Polity*. Cham: Palgrave.

Zimmermann, A. & A. Favell, 2011: Governmentality, Political Field or Public Sphere? Theoretical Alternatives in the Political Sociology of the EU. *European Journal of Social Theory* 14(4):489–515.

Part IV: **An Emerging European Society:**
       Institutions, Structures, and Interactions

Stefanie Börner
10 Social Policy and Solidarity

Social policies are policies that strive to modify or abolish market-induced outcomes or unfavorable conditions (such as social inequalities or hazardous workplaces) by setting social standards and providing social transfers, rights, or services. The questions, however, of *when* a social inequality can be dealt with politically, *which groups* social policies should benefit and *what* these policies *aim* to achieve are highly controversial, and states vary in their responses to these matters. The development, implementation, and effects of social policy are closely linked to society as a whole. Social policies entail a whole apparatus of social-insurance and social-assistance schemes, social services, and labor-market regulations; this apparatus we call 'the welfare state'.

Each welfare state runs an intricate mix of schemes and regulations that take effect in the event of poverty, unemployment or low wages, sickness, invalidity or disability and old age. The *British National Health Service* is an example of a tax-funded social service that provides medical treatment to citizens in the case of ill health. Some countries rely on contributory social insurance, and yet others try to intervene as little as possible in individual lives and market outcomes (see Info-box 10.1 below). Thus, social policies have quite an impact on our lives because they affect (often unnoticed) individual life courses 'from the cradle to the grave'. However, from the individual point of view as well as from a macro-analytical perspective, social policy is a major ingredient of modern societies, which are marked by high degrees of individual autonomy, mobility (both social and geographic), and social diversity. Thus, through a dense network of sometimes very straightforward, sometimes extremely complex regulations and redistributive mechanisms, social policies link (otherwise unrelated) individuals to each other as well as to the state. This renders the politics of social policy not only a particularly important but also a highly delicate matter, as political actors and national governments rely on social policies as a key source of political legitimacy and citizens' loyalty towards the state.

But what does solidarity have to do with social policy? Solidarity is linked to social policy in at least three ways: First, modern social policy draws on *traditional ideas of solidarity* – that is, ideas of brotherly support and mutual responsibility such as those found in catholic social teachings. Second, to many scholars, the welfare state is a system of *institutionalized solidarity*. This conclusion is by no means self-evident. On the contrary, before social policy started to become a public matter at the end of the 19th century, people used to take care of each other in the private sphere (namely, within the family, the neighborhood,

https://doi.org/10.1515/9783110673630-010

the workshop or the local or religious community) (Börner 2013). Over the history of social security, matters of social welfare then shifted from being a private to a public concern. During this process, social solidarity ceased to take place exclusively within the narrow social sphere in which traditional norms required people to support each other and instead moved towards becoming a state responsibility. Social scientists describe this as the transformation from face-to-face solidarity to a solidarity among strangers. This abstract form of solidarity basically refers to the established relations of mutual support within society that link people from different social backgrounds and with different needs to each other. Thus, third, seen from a functionalist perspective, solidarity has become an important *source* of a society's social cohesion. Today, the Western welfare state is the most advanced expression of a system of solidarities and policies that strive to improve individual life chances, alleviate social need, or help people to organize their life in a self-responsible way. These questions of resource allocation and redistribution have always been at the heart of the debates, ideas and thinking in social policy.

With this in mind, accurately reflecting on EU social policies means both understanding the social and political circumstances that shape these policies and being aware of the historical dimension of social policy and solidarity. The emergence of a new supranational political order in Europe 60 years ago and the European economic and social integration that results from this order have triggered controversial debates about the right place and proper extent of social policy and transformed many of the conflicts within the EU into conflicts of solidarity. To better characterize the European version of social policy, this chapter asks how EU social policy affects these historically grown institutional arrangements of solidarity – the welfare state – and hence the social relations within our society in a transnational fashion and what kind of supranational policies and transnational solidarities are evolving. In introducing the basic social-policy paths that have been adopted by European actors and their specific governance approaches (i.e., the *dynamics* of European integration as regards social policy), the following section will help the reader understand the fundamental differences between national and European social policymaking. In the following, I will first provide a brief overview of how scholars have explained this development and presents the most important controversies in the field. Then, it will be further discussed how member states' welfare policies are affected by this process and whether new transnational solidarities are evolving.

Info-Box 10.1: Esping-Andersen's three worlds of welfare
To systematically distinguish the different approaches towards public welfare, the Danish sociologist Gøsta Esping-Andersen (1990) designed a threefold typology that is, although not the first typology, the most popular and widely used welfare state typology until today.

At the very core of this typology is decommodification, a concept that refers to the degree a welfare state reduces the status of individuals *vis-a-vis* the market via social transfers and services. Another of his key insights that informs the three ideal types is the idea that "the welfare state is a system of stratification" (Esping-Andersen 1990: 49). This means that welfare states modify the respective society's class structure through redistribution, which might raise the standard of living or diminish existing inequalities while at the same time prevailing class structures or status groups might remain untouched. This means the more means are redistributed the lower the degree of stratification in a welfare society.

The three groups of countries Esping-Andersen (1990) introduced are the social democratic, the conservative and the liberal welfare state. The social democratic regime prevailing in Northern Europe relies on a strong tradition of public interventions and is marked by the lowest degree of social stratification and a higher degree of decommodification. This results from universal and relatively high social benefits that require a high level of taxation. The liberal regime type consisting of the Anglo-Saxon nations are marked by the highest degree of stratification and low decommodification which gives the market a relative dominance in solving social problems given the low assistance levels. Means-testing is more wide-spread here than in the other two models. In between these two models is the conservative – or corporatist – welfare state that is made up of the continental European countries, such as Austria, Belgium, France, and Germany. Here, the role of the family as welfare provider is emphasized stronger than in the other two which is why it is also referred to as male breadwinner/female care giver-model. Instead of a universal system covering the entire resident population, social insurance is organized in distinct occupational and status-based schemes (like special pension programs for civil servants). Between these schemes, benefit levels and thus decommodification can vary considerably which is why stratification remains at a medium or even relatively high level compared to the social democratic model.

Although Esping-Andersen assigned the eighteen welfare states of his study to one of the three ideal typical models, each state entails features of the other models as well. The three-worlds approach proved so useful in comparing different welfare state, since it goes beyond the mere comparison of expenditure levels or instruments, and sheds light on aspects, such as the cultural rootedness of social security or the aims and guiding principles implicit to public schemes. However, when using the approach today one should know welfare states are in constant flux.

EU Social Politics: A New Generation of Social Policymaking?

The EU's social dimension is highly controversial – not only in normative terms (i.e., whether the EU *should* entail a social dimension at all) but also in empirical terms (i.e., whether there already *is* such a thing as a social dimension). Here, academic positions range from skeptical voices who say the EU's social dimension is a myth (Höpner 2018) to those who claim that this social dimension is slowly but surely unfolding. Among the first scholars to put EU social policy center stage were Paul Pierson and Stephan Leibfried (1995: 3), who claimed that

> [. . .] the absence of social policy initiatives at the EU level has been one of the clearest signs of its limited role. After all, the development of social policy was a key element in the history of European state building, and the welfare state is a central component of all advanced industrial nations. [. . .] Nevertheless, the Union has gradually assumed considerable authority in policy domains beyond those directly tied to the creation of a common market.

Even 25 years ago, the authors were claiming that a social dimension of Europe existed because the EU had been busy establishing quite a few social regulations and was active in matters of redistribution even then (Pierson & Leibfried 1995: 3).[1] The following section briefly examines this social dimension to better understand the nature of these policies. Essentially, the EU engages in four major social-policy activities: harmonizing, funding, coordination, and cooperation:

(1) Harmonization means that national differences in social regulation are being levelled to facilitate economic cooperation between member states. This *regulatory approach* formed part of the European integration process from the very beginning when the initial six member states signed the Treaty of Rome, which established the European Economic Community in 1957. To promote "throughout the Community a harmonious development of economic activities, a continuous and balanced expansion, an increased stability, an accelerated raising of the standard of living and closer relations between its member states", as set out in Article 2 of the founding treaty, it was not only necessary to abolish direct trade barriers, such as tariffs and customs. The formation of the common market also required the removal of barriers to competition through shared standards with respect to gender equality. The 1986 Single European Act, the first treaty revision, strengthened the Union's regulatory power in the field of occupational safety and started a transnational dialogue between trade unions and employers' associations. Examples of social regulations harmonizing the member states' policies are Directive 90/270/EEC on 'display screen equipment' (1990) and the 1992 directive on 'pregnant workers' (92/85/EEC). The European Council

---

1 Although primarily of symbolic value, joint commitments such as the Community Charter of Fundamental Social Rights for Workers (1989) or the Social Protocol (1992) belie sceptical voices that maintain that there is no such thing as social policy at the European level. These kinds of agreements are typical instruments of international organizations and form the skeleton of the EU's social dimension; however, as the following paragraph shows, there is more to EU social policy.

has since decided on more than 70 regulations in the field of health and safety.[2] The individual directives had an enormous impact on national labor-law provisions. According to a European Commission report (2004), only the Scandinavian countries were spared a comprehensive transposition of EU regulations into national law given that their existing rules were already in line with the directives. Although the regulations continue to have a considerable effect on workers' rights and the work environment, the regulatory strategy's primary addressee is the member states' macro economies (Börner 2020).

(2) In contrast to *redistributive measures,* regulatory policies do not provide social transfers to individuals that usually form the heart of modern social policy. Since the EU lacks the sovereignty to raise taxes or contributions, there is no such thing as European social benefits for the poor or the elderly. One exception is the EU's Common Agricultural Policy (CAP), which provides income support to agricultural workers. According to the sociologist Elmar Rieger, who was the first to study the CAP from a social-policy perspective, the CAP "influenced and formed life chances in the field of agriculture in a way unparalleled in other fields of Community activity. As for its economic and social consequences, the CAP functions as an agent of 'decommodification' of agricultural markets" (Rieger 1995: 222). The fact that Western and, later, Eastern agricultural workers used to be the precariat of the post-war era in Europe explains why farmers are the only group to which the EU provides direct income payments.

Apart from this sector-specific regime, EU-wide redistribution does not, unlike in most welfare states, take place between social groups but among regions. This redistributive approach is represented by the EU's structural and regional policies. Besides the large structural funds, such as the European Regional Development Fund (ERDF) or the Cohesion Fund, the European Social Fund (ESF) is of the utmost importance in the social-policy arena. Introduced as early as 1957, this employment-policy instrument is a typical product of the EU's multilevel politics: It is institutionally located directly within the European Commission, and several transnationally, locally, or nationally operating interest groups have targeted the ESF in recent decades to shape its legal framework, programs, and objectives (Kopp-Malek & Lackowska 2011). Because it is tailored towards "promoting the development and structural adjustment of the regions whose development is lagging behind" as well as "combating long-term unemployment" (EEC 1988: 9), the ESF provides support depending on regional and not individual labor-market performance or need. The assistance

---

2 See the website of the European Agency for Safety and Health at Work (https://osha.europa. eu/en/safety-and-health-legislation/european-directives; accessed February 26, 2020).

provided is project-based (i.e., it is defined by a competitive partial financing of regional projects), which at best supplements national labor-market policies. A wide range of local civil-society organizations, public agencies, and private companies implement these projects (Büttner & Leopold 2016).

In 2006, the European Globalization Adjustment Fund (EGF) was launched. It can also benefit workers who have lost their means of employment owing to structural economic changes. The EGF and ESF are the only structural policies that support (among others) individuals who belong to vulnerable groups, such as the long-term unemployed, single parents or migrants. This support comes in the form of, for example, case-specific job training, mentoring or assistance in finding an apartment or a childcare. By the ESF's own account, ESF-funded projects have supported an average of 11.7 million individuals annually between 2007 and 2014.[3] However, the funds do not establish a social right to support, which means that individuals are not legally entitled to any EU-based active labor-market support.

(3) Flourishing economic integration and increasing intra-EU mobility have enhanced the significance of the third EU social-policy approach, which is related to the free movement of workers. Article 48 of the EEC Treaty (1957) already abolished "any discrimination based on nationality between workers of the member states as regards employment, remuneration and other conditions of work and employment." The common market then unleashed several unintended policy outcomes that resulted in an unprecedented *supranational regime of social security coordination* (Threlfall 2003). The set of social rights for mobile citizens established in the process has been extended incrementally over the years and, after Maastricht, even included the economically non-active (Eigmüller 2013). It not only grants workers the right to accumulate the entitlements that they have acquired in different member states or pensioners the possibility of exporting their old-age benefits to another country. Vice versa, it also permits patients to have their medical expenses reimbursed after being treated in another member state (as regulated by the 2011 Cross-Border Health Care Directive). Workers sent by their employers to work in another EU member state for a limited period also fall under the category of mobile citizens. They are covered by the *Posted Workers Directive* (see info-box 10.2 below). Rather than establishing new social rights, this coordination regime improves the effectiveness of the existing national social rights within a transnational framework. This construction has intensified the mutual interdependence of European welfare states

---

3 According to information provided by the European Commission on the European Social Fund at https://ec.europa.eu/esf/main.jsp?catId=66&langId=en (accessed February 27, 2021).

tremendously and involves a loss of sovereignty for national welfare states, which now have to meet the requirements inherent to free movement. In contrast to the transnational regulations mentioned above (approach 1) that are designed to cover all individuals working in the EU, this coordinating action only targets *mobile* EU citizens, that is, citizens who are active across borders and whose mobility falls under the four market freedoms (the free movements of persons, goods, capital, and services) or the ensuing jurisdiction.

The 2000s witnessed a highly controversial series of case laws in this area (e.g., cases *Viking, Laval, Rüffert*) that strengthened the rights of transnational firms and the freedom of services to the detriment of trade unions' collective action and workers' social protection. As this constrained member states' abilities to regulate the labor market and the rights of trade unions, these cases received a great deal of negative attention. What is more, they show that another instrument has been gaining importance in EU social policy: rulings by the European Court of Justice (ECJ). The court's unpredicted but growing social legislation set off an avalanche of profoundly critical interpretations of European (social policy) integration. Some authors discussed the "asymmetric potentials of disembedding markets at the national level and re-embedding them supranationally" (Höpner & Schäfer 2012: 450). These works accused the EU of following a liberal market agenda that emphasizes individual rights – a process that harms national-level social protection and redistribution (Scharpf 2002, 2010). Others have argued that the field of social-security coordination has contributed to a stratification of EU social policies (Bruzelius et al. 2017) given the small numbers of this target group of transnationally mobile Europeans and the vast differences in the levels of social security among member states. This renders the third approach a policy strategy that benefits the most mobile instead of one that benefits the most vulnerable.

Info-Box 10.2: Posted workers – the new precariat in the EU
Posted workers are temporary foreign workers sent by their employers to another EU member state while they remain employed in the sending country. This specific constellation raises such questions as 'Who is responsible?' or 'Which law and wage level apply?'; questions of solidarity in short. The practice is especially widespread in sectors such as construction or the meat industry. It is inherent in the rationale of posting that the process moves in the direction from low-wage countries to countries that are usually said to have high labor standards, such as Belgium, Denmark, or Germany. The Posted Workers Directive of 1996 established that the employment conditions must comply with the legal provisions laid down in the host country (e.g., minimum wage, health and safety, holiday), whereas the sending country provides the framework for the worker's social insurance and taxation. Even though the directive defines the rights and social standards of posted workers, these are often inaccessible to or unenforceable for them. The result is that this type of mobile worker inhabits a "contingent conditional, and even vague place" within the national framework. They often face housing conditions below the standard, receive low

wages, are not covered by labor laws, and lack a voice that represents their interests (Wagner 2018: 5). They thus belong to the most vulnerable of all workers in the EU. This effect was even reinforced in 2005 when the ECJ interpreted the minimum rights set out in the directive as maximum rights (*Laval*, Case C-341/05). This basically makes it impossible for member states to define labor standards for posted workers *above* the legal minimum (see Höpner & Schäfer 2012: 443). This transnational version of atypical employment, which often results in precarious working and living conditions, is indicative of the solidarity conflicts, rebordering processes and in-between spaces that European integration sometimes produces. Together with the free movement of workers, the freedom to provide services has created a "transnational European market for low-skilled labor" (Dølvik & Visser 2009: 499). This poses a new transnational social question that EU social policy has thus far been unable to tackle (Faist & Bilecen 2015).

The political sociology of Europe, especially more recently, is interested not only in the political negotiation processes, institutional change and the conflicts between different political levels and actors but also in the interaction between actors and institutions and the way they (fail to) draw on European provisions and their *'Doing Europe'* (Woll & Jacquot 2010; Zimmermann 2016; Wagner 2018). These works show that it is important to also shed light on everyday experiences and people's encounters with institutional settings from a micro perspective. This development takes the profoundly sociological insight that social institutions have both restraining and enabling effects on actors into account.

(4) The EU began to pursue its fourth social-policy approach during the 1990s; it was codified in the 1997 Treaty of Amsterdam and institutionalized in the Lisbon Process in 2000. The treaty promotes "a coordinated strategy for employment and particularly for promoting a skilled, trained and adaptable workforce and labor markets responsive to economic change" (Art. 145 TFEU). These activities were associated with the emerging mass unemployment in Western Europe and the growing concerns that the finalization of the monetary union would entail further negative labor-market effects (Anderson 2015: 113). The European Employment Strategy (EES) aimed to promote good governance in matters of employment policy through "full employment, quality and productivity at work, and social cohesion and inclusion" (EC 2003). The framework that was to implement these ideas was the so-called Open Method of Coordination (OMC), a rather "experimental method of policy-making" (Rhodes 2005: 290) that tried to influence member states' social policies in fields where the EU has the least competencies and unleash a competition for the best policies. It intends for national governments to *voluntarily* commit to policies and reforms that comply with the guidelines formulated by the Commission. However, there are no law-enforcement procedures, only instruments borrowed from the new-public-management toolkit, such as benchmarking, monitoring, or best-practice models. Therefore, public authorities are likely to make use of the method only in areas where it matches their domestic policy preferences (Majone 2014: 271). Other

areas in which the OMC is applied are pensions, social inclusion, health, and migration. Compared to the other three approaches, the participative and policy-making elements constitutive of the OMC are institutionalized to a lesser degree, which goes back to the soft character of this method. More generally, the *soft-law approach* has often been criticized for its non-binding nature (i.e., that there are no instruments or sanctions to enforce members states' commitments to the objectives), although it did encourage transnational learning processes (Heidenreich & Zeitlin 2009: 3) and even provided a "collectively shared mental map" that allowed member states "to move in the same direction, at different intensity, and with varying success" (Visser 2009: 42, 55).

In accordance with the four social-policy approaches introduced above, the EU can be described as a "regulatory state" (Majone 1997): instead of redistribution via taxing and spending, harmonizing, and coordinating activities prevail. This form of exercising power does not require huge social expenditures (EU member states spend between 20 and 30 per cent of their overall budget on social policies) because the member states and companies that must comply with the new regulations bear the main costs. These policies and methods do not substitute national social policies but rather modify or supplement them in specific areas that are subject to transnationalization. Most of the EU's social policy initiatives are thus very much the fruit of economic integration. In particular, the regulatory and the coordinating approaches that address 'market compatibility requirements' have been characterized as market-making EU social policies (see Table 10.1) given that they do not compensate for market failures but are meant to allow for a smooth transition towards a common market (Pierson & Leibfried 1995: 3; Leibfried 2010). In contrast, the regional or sector-wide funds address the structural imbalances within the EU, whereas the OMC tackles member states' social and employment problems that might occur from market integration. Hence, to a certain extent, the redistributive and the soft-law approach try to compensate for market anomalies, although with limited efficacy.

Analysts also differ in their overall assessment of EU social policy: For some, the EU's constitutionalized general mission to advance "the well-being of its peoples", "combat social exclusion and discrimination" and "promote social justice and protection, equality between women and men, solidarity between generations and protection of the rights of the child" (Art. 3 III TEU) renders the integration project a social undertaking and an unexpectedly expansive one at that (Threlfall 2003; Vandenbroucke 2017). This perspective concentrates on the EU's ability to "enhance its own legitimacy by strengthening individual social rights" (Caporaso & Tarrow 2009). Based on the standards set by *national* welfare states, other analysts have focused on the deficient aspects of EU social policy and declared 'Social Europe' a failure given the fundamental

Table 10.1: The EU's four main social-policy approaches (NGs = national governments).

REGULATORY APPROACH	REDISTRIBUTIVE APPROACH
– Aim: Governance through harmonization – Instruments: Regulations that have to be transposed to national law – Legal basis: Treaty, binding directives and regulations – Responsible for implementation: NGs	– Aim: Governance through supporting structurally weak regions – Instruments: Projects – Legal basis: EU Treaty and specifying regulations – Responsible for implementation: Local public or private organizations and actors
COORDINATING APPROACH	SOFT-LAW APPROACH
– Aim: Governance through coordination of national social law to secure mobility within the common market – Instruments: relevant national social policies – Legal basis: Binding directives and regulations, ECJ case law – Responsible for implementation: ECJ, NGs	– Aim: Governance through soft law (i.e., providing incentives for national reforms) – Instruments: Benchmarking, monitoring, best practice (embedded in the OMC) – Legal basis: None (non-binding) – Responsible for implementation: NGs
Market-making EU social policy	Market-compensating EU social policy

structural asymmetries (Scharpf 2010) that prevail at the European level and that have left EU social policy "to the judges and the markets" (Leibfried 2010: 253; Scharpf 2002; Höpner & Schäfer 2012; Rödl & Callsen 2014). The most recent decade has yielded a new train of thought that discusses the stratifying effects of EU social policy, especially with respect to social rights and free movement (Carmel at al. 2016; O'Brien 2016; Bruzelius et al. 2017; Farahat 2017; Bauböck 2019; Börner 2020). This research tries to identify the weaknesses in the construction of EU social policy and discusses existing potentials and feasible alternatives to EU social policy. For example, Thym (2019: 106) has argued that the EU needs "a vision of social justice for the Union as a whole, not only for those moving to other Member States."

Explaining Supranational Social Policies in the EU

The largely unintended, incremental, and highly controversial development of EU social policy described in the previous section is a major puzzle given the EU's weak – although growing – mandate, the lack of financial autonomy and the possessiveness that national authorities have exhibited towards social-policy competencies (Obinger et al. 2005). This question has mainly been tackled by political scientists. What makes it an interdisciplinary endeavor, however, is the fact that existing theories have entered sociological studies, and in turn sociological concepts informed these explanations from the very beginning as well.

Neofunctionalist integration theory considers EU social policy to be a result of so-called 'spill-over effects' from economic integration to other fields (Haas 1958; Schmitter 1969). In this line of explanation, social policies at the supranational level are a side effect of market integration. Accordingly, a host of research since the 1990s has referred to the emerging social measures as market-making (instead of market-compensating) social policies for "the construction of markets so visibly and intensively shaped the trajectory of social policies" (Leibfried 2010: 279). In line with a heuristic introduced by Wolfgang Streeck (1995: 34), the main function of EU social policies is the removal of trade barriers, as is the case in the regulatory and the coordinating approach that evolved in direct dialogue with the four freedoms of the common market, a process called 'negative integration'. In contrast, the OMC and the EU's structural polices are outcomes of positive integration, which is more demanding since it requires a political consensus (Scharpf 1996: 20f.).

For *intergovernmentalists* there is no such automatism that drives EU social policy. Rather, they emphasize the EU's weak policy-making capacities, which stem from the conflicting national interests that must be aligned to push European integration ahead (Moravcsik 1993). This renders the EU's social policy-making a cumbersome process since national governments remain the main actors in European integration. Because policies that result from multilevel systems are likely to be suboptimal (Scharpf 1988), this perspective focuses on the institutional barriers and explains why EU social policies lack efficacy or tend to be highly technocratic. Thus, policy instruments such as the European Employment Strategy appear to be ineffective and bureaucratic because they employ a soft-law approach that does not allow for the enforcement of policy measures or sanctioning of noncompliance.

In contrast to intergovernmentalism's state-centered theoretical perspective, which neglects the EU's genuinely supranational policymaking mechanisms, *multilevel governance* takes the complex negotiation processes and the shifting power balances at the European level into account (Marks et al. 1996; Hooghe & Marks 2001). Because actors with their particular interests are no longer seen only as a function of their national governments but as players in "a multitiered system of governance" (Pierson & Leibfried 1995: 3), EU social policy is understood as a result of unexpected dynamics and political conflicts between the central level and the constituent units. Adopting this perspective has enabled researchers to explain unexpected outcomes of EU social policymaking. Falkner (1998), for example, showed that the involvement of organized interests was key to advancing EU social policy during the 1990s. Another new actor in supranational social policy was the ECJ; its *Eurolegalism* (Kelemen 2006) became an important driving force of European *integration through law*. Authors who highlight the "growing judicial role in shaping policy" (Kelemen 2006: 5) have analyzed both the extent to which the EU calls on citizens to claim their transnational rights and, vice versa, how EU citizens call on it to enforce their individual rights that derive from the freedom of services and freedom of mobility of workers – and as of 1992 even of the economically inactive. The Cross-Border Health Care Directive, for instance, which is a part of the EU's social security coordination, was only initiated after several citizens invoked European law to claim their mobility rights (Eigmüller 2013). Caporaso and Tarrow (2009: 595) have argued that ECJ decisions not only helped to complete the market but also "to embed the market in what it [the ECJ] considers the legitimate social purpose of protecting the rights of workers and their families". On the other hand, although the more than 1,000 social-policy rulings over the last fifty years make it the policy area with the third most ECJ court cases (Martinsen 2015: 11), the growing judicial role in promoting social policy has also been seen to have destructive effects for national welfare states and collective social rights as they free "individuals from collectively imposed obligations" instead of socially embedding the market more comprehensively (Höpner & Schäfer 2012: 432; Rödl & Callsen 2014).

More recently, sociological perspectives on EU social policy have considered the emergence of different social-policy fields or concepts and emphasized the constructivist nature of these processes. These approaches shed light on the strategies, resources, and context factors that enabled EU social policy to find "a *raison d'être* alongside national social policies" (Bernhard 2011: 441, original emphasis). In showing how transnational social spaces emerge, they bring another type of actor – namely, EU-wide organizations, social movements, and other non-state actors (e.g., experts) – to the fore and highlight how this field functions. This research has been useful in uncovering the mechanisms that have given rise to the neoliberal consensus that underlies the Lisbon strategy or the Europe 2020 framework (Rowell 2011) and explaining how statistical and legal categories that emerge during EU social policymaking are constructed (Tietze 2019). In a similar way, *historical sociological perspectives* such as diachronic comparisons or historical institutionalist approaches provide explanations for existing lines of conflict and institutions by focusing on the processuality of social policymaking, path-dependent development, and the formation of social categories (Marks 1997; Börner 2013; Börner & Eigmüller 2015; Anderson 2015). From such a perspective, EU social policies are considered to be the result of contingent rescaling processes that are shaped by all kinds of actors against the backdrop of member states' centrifugal forces and historical legacies on the one hand and the centralizing powers and autonomous aspirations of the EU on the other. Theresa Wobbe and Ingrid Biermann (2007), for instance, have analyzed the emergence of "the principle of equal pay for male and female workers" (Art. 119, ECC Treaty) being subject to the regulatory approach. They show how the principle transformed from member states' economic interest in avoiding unfair competition to a supranational norm enforced by the EU, and how this norm became an increasingly independent political factor that comes with an agenda of its own.

National Welfare States and European Social Policies

For a long time, social policy in the EU used to be a side product of market integration that was only necessary to eliminate competitive disadvantages and co-ordinate the social security of mobile workers within the common market. Whereas member states' social policies are meant to protect individuals from the market (i.e., the typical risks individuals face in industrialized and post-industrial societies), EU-level social policies have sought to regulate the emerging social-security flaws that result from a transnational lifestyle. Thus, when we compare the role of social policies in the nation-building process during the 19th century with the character of EU social policies, they do not have much in common. It is not social but economic policies that were the main drivers of Europe's unification process after the Second World War. In contrast, in the national model of social integration, which is marked by a congruence between state, territory and society, social policies played a crucial role in democratic legitimacy, citizens' loyalty and national identity. Today, national "social policy is the single largest area of government activity" (Anderson 2015: 8). Public social spending is high in most member states, especially compared to other regions of the world, with an EU27 average of around one fifth of GDP in 2018 according to Eurostat data.[4] Emphasizing the enormous significance of national social policies helps us to better understand why the supranational activities in the social-policy arena have created a conflictual relationship between national and EU social policy. EU social policy has neither replaced national social policies nor has it made them redundant. Instead, EU social policy has restricted

---

4 Eurostat: Government expenditure on social protection (gov_10a_exp).

the leeway of national political actors, shaped national welfare reforms and co-ordinated national provisions so that they all can operate under transnational conditions.

Although, in theory, "[t]he member states remain masters of their own welfare states" (Anderson 2015: 7), this mastery is impaired in at least three ways according to a heuristic suggested by Stephan Leibfried (2010: 255). First of all, the EU has gained more and more competencies in the social arena. In addition to qualified majority voting being extended to more and more areas, each treaty has also widened the EU's social-policy mandate (for an overview Anderson 2015: Ch. 3). Consequently, national actors must take into consideration European primary law, directives and regulations when initiating social reforms. National social law also must fulfil the *market-compatibility requirements* derived from the four freedoms. Hence, "a whole range of social policy designs that would be available to sovereign welfare states – and belong to the traditional policy 'toolkit' – are prohibited, or made more costly, to member states within the EC's multi-tiered polity" (Leibfried 2010: 274). National redistributive policies are especially affected by the EU's social-security coordination because member states might react to the perceived budget pressure that arises from the transnationalization of social rights. This, however, is more likely to have consequences for the non-mobile citizens (i.e., for the group of individuals who benefit the least from these rights) (Börner 2020: 10). A second source of this loss of sovereignty are the *direct policy pressures* that mainly stem from the regulative and the soft-law approach – for example, in the field of gender equality or health and safety at work. Last but not least, *market integration* itself exerts *indirect pressures* that lead national actors to adapt their welfare states to EU rules (e.g., when competitive disadvantages that date back to national social standards, such as high social-security contributions, are anticipated). The assumption that this could trigger a downward convergence between member states gave rise to the race-to-the-bottom thesis (Kvist 2004).

One of the most influential EU social-policy analyses, by Maurizio Ferrera, has examined territorial shifts and rescaling processes and has provided us with a thorough understanding of the macro processes that underlie European social-policy integration. Ferrera (2005: 7) has described them as "destructuring processes" that are "redrawing the boundaries of national welfare states". In contrast to the boundary-drawing of welfare states, European integration engenders the opening and shifting of boundaries. As a result, EU citizens can exit their domestic schemes without losing social protection and enter the social systems of other member states as social citizens. Not only does this put enormous pressure on domestic social budgets, it also restricts the exclusionary prerogatives of nation states because the structural dynamics put the "long-standing patterns of institutionalized solidarity" under pressure (Ferrera 2005: 207, 8): "The sovereign 'right to bound' is still there, but it is no longer an absolute right, subject as it is to the limits imposed by EU competition and coordination regimes – which specify the conditions under which it can be legitimately exercised – and by the judicial review of the ECJ" (Ferrera 2005: 207). Ferrera's long-term perspective allows EU social policy to be considered in a new light because it focuses both the restrictions on national sovereignty as well as the chances for a less exclusive EU-wide social policy.

This leaves us with one fundamental question to be discussed in the final section – that is, whether new forms of solidarity will emerge at the supranational level that are able to close the welfare gaps and heal the social deficit.

The Transfer of Social Solidarity to the EU?

For many observers, the transfer of social-policy competencies to the European level together with the increasing interactions between EU citizens fueled the hope that social solidarity, which seems so closely wedded to national welfare systems, might begin to open towards other European states as well. Using the sociological toolkit of Émile Durkheim, Richard Münch argued that European integration has unleashed a shift in solidarities that is comparable to the shift from local private to national public solidarity described at the beginning of this chapter. Advancing supranational integration and transnational exchange have resulted in an increasing division of labor in Europe that is also likely to relocate the established solidarities from the national to the European sphere. However, this *network solidarity* is bound to be weaker and more abstract given the vast socio-economic differences between member states and the liberal bias of EU regulation and legislation (Münch & Büttner 2006: 74). In this European network, solidarity is based on ever tighter economic connections that lack an EU-wide collective consciousness. While national social policy is characterized by "sharing arrangements based on interpersonal transfers and individual social entitlements", EU social policy must rely on modest regional redistributive mechanisms as well as its regulating and coordinating role (Ferrera 2005: 177). The EU has created a new transnational social-policy paradigm that "supports the employability of the single individual instead of job security, equal opportunities instead of equal results, and the justice of achievement instead of status security" (Münch 2006: 94). This lack of redistributive solidarity increases the competition between member states, regions, European citizens and so forth. This leads Streeck (1999) to speak of a *competitive solidarity* that centers on a marketization process that covers all areas of society and turns social policies into economic policies. What we see here is that, although sociologists and political scientists employ different concepts, they agree in their diagnoses that the emerging solidarity at the European level is weaker, less cohesive, and collective in nature. These macro analyses provide insightful interpretations of the existing European social policy regime. However, it is appropriate to exercise caution and not overstate or romanticize the notion of redistributive solidarities and the national welfare state.

Another important aspect of transnational solidarity in the EU is citizens' willingness to provide for others, even across borders, or to widen the EU's policy competencies in that area. Empirically, solidarity does not seem to be among the shared values of Europeans. In a survey conducted by the European Commission (2019a: 67) itself only 15 per cent of the respondents chose solidarity from a list of 12 items, putting it in ninth place. Nevertheless, a slim majority of Europeans thinks that more decisions on social security should be made at the European level (European Commission 2019b: 177). Yet these data approach transnational solidarity only very roughly. A recent study sheds more light on this question. It suggests that an overwhelming majority of Europeans supports transnational solidarity: 80 per cent of the respondents thought that the EU should reduce income differences between the rich and poor, and most of them welcomed the idea of the EU guaranteeing a decent standard of living for the elderly (90 per cent) and the unemployed (77 per cent) (Gerhards et al. 2019: 144, 147). This result might surprise many readers as it seems to neglect the multifaceted conflict lines that European society (or rather, societies) is facing now. It seems to be the result of the pre-existence of welfare states and their still-increasing embeddedness as well as the growing interdependence of national societies rather than outright approval of a European welfare state.

Didactical Section

Key Learning Points

- Social policy is not by nature but by historical development a national endeavor, however, European integration challenges and weakens this arrangement.
- Even though there is no supranational welfare state, the EU has become an important actor in the field of social policy. We can distinguish between four different approaches to social policy at the European level: regulatory, redistributive, coordinating, and soft law. They do not substitute national social policies but modify or supplement them in specific areas that are subject to transnationalization.
- In contrast to national social policies EU social policy is less redistributive and more regulatory. Therefore, we speak of market-making instead of market-compensating policies. They differ from national approaches with respect to scope, size of the budget and administrative body as well as the instruments employed.
- Given the enormous significance of national social policies the growing supranational activities in the social-policy arena have created a conflictual relationship between national and EU social policy. Major difficulties arise from the fact that member states must fulfil market-compatibility requirements that restrict national sovereignty.
- Existing theoretical approaches that explain EU social policy diverge in the way they interpret the EU's political power, the main actors, and major drivers of social policy.

Further Readings

For an introduction to individual social-policy fields: Anderson, K., 2015: *Social Policy in the European Union*. London: Palgrave.

Already one of the classics, this work provides an overview of how and why EU social policy differs from national ones: Pierson, P. & S. Leibfried, 1995: Semi-sovereign welfare states: Social policy in a multi-tiered Europe. In: Leibfried, S. & P. Pierson (eds.), *European Social Policy: Between Fragmentation and Integration*, pp. 43–77. Washington: Brookings.

The following two papers introduce the basic debate between the progressive and the critical approach in this field: Caporaso, J. & S. Tarrow, 2009: Polanyi in Brussels: Supranational institutions and the transnational embedding of markets. *International Organization* 63(3):593–620. Höpner, M. & A. Schäfer, 2012: Embeddedness and regional integration: Waiting for Polanyi in a Hayekian setting. *International Organization* 66(3):429–455.

Questions for Discussion

- Why is it so difficult to establish social policy at the EU level? List three reasons.
- A friend of yours read about the idea to introduce a supranational unemployment scheme in the EU. She is confused by this given that she thought that social insurance, social assistance, and social services were supposed to be regulated at the national level. Now she would like to know whether a (supranational) European welfare state exists. Provide a brief answer.
- What does integration by law mean?
- The Working Time Directive (2003) sets minimum standards with respect to weekly working hours, breaks and holiday for all employees who work within the EU. It is a binding instrument that member states must comply with and transpose into national law. Which of the four social policy approaches does it match (Table 10.1)?

References

Anderson, K., 2015: *Social Policy in the European Union*. London: Palgrave Macmillan.

Bauböck, R. (ed.), 2019: *Debating European Citizenship*. Cham: SpringerOpen.

Bernhard, S., 2011: Beyond Constructivism: The Political Sociology of an EU Policy Field. *International Political Sociology* 5(4):426–445.

Börner, S., 2013: *Belonging, Solidarity and Expansion in Social Policy*. Basingstoke: Palgrave.

Börner, S., 2020: Marshall revisited. EU social policy from a social-rights perspective. *Journal of European Social Policy* 30(4):421–435. https://doi.org/10.1177/0958928720904330.

Börner, S. & M. Eigmüller (eds.), 2015: *European Integration, Processes of Change and the National Experience*. Basingstoke: Palgrave.

Bruzelius C., C. Reinprecht & M. Seeleib-Kaiser, 2017: Stratified social rights limiting EU Citizenship. *Journal of Common Market Studies* 55(6):1239–1253.

Büttner, S. M., & L. M. Leopold, 2016: A 'new spirit' of public policy? The project world of EU funding. *European Journal of Cultural and Political Sociology* 3(1):41–71.

Caporaso, J. & S. Tarrow, 2009: Polanyi in Brussels: Supranational institutions and the transnational embedding of markets. *International Organization* 63(3):593–620.

Carmel, E., B. Sojka & K. Papiez, 2016: Free to move, right to work, entitled to claim? Governing social security portability for mobile Europeans. *WSF Working Paper Series* 1/2016.

Dølvik, J. E. & J. Visser, 2009: Free movement, equal treatment and workers' rights: can the European Union solve its trilemma of fundamental principles? *Industrial Relations Journal* 40(6):491–509.

Eigmüller, M., 2013: Europeanization from below: The influence of individual actors on the EU integration of social policies. *Journal of European Social Policy* 23(4):363–375.

Esping-Andersen, G., 1990: *The Three Worlds of Welfare Capitalism*. Princeton: Princeton University Press.

European Commission, 2004: Communication from the Commission to the European Parliament, the Council, the European Economic and Social Committee and the Committee of Regions on the practical implementation of the provisions of the Health and Safety at Work Directives 89/391 (Framework), 89/654 (Workplaces), 89/655 (Work Equipment), 89/656 (Personal Protective Equipment), 90/269 (Manual Handling of Loads) and 90/270 (Display Screen Equipment). *COM/2004/0062 final*. Brussels.

European Commission, 2019a: *Standard Eurobarometer* 91. Spring 2019. European citizenship. Brussels. https://ec.europa.eu/commfrontoffice/publicopinion/index.cfm/ResultDoc/download/DocumentKy/88100 (accessed February 9, 2021).

European Commission, 2019b: *Standard Eurobarometer* 91. Spring 2019. First Results: Public opinion in the European Union. Brussels. https://ec.europa.eu/commfrontoffice/publicopinion/index.cfm/ResultDoc/download/DocumentKy/88107 (accessed February 9, 2021).

EEC, 1999: Council Regulation (EEC) No 2052/88 of 24 June 1988 on the tasks of the Structural Funds and their effectiveness and on coordination of their activities between themselves and with the operations of the European Investment Bank and the other existing financial instruments. *Official Journal* L 185, 9–20.

Faist, T. & B. Bilecen, 2015: Social Inequalities Through the Lens of Social Protection: Notes on the Transnational Social Question. *Population, Space and Place* 21(2):282–293.

Falkner, G., 1998: *EU Social Policy in the 1990s: Towards a Corporatist Policy Community*. London and New York: Routledge.

Farahat, A., 2017: Wettbewerb um Migranten? Die Stratifikation von Freizügigkeitsrechten in der EU. In: Kadelbach, S. (ed.), *Wettbewerb der Systeme – System des Wettbewerbs in der EU*, pp. 101–122. Baden-Baden: Nomos.

Ferrera, M., 2005: *The Boundaries of Welfare. European Integration and the New Spatial Politics of Social Protection*. Oxford: Oxford University Press.

Gerhards, J., H. Lengfeld, Z. S. Ignácz, F. Kley & M. Priem, 2019: *European Solidarity in Times of Crisis In-sights from a Thirteen-Country Survey*. London and New York: Routledge.

Haas, E. B., 1958. *The Uniting of Europe: Political, Social and Economic Forces, 1950–57*. London: Stevens.

Heidenreich, M. & J. Zeitlin, 2009: The Open Method of Coordination: a pathway to the gradual transformation of national employment and welfare regimes? In: Heidenreich, M. & J. Zeitlin. (eds.), *Changing European Employment and Welfare Regimes. The Influence of the Open Method of Coordination on National Reforms*, pp. 10–36. London: Routledge.

Hooghe, L. & G. Marks, 2001: *Multi-Level Governance and European Integration*. Lanham: Rowman & Littlefield.

Höpner, M. & A. Schäfer, 2012: Embeddedness and regional integration: Waiting for Polanyi in a Hayekian setting. *International Organization* 66(3):429–455.

Höpner, M., 2018: *Social Europe is a myth*. https://www.socialeurope.eu/social-europe-is-a-myth (accessed February 16, 2021).

Kelemen, D., 2006: Suing for Europe: Adversarial legalism and European governance. *Comparative Political Studies* 39(1):101–127.

Kopp-Malek, T. & M. Lackowska, 2011: Structual Funds. In: Heinelt, H. & M. Knodt (eds.), *Policies within the EU Multi-Level System*, pp. 153–170. Baden-Baden: Nomos.

Kvist, J., 2004: Does EU Enlargement Start a Race to the Bottom? Strategic Interaction among EU Member States in Social Policy. *Journal of European Social Policy* 14(3):301–318.

Leibfried, S., 2010: Social policy: Left to the judges and the markets? In: Wallace, W., H. Wallace & M.A. Pollack (eds.), *Policy- Making within the European Union*, pp. 243–278. Oxford: OUP, 5th edition.

Majone, G., 1997: From the positive to the regulatory state: Causes and consequences of changes in the mode of governance. *Journal of Public Policy* 17(2):139–167.

Majone, G., 2014: *Rethinking the Union of Europe Post- Crisis: Has Integration Gone Too Far?* Cambridge: CUP.

Marks, G., 1997: A Third Lense: Comparing European Integration and State Building. In: Klausen, J. & L. A. Tilly (eds.), *European Integration in Social and Historical Perspective: 1850 to the Present*, pp. 23–43. Lanham: Rowman & Littlefield.

Marks, G., L. Hooghe & K. Blank, 1996: European integration from the 1980s: State-centric vs multi-level governance. *Journal of Common Market Studies* 34(3):341–377.

Martinsen, D. S., 2015: *An Ever More Powerful Court? The Political Constraints of Legal Integration in the European Union*. Oxford: OUP.

Moravcsik, A., 1993: Preferences and Power in the European Community: A Liberal Intergovernmentalist Approach. *Journal of Common Market Studies* 31(4),473–523.

Münch, R., (2006): Solidarity and Justice in the Extended European Union. In: Bach, M., C. Lahusen & G. Vobruba (eds.), *Europe in Motion. Social Dynamics and Political Institutions in an Enlarging* Europe, pp. 79–95. Berlin: edition sigma.

Münch, R. & S. Büttner, 2006: Die europäische Teilung der Arbeit. Was können wir von Émile Durkheim lernen? In: Heidenreich, M. (ed.), *Die Europäisierung sozialer Ungleichheit. Zur transnationalen Klassen- und Sozialstrukturanalyse*, pp. 65–107. Frankfurt and New York: Campus.

O'Brien, C., 2016: Civis capitalist sum: Class as the new guiding principle of EU free movement. *Common Market Law Review* 53(4):937–978.

Obinger, H., S. Leibfried & F. G. Castles, 2005: Bypasses to a Social Europe? Lessons from federal experience. *Journal of European Public Policy* 12(3):545–571.

Pierson, P. & S. Leibfried, 1995: Semi-sovereign welfare states: Social policy in a multi-tiered Europe. In: Leibfried, S. & P. Pierson (eds.), *European Social Policy: Between Fragmentation and* Integration, pp. 43–77. Washington: Brookings.

Rhodes, M., 2005: Employment Policy. Between Efficacy and Experimentation. In: Wallace, W., H. Wallace & M. A. Pollack (eds.), *Policy-Making Within the European* Union, pp. 279–304. Oxford: OUP, 5th edition.

Rieger, E., 1995: Protective Shelter or Straitjacket: An Institutional Analysis of the Common Agricultural Policy of the European Union. In: Leibfried, S. & P. Pierson (eds.), *European Social Policy: Between Fragmentation and Integration*, pp. 194–230. Washington: Brookings.

Rowell, J., 2011: The instrumentation of European disability policy: Constructing a policy field with numbers. In: Rowell J. & M. Mangenot (eds.), *A Political Sociology of the European Union*, pp. 243–262. Manchester: MUP.

Rödl, F. & R. Callsen, 2014: The struggle for Union rights under the euro and the dialectics of social integration. In: Joerges, C. & C. Glinsky (eds.), *The European Crisis and the Transformation of Transnational Governance*, pp. 101–121. Oxford: Hart Publishing.

Scharpf, F. W., 1988: The Joint-Decision Trap: Lessons from German Federalism and European Integration. *Public Administration* 66(3):239–278.

Scharpf, F. W., 1996: Negative and Positive Integration in the Political Economy of European Welfare States. In: Schmitter, P. C. & W. Streeck (eds.), *Governance in the European Union*, pp. 15–39. London: Sage.

Scharpf, F. W., 2002: The European Social Model: Coping with the Challenges of Diversity. *Journal of Common Market Studies* 40(4):645–670.

Scharpf, F. W., 2010: The asymmetry of European integration, or why the EU cannot be a 'social market economy'. *Socio- Economic Revue* 8(2):211–250.

Schmitter, P., 1969. Three Neo-functional Hypotheses About International Integration. *International Organization* 23(1): 161–166.

Streeck, W., 1995: Neo-voluntarism: A new European social policy regime. *European Law Journal* 1(1):31–59.

Streeck, W., 1999: *Competitive Solidarity: Rethinking the "European Social Model"*. Köln: Max-Planck-Institut für Gesellschaftsforschung.

Threlfall, M., 2003: European Social Integration: Harmonization, Convergence and Single Social Areas. *Journal of European Social Policy* 13(2):121–139.

Thym, D., 2019: The failure of Union citizenship beyond the single market. In: Bauböck, R. (ed.), *Debating European Citizenship*, pp. 101–106. IMISCOE: Springer.

Tietze, N., 2019: *Legal Imagination* am Europäischen Gerichtshof: Erzählungen europäischer Richter über Gleichbehandlung und Kategorisierungen des Sozialen. In: Fertikh, K., H. Wieters & B. Zimmermann (eds.), *Ein soziales Europa als Herausforderung. Von der Harmonisierung zur Koordination sozialpolitischer* Kategorien, pp. 323–349. Frankfurt/ Main: Campus.

Vandenbroucke, F., 2017: The idea of a European social union. In: Vandenbroucke F., C. Barnard & G. De Baere (eds.), *A European Social Union after the Crisis*, pp. 3–46. Cambridge: CUP.

Visser, J., 2009: Neither convergence nor frozen paths: Bounded learning, international diffusion of reforms and the Open Method of Coordination. In: Heidenreich, M. & J. Zeitlin (eds.), *Changing European Employment and Welfare Regimes. The Influence of the Open Method of Coordination on National Reforms*, pp. 37–60. London: Routledge.

Wagner, I., 2018: *Workers Without Borders. Posted Work and Precarity in the EU*. Cornell: Cornell University Press.

Wobbe, T. & Biermann, I., 2007: Die Metamorphosen der Gleichheit in der Europäishcen Union. *Kölner Zeitschrift für Soziologie und Sozialpsychologie* 59(4):565–588.

Woll, C. & S. Jacquot, 2010: Using Europe: Strategic action in multi-level politics. *Comparative European Politics* 8(1):110–126.

Zimmermann, K., 2016: Local Responses to the European Social Fund. *Journal of Common Market Studies* 54(6):1465–1484.

Zsófia S. Ignácz & Eleonora Vlach

11 Socio-structural Developments and Inequalities in Europe

The study of social structure is one of the fundamental areas of sociology and has been present since the discipline's earliest stages (Durkheim [1893] 1933; Marx & Engels [1848] 2015; Weber [1922] 2013). *Social structure* refers to the presence of relations of dominance and subordination between individuals, between groups, and between the social roles of members of society (e.g., employers and employees, politicians and voters, rich and poor, teachers and students). *Structure* inherently refers to the long-term nature that a 'system of social stratification' has. In fact, relations of dominance and subordination characterize every society, even the simplest and most ancient ones (think of the distinction between hunters and gatherers at the onset of human settlements, for example) (Lenski 1966). The highest **social positions** have long been defined by the same occupations – businessmen/women, politicians, and doctors. In addition, a country's social structure is likely to remain unchanged during an individual's life, even if that individual's social position may change during their lifetime (e.g., by accessing a more prestigious job than their parents, i.e., the difference between *social origin* and *social destination*). Thus, the term social structure describes the social order of a society from a bird's and a worm's-eye view. It identifies the main arrangements typical in that society (whether it be hierarchies, groups, or networks) and it helps assess the individuals' position in social hierarchies and social groups.

The study of social structure has focused exclusively on the arrangements within national borders since the birth of nation states in the past two centuries. However, Europeanization processes have contributed a great deal in shaping social structures (Delhey & Kohler 2005; Mau & Verwiebe 2010; Kuhn 2015, Heidenreich 2016a). It prompts us to view social structure beyond the nation state and it is meaningful to expand the established single-country perspective to a European perspective. The study of *European social structure* means examining social structures across European countries and acknowledging the role that European integration plays in existing systems of social stratification.

Overall, studying the socio-structural developments of Europe connects two bodies of literature. The concepts stem from social stratification and social policy research, while the analytical approach of the field views societies through transnational lenses inherited from the sociology of Europe and Europeanization theory (Beck & Grande 2007; Díez Medrano 2010; Favell & Guiraudon 2011; Delhey et al. 2014; Kuhn 2015; Recchi 2019). The combination of these research areas is

https://doi.org/10.1515/9783110673630-011

unique: investigating a European social structure (its existence and development) weds one of sociology's oldest areas with one of its newest.

Approaches to Modelling European Social Structure(s)

How should European social structure be regarded? The discussion of European social structure is highly dependent on the approach depicting European countries and their societies. We can roughly identify four approaches (compartmentalist, comparativist, transnationalist, and pan-European), which can be ordered between two poles in regard to how national societies and social positions are connected beyond the national container. These approaches touch questions about whether we speak of European societies in the plural or of a singular European society, and how connected nation states are to one other?[1] Figure 11.1 depicts these different approaches.

Info-Box 11.1: Gilbert-Kahl model

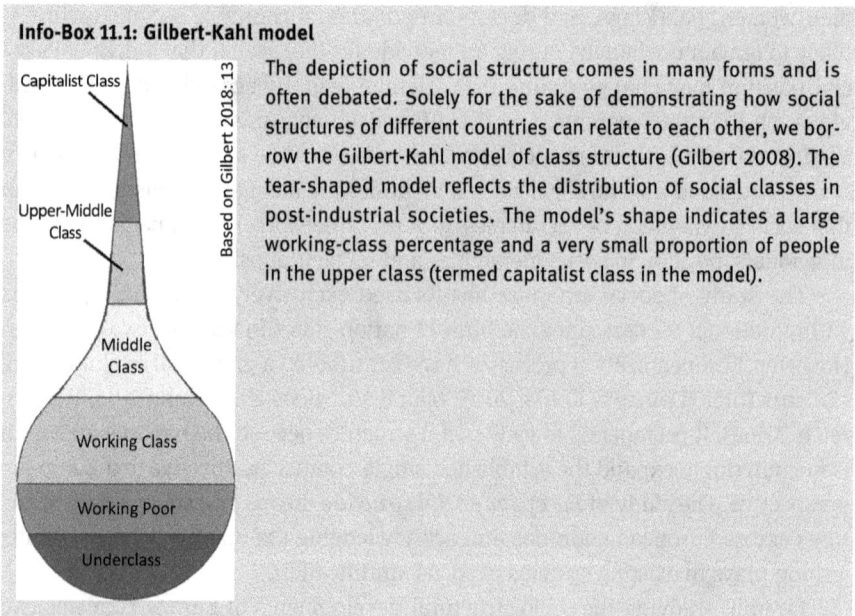

The depiction of social structure comes in many forms and is often debated. Solely for the sake of demonstrating how social structures of different countries can relate to each other, we borrow the Gilbert-Kahl model of class structure (Gilbert 2008). The tear-shaped model reflects the distribution of social classes in post-industrial societies. The model's shape indicates a large working-class percentage and a very small proportion of people in the upper class (termed capitalist class in the model).

Capitalist Class

Based on Gilbert 2018: 13

Upper-Middle Class

Middle Class

Working Class

Working Poor

Underclass

---

1 Discussions also target the definition of Europe: is it EU member states or those geographically within the European subcontinent? This chapter does not aim to respond to this debate, however.

(A) *Compartmentalist approach*: European societies are completely disconnected entities. Nation states' social structures are analyzed individually and compared to each other against baseline markers of social structure. This approach applies methodological nationalism: It seals societies off from one another and ignores the relevance of European institutions in the dynamics of social structure. Units do not constitute a whole, as they are only loosely linked due to geography and proximity.

(B) *Comparativist approach*: Societies in Europe are separate entities, where national borders are relevant and significant, but societies are linked via European integration. Nation states' social structures are analyzed individually and compared to each other with convergence patterns, baseline markers, and already include European benchmarks that stem from summarizing markers such as EU15, EU27, or EU28 countries (e.g., the aggregate fertility ratefor the EU15 or the aggregate poverty rate for the EU28). This approach acknowledges the top-down influence of EU institutions (i.e., vertical Europeanization). Individual units add up to a whole.

(C) *Transnationalist approach*: Societies in Europe are separate entities, but the relevance of national borders is diminishing. This approach mirrors the multi-level governance of the European Union and considers both national and transnational convergence patterns; baseline markers include European benchmarks (stemming from summarizing the marker in question with EU15, EU27, or EU28 countries). Social structure beyond that defined by nation states exists via horizontal, cross-border connections on top of the vertical influence of supranational EU institutions. The individual units add up to a whole and produce supranational structures on top of the national structures.

(D) *Pan-European approach*: Societies in Europe are one unified entity, where national borders are deemed irrelevant, and a single European society exists (imagine the nations of Europe melting into a single social entity!). This approach disregards the multi-level governance of the European Union and focuses only on supranational patterns. Instead of aggregate European benchmarks, social indicators refer to smaller regional units (regardless of national borders) of the EU. There is one single unit, which is a supranational structure.

A – Compartmentalist

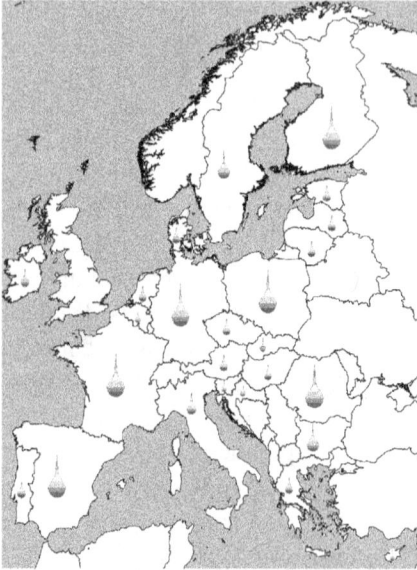

B – Comparativist

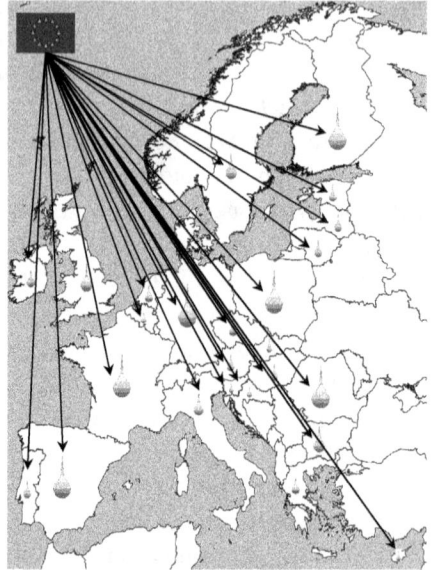

C – Transnationalist

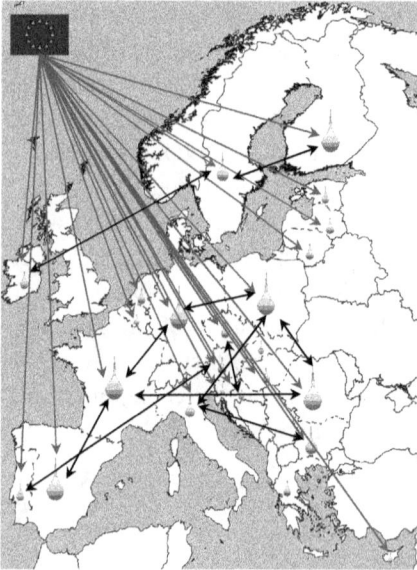

D – Pan-European

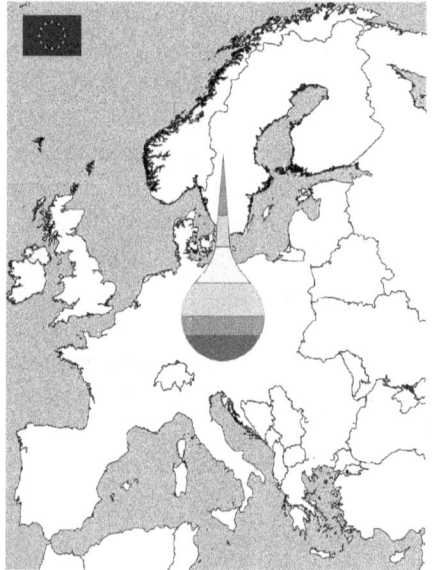

Figure 11.1: Overview of approaches to depict European societies. © EuroGeographics for the administrative boundaries.
Source: Own depiction. Map created by authors from shapefiles provided by

These approaches acknowledge European integration to different degrees. The most important contrast between the *compartmentalist* and *comparativist* approach is what role they ascribe to the European Union and the processes related to European integration. The *compartmentalist* approach does not see an active role of the EU and its institutions, while the *comparativist* approach does. The *transnationalist* approach models the complexity of European integration in the most comprehensive way, by acknowledging the vertical and horizontal Europeanization. Lastly, the pan-European approach leaves behind the complexity represented by the *transnationalist* approach, as it simplifies the study of European countries by only focusing on European society as a whole. In a way, this approach disregards national processes (or it prioritizes European processes) and concentrates on the result of European integration and deals with EU regional differences.

The *compartmentalist* and *comparativist* approaches employ methodological nationalism by dealing with societies as the national containers and investigating them along three guidelines: (1) comparatively, (2) the analysis of the endogenous convergence of nation states' social structures, (3) intersections between the commonalities (Beck & Grande 2007: 95–96). In contrast, the *transnationalist* approach deals with processes beyond the national containers and addresses cross-border dynamics between the member states.

Another distinction between the approaches is the recognition of *a* European society (or lack thereof). *Compartmentalist* and *comparativist* approaches speak of European societies only in plural. *Transnationalist* and *pan-European* approaches utilize the notion of a European society. The *transnationalist* understanding is that a European and national societies are developing side-by-side via transnationalization of the social space (i.e., horizontal Europeanization), while the *pan-European* approach overrides nation states in favor of a European society.

While these approaches allow us to study European countries from different points of view, there is a growing consensus, first spearheaded in the 2000s, that an *exclusive* comparativist approach is outdated because an outline of a European society is emerging (or is expected to) (Delhey & Kohler 2005; Díez Medrano 2011; Kuhn 2015).

Regardless of how European social structures are examined, all of these approaches are united by the research question. Thus, the following section focuses on topics central to stratification research: poverty and income inequality, the labor market, education, demographics, and subjective well-being. As such, it addresses traditional areas of stratification research as well as some new developments. Using the traditional *comparativist* approach as the baseline, it highlights convergence processes while also showing where a *transnationalist* or *pan-European* approach is particularly insightful.

Comparing Socio-Structural Developments

The section first examines demographic trends in Europe. Demography studies the population, which features those who live in the social structure. Second, it examines how resources are divided in the population, i.e., the phenomena of poverty and inequality. Next, it addresses fundamental *processes of social stratification* by dedicating a section to the dynamics of employment and unemployment. Additionally, the labor market has dramatically changed over the past several decades and educational skills have a growing importance to secure well-remunerated jobs. Thus, education and equality of educational opportunities in Europe are also examined. Finally, Europeans' social well-being is discussed to reflect the latest development in social stratification research.

Demography

Demography studies qualities of human populations and their trends over time. Births, deaths, and migration flows shape human populations (Murphy 2017), and their observation helps assess how population increases or declines and how the age structure changes. As a younger population means more individuals actively participate in the production of goods and services, countries with older populations report a higher share of people at risk of poverty (due to difficulty of labor market participation for the elderly).

According to the demographic transition theory, population growth has several stages (cf. Kirk 1996). In the first stage, natality and mortality are high, and population increases slowly. This characterized Europe until the mid-1800s. Then, industrialization improved living conditions, so mortality levels decreased while birth rates remained high, resulting in a population boom in Europe for the successive century. Post-war Europe entered a demographic stage of low fertility and mortality rates, meaning slower population growth and population aging. This stage culminates with population decline when there are fewer newborns than the number of deceased. Demographers expect the European population to grow until roughly 2045, after which it will start to decline. The Baltic states as well as Eastern and Southern European countries are already exhibiting losses in population. In contrast, many countries beyond Europe have yet to reach this last stage.

Diffuse economic prosperity, stable political conditions, technological developments, and medical progress all increase life expectancy. Currently, European newborns can expect to live around 80 years. Correspondingly, the rate of individuals celebrating their 65th birthday is growing faster than birth rates in every European country. It is estimated that by 2050 the share of people above

65 years of age (i.e., potentially outside the labor force) may reach one-third of the overall population (Eurostat 2019). Globally, these tendencies put Europe (and European countries) at the frontline for population aging (joined only by Japan). Within Europe, Southern European countries are most affected, but other European countries (such as Germany) trail closely behind.

Fertility patterns are also responsible for driving European population decline. A **fertility rate** of 2.1 or higher guarantees simple, one-to-one population replacement. More than half of nation states worldwide fall short of this threshold, and the majority of the global population lives in one of these low-fertility countries (Murphy 2017). Every European country has remained below the threshold since the 2000s. Southern European countries have the lowest fertility rates, while Eastern European countries report values around the European average. Countries initially featuring a more favorable situation converged to the average below-replacement value during the last decades.[2]

Reasons behind the decline of fertility rates are disputed. Scholars suggest that broader processes of urbanization, secularization and modernization alter females' social role in society, which then influences family structures and, in turn, fertility (Peterson & Bush 2013). Further factors include women's increased participation in education (in every country) and the labor market (especially in Scandinavian and Anglo-Saxon countries); the increased age at first partnership formation (especially in Western Europe) and the growing share of one-person families (especially in Northern and Western Europe) (Adsera 2011; Mau & Verwiebe 2010). The role of public policies is also important: the lack of care facilities (especially in Southern Europe) affect decisions to give birth, as well as labor market participation for both parents.

Dynamics of demographics are strongly anchored in nation states. Nonetheless, there is evidence that the transnational nature of European societies impact fertility rates (Marczak, Sigle & Coast 2018): cross-border reference groups influence childbearing intentions.

Poverty and Income Inequality

Poverty and income inequality are outcomes of stratification processes. Poverty means individuals lack valuable resources, such as money, assets, and goods. Income inequality refers to the unequal distribution of economic resources

---

2 For statistics on each EU member state see the Eurostat, Key Figures on Europe. Statistics Visualised. https://ec.europa.eu/eurostat/cache/digpub/keyfigures/ (accessed March 24, 2021).

among individuals within a given territory. In other words, it describes the distance between poor and wealthy individuals within society.

Info-Box 11.2: Gini index

One of the most widely used measures of income inequality is the Gini index. This index compares the total income produced to the number of individuals and then calculates how far away that picture is from a hypothetical situation of perfect equality, in which every person receives the same amount of income. The Gini index ranges from 0 (meaning zero distance to the abstract situation, i.e., all members of society possess an equal number of resources) and 100 (meaning maximal distance, i.e., one person possesses all the resources).

Inequality has many sources. Labor market position is important. Unemployed persons without income are at great risk of becoming poor. However, jobs have different conditions and remuneration, so access to valuable resources varies. Low-paying jobs can still leave people in poverty. Moreover, economic resource possession reproduces itself across generations: Children of impoverished parents face a greater risk of becoming poor than those whose parents are not poor. Parental poverty hinders children's educational success, their future occupational opportunities and, thus, the availability of economic resources to them (Blau & Duncan 1967).

Mitigating poverty (to reduce inequality) is one of European countries' primary aims. On the one side, high **poverty rates** in the population hinder national economic dynamism. On the other side, countries with low economic prosperity lack economic means to effectively fight poverty in their population. Welfare transfers can provide a way out of poverty for individuals, but the generosity of welfare varies greatly across countries (see also Chapter 10 in this volume).

Compared to the rest of the world, European countries exhibit low to average levels of income inequality. Income inequality levels have followed global trends since the 1960s: they decreased until 1990 and then stagnated in the 1990s and 2000s. There has been a slight increase in inequality since the Great Recession in 2008 to 2009, but it has not been as drastic as in non-EU countries with narrow-range welfare states (Beckfield 2019). Beyond the overall stability of European patterns, we can observe clear signs of convergence between the member states, while country-specific trends do persist. Southern Europe, Baltic and new Balkan member states have the highest levels of inequality within Europe. Scandinavia boasts the most equal societies in Europe thanks to their effective redistributive welfare system, as do some Central Eastern European countries (e.g., Slovakia, Slovenia, and the Czech Republic).

Figure 11.2 below reports the share of Europeans at risk of poverty. Poverty in Europe exhibits a positive trend over time. Most European countries show stable or decreasing rates of poverty risk since joining the EU. The amelioration is particularly strong for Eastern Europe and the Baltic countries. For example, in 2006, 60 per cent of the Bulgarian population was poor, but this rate halved after the country joined the EU. Other countries experienced drops in their poverty rates after joining the EU as well.

In the EU, individuals are no longer isolated in their social position within their nation state thanks to open borders. So, a pan-European approach can be adopted for studying poverty and income inequality. Both EU-wide poverty measures (Berthoud 2012) and an EU-wide Gini index exist. These pan-European measures echo the convergence/divergence trends reported by national accounts, but with nuanced background information (Brandolini & Rosolia 2019). Furthermore, studying a person's social status relative to their fellow Europeans (instead of just their fellow countrymen) is meaningful for understanding the relevance of social status on well-being (Heidenreich 2016c).

Labor Market Inequality

The labor market is the arena where employers and employees exchange labor for valuable resources: foremost money, but also social prestige and human capital (as working experiences expands one's curriculum). In contemporary European countries, the vast majority of the population relies exclusively on paid work to satisfy their primary needs (e.g., food, clothing, and rent) and to enjoy leisure and social activities (which often imply costs). Inequality and poverty levels greatly depend on the dynamics of the economy and labor market. The risk of unemployment is unequally distributed across individuals. Vulnerable groups, such as young, uneducated individuals with migration background, have an especially high risk of being unemployed across all European countries

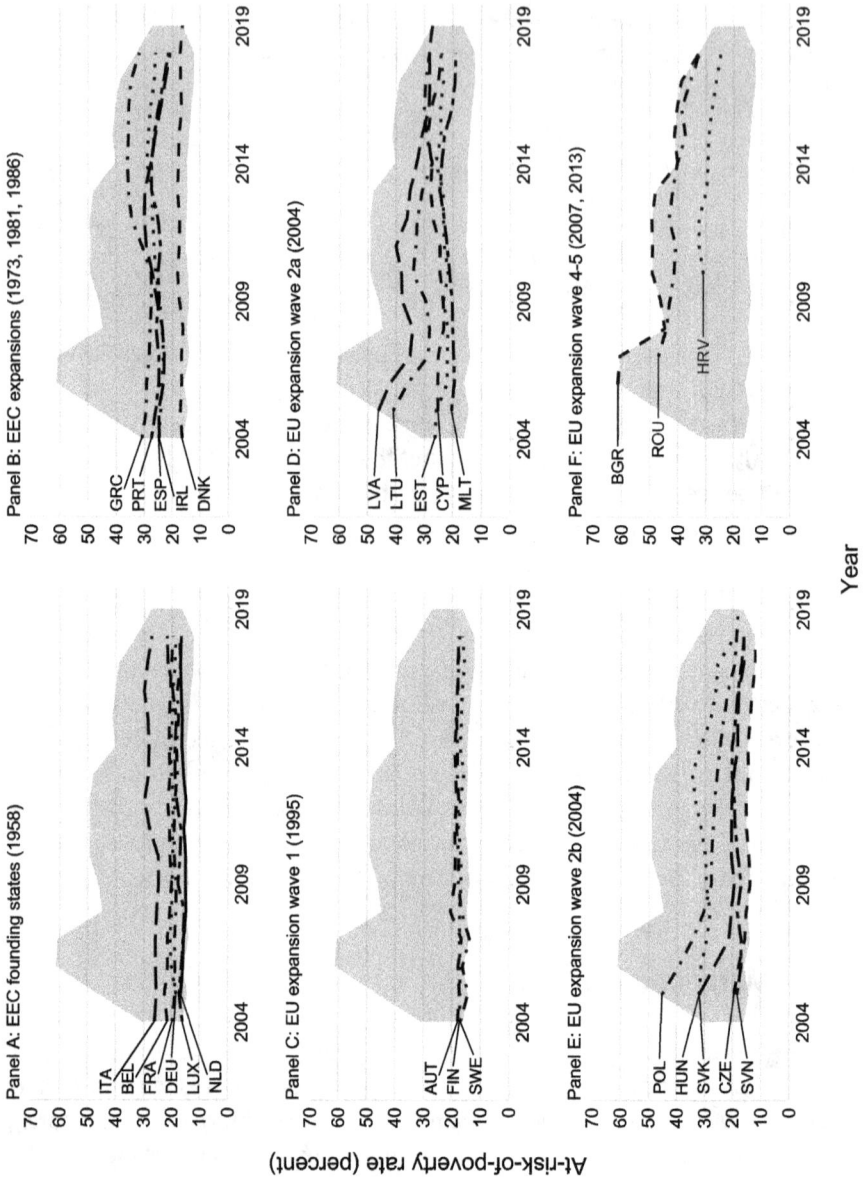

Figure 11.2: At risk of poverty rates, 2004–2019.
Source: Own depiction of Eurostat data [Table ilc_peps01].

(Heidenreich 2015). Increased liberalization of the European labor market over the last decades has substantially increased the number of individuals working in temporary contracts and/or part-time (Gebel & Giesecke 2011; Hall & Soskice 2001). Unemployment, working in precarious situations or being outside the labor market all potentially lower well-being and increase the risk of poverty and social exclusion. At a societal level, participating in the labor market (as an employer or employee) means directly contributing to the national production of goods and services (thus to a country's gross domestic product), while simultaneously subsidizing the welfare state by paying taxes. Thus, labor market activity and lack thereof are important issues for policy makers.

Activity rates show an increase in every European country over time (see Figure 11.3). A common driver of these increasing rates is the growing number of women joining the labor force due to modernization processes. Scandinavian and Baltic countries, together with the Netherlands, Germany and Denmark, have the most active work forces. Values below the average are instead frequent in Southern Europe and in the new Central European member states. However, the distance between the countries with the highest and lowest rates (the grey field) decreased from 22 to 17 percentage points over the last 20 years. Thus, they have converged.

Both employed individuals and those searching for a job (the unemployed) are considered active in the labor market. So, *unemployment rates* tell the second part of the story. Unemployment rates show little convergence across European countries. While founding member states report relative stability over the last 20 years, the same does not hold true for new member states. Contrary to activity rates, short and medium-term events drive change in unemployment rates: primarily financial and economic crises, i.e., member states' varying abilities to cope with economic downturns quickly, but also technological innovations affecting how people work (think of the changes accompanying the advent of the Internet!). For example, European prosperity and job availability decreased significantly during and after the Great Recession of 2008/2009 and it took nearly ten years for the average unemployment rates to return to pre-crisis values. At the height of the crisis, the unemployment rates remained favorable in some countries (e.g., Germany, the Netherlands, and Poland), while other countries suffered dramatic shifts: reported rates were in the two-digits. In fact, in Spain and Greece the rates were even above 20 per cent. Beyond the short and medium-term drivers, gaps in unemployment rates are systematic across European Union countries (Heidenreich 2016b). Countries' center-periphery position in Europe contribute to the long-term challenges of labor market. Southern Europe, situated at the periphery, will continue to exhibit less favorable levels of

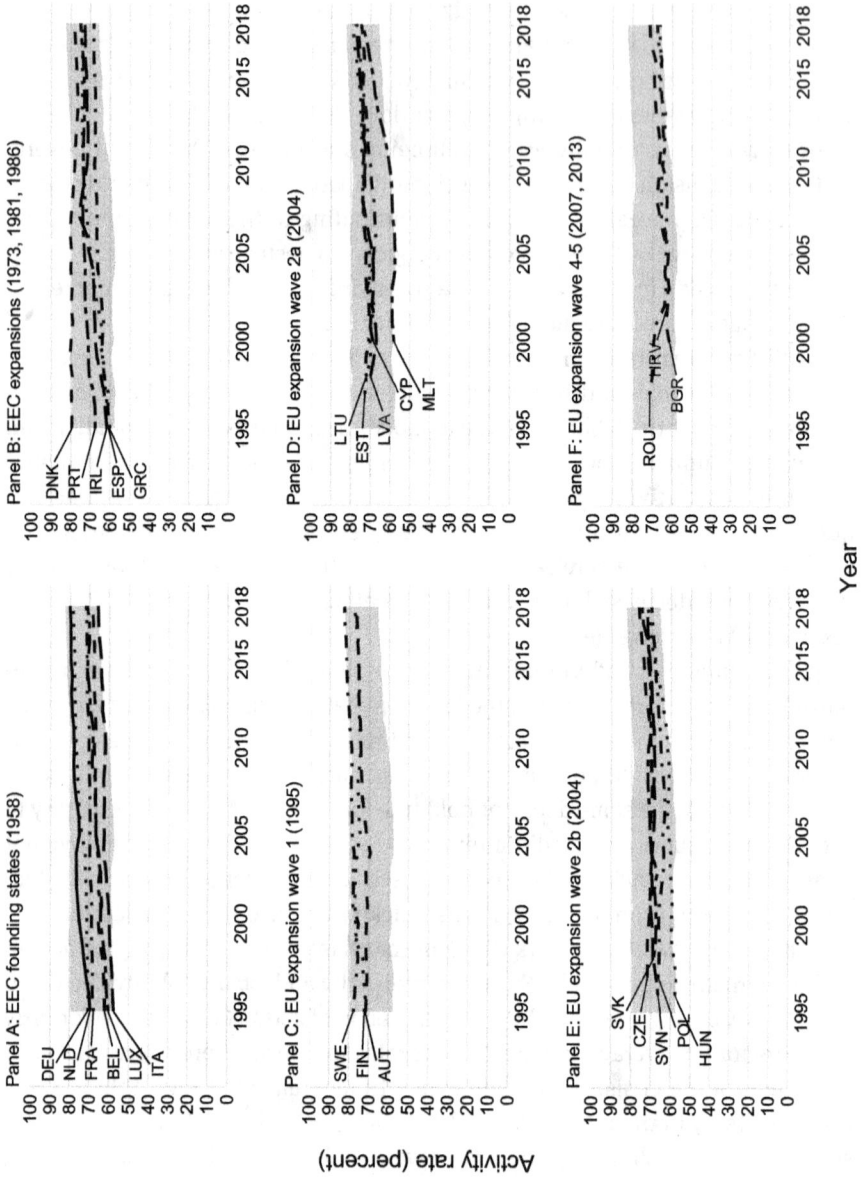

Figure 11.3: Activity rates, 1995–2018.
Source: Own depiction of Eurostat data [Table lfsa_pganws].

unemployment beyond imminent crises. This is known as double dualization: inequalities are maintained within and between countries.

Educational Inequality

Education is one of the most relevant factors determining participation in the labor market (Blau & Duncan 1967; Boudon 1974). School transfers technical and social skills to new generations and provides people with official educational credentials, to which employers assign great value. As official educational degrees are one of the greatest drivers of individuals' labor market opportunities, it is important that barriers to educational participation (e.g., lack of family support) are minimized (e.g., by free mandatory schooling and study grants).

Knowing how many young individuals in society are excluded from full-time education provides an early glimpse at how many individuals might become unemployed or working-but-poor later in life. The share of young adults (18–24 years) who prematurely quit education reveals that the educational outcomes of European societies have become more similar than only 20 years ago (Figure 11.4). The steepest convergence is reported by Southern European countries, which successfully brought initially alarming numbers (more than one out of three students left education prematurely) to a rate closer to the European average. Figure 11.4 demonstrates the positive effects of the EU's Europe 2020 strategy adopted in 2010, which aimed to lower the share of early school leavers to 10 per cent by 2020.

While European countries are converging in terms of educational participation, the same cannot be said for their educational systems, i.e., reigning educational regulations. While the European Union has made a conscious effort to equalize requirements and the value of university degrees (i.e., the implementation of the Bologna Process reform from the beginning of 2000s), students' pre-university experiences still differ across countries. Results of standardized international competency tests, the most famous of which is the OECD-PISA, demonstrate that these experiences are largely determined by the selectivity function of a country's schools, i.e., comprehensive systems (typical in Northern European and Anglo-Saxon countries) and stratified systems (frequent in Continental and Southern Europe) (van de Werfhorst & Mijs 2010). Countries with comprehensive educational systems, which first divide students into tracks at age 16, occupy the top positions in terms of average test scores. In addition, in stratified school systems the difference in test scores is higher than in comprehensive systems. Thus, stratified systems help sustain social inequality.

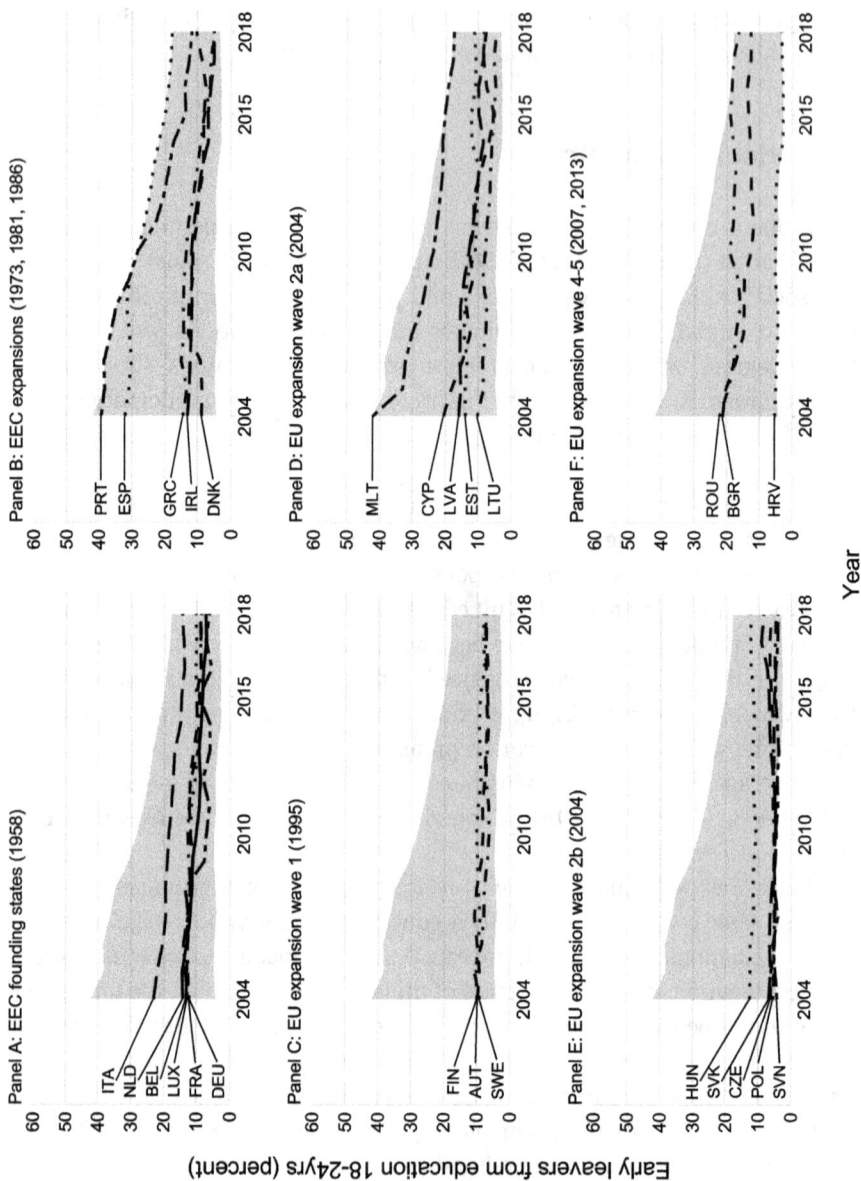

Figure 11.4: Early leavers from education, 2004–2019.
Source: Own depiction of Eurostat data [Table edat_lfse_14].

Subjective Well-Being

Subjective well-being is a function of numerous characteristics of an individual and of the country in which they live. Personal factors relevant for subjective well-being range from socio-economic measures, such as the objective quality of life measures (e.g., living conditions), individual's social position, but including 'softer' factors, such as quality of social ties, or individual's perceived relative position to others in society (i.e., reference groups). Beyond such personal factors, an individual's subjective well-being is also influenced by the quality of the society in which they live, including factors such as economic development (Sacks, Stevenson & Wolfers 2013), the level of inequality (Kragten & Rözer 2017), openness of a society (Helliwell & Huang 2008), and level of cohesion (Delhey & Dragolov 2016).

Figure 11.5 depicts average levels of subjective well-being across the EU member states. Many exhibit stable average levels of subjective well-being over time, while some exhibit upward and downward trends. Several member states that joined the EU in 2004 or later show improving average levels of well-being (e.g., the Baltic countries, Malta, and Bulgaria). In addition to *intranational* trends, some *international* tendencies emerge in the level of well-being as well. Scandinavian countries (Sweden, Norway, Denmark) and the Benelux countries exhibit the highest levels of average subjective well-being. The ranks of countries in the lower tier are less clear. Overall, however, levels of well-being converge: the range across member states is somewhat smaller in the last recorded year than it was at the first point in time.

While subjective well-being is a personal matter, EU integration shapes the well-being of Europeans as well. First, due to Europeanization, a transnational social structure is emerging in which one's personal *transnational* social position can affect their subjective well-being. There is a clear connection between transnational income position and subjective risk assessment (Heidenreich 2016c). Second, EU integration creates a new frame of reference for individuals to assess their well-being through cross-border references. Individuals cognitively expand their understanding of a milieu to become a cross-border milieu, and their imagined community reaches beyond their own national borders. Living conditions in other countries thus become relevant markers that individuals use to assess their subjective well-being. Overall, Europeans have well-founded, fundamental impressions about the living conditions in other countries (Delhey & Kohler 2005) but are also prone to cherry-pick the countries that they compare themselves with, i.e., primarily upward comparisons influence individuals' subjective well-being. Thus, people's life satisfaction is negatively affected, as they tend to consider better-off societies (Lahusen & Kiess 2019).

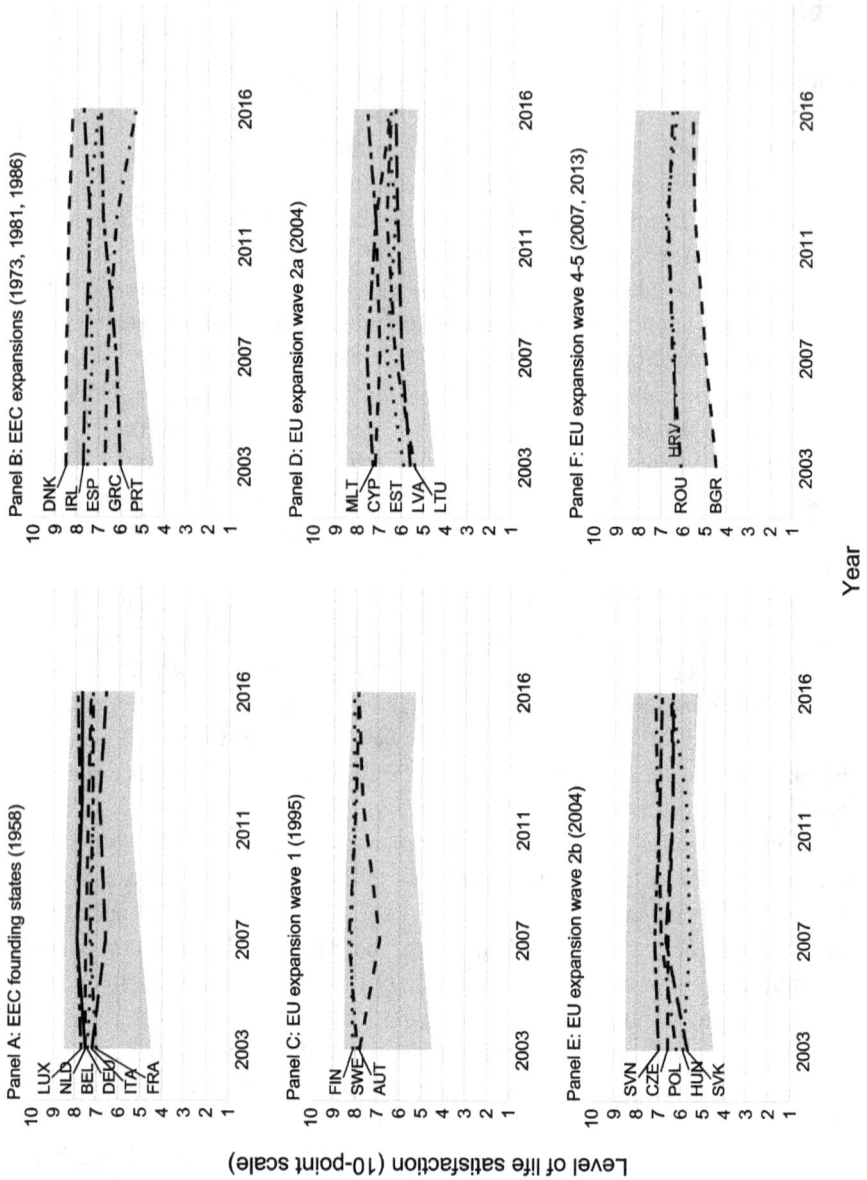

Figure 11.5: Average subjective well-being, 2003–2016.
Source: Own depiction of Eurofound data [https://www.eurofound.europa.eu/data/european-quality-of-life-survey].

The Transnationalization of European Societies

Establishing the transnational nature of European societies is an important tail-wind for the transnationalist and pan-European approaches. That is, that individuals in national societies are embedded transnationally; they are connected across and their affairs reach beyond their own national borders, they are able to, willing to and interested in engaging in cross-border interactions. Overall, there are three ways in which European societies can be transnationally connected: 1) structurally, 2) affectively, and 3) cognitively.

1) *Structural.* European social structures can be connected by how active individuals are across national borders. Individuals who engage in transnational practices and are less confined to national containers also have a greater chance of creating and moving in European social space. Authors identify transnational backgrounds and transnational human capital (i.e., speaking foreign languages) to be linked to transnational practices (Kuhn 2015). The theoretical underpinnings of this dimension stems from Karl Deutsch's **transactionalist theory**. Furthermore, the structural connectedness of European societies is also connected to the social structure of national societies. Studies show that those that engage in transnational practices are more likely to be affluent in their own country (Mau & Mewes 2009; Delhey et al. 2015; Kuhn 2015; Gerhards et al. 2017), thus structural transnationalism can also be seen as an extension of social structure bounded by nation states.

2) *Affective.* The affective connection of European societies underlines value and affectual association with a transnational European community. A main marker of cultural transnationalization is cross-border identity, that is, identifying with Europe. Based on the theoretical underpinnings from Weber, identification as a European is an important indicator for the existence of a European social class (and hence a European society) (Díez Medrano 2010, 2011).

3) *Cognitive.* Cognitive transnationalism refers to individuals considering a frame of references beyond their own national borders. Since being introduced by Delhey and Kohler (2005), scholars have often revisited this question (Whelan & Maître 2009; Goedemé & Rottiers 2011; Lahusen & Kiess 2019). Evidence suggests that other European countries serve as reference points for individuals and this also shapes social structural trends.

So, how transnational are European societies? Findings still report relatively few individuals engaging in transnational practices for a European society (Kuhn 2015) and this is in the way of the development of strong European ties, despite growing number of self-identification with Europe. And while employing a pan-European approach to European societies is not yet justified, the transnational aspect of European societies is an important aspect. In particular, Delhey and colleagues (2015) suggest that individuals' transnationalism seems to be a new dimension added to one's social position. Similarly, Díez Medrano (2010) assesses a European middle class by pinpointing those members of national societies who are in the middle class *and* identify with Europe primarily.

Didactical Section

Key Learning Points

- European society can be conceptualized as European national societies being interlinked or as a society of individuals in Europe who are transnationally connected beyond their national borders.
- Outcomes of social stratification are more comparable across European countries: they can be extended beyond national borders for understanding the overall level for all European people, instead of only the aggregate of European national levels.
- Processes of social stratification (labor market and education) are unique to European societies: the European Union consists of countries with different histories, cultures, norms and values, which all are reflected in the set-up of social stratification processes.
- Subjective well-being is of growing relevance for European social structure.
- The relevance of other European countries to individuals is selective upwards: better-off European countries serve as anchors.

Glossary

Activity rate: Indicator referring to how many individuals of a specific age over the same-aged population are employed or are currently seeking a job in the labor market.

Fertility rate: Ratio of the total births to the number of females in the population.

Poverty rate: Share of individuals whose income falls below the poverty threshold (customarily set at 60 per cent of the national median income), after taxes, with welfare transfers and family composition (as family members share resources and costs).

Social positions: Groups of individuals within society having similar levels of valuable resources (such as economic capital, social status, or prestige).

Subjective well-being: A purely subjective quality of life indicator referring to individuals' sense of satisfaction and feeling of happiness related to their own life and living conditions. This personal assessment reflects one's own position and can relate to physical and mental well-being with cognitive and affectual dimensions (cf. Veenhoven 2000). It is considered a multi-dimensional indicator because it can relate to many domains of social and personal life (Fischer 2009).

Unemployment rate: Proportion of the total active population actively searching for a job and that would be available to start working right away, i.e., they are not employed.

Transactionalist theory: The more that individuals experience cross-border interactions, the more transnational individuals are, which will result in a supranational European society (cf. Deutsch 1979; Mau & Mewes 2009; Kuhn 2015).

Further Readings

Beckfield, J., 2019: *Unequal Europe. Regional Integration and the Rise of European Inequality.* Oxford: Oxford University Press.

Carmo, R. Md., C. Rio & M. Medgyesi (eds.), 2018: *Reducing Inequalities. A Challenge for the European Union?* Basingstoke: Palgrave Macmillan.

Heidenreich, M (ed.), 2016: *Exploring Inequality in Europe. Diverging Income and Employment Opportunities in the Crisis.* Cheltenham: Edward Elgar.

Mau, S. & R. Verwiebe, 2010: *European Societies. Mapping Structure and Change.* Bristol: Policy Press.

Milanović, B., 2018: *Global Inequality. A New Approach for the Age of Globalization.* Cambridge: The Belknap Press of Harvard University Press.

Piketty, T. & A. Goldhammer, 2017: *Capital in the Twenty-First Century.* Cambridge: The Belknap Press of Harvard University Press.

Sorenson, A.B., 2000: Toward a Sounder Basis for Class Analysis. *American Journal of Sociology* 105(6):1523–1558.

Teney, C. & E. Deutschmann, 2018: Transnational Social Practices: A Quantitative Perspective In: Scott R.A., S. Kosslyn & M.C.B. Buchmann (eds.), *Emerging Trends in the Social and Behavioral Sciences,* pp. 1–15. Hoboken: John Wiley & Sons.

Additional Web-Sources

Eurostat (Key Figures on Europe). The Statistical Office of the European Union collects extensive data to describe the European population and European societies on an annual basis. Data on individuals, education, labor market, wealth, living conditions and much more (including those used in this chapter) can be explored online free of charge. Link: https://ec.europa.eu/eurostat/cache/digpub/keyfigures/

OECD database. The Organization for Economic Co-operation and Development aims to support European and non-European governments in designing policies to solve social problems, such as poverty and inequality of opportunities. The data is also available to the public through a series of interactive charts and maps comparing countries on a wide range of indicators. Link: https://data.oecd.org/

Luxembourg Income Study. The LIS is a cross-national data center that regularly collects information on wealth, income, and poverty in Europe and beyond. Interactive and colorful world maps make international comparisons of socio-economic indicators simple and user-friendly. Link: https://www.lisdatacenter.org/

Human Development Index. Sponsored by the United Nations Development Program, this resource provides comparable indicators of societies' achievements in terms of wealth, full education, and equality of opportunities, as well as socio-economic sustainability, human security, gender inequality, vulnerability and living conditions. Link: http://hdr.undp.org/en/data

The Standardized World Income Inequality Database. The SWIID is an on-going research project to create a database of reliable and comparable measures on income inequality worldwide. It covers 198 countries, is regularly revised, and updated, and the data goes back several decades. See Slot 2020. Link: https://fsolt.org/swiid/

The World Factbook. Published by the Central Intelligence Agency (CIA) of the United States. Provides basic information on various social economic, political, geographic, and infrastructural as well as transnational issues for 266 world entities. https://www.cia.gov/the-world-factbook/

Questions for Discussion

– Compare Figures 11.2 and 11.5. Would you say the data support or contradict the following statement? The countries where subjective well-being is higher are also the countries where the risk of poverty is lower.

– How transnational are you? Fill out the self-assessment quiz about your transnationality (download here: https://www.degruyter.com/books/9783110673630). Discuss your score with a classmate. How much do you think it influences your association with the European Union?

References

Adsera, A., 2011: Where Are the Babies? Labor Market Conditions and Fertility in Europe. *European Journal of Population/Revue Europeenne de Demographie* 27(1):1–32.

Beck, U. & E. Grande, 2007: *Cosmopolitan Europe*. Oxford: Polity Press.

Beckfield, J., 2019: *Unequal Europe. Regional Integration and the Rise of European Inequality*. Oxford: Oxford University Press.

Berthoud, R., 2012: Calibrating a Cross-European Poverty Line. ISER Working Paper Series 2012–02, Institute for Social and Economic Research (ISER), Colchester. https://www.econstor.eu/handle/10419/65964 (accessed February 23, 2021).

Blau, P. M. & O. D. Duncan, 1967: *The American Occupational Structure*. New York: John Wiley & Sons.

Boudon, R., 1974: *Education, Opportunity, and Social Inequality. Changing Prospects in Western Society*. New York: Wiley.

Brandolini, A. & A. Rosolia, 2019: The Distribution of Well-Being among Europeans. SOEP papers on Multidisciplinary Panel Data Research 1052, Deutsches Institut für Wirtschaftsforschung (DIW), Berlin. https://ideas.repec.org/p/diw/diwsop/diw_sp1052. html (accessed February 23, 2021).

Delhey, J. & G. Dragolov, 2016: Happier Together: Social Cohesion and Subjective Well-Being in Europe. *International Journal of Psychology* 51(3):163–176.

Delhey, J. & U. Kohler, 2005: From Nationally Bounded to Pan-European Inequalities? On the Importance of Foreign Countries as Reference Groups. *European Sociological Review* 22 (2):125–140.

Delhey, J., E. Deutschmann & K. Cirlanaru, 2015: Between 'Class Project' and Individualization: The Stratification of Europeans' Transnational Activities. *International Sociology* 30(3): 269–293.

Deeley, J., E. Deutschmann, T. Graf & K. Richter, 2014: Measuring the Europeanization of Everyday Life: Three New Indices and an Empirical Application. *European Societies* 16(3): 355–377.

Deutsch, K. W., 1979: *Tides among Nations*. New York: Free Press.

Díez Medrano, J., 2010: A New Society in the Making. European Integration and European Social Groups. KFG Working Paper 12, Kolleg-Forschergruppe (KFG) "The Transformative Power of Europe", Freie Universität Berlin, Berlin. https://ideas.repec.org/p/erp/kfgxxx/ p0012.html (accessed February 23, 2021).

Díez Medrano, J., 2011: Social Class and Identity. In: Favell A. & V. Guiraudon (eds.), *Sociology of the European Union*, pp. 28–49. Palgrave Macmillan, Basingstoke.

Durkheim, É., [1893] 1933: *The Division of Labor in Society*. Macmillan, New York.

EQLS, 2003: *European Quality of Life Survey*, Dublin. https://www.eurofound.europa.eu/sur veys/european-quality-of-life-surveys/european-quality-of-life-survey-2003 (accessed March 24, 2021).

EQLS, 2007: *European Quality of Life Surveys (EQLS)*, Dublin. https://www.eurofound.europa. eu/surveys/european-quality-of-life-surveys/european-quality-of-life-survey-2007 (accessed March 24, 2021).

EQLS, 2012: *European Quality of Life Surveys (EQLS)*, Dublin. https://www.eurofound.europa. eu/surveys/european-quality-of-life-surveys/european-quality-of-life-survey-2012 (accessed March 24, 2021).

EQLS, 2016: *European Quality of Life Surveys (EQLS)*, Dublin. https://www.eurofound.europa. eu/surveys/european-quality-of-life-surveys/european-quality-of-life-survey-2016 (accessed March 24, 2021).

Eurostat, 2019: *Ageing Europe. Looking at the Lives of Older People in the EU*, Publications Office of the European Union, Luxembourg.

Favell, A. & V. Guiraudon, 2011: Sociology of the European Union. An Introduction. In: Favell A. & V. Guiraudon (eds.), *Sociology of the European Union*, pp. 1–24. Basingstoke: Palgrave Macmillan.

Fischer, J. A., 2009: *Subjective Well-Being as Welfare Measure. Concepts and Methodology*. Munich Personal RePEc Archive. https://mpra.ub.uni-muenchen.de/16619/ (accessed February 23, 2021).

Gebel, M. & J. Giesecke, 2011: Labor Market Flexibility and Inequality: The Changing Skill-Based Temporary Employment and Unemployment Risks in Europe. *Social Forces* 90(1): 17–39.

Gerhards, J., S. Hans, & S. Carlson, 2017: *Social Class and Transnational Human Capital. How Middle and Upper Class Parents Prepare their Children for Globalization*. London: Routledge.

Gilbert, D. L., 2008: *The American Class Structure in an Age of Growing Inequality*. Thousand Oaks: Pine Forge.

Goedemé, T. & S. Rottiers, 2011: Poverty in the Enlarged European Union: A Discussion about Definitions and Reference Groups. *Sociology Compass* 5(1):77–91.

Hall, P. & D. Soskice, 2001: *Varieties of Capitalism. The Challenges Facing Contemporary Political Economies*. Oxford: Oxford University Press.

Heidenreich, M., 2015: The End of the Honeymoon: The Increasing Differentiation of (Long-Term) Unemployment Risks in Europe. *Journal of European Social Policy* 25(4):393–413.

Heidenreich, M. (ed.), 2016a: *Exploring Inequality in Europe. Diverging Income and Employment Opportunities in the Crisis*. Cheltenham: Edward Elgar.

Heidenreich, M., 2016b: Introduction: The Double Dualization of Inequality in Europe. In: Heidenreich, M. (ed.), *Exploring Inequality in Europe. Diverging Income and Employment Opportunities in the Crisis*, pp. 1–21. Cheltenham: Edward Elgar.

Heidenreich, M., 2016c: The Europeanization of Income Inequality before and during the Eurozone Crisis: Inter-, Supra-, and Transnational Perspectives. In: Heidenreich, M. (ed.), *Exploring Inequality in Europe. Diverging Income and Employment Opportunities in the Crisis*, pp. 22–47. Cheltenham: Edward Elgar.

Helliwell, J. F. & H. Huang, 2008: How's Your Government? International Evidence Linking Good Government and Well-Being. *British Journal of Political Science* 38(4):595–619.

Kirk, D., 1996: Demographic Transition Theory. *Population Studies* 50(3):361–387.

Kragten, N. & J. Rözer, 2017: The Income Inequality Hypothesis Revisited: Assessing the Hypothesis Using Four Methodological Approaches. *Social Indicators Research* 131: 1015–1033.

Kuhn, T., 2015: *Experiencing European Integration. Transnational Lives and European Identity*. Oxford: Oxford University Press.

Lahusen, C. & J. Kiess, 2019: 'Subjective Europeanization': Do Inner-European Comparisons Affect Life Satisfaction? *European Societies* 21(2):214–236.

Lenski, G. E., 1966: *Power and Privilege. A Theory of Social Stratification*. New York: McGraw-Hill.

Marczak, J., W. Sigle & E. Coast, 2018: When the Grass Is Greener: Fertility Decisions in a Cross-National Context. *Population Studies* 72(2):201–216.

Marx, K. & F. Engels, [1848] 2015: *The Communist Manifesto*. London: Penguin Books.

Mau, S. & J. Mewes, 2009: Class Divides within Transnationalisation: The German Population and Its Cross-Border Practices. In: Ohnmacht T., H. Maksim & M. M. Bergman (eds.), *Mobilities and Inequality*, pp. 165–186. Farnham: Ashgate.

Mau, S. & R. Verwiebe, 2010: *European Societies. Mapping Structure and Change*. Bristol: Policy Press.

Murphy, M., 2017: Demographic Determinants of Population Aging in Europe since 1850. *Population and Development Review* 43(2):257–283.

Peterson, G. W. & K. R. Bush, 2013: *Handbook of Marriage and the Family*. Boston: Springer.

Recchi, E., 2019: Is Social Transnationalism Fusing European Societies into One? In: Recchi, E., F. Apaydin, R. Barbulescu, A. Favell, M. Braun & I. Ciornei (eds.), *Everyday Europe. Social Transnationalism in an Unsettled Continent*, pp. 255–290. Bristol: Policy Press.

Sacks, D., B. Stevenson & J. Wolfers, 2013: Subjective Well-Being, Income, Economic Development, and Growth. In: Sepúlveda C., A. Harrison & J. Yifu Lin (eds.), *Annual World Bank Conference on Development Economics 2011. Development Challenges in a Post-Crisis World*, pp. 283–315. Washington, D.C: The World Bank.

Solt, F., 2020: Measuring Income Inequality Across Countries and Over Time: The Standardized World Income Inequality Database. *Social Science Quarterly* 101(3): 1183–1199.

van de Werfhorst, H. G. & J. J. Mijs, 2010: Achievement Inequality and the Institutional Structure of Educational Systems: A Comparative Perspective. *Annual Review of Sociology* 36(1):407–428.

Veenhoven, R., 2000: The Four Qualities of Life: Ordering Concepts and Measures of the Good Life. *Journal of Happiness Studies* 1(1):1–39.

Weber, M., [1922] 2013: *Economy and Society. An Outline of Interpretive Sociology*. Berkeley: University of California Press.

Whelan, C. T. & B. Maître, 2009: The 'Europeanisation' of Reference Groups. *European Societies* 11(2):283–309.

Emanuel Deutschmann & Ettore Recchi

12 Europeanization via Transnational Mobility and Migration

Mobility and migration between countries in Europe are central elements of Europeanization and have played an important role in uniting the continent over the last decades. By being mobile across borders, Europeans have come into contact with each other, generated social bonds and exchanged ideas, thereby creating a dense web of transnational social interaction that contributed to European society-building 'from below' (Mau & Büttner 2009; Deutschmann & Delhey 2015; Kuhn 2015; Recchi et al. 2019a; Heidenreich 2019). At the same time, mobility and migration have also created new fault lines and caused shifts in political landscapes. Brexit, an extreme example of such a rift, even contributed to the partial breakup of the European Union. Regardless of how one weighs these consequences, one thing is clear: mobility and migration matter!

When we speak of *mobility* in this chapter, we mean physical movements of people between countries.[1] *Migration* is a sub-form of such mobility. According to the United Nations, international migration occurs when someone changes their country of usual residence, irrespective of the reason or the legal status in the destination country. Conventionally, this migration is regarded as 'long-term' when the international migrant has lived in the destination country for a period of at least one year (UN 2020). In a nutshell: *migration = mobility + settlement.*

How many people move and migrate between countries in Europe? Figure 12.1 illustrates trends between 2011 and 2018 (i.e., before the Covid-19 pandemic). Panel A shows estimated transnational trips, an indicator for mobility that combines tourism statistics and air traffic data and is thus quite comprehensive (Recchi et al. 2019b). It reveals that both within the EU-28 and Europe at large, the amount of transnational mobility has strongly increased between 2011 and 2016, rising by

---

1 Research under the "new mobilities paradigm" (Urry 2000) differentiates between physical and virtual mobilities. The latter category includes, e.g., online friendships and phone calls between countries, which allow contact without changing one's location physically. For more details on this form of mobility, which is excluded here, see e.g., Kellerman (2006) and Recchi et al. (2014).

Acknowledgements: We would like to thank Sebastian Büttner, Monika Eigmüller and Susann Worschech for helpful feedback and Aditya Srinivasan for rigorous proof-reading and suggestions that improved the quality and readability of the text a lot. We are also indebted to Klaus Spiekermann for kindly permitting us to reproduce his maps in this chapter.

https://doi.org/10.1515/9783110673630-012

A. Transnational trips

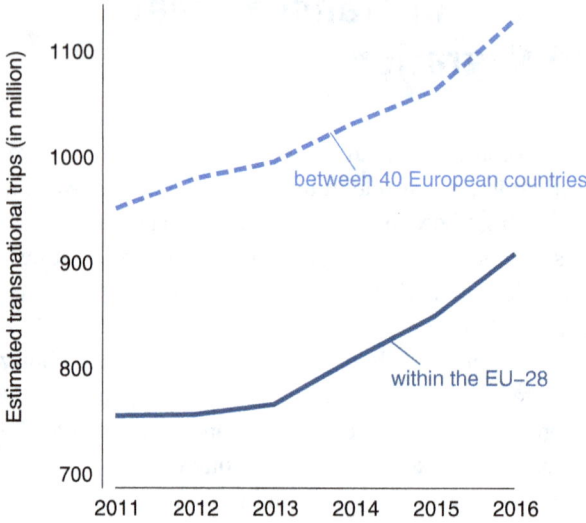

Estimated transnational trips (in million)

between 40 European countries

within the EU–28

2011   2012   2013   2014   2015   2016

B. Migration within the EU–28

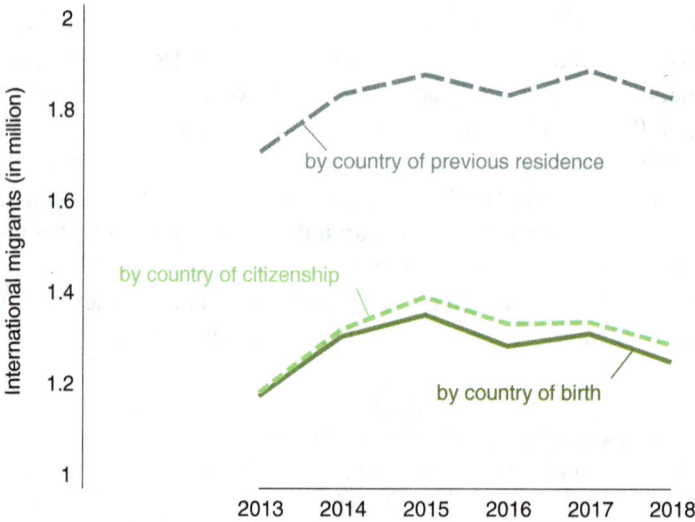

International migrants (in million)

by country of previous residence

by country of citizenship

by country of birth

2013   2014   2015   2016   2017   2018

Figure 12.1: Trends in mobility and migration flows within Europe over time.
Note: Based on data from the GMP Global Transnational Mobility Dataset (Recchi et al. 2019b) and Eurostat immigration data (2020). Values to and from Cyprus missing in the former dataset; no missing values in the latter.

about 20 per cent in just five years. Panel B, by contrast, illustrates that for yearly migration flows within the EU-28 (based on Eurostat data), there is no clear trend over time. Depending on how migrants are categorized, the overall number of intra-EU-28 immigrants oscillates around 1.3 million (counted by country of birth or citizenship) or 1.8 million (by country of previous residence). This implies that, given a population of 510 million, roughly 0.3 per cent of the EU-28 population migrated to another EU-28 country in 2016. Although comparisons to intra-national migration must be treated with caution, it is interesting that this rate is exactly the same as the migration rate from Quebec to the rest of Canada (Fries-Tersch et al. 2017: 43). In the US, by contrast, 1.7 per cent of the US population moved to another US state in 2016 (White 2019). Linguistic barriers may partly explain the lower migration rates in the former two cases.

A comparison of the stated estimates between the two graphs in Figure 12.1 showcases that migration is indeed only a small subset of all mobility: for every migratory move, approximately 500 to 700 transnational trips occurred within the EU-28 in 2016. Our mobility indicator does not take daily cross-border commuting into account – it is hard to measure since it is not registered – rendering this estimate conservative.

Drivers of Mobility and Migration in Europe

Human mobility may be seen as the product of four major factors: politics, technology, the economy, and culture. Each of these macro-factors can either limit or enhance the potential movements of individuals out of their places of birth or residence. Moreover, these factors interact with each other. For instance, political decisions may facilitate innovations in transportation means, while economic development may trigger cultural changes that favor human mobility. In Europe, these underlying factors jointly generated four significant trends affecting mobility and migration post World War II: the deepening and enlargement of the *free movement regime*, the expansion of the *transportation infrastructure*, *economic development*, and the rise of *individual freedom and an ethos of mobility*.

The Free Movement Regime

The expansion of mobility and migration in Europe owes much to the political integration of the continent (Recchi 2015; Geddes et al. 2020). Since the earliest incarnation of the EU – i.e., the European Coal and Steel Community (ECSC) uniting France, Germany, Belgium, the Netherlands, Luxembourg, and Italy in 1951 – the focus on a customs-free common market of raw materials was accompanied by a clause allowing workers in the coalmining and steel-making sectors to get jobs in other member states freely. Although the enactment of this policy proved particularly difficult in the following years, the free movement of workers became a flagship principle of the more ambitious European Economic Community in 1957. It was given legal backing in 1968, with the important add-on of non-discrimination of mobile workers vis-à-vis nationals. In the 1970s and 1980s, the right to resettle across the entire supranational space of the Community was disjointed from individuals' employment status, and granted to students, retirees, and the unemployed as well. Eventually, the 1992 Maastricht Treaty, which turned the European Community into the European Union, generalized the right from "workers to citizens", making it the cornerstone of the newly founded "European citizenship" (Maas 2007). From this point on, every citizen of an EU member state automatically gets European citizenship on top of the national one and can thus enjoy freedom of movement across the Union.

What is commonly called 'freedom of movement' consists, in fact, of three different types of rights:

a. The right to cross the border of other EU member states without a visa and even without a passport (an identity card suffices).
b. The right to settle freely in any EU member state, conditional on having a health insurance and sufficient resources not to be an immediate burden for social assistance in the receiving country.
c. The enjoyment of the same rights as nationals of the receiving country, apart from voting in national elections.

The process by which free movement rights have enlarged their scope and become less conditional over time is dubbed 'deepening' in EU jargon. In parallel, freedom of movement has gone through a 'widening' of the geographical space and populations involved – from 6 up to 28 different sovereign states (until Brexit). Deepening and widening of free movement are, however, not independent of one another. The number of intra-EU migrants stagnated until the early 2000s, when it soared on the eve of the 2004 and 2007 enlargements of the EU (Recchi 2015: 49–70). Before the rise of the intra-EU migration flows of the 2000s, the deepening of movers' rights was therefore relatively unproblematic, touching upon a small-scale population. As soon as the stock of (mostly Central and Eastern) European migrants swelled, their access to the same social rights – unemployment, housing, social assistance – as nationals became increasingly contested. While there is evidence that intra-EU migrants did not tap more welfare benefits than nationals (ECAS 2014), not the least because their younger age profile makes them less likely to need healthcare and retirement pensions, 'welfare chauvinism' gained traction in several receiving countries – notably the UK – and fed into social policies that limited such benefits, in contrast with EU legislation (Bruzelius et al. 2017; Barbulescu and Favell 2019). Even the European Court of Justice, traditionally at the forefront of the deepening of free movement rights, tempered its stance on EU migrants' access to welfare in several controversial judgments (Thym 2017). The free movement of people has not lost its legal prominence in the EU, alongside the other three foundational freedoms of movement of goods, capital, and services, but its symbolic aura looks less uncontroversial now than it used to after the introduction of European citizenship.

Overall, free movement in the EU may be considered a "mobility regime" (Engbersen et al. 2017), because mobility rights are complemented by additional policies that shape and encourage cross-state population movements. A common currency, the EU-wide recognition of educational and professional qualifications, a common template for higher education, research, and student mobility grants (like Erasmus), and, especially, the Schengen agreement on border management are examples of such policies. The latter is perhaps the single most important of these accessory regulations. It takes its name from the town in Luxembourg where it was first discussed by European government representatives in the 1980s. Now an integral part of EU legislation, the Schengen Agreement harmonizes the control of external and internal borders of its signatories (22 out of the 27 EU member states plus Iceland, Norway, Switzerland, and Liechtenstein).[2] As for external borders, the Agreement provides a framework (the so-called Schengen visa) for third-country nationals wishing to enter the EU and caters for a shared information system for policing access into the Union territory. As regards internal borders, Schengen sets a principle of 'no border control', except in case of external threats (like terrorist attacks or public health emergencies). Much of the image of the EU as a seamless and unitary geographical space is due to this Schengen rule, whose suspension – as during the COVID-19 crisis – is symbolically perceived as a lethal strike against free movement altogether. Such suspensions are unilaterally decided by member states. They therefore retain a last resort control over their borders – an ultimate proof of their primordial sovereignty over national territories.

---

2 The UK and Ireland opted out of the Schengen agreement from the start. Bulgaria, Croatia, Cyprus, and Romania are committed to join in at some point.

Transportation Infrastructure

Human mobility is predicated on the development of transportation systems. For instance, some technological improvements in steam-shipping increased the capacity of ocean liners by the end of the 19th century, thus reducing costs and permitting large transatlantic migration flows from Europe to the US, South America, and Australia. Technology, however, is a necessary but not sufficient condition for long-distance human mobility. Politics plays a major part in the promotion of technological innovation and the deployment of mobility infrastructures. On a regional scale, the success of the EU and its predecessors lies behind two critical political decisions that have greatly eased movement across the continent. The first is the allocation of substantial funding to the development of cross-country land transportation 'corridors'. The second is the liberalization of commercial flight transportation (Mau & Büttner 2009). Let us review both these factors in greater detail.

Article 3 of the Treaty of Rome (1957) specifies that the European Commission (EC) is in charge of common policies concerning land transportation. In the first three decades of European integration, member states were reluctant to initiate any coordination on this front. Things started to change in the 1990s, when the EC promoted the development of a Trans-European Transport Network (TEN-T), with priority projects and generous funding, particularly for the poorest member states. Ever since, European institutions have persistently strived to strengthen transportation infrastructures, with an emphasis on highways in the last decade of the century and high-speed rail later on. Massive investments have been premised on the goal of convergence: transportation from and to less developed regions would help these regions come closer – physically but also economically – to more developed ones. The effort to create a common transportation space has targeted accession countries in the 2000s and, since 2017, even candidate member states are eligible for funding. According to the EC (2020) itself,

> [t]he EU aims to build a modern integrated transport system that strengthens its global competitiveness [. . .] [through] a well-functioning infrastructure that can transport people and goods efficiently, safely, and sustainably. In 2017, the EU's physical infrastructure counts over 217,000 km of railways, 77,000 km of motorways, 42,000 km of inland waterways, 329 key seaports and 325 airports.

Whether – and to what extent – these efforts can counter existing divergences in infrastructure between the richer and the poorer parts of the continent is an open question. Yet, undeniably, the time-space map (also called an 'isochronic map') of Europe has shrunk considerably. Figure 12.2 illustrates the evolution of travel distances by railways, which is a major part of this story, as it traces the building of new lines and the introduction of faster trains (Spiekermann & Wegener 1994). Does this development create an 'ever closer Union' in mobility terms? Yes, but with marked territorial differences reflecting a 'hub effect': "[O]nly cities that are nodes of the high-speed rail network gain accessibility, while the areas between nodes and those not on the network or at its edges do not" (Puga 2002: 398). Figure 12.2 visualizes this unequal development: some squares on the map shrink faster than others, resulting in a highly distorted time-space grid.

The second significant change in the landscape of transportation infrastructure is the proliferation of flight connections across Europe, which resulted from the spectacular success of low-cost airlines from the 1990s onwards. EU institutions, once more, spearheaded this change. In 1988, 1990 and 1993, the European Commission launched three 'liberalization packages' that dismantled the route and slot monopolies of national airlines (Button 2001). New commercial low-cost carriers invaded the EU-wide market and fares fell across the board. Provincial airports, offering convenient costs to these airlines, widened the number of destinations and improved access to off-the-beaten track destinations – mostly to tourists, but also to workers and business travelers. Demand for airline transportation was further boosted by the EU enlargements, which created a brand-new clientele of Central and Eastern intra-EU migrants. The very existence of cheap East-West airline routes contributed to intra-EU migration embodying short-term and circular-like patterns to a large extent (Gabrielli et al. 2019; Fries-Tersch et al. 2020).

In the 2010s, the liberalization of international flights served as a model for a similarly sharp development in the long-distance bus service sector in continental Europe (and particularly in Germany in 2013 and France in 2015), as well as the progressive deregulation of domestic railway markets. The impact of the liberalization in coach transportation was remarkable: from 2012 to 2015, the bus travel supply in Germany grew from 26 to 220 million kilometers (Grimaldi et al. 2017). Two companies – *Eurolines* and *Flixbus* – have come to dominate the intra-European network routes, becoming particularly popular with young and low-budget passengers.

Economic Development

Mobility comes with a price. The affordability of travel is mostly a function of two factors: the costs of transportation and border-crossing (including visas: Recchi et al. 2021) and the prosperity of would-be movers. From the previous sections, we know that the EU free movement regime has slashed border-crossing costs

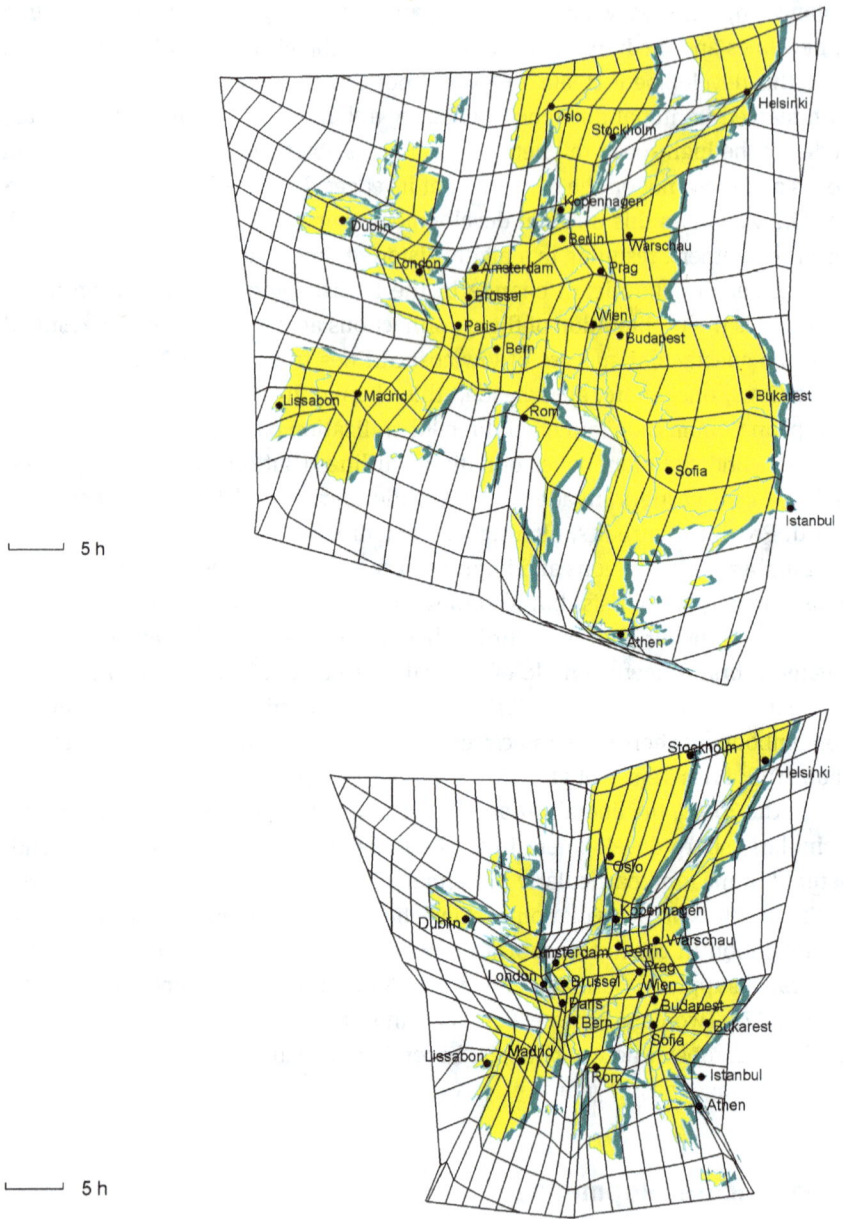

5 h

5 h

Figure 12.2: Time-space maps of railway distances in Europe in 1993 (top) and 2020 (bottom). Source: http://www.spiekermann-wegener.com/mod/time/time_e.htm (accessed 9 June 2020), reproduced with kind permission from Klaus Spiekermann. See the link for an undistorted base map and further details.

and the liberalization of commercial flights has taken down airline price tickets in Europe. Here, we focus on the impact of economic development on the propensity of Europeans to cross borders – either as tourists, economic migrants, business travelers or lifestyle movers.

The first thing to note is that income and wealth do not necessarily have the same impact on short-term movements and longer-term migration. As people grow richer, they may wish to visit other countries. Travel in the form of *tourism*, then, often becomes a consumption good –like fine dining or going to a concert. Figure 12.3 describes this positive relationship between prosperity and mobility across European countries by correlating GDP with the number of outgoing trips (both per capita). The correlation is indeed quite strong (r=.69, p<.001).

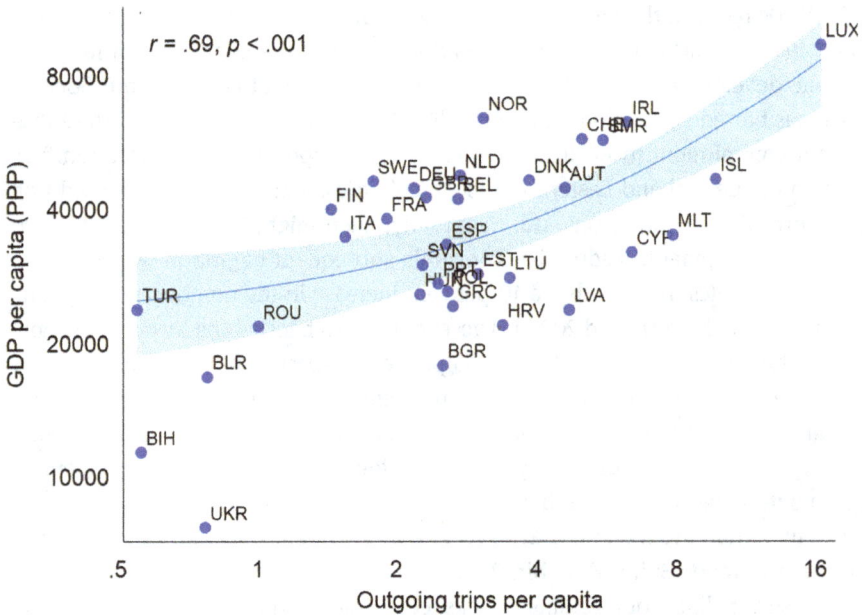

Figure 12.3: The relation between GDP per capita and outgoing trips per capita in 2016. Note: Both axes are logarithmic. Based on data from the World Bank and the GMP Global Transnational Mobility Dataset (Recchi et al. 2019b). GDP per capita in USD at PPP (Purchasing Power Parity).

Economic migration, by contrast, is often viewed as an investment decision. In economists' models, the decision to migrate discounts earning differentials – as well as other costs – between the country of origin and the country of destination. In this case, what counts is not economic well-being per se, either at home or at destination, but rather the gap between the two. Migrants may also consider the dynamic aspect of this gap: A sending country on a recession path may be an incitement to leave (a push factor) as much as a potential receiving country undergoing sustained growth (a pull factor). Indeed, both mechanisms showed up in Europe in the last decades – think, on the one hand of labor migration from Southern Europe during the Euro-crisis, and on the other, the spectacular 'Celtic Tiger' growth of the Irish economy in the early 2000s.

Of course, these are just two ideal types and sometimes the situation is the opposite: short-term *business* and *educational trips* can also serve as investments and *lifestyle migration* (see below) could be interpreted as a form of consumption. The economic development-migration nexus is also complex and the subject of extensive research and debate (for a review with a European focus, see King and Collyer 2016). In Western Europe, economic convergence between countries after the 1970s reduced the incentives to follow the mass migration routes of the 1950s and 1960s – particularly from the Southern part of the continent. In fact, economic development lagged behind in Eastern Europe after WWII, but Socialist regimes barred emigration westbound. The fall of the Iron Curtain and the subsequent commitment to EU accession created an opportunity for migration from the poorer Central and Eastern European countries, which fully materialized from the turn of the century onward. Eventually, such migration flows affected economic development, feeding back towards subsequent migration waves. Econometric estimates indicate that a 10 per cent increase in the number of immigrants coming from the 2004 and 2007 EU accession states boosted the income per capita in the host countries by 0.30 and 0.55 per cent respectively (Kahanec et al. 2013: 56). The effects of emigration are more problematic for the sending countries, as a **brain drain** and the resulting lack of young, educated people affects the depopulated parts of Eastern Europe negatively (Krastev 2020). Yet, since the enlargement, both out-migration and GDP have grown, which suggests that remittances and return migration are likely to have accelerated economic development in Central-Eastern Europe (Buiter & Lubin 2019: 34). Following this trend, in absence of major sociopolitical or economic shocks, economic convergence is likely to attenuate East-West migration in Europe in the future.

Individual Freedom and the Mobility Ethos

As societies become more prosperous and secure, people increasingly value their own self-realization and empowerment (Welzel 2013; Inglehart 2018) – which, from a different theoretical angle, is referred to as 'individualization' (Beck & Beck-Gernsheim 2002). Among all different forms of freedom, several philosophers – from Hobbes to Pascal and Arendt to Walzer – have highlighted the primacy of freedom of movement (Blitz 2014). Indeed, peoples' rising appetite for this particular freedom is an ingredient of the expansion of mobility and migration in Europe (and elsewhere). The wish to experience different places and cultures first-hand through mobility is a trope of contemporary culture. As Cresswell (2006: 20) puts it, "mobility is central to what it is to be modern".

Europeans highly value the freedom of cross-national movement that the EU grants them. In spite of mounting anti-immigration sentiments, almost all the Eurobarometer surveys conducted between 2012 and 2019 found that "free movement" ranked on top of the "most positive outcomes of the EU", regularly even more valued than "peace" in the continent.[3] An overwhelming majority of 82.4 per cent of EU citizens appreciated the principle of free movement between 2015 and 2017, and even 72.7 per cent did so in the UK, where Brexit was in fact won on the basis of anti-immigration and anti-EU platforms (Vasilopoulou & Talving 2019). The fact that support for freedom of movement is higher than support for the EU itself indicates that individuals' love of the opportunity to be mobile internationally bolsters EU legitimacy substantially.

This widespread attachment to free movement is also reflected in migration choices. While intra-EU migration has been mostly fueled by labor migration out of the poorest areas of the continent (the East and the South), a small but significant section of the migrating population does not correspond to economic incentives and may be called 'lifestyle migration' (Benson 2016). Especially among Western Europeans, the prevailing motivations to resettle in another EU member state are not strictly income- or labor-related, as upward social mobility is more the exception than the rule (Recchi 2009). In fact, personal relationships and romance drive many Europeans' migration projects (Santacreu et al. 2009; Díez Medrano 2020), as well as the desire to live in a milder climate by the sea or in the countryside (King et al. 2000). In some cases, migration may even be driven by a more deep-seated aspiration of a borderless existence (Favell 2008). For many, transnational mobility is, at the end of the day, a prized freedom that paves the way towards the enjoyment of most other individual liberties.

---

3 The Eurobarometer is a public opinion survey conducted regularly on behalf of the European Commission in all EU member states and additional European countries. The long-term response pattern with respect to what Europeans regard as 'the most positive results of the EU' can be found here: https://bit.ly/2BmyWrf (accessed June 12, 2020).

Sociological Perspectives on Mobility and Migration in Europe

Having discussed background conditions in the preceding section, we now highlight several aspects of mobility and migration in Europe that have been subject to vivid sociological research in the last years, starting with the issue of inequality.

Inequality in Mobility and Migration in Europe

Migration and mobility are distributed very unequally within and between countries in Europe. *Within* countries, a considerable **class gap** exists, with the upper social strata (i.e., those with a higher occupational class, better education, etc.) engaged in more cross-border mobility and other transnational activities (Fligstein 2008; Kuhn 2016; Salamonska & Recchi 2019). In 2010, for example, one third of upper-class residents of the EU declared that they spend their holidays abroad regularly, as opposed to only 22 per cent of middle-class respondents and 15 per cent of working-class people (Baglioni & Recchi 2013: 54). Class is not the only stratifying force, however: men are more transnationally active than women, urban residents more than people from the countryside, and people with a migration background more than those without (Delhey et al. 2015). One important mechanism that helps create this stratification is **transnational linguistic capital**: speaking foreign languages makes transnational mobility easier (Gerhards 2012), in particular in a multilingual continent such as Europe. Differences in endowment of economic resources, existing cultural ties to other countries and job-related opportunities for cross-border mobility may be other central explanatory factors.

Between countries, mobility and migration are also distributed unequally, as the two maps in Figures 12.4 and 12.5 reveal. Figure 12.4 shows the intra-EU-28 network of estimated mobility flows in 2016. Whereas the size of the country nodes is proportional to the amount of incoming and outgoing mobility, the node color corresponds to the amount of incoming mobility only, ranging from largest (blue) to smallest (red), with white denoting a medium amount of incoming mobility. Thicker arrows denote larger flows. The mobility network contains a distinctive core of 'blue countries' with a lot of incoming mobility, centered around Germany, the UK, Spain, France, and – to lesser extents – Italy and Poland. Surrounding this core is a set of smaller, peripheral 'red countries' with very little incoming mobility. The European mobility network thus appears highly unequal and features a clear core-periphery structure. Interestingly, a similar structure is found when exploring Europeans' sense of familiarity with other countries (Savage et al. 2019).

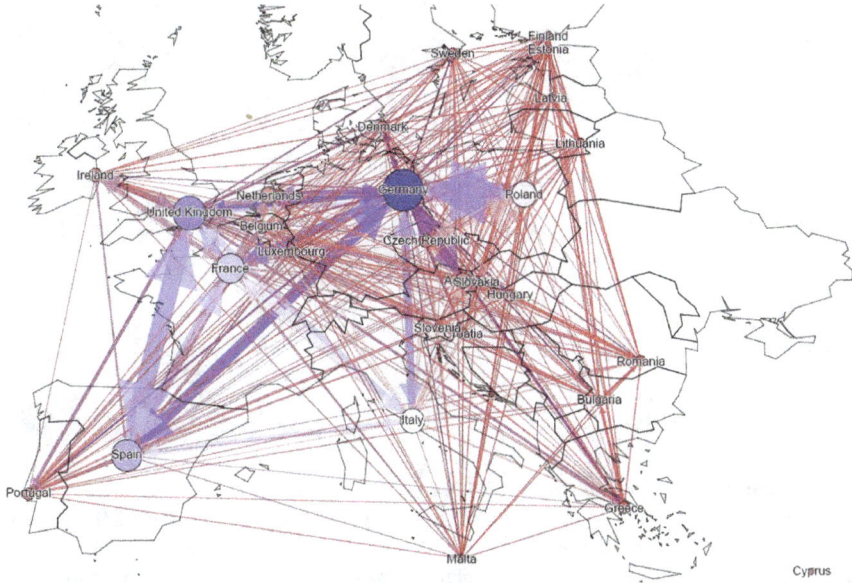

Figure 12.4: Mobility flows in the EU-28, 2016.
Note: Based on the GMP Global Transnational Mobility Dataset (Recchi et al. 2019b). Arrow size corresponds to the number of trips, node size corresponds to the weighted degree and node color corresponds to the weighted indegree, ranging from largest (blue) to smallest (red), with white denoting a medium weighted indegree. Values for Cyprus are missing. Coloring is directly comparable between Figures 12.4 and 12.5, arrow sizes are not.

Figure 12.5 shows a similar representation for migration flows in the EU-28 in 2016. Here, the network appears even more centralized. The UK stands out as *the* main receiver country and Romania as *the* main sender country of migrants. Most major migration flows are one-sided, e.g., from Romania to the UK, Italy, and Spain, or from Poland to the UK and the Netherlands, but not vice versa. An exception is the tie between Spain and the UK, which is meaningful in size in both directions. Windzio et al. (2019) examined – for earlier years, in which Germany stands out as a second central receiver country next to the UK – why the intra-EU migration network takes such a shape and found that national economic performance explains inflows, whereas unemployment rate explains outflows well (see above). Political regulation also seems to play a role, although apparently a weaker one than the economic factors.

Figure 12.5: Migration flows in the EU-28, 2016.
Note: Based on Eurostat data on immigrants by citizenship, retrieved from the KCMD Dynamic Data Hub (https://bluehub.jrc.ec.europa.eu/catalogue/dataset/0026, accessed 4/5/2020). Arrow size corresponds to the number of migrants moving, node size corresponds to the weighted degree and node color corresponds to the weighted indegree, ranging from largest (blue) to smallest (red), with white denoting a medium weighted indegree. Coloring is directly comparable between Figures 12.4 and 12.5, arrow sizes are not.

To achieve further clarity on the amount of inequality in these networks, we may look towards the Gini coefficient for various indicators. While Gini coefficients are often used to measure income inequality, they can also be applied to describe inequality in mobility networks (Delhey et al. 2020; Deutschmann et al. 2021). This measure can range from 0 (denoting a perfectly equal distribution) to 1 (the most unequal distribution possible). In 2016, the Gini coefficient for the distribution of movements across country pairs in the EU-28 was .80 for mobility and .84 for migration.[4] For an assessment of the magnitude of these degrees of inequality, consider that for income inequality the coefficient ranged

---

4 One could object that a certain inequality is to be expected since the population size varies between countries and larger countries will yield more mobile people. To take this *baseline inequality* into account, we can adjust the flow sizes by the population size of the sender country. When this is done, the inequality shrinks only slightly. With Gini coefficients of .78 for mobility and .79 for migration, it is still very high.

from .24 (Slovakia) to .38 (Bulgaria) in the EU-28 countries in 2016 (Eurostat 2020). Hence, while the inequality of income within countries is already considerable, it is dwarfed by the extreme inequality of mobility and migration in their distribution across country pairs in the EU. This unequal participation in transnational mobility – both within and between countries – can have substantial social implications, as we will see in the following section.

Social Consequences of Mobility and Migration

Why should we care about the unequal distribution of mobility and migration? What are their social consequences? One reason is that mobility to other countries generates **transnational human capital**, a new marker of distinction and a resource that is increasingly in demand in labor markets today (Gerhards et al. 2017). Experience abroad is seen as positive as it signals intercultural competence – to start with, improved foreign language proficiency. Thus, participating in mobility and migration across borders can influence opportunities in life and plays a significant role in (re-)producing social stratification.

Going abroad can also have positive consequences for one's social position when the move is permanent, i.e., when one migrates. This phenomenon is called **social spiralism**: by moving from provincial places in Europe's periphery to urban centers in the core, migrants can potentially "spiral [. . .] up through society by taking a detour away from their place of origin" (Favell & Recchi 2011: 53). Thus, moving abroad spatially may boost upward social mobility. However, this transition is far from easy. Empirically, it is only achieved by a minority of migrants and often only after a difficult transition phase that may even entail temporary downward mobility.

Another consequence of mobility and migration is the creation of a *transnational sense of community*. By moving across borders, people from different nationalities come into contact. According to the **contact hypothesis** (sometimes also called *intergroup contact theory* or *transactionalist theory*), this increased interaction leads to a we-feeling as a former out-group becomes part of a new common in-group. A shared identity develops, possibly leading to increased solidarity, trust, and attachment to other countries (Deutsch et al. 1957). Several empirical studies support this hypothesis (Mau et al. 2008; Kuhn 2011; Recchi 2015; Deutschmann et al. 2018).

Others have hypothesized – in stark contrast to the above arguments – that mobility and migration across borders can lead to emerging societal conflicts, a position we may call the **conflict hypothesis**. This idea is particularly pronounced for permanent, (allegedly) poverty-driven moves. As already mentioned above, migration from Central and Eastern Europe to the UK was a prominent point of contention that drove the Brexit campaign (Sudarshan 2017), and in Western Europe at large it has contributed to the perception of immigration as an economic threat (Jeannet 2020). Social conflicts can also result from other forms of mobility such as tourism. Examples include citizen protests as a reaction to congested housing markets and rising rents due to Airbnb and the negative impact of **overtourism** (Clancy 2020; Delhey et al. 2020).

Thus, there appears to be a paradoxical situation in which mobility and migration have both unifying (growing sense of community) and dividing (new conflicts) effects. How can this seemingly intractable paradox be resolved? First, society is complex, and it is well possible that some social groups welcome increasing exchange across borders and perceive it as enriching in both economic and cultural terms, whereas other groups see it negatively, be it for fear of labor market competition or threatened cultural identities. The labels 'cosmopolitan' and 'local' (Merton 1949; Recchi 2005; Helbling & Teney 2015) have been used to describe these two archetypes. Transnational mobility and migration can thus lead to a sense of community in some social milieus and to resentment and conflict in others.

Second, it is important to consider that, following a counterintuitive perspective that was first introduced by Simmel (1904), both an increased sense of community and new social conflicts can be understood as indicators of social integration. While it can often feel disintegrative for the individuals involved, a conflict also represents a form of social interaction – and thus a sociation (i.e., 'society-making') force in Simmel's terms. A well-functioning society is one in which there is room for some conflict. For Europe, the social consequences of intra-European mobility and migration could thus be regarded as integrative in this sense, i.e., as signs of *horizontal Europeanization*, regardless of whether they are directly unifying or conflictive. This theoretical argument is visualized in Figure 12.6. Following a similar logic, El-Mafaalani (2018) has recently argued that it is precisely when the integration of migrants is successful that more (not less!) social conflicts occur, a situation he calls the **integration paradox**.

Looking beyond Europe to Learn about Europe

The European networks of mobility and migration are actually not closed systems as depicted in Figures 12.4 and 12.5. In reality, Europeans also move to other parts of the world and people from all over the planet come to Europe (Mau & Büttner 2009). Furthermore, people are also transnationally mobile in other world regions.

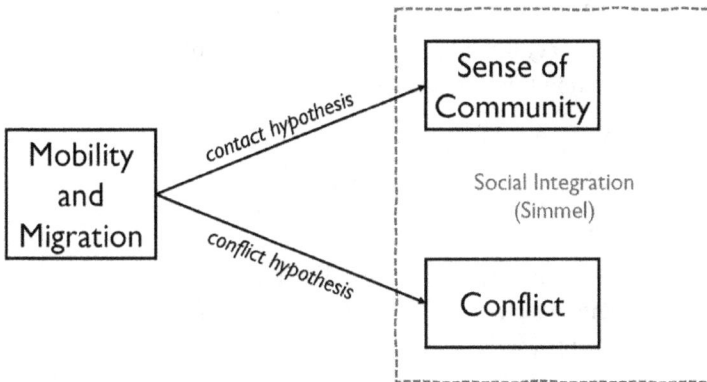

Figure 12.6: Seemingly paradoxical consequences of mobility and migration.

The actual density or sparseness of intra-European networks of transnational mobility and migration may only be determined – one may argue – by comparing it to similar networks in other world regions, i.e., via an external benchmark, in line with a **comparative sociology of regional integration** (Deutschmann 2021). In other words, we need to look beyond Europe to learn about Europe.

Doing so reveals, on the one hand, that more transnational mobility takes place within Europe than within other world regions (Recchi et al. 2019b). On the other hand, however, the *density* (i.e., the share of country pairs that feature a substantial mobility flow) is not low but also not exceptionally high in the European mobility network compared to other world regions. This has to do with the high inequality observed above: while a few country pairs in Europe feature extremely large flows of mobility and migration, most see only small flows (see the many thin red ties in Figures 12.4 and 12.5). Hence, this highly unequal participation in cross-border mobility and migration diminishes the overall density, or *regionalism*, of interaction in Europe compared to other world regions (Deutschmann 2021).

Another important factor is that Europe is more globally integrated through inter-continental ties of mobility and migration than other world regions. Thus, whereas some world regions (e.g., Latin America) are only strongly connected internally, Europe is relatively well-connected internally *and* globally. In other words, it is *both Europeanized and globalized*, which mitigates its regionalism in relative terms (Deutschmann 2019). This is also visible in longitudinal comparative analyses of migration stocks that show that Europeans increasingly tend to stay in Europe when moving abroad: whereas only 40 per cent of emigrants from European countries moved within Europe (as opposed to out of Europe) in 1960, this share increased to 60 per cent in 2017. At the same time, migrants from outside Europe as a share of all migrants moving into European countries also increased from 40 per cent in 1960 to 60 per cent in 2017. These two trends taken together again suggest a double process of *Europeanization from within* and *globalization from outside* (Delhey et al. 2019, 2020).

Conclusion

Modern societies are not demographically 'closed containers'. Rather, commodities, messages, and, not least, people constantly move between countries around the planet. In Europe, mobility and migration across borders are a central aspect of horizontal Europeanization (Mau & Mewes 2012). This chapter provided an overview of the central drivers behind this process and gave insights into some sociological perspectives on the topic. There are two final aspects that we wish to highlight in this conclusion.

The first is the interplay of migration and short-term mobility: rather than being separate phenomena, increased migration can trigger increased short-term movement through circular mobility of migrants. Typically, migrants do not move into a receiving society once and for all, but rather tend to move back and forth, thereby creating 'transnational social spaces', a view that is highlighted in transnational migration research (Waldinger 2015). At the same time, short-term mobility may usher in prospects of settlement and thus translate into migration. Second, there can be complex interplays of factors boosting and constraining mobility and migration. A good example is the global Covid-19 pandemic: a health crisis led to political decisions to block (cross-border) mobility, which engendered an economic crisis, which, in turn, may lead to new pressures in favor of migration. Another example is the climate crisis: transnational mobility is still emission-intensive today and thus a major contributor to the looming climate catastrophe, which, in turn, may globally force one billion people to migrate (Spratt & Dunlop 2019). These complex entanglements will have to be studied closely in the coming years, in Europe and beyond.

Didactical Section

Key Learning Points

- Mobility and migration are central mechanisms by which Europeans are brought into contact with each other, thus facilitating horizontal Europeanization.
- Mobility and migration are distributed very unequally between social strata within societies and extremely unequally across country pairs in Europe.
- Mobility and migration can lead to a sense of community and generate new social conflicts, both of which can be seen as contributing to social integration in Europe.

Glossary

Brain drain: negative consequences of massive emigration due to the lack of human capital in the sending country.

Class gap: the higher social strata are more transnationally mobile than the lower ones (e.g., Fligstein 2008; Delhey et al. 2015).

Comparative Sociology of Regional Integration: comparing mobility and migration patterns across world regions can lead to new insights through external benchmarks (Deutschmann 2019, 2021).

Contact hypothesis: intergroup contact leads to a sense of community (Allport 1954); mobility and migration between countries lead to a transnational sense of community (Deutsch et al. 1957).

Conflict hypothesis: intergroup contact (e.g., through mobility and migration) leads to social conflicts (Campbell 1965).

Integration paradox: the successful integration of migrants into a host society leads to new social conflicts (El-Mafaalani 2018).

Overtourism: too much tourism has negative social, economic, and ecological consequences for the hosting environment (e.g., Clancy 2020).

Social spiralism: potential upward social mobility achievable through (transnational) spatial mobility (Favell & Recchi 2011).

Transnational linguistic capital: skills and resources linked to speaking foreign languages (Gerhards 2012).

Transnational human capital: skills and resources derived from experiences abroad (Gerhards et al. 2017).

Further Readings

Delhey, J., M. Verbalyte, A. Aplowski & E. Deutschmann, 2019: Free to Move: The Evolution of the European Migration Network, 1960–2017. In: M. Heidenreich (ed.), *Horizontal Europeanisation: The Transnationalisation of Daily Life and Social Fields in Europe*, pp. 63–88. New York: Routledge.

Geddes, A., L. Hadj-Abdou & L. Brumat, 2020: *Migration and Mobility in the European Union*. Basingstoke: Palgrave.

Recchi, E., 2015: *Mobile Europe: The theory and practice of free movement in the EU*. Basingstoke: Palgrave.

Recchi, E. & A. Favell (eds.), 2009: *Pioneers of European integration: Citizenship and mobility in the EU*. Cheltenham: Edward Elgar.

Recchi, E., A. Favell, F. Apaydin, R. Barbulescu, M. Braun, I. Ciornei, N. Cunningham, J. Díez Medrano, D. N. Duru, L. Hanquinet, S. Pötzschke, D. Reimer, J. Salamońska, M. Savage, J. Solgaard Jensen & A. Varela, 2019: *Everyday Europe: Social transnationalism in an unsettled continent*. Bristol: Policy Press.

Additional Web-Sources

Global Mobilities Project: The GMP at the Migration Policy Centre of the European University Institute (EUI) collects data on transnational mobility and the structural factors that form it. The Global Transnational Mobility Dataset, which was used in this chapter, can be downloaded for free to explore mobility flows within Europe and beyond: http://www.migrationpolicycentre.eu/globalmobilities

KCMD Dynamic Data Hub: This website, created by the European Commission's Knowledge Centre on Migration and Democracy, allows you to explore various mobility and migration datasets (including the ones used in this chapter) on an interactive world map. The data can be downloaded by pressing the 'D' key on your keyboard: https://bit.ly/2LdjNwK

Network Europe: This website, built to accompany the book *Netzwerk Europa* (Delhey et al. 2020) allows you to explore visually the development of migration, student exchange, and tourism flows as well as international phone calls in Europe in their development over time: www.network-europe.eu

Questions for Discussion

1. Are you from Europe and have you been to other European countries? If yes, do you feel these stays abroad have made you feel more 'European'?

2. During the Covid-19 pandemic, international mobility decreased a lot as many borders were closed. How do you think this may have affected processes of Europeanization?
3. What do you think: Is mobility between countries primarily a path to peaceful integration or rather a source of new social conflicts?

References

Allport, G. W., 1954: *The Nature of Prejudice*. New York: Addison-Wesley.

Baglioni, L. G. & E. Recchi, 2013: La classe media va in Europa? Transnazionalismo e stratificazione sociale nell'Unione Europea. *SocietàMutamentoPolitica* 4(7):47–69.

Barbulescu, R. & A. Favell, 2019: A citizenship without social rights? EU freedom of movement and changing access to social rights. *International Migration* 58(1):151–165.

Beck, U. & E. Beck-Gernsheim, 2002: *Individualization: Institutionalized individualism and its social and political consequences*. London: Sage.

Benson, M., 2016: *Lifestyle migration: Expectations, aspirations and experiences*. London: Routledge.

Blitz, B.K. (ed.), 2014: *Migration and freedom: Mobility, citizenship and exclusion*. Edward Elgar Publishing.

Bruzelius, C., C. Reinprecht, & M. Seeleib-Kaiser, 2017: Stratified social rights limiting EU citizenship. *Journal of Common Market Studies* 55(6):1239–1253.

Buiter, W. & D. Lubin, 2019: Did EU membership bring economic benefits for CESEE member states? In: Székely, I. P. (ed.), *Faces of Convergence*, pp. 33–37. Vienna: WIIW.

Button, K., 2001: Deregulation and liberalization of European air transport markets. *Innovation* 14(3):255–275.

Campbell, D. T., 1965: *Ethnocentric and Other Altruistic Motives*. Lincoln: University of Nebraska Press.

Clancy, M., 2020: Overtourism and resistance: Today's anti-tourist movement in context. In: Pechlaner, H., E. Innerhofer & G. Erschbamer (eds.), *Overtourism*, pp. 14–24. New York: Routledge.

Cresswell, T., 2006: *On the Move: Mobility in the Modern Western World*. New York: Routledge.

Delhey, J., E. Deutschmann & K. Cîrlănaru, 2015: Between 'Class Project' and Individualization: The Stratification of Europeans' Transnational Activities. *International Sociology* 30(3):269–93.

Delhey, J., E. Deutschmann, M. Verbalyte & A. Aplowski, 2020: *Netzwerk Europa: Wie ein Kontinent durch Mobilität und Kommunikation zusammenwächst*. Wiesbaden: Springer VS.

Delhey, J., M. Verbalyte, A. Aplowski & E. Deutschmann, 2019: Free to Move: The Evolution of the European Migration Network, 1960–2017. In: M. Heidenreich (ed.), *Horizontal Europeanisation: The Transnationalisation of Daily Life and Social Fields in Europe*, pp. 63–88. New York: Routledge.

Deutsch, K.W., S. Burrell, R. Kann, M. Lee Jr., M. Lichterman, R. E. Lindgren, F. L. Loewenheim, R. W. Van Wagenen, 1957: *Political Community and the North Atlantic Area*. Princeton: Princeton University Press.

Deutschmann, E., 2019: Regionalization and Globalization in Networks of Transnational Human Mobility, 1960–2010. *SocietàMutamentoPolitica* 10(20):137–52.

Deutschmann, E., 2021: *Mapping the Transnational World: How We Move and Communicate across Borders, and Why It Matters*. Princeton: Princeton University Press.

Deutschmann, E. & J. Delhey, 2015: People Matter: Recent Sociological Contributions to Understanding European Integration from Below. *Perspectives on Europe* 45(2):25–32.

Deutschmann, E., J. Delhey, M. Verbalyte & A. Aplowski, 2018: The Power of Contact: Europe as a Network of Transnational Attachment. *European Journal of Political Research* 57(4):963–88.

Deutschmann, E., E. Recchi & F. Bicchi, 2021: Mobility Hub or Hollow? Cross-border Travelling in the Mediterranean, 1995–2016. *Global Networks* 21(1):146–169.

Díez Medrano, J., 2020: *Europe in Love: Binational Couples and Cosmopolitan Society*. New York: Routledge.

ECAS (European Citizens' Action Service), 2014: *Fiscal Impact of EU Migrants in Austria, Germany, the Netherlands and the UK*. Brussels: ECAS.

El-Mafaalani, A., 2018: *Das Integrationsparadox: Warum gelungene Integration zu mehr Konflikten führt*. Köln: Kiepenheuer & Witsch.

Engbersen, G., A. Leerkes, P. Scholten & E. Snel, 2017: The intra-EU mobility regime: Differentiation, stratification and contradictions. *Migration Studies* 5(3):337–355.

European Commission, 2020: *Infrastructure and investment*. DG Mobility and Transport. https://ec.europa.eu/transport/themes/infrastructure_en (accessed June 7, 2020).

Eurostat (ed.), 2020: *Database*. https://ec.europa.eu/eurostat/data/database (accessed May 23, 2020).

Favell, A., 2008: *Eurostars and Eurocities: Free movement and mobility in an integrating Europe*. Oxford: Blackwell.

Favell, A. & E. Recchi, 2011: Social mobility and spatial mobility. In: Favell, A. & V. Guiraudon (eds.), *Sociology of the European Union*, pp. 50–75. Basingstoke: Palgrave Macmillan.

Fligstein, N., 2008: *Euroclash: The EU, European identity, and the future of Europe*. Oxford: Oxford University Press.

Fries-Tersch, E., T. Tugran & H. Bradley, 2017: *2016 Annual Report on Intra-EU Labour Mobility*. Brussels: European Commission.

Fries-Tersch, E., T. Tugran & H. Bradley, 2020: *2019 Annual Report on Intra-EU Labour Mobility*. Brussels: European Commission.

Gabrielli, L., E. Deutschmann, E. Recchi, F. Natale & M. Vespe, 2019: Dissecting Global Air Traffic Data to Discern Different Types and Trends of Transnational Human Mobility. *EPJ Data Science* 8(26):1–24.

Geddes, A., L. Hadj-Abdou & L. Brumat, 2020: *Migration and Mobility in the European Union*. Basingstoke: Palgrave.

Gerhards, J., 2012: *From Babel to Brussels. European Integration and the Importance of Transnational Linguistic Capital*. Berlin Studies on the Sociology of Europe (BSSE). No. 28. Berlin: Freie Universität Berlin.

Gerhards, J., S. Hans & S. Carlson, 2017: *Social class and transnational human capital: How middle and upper class parents prepare their children for globalization*. New York: Routledge.

Grimaldi, R., K. Augustin & P. Beria, 2017: Intercity coach liberalisation. The cases of Germany and Italy. In: *World Conference on Transport Research-WCTR 2016*, pp. 474–490. Amsterdam: Elsevier.

Heidenreich, M. (ed.), 2019: *Horizontal Europeanisation: The Transnationalisation of Daily Life and Social Fields in Europe*. New York: Routledge.

Helbling, M. & C. Teney, 2015: The cosmopolitan elite in Germany. Transnationalism and postmaterialism. *Global Networks* 15(4):446–468.

Inglehart, R., 2018: *Cultural evolution: people's motivations are changing, and reshaping the world*. Cambridge: Cambridge University Press.

Jeannet, A., 2020: A threat from within? Perceptions of immigration in an enlarging European Union. *Acta Sociologica* 63(4):343–360.

Kahanec, M., K. Zimmermann, L. Kurekova & C. Biavaschi, 2013: Labour migration from EaP Countries to the EU–Assessment of costs and benefits and proposals for better labour market matching. *IZA Research Report* 56. Bonn: IZA.

Kellerman, A., 2006: *Personal Mobilities*. London and New York: Routledge.

King, R. & M. Collyer, 2016: Migration and development framework and its links to integration. In: Garcés-Mascareñas, B. & R. Penninx (eds.), *Integration Processes and Policies in Europe*, pp. 167–188. Cham: Springer.

King, R., A. M. Warnes & A. M. Williams, 2000: *Sunset Lives: British Retirement Migration to the Mediterranean*, Oxford: Berg.

Krastev, I., 2020: *After Europe*. Updated Edition. Philadelphia: University of Pennsylvania Press.

Kuhn, T., 2011: Individual transnationalism, globalisation and euroscepticism: An empirical test of Deutsch's transactionalist theory. *European Journal of Political Research* 50(6):811–837.

Kuhn, T., 2015: *Experiencing European integration: Transnational lives and European identity*. Oxford: Oxford University Press.

Kuhn, T., 2016: The social stratification of European schoolchildren's transnational experiences: A cross-country analysis of the International Civics and Citizenship Study. *European Sociological Review* 32(2):266–279.

Maas, W., 2007: *Creating European Citizens*. Lanham, MD: Rowman & Littlefield.

Mau, S. & S. Büttner, 2009. Transnationality. In: Immerfall, S. & G. Therborn (eds.), *Handbook of European Societies*, pp. 537–570. New York: Springer.

Mau, S. & J. Mewes, 2012: Horizontal Europeanisation in contextual perspective: What drives cross-border activities within the European Union? *European Societies* 14(1):7–34.

Mau, S., J. Mewes & A. Zimmermann, 2008: Cosmopolitan attitudes through transnational social practices? *Global Networks* 8(1):1–24.

Merton, R. K., 1949: Patterns of influence: Local and cosmopolitan influentials. In: Lazarsfeld, P. & F. N. Stanton (eds.), *Communication Research 1948–1949*, pp. 180–219. New York: Harper.

Puga, D., 2002: European regional policies in light of recent location theories. *Journal of Economic Geography* 2(4):373–406.

Recchi, E., 2005: Migrants and Europeans: An Outline of the Free Movement of Persons in the EU. *Academy of Migration Studies (AMID) Working Paper* No. 38. Aalborg: AMID.

Recchi, E., 2009: The social mobility of mobile Europeans. In: Recchi, E. & A. Favell (eds.), *Pioneers of European integration: citizenship and mobility in the EU*, pp. 72–97. Cheltenham: Edward Elgar.

Recchi, E., 2015: *Mobile Europe: The theory and practice of free movement in the EU*. Basingstoke: Palgrave.

Recchi, E. & A. Favell (eds.), 2009: *Pioneers of European integration: Citizenship and mobility in the EU*. Cheltenham: Edward Elgar.

Recchi, E., J. Salamońska, T. Rossi & L. G. Baglioni, 2014: Cross-border mobilities in the European Union: an evidence-based typology. In: Recchi, E. (ed.), *The Europeanisation of Everyday Life: Cross-Border Practices and Transnational Identifications among EU and Third-Country Citizens – Final Report*, pp. 8–30. https://nbn-resolving.org/urn:nbn:de:0168-ssoar-395269 (accessed March 24, 2021).

Recchi, E., A. Favell, F. Apaydin, R. Barbulescu, M. Braun, I. Ciornei, N. Cunningham, J. Díez Medrano, D. N. Duru, L. Hanquinet, S. Pötzschke, D. Reimer, J. Salamońska, M. Savage, J. Solgaard Jensen & A. Varela, 2019a: *Everyday Europe: Social transnationalism in an unsettled continent*. Bristol: Policy Press.

Recchi, E., E. Deutschmann & M. Vespe, 2019b: Estimating transnational human mobility at a global scale. *EUI RSCAS Working Paper* 2019/30. Florence: European University Institute.

Recchi, E., E. Deutschmann, L. Gabrielli & N. Kholmatova, 2021: The Global Visa Cost Divide: How and Why the Price for Travel Permits Varies Worldwide. *Political Geography* 86:1–14.

Salamonska, J. & E. Recchi, 2019: The Social Structure of Transnational Practices. In: Recchi, E., A. Favell, F. Apaydin, R. Barbulescu, M. Braun, I. Ciornei, N. Cunningham, J. Díez Medrano, D. N. Duru, L. Hanquinet, S. Pötzschke, D. Reimer, J. Salamońska, M. Savage, J. Solgaard Jensen & A. Varela, *Everyday Europe: Social Transnationalism in an Unsettled Continent*, pp. 61–86. Bristol: Policy Press.

Santacreu, O., E. Baldoni & M. C. Albert, 2009: Deciding to move: migration projects in an integrating Europe. In: Recchi, E. & A. Favell (eds.), *Pioneers of European integration: citizenship and mobility in the EU*, pp. 52–71. Cheltenham: Edward Elgar.

Savage, M., N. Cunningham, D. Reimer & A. Favell, 2019: Cartographies of social transnationalism. In: Recchi, E., A. Favell, F. Apaydin, R. Barbulescu, M. Braun, I. Ciornei, N. Cunningham, J. Díez Medrano, D. N. Duru, L. Hanquinet, S. Pötzschke, D. Reimer, J. Salamońska, M. Savage, J. Solgaard Jensen & A. Varela, *Everyday Europe: Social transnationalism in an unsettled continent*, pp. 35–59. Bristol: Policy Press.

Simmel, G., 1904: The Sociology of Conflict. *American Journal of Sociology* 9(4):490–525.

Spiekermann, K. & M. Wegener, 1994: The Shrinking Continent: New Time Space Maps of Europe. *Environment and Planning B: Planning and Design* 21(6):653–673.

Spratt, D. & I. Dunlop, 2019: *Existential Climate-Related Security Risk: A Scenario Approach*. Melbourne: Breakthrough – National Centre for Climate Restauration.

Sudarshan, R., 2017: *Understanding the Brexit Vote: The Impact of Polish Immigrants on Euroscepticism*. https://www.humanityinaction.org/knowledge_detail/understanding-the-brexit-vote-the-impact-of-polish-immigrants-on-euroscepticism/?lang=de (accessed September 11, 2019).

Thym, D. (ed.), 2017: *Questioning EU Citizenship: Judges and the Limits of Free Movement and Solidarity in the EU*. London: Bloomsbury.

UN (ed.), 2020: *Refugees and Migrants: Definitions*. https://refugeesmigrants.un.org/definitions (accessed May 23, 2020).

Urry, J., 2000: *Sociology beyond Societies: Mobilities for the Twenty-first Century*. London: Routledge.

Vasilopoulou, S. & L. Talving, 2019: Opportunity or threat? Public attitudes towards EU freedom of movement. *Journal of European Public Policy* 26(6):805–823.

Waldinger, R., 2015: *The Cross-Border Connection: Immigrants, Emigrants, And Their Homelands*. Cambridge, MA: Harvard University Press.

Welzel, C., 2013: *Freedom Rising*. Cambridge: Cambridge University Press.

White, M., 2019: *US Moving Statistics for 2019*. https://www.moving.com/tips/us-moving-statistics-for-2019/ (accessed May 27, 2020).

Windzio, M., C. Teney & S. Lenkewitz, 2019: A network analysis of intra-EU migration flows: How regulatory policies, economic inequalities and the network-topology shape the intra-EU migration space. *Journal of Ethnic and Migration Studies* 47(5):951–969.

Part V: Conflictual Dynamics: Cleavages, Civil Society, and Social Movements

Christian Lahusen

13 The (un)loved Union: Social and Political Cleavages

Political dissent among citizens is a normal aspect of political life, particularly in democratic societies. Citizens disagree regarding how politicians undertake their political responsibilities, the problems they consider to be most urgent and the solutions they prefer, among other contentious issues. This dissent is not a setback for modern societies because it ensures a critical evaluation of institutional politics and motivates public participation in politics. It also guarantees the continuous replacement of public officials and it promotes political and institutional reform. However, political dissent is a productive force only as long as lines of disagreement are mutable and numerous. It can become troublesome when societies develop structural fault lines between groups of citizens that engage in constant and systematic conflict about interrelated issues and fundamental questions. Regarding the European Union, this problem is equally relevant for the nation state, but more consequential, given that European citizens might be systematically divided regarding their preferences and opinions. Depending on their national residence, their political orientations and living conditions, they might profess contrasting views about the European Union, its institutions and policies.

Sociology is interested in these cleavages and conflicts as a proper field of research, thus showcasing its potential contribution to the study of the European Union and European integration. On the one hand, sociology has been able to show that conflicts are both a destructive and a productive force, able to contribute to social order and change (Simmel 1903; Coser 1956; Dubiel 1986). The building of the European Union conforms to this general lesson insofar as it is the product of innumerable disputes and contentions that enmesh and tie opposing parties into ongoing social relations, particularly if they are institutionally contained and regulated (Münch 1996; Vobruba 2012). With European enlargement and integration, the number of member states, political parties and interest groups has steadily increased, thus contributing to what scholars have called the growing 'politicization' of the European Union (Hooghe & Marks 2009; de Wilde & Zürn 2012; Hutter & Kriesi 2019). This process can encourage defection (e.g., the United Kingdom leaving the EU), but has not necessarily impeded further integration processes. What we can say unequivocally is that it has increased the contentiousness of political negotiations and the incremental and piece-meal approach of European policy making and institution building.

https://doi.org/10.1515/9783110673630-013

Additionally, politicization has also affected the relations between the EU and its citizens, given that public opinion is increasingly divided regarding policy issues, and the future of the EU in general.

Sociology not only contributes to the identification of integrative and disintegrative conflicts, their causes, dynamics and implications, but has also been interested, on the other hand, in the analysis of **social inequalities**, divisions and cleavages that nurture such conflicts. While these divisional lines do not predetermine (political) conflicts, they have been of great interest in previous research given that they help to identify those fault lines that temporarily or systematically divide individuals, groups or societies. Scholars have been particularly interested in structural cleavages because not only do they delineate the fault lines along which (political) conflicts might erupt, they also predetermine their severity, dynamics and outcomes. For the study of European integration and the European Union, the identification of societal cleavages has thus become a particularly important and interesting venture (Kriesi et al. 2012; Hooghe & Marks 2018; de Wilde et al. 2019). It allows us to spot the divisional lines nurturing the politicization of the EU, while helping to differentiate supporters and opponents, and explain their political preferences and practices.

The following chapter aims to condense available knowledge about the growing contentiousness of the European Union by focusing on public opinion. Firstly, I will portray the increasing politicization of public opinion across time, elucidating on how previous research has tried to explain the divisions between Europeans and the main factors that are responsible for their perceptions and assessments of the EU. Secondly, I will highlight the role of societal cleavages, given that this approach is closely linked to a sociological research agenda.

Politicization of Public Support of the EU across Time

Numerous studies have attested to a gradual politicization of the European Union, a situation that stands in contrast to the 'permissive consensus' within the public sphere (Hooghe & Marks 2009; de Wilde 2011) during the first decades of the European Communities (EC), and which was generally favourable to the European idea and allowed for consecutive steps of integration and institution building. The subsequent politicization seems to touch all aspects of the EU because political contentions emerge regarding policy issues, persons and organizations, institutional procedures and rules, and the legitimacy of the EU as such. Scholars have assembled a series of explanations for this process, and they all tend to merge in the assumption that this development is a product of the EU's own success. The consecutive steps of enlargement of the EC/EU increased the number of member states from the six founding members to 16 Western European countries by 1995 – with the addition of a further 12 Eastern European countries by 2007. This enlargement has contributed to the horizontal differentiation of the EU, increasing the complexity of intergovernmental negotiations, and has generated more disagreements between member state governments (Schimmelfennig et al. 2015). Additionally, the deepening of the European integration process has conferred on the EU more competencies in a greater number of policy fields, making European politics more consequential and more salient for the mass media, political parties, interest groups and citizens. Consequently, the EU is more directly exposed to the ideological divisions within the member states' public sphere (de Wilde 2011), particularly since political groups and parties started to rally and mobilize against the EU (Kriesi 2016). Party politics and related conflicts also play a greater role within European institutions themselves, not only due to the greater role of the European Parliament in decision-making, but also within the European Commission and the working groups of the European Council (Beyers & Kerremans 2004). Finally, the politicization of the EU is also a product of various crises (e.g., the economic and financial recession since 2008, the so-called refugee crisis since 2015, the Covid19-related crisis) that highlighted the limited problem-solving capacities of the EU and thus contributed to growing scepticism about the governance capacity and legitimacy of the EU (Zeitlin et al. 2019).

Unsteady Support of the European Union across Time

It is not surprising that the growing contentiousness of European politics has impacted on public opinion within and across the European member states. However, this process is not as linear and unequivocal as might be assumed because public support of the EU has experienced ups and downs since the early 1970s. This is what available survey data show. In fact, citizens of the European member states have been asked recurrently to assess their country's membership in the EC/EU (see Figure 13.1), thus providing insights into a slowly growing community of 27 member states. The surveys show that until now, the group of supporters continues to be consistently larger than the group of opponents. However, public approval has become more conditional across time. This is not only due to increasing numbers of respondents testifying that membership is a bad thing; the more notable development is the increasing number of undecided citizens potentially open to assessing the EU negatively.

In general, Europeans are more opinionated about EU membership given that the share of people not knowing what to answer is shrinking considerably.

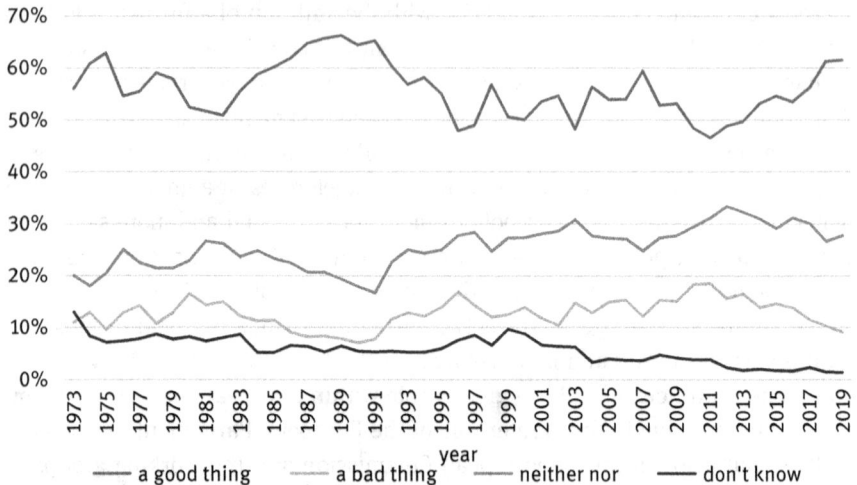

Figure 13.1: Generally, the membership of [country] in the EU is . . . (1973–2019). Source: Eurobarometer data.

Info-Box 13.1: The European Union's interest in public opinion: curse and blessing

Scholars working on public opinion within EU member states are in a very comfortable situation, because they can rely on a number of surveys that are issued on a regular basis (e.g., Eurobarometer surveys, European Value Study or the World Values Survey, the European Social Survey, the European Elections Study or EU-Silc). This situation, however, is not only a consequence of scientific demand and initiatives; the main drivers behind the establishment and realization of many opinion polls are political self-interests. This is clearly evident in regard to the Eurobarometer surveys, which have been providing data on citizens' opinions since 1973 for all of its member states. It is no coincidence that the Commission of the European Communities, founded in 1967, developed a pronounced interest in opinion polls at an early stage. Scientific research institutes had already conducted individual surveys in the six founding countries of the EC during the 1960s. However, such surveys became a regular exercise as early as 1973 when the Commission, with the support of the European Parliament, established the Eurobarometer programme, which since then has conducted two surveys per year in all member states – initially six, then 15, and finally 28 member states. The considerable effort involved is explained by the objectives that the EU Commission attaches to this instrument. On the one hand, the interest in public opinion is an instrument of policy advice; on the other, European opinion research is also subject to the objective of the European Commission's aim to contribute to building a European public by improving the level of information, harmonising it across countries and generating Europe-wide public opinions, thus breathing life into the idea of a 'Union of the peoples of Europe' (Signorelli 2012: 14–47; Nissen 2014).

Hence, the use of Eurobarometer surveys – and similar public opinion polls at national level – requires caution, given that public opinion research is enmeshed in political demands and debates. Eurobarometer data has been justifiably criticized for not conforming to scientific standards and for being too closely tied to the institutional needs of the EU. Critics, in particular, highlight methodological flaws, among them the intransparent methodological documentation, low response rates and simple operationalizations (Katz 1985; Schmitt 2003; Nissen 2014; Höpner & Jurczyk 2015). These flaws have consequences for the representativity of the data. For instance, it is to be expected that low response rates cause a bias towards citizens willing to participate in an (EU-related) survey. This bias might explain why Eurobarometer data paint a partially more positive picture in favour of EU membership, when compared to other opinion polls (e.g., Pew Research Center 2012; YouGov 2016, Lahusen 2021: 142). However, if we assume that this bias is systematic across time, we can make use of these surveys to trace changes across time, albeit with caution regarding the interpretation of findings.

The development of public opinion seems to reflect progress and failure. The best approval rates were achieved in 1991 and mirror political efforts to deepen the European integration process and overcome the division of Europe after the end of the East-West confrontation. However, approval levels fell to 50 per cent in only six years, most likely due to the economic downturn in the internal market and the return of mass unemployment within the member states. Figures recovered temporarily until 2007, for which the pro-European attitude in the ten new eastern and central European member states was likely responsible. However, with the outbreak of the global financial and economic crisis in 2008, support rates collapsed again, with those years producing the worst results for the EU since the beginning of the Eurobarometer surveys. In 2011, only 46.6 per cent of those surveyed saw membership as a good thing, 18.5 per cent as a bad thing. The reasons for this loss of acceptance are undoubtedly the severity and duration of the economic and financial crisis, which hit people in the southern European member states especially hard. This crisis quickly turned into a political crisis, as the member states and EU institutions did not find convincing solutions to the economic slumps and overindebted public budgets. EU support collapsed, particularly in countries such as Italy and Greece, hit hard by both crises. Since 2015, approval levels have recovered slightly, but it remains unclear how stable they will be in the future.

The dramatic change in mood is instructive because it has affected countries that were strong supporters of the European Union for a long period. Until the early 2000s, studies repeatedly confirmed that the populations in Luxembourg, Ireland, the Netherlands, and most southern European countries were among the supporters of the EU, while the British, Swedish, Austrian and Baltic citizens were consistently more critical of the EU (Weßels 2007; Hooghe & Marks 2007). EU-supporters have been thinning out, particularly among the more EU-friendly countries. Figure 13.2 summarizes the trends for countries that either represent a traditionally EU-friendly stance (the Netherlands) or an EU-sceptical population (the UK), and two countries that changed sides (Italy and Greece). Consistently high support rates are true for Dutch citizens, even though the fluctuations mentioned before can also be observed there. The same fluctuations are true for British citizens as well, but the share of citizens rejecting or questioning their country's membership exceed the EU-friendly voices. The change of opinion is most pronounced in Italy and Greece, where a decline in approval levels began in 1991 and has been significantly gathering pace since 2007, meaning that the economic and financial crisis may have grown into a legitimacy crisis for the EU in these countries.

The developments corroborate that scholarly writing is correct in arguing that the EU is exposed to a process of politicization (Hooghe & Marks 2009; de Wilde & Zürn 2012; Hutter & Kriesi 2019). This politicization is not only mirrored in public opinion polls but has moved to the forefront during the almost 50 referendums on EU-related issues, with the latter unleashing considerable controversy in the respective member states. Referenda about each country's accession to the EC/EU were successful in most countries where the population was called to the ballet box. However, this was not the case in Norway, where the majority of people opposed membership twice (September 1972 and November 1994). The Maastricht Treaty failed in Denmark in June 1992 and had to be renegotiated before the referendum in May 1993 was positive. The same applies to the Treaties of Nice and Lisbon, which were only approved in Ireland on the second attempt (October 2002 and October 2009, respectively). Referenda about the introduction of the euro also failed in Denmark and Sweden (September 2002 and 2003, respectively), and consequences were even more drastic for the EU when the referendums about the proposed European Union Constitution were cancelled after the negative votes in the Netherlands and France (May and June 2005). The biggest shock wave, however, was the British referendum about the country's EU membership, since the referendum ended in June 2016 with 51.9 per cent of the votes in favour of withdrawal.

Differentiated Support: Public Trust in European and National Institutions

The politicization of the EU needs to be put in context to prevent overly hasty conclusions. In fact, EU citizens might be considerably more sceptical about the EU, but this development is not restricted to European politics, given that citizens are more disparaging of institutionalized politics at large. While citizens might

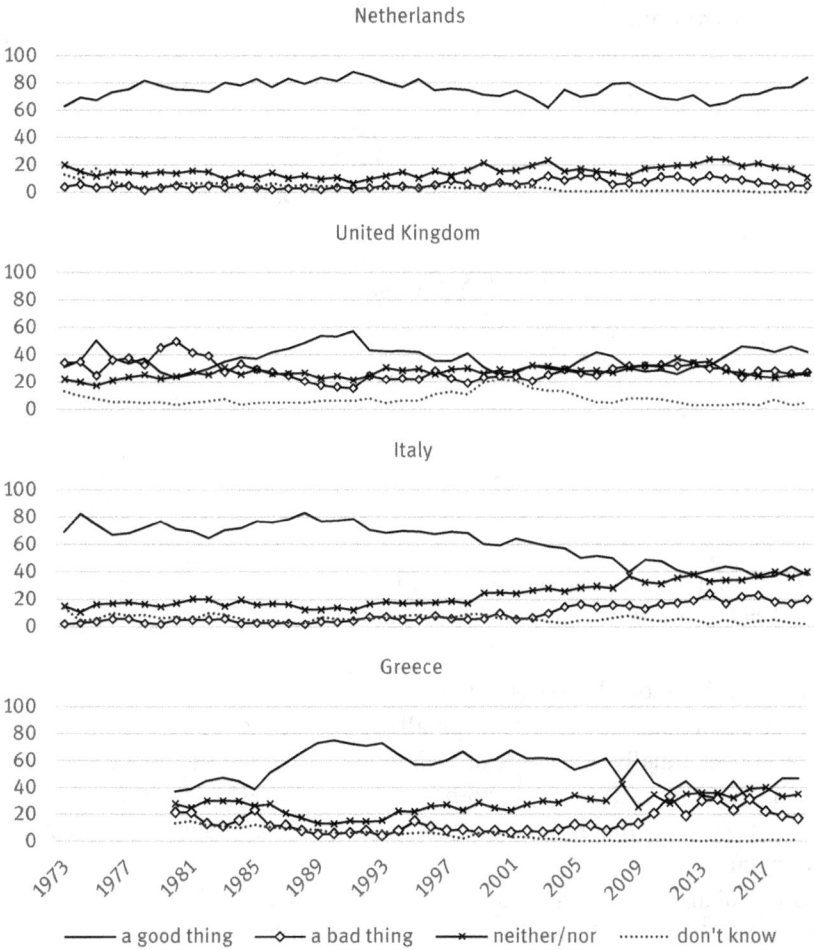

Figure 13.2: Attitude towards EU membership: country selection.
Source: Eurobarometer data.

be more disillusioned in regard to the EU, they are also less supportive of national politics. This observation also applies when considering survey data that asks respondents to indicate the extent to which they trust political institutions. Figure 13.3 summarizes available data since the year 2001 or 2003, respectively, showing that there has been a general decline in trust regarding political institutions at the European and national levels since the outbreak of the financial and economic crisis, even though figures have gradually recovered since 2015. It is noteworthy that the EU garners more citizen trust than national

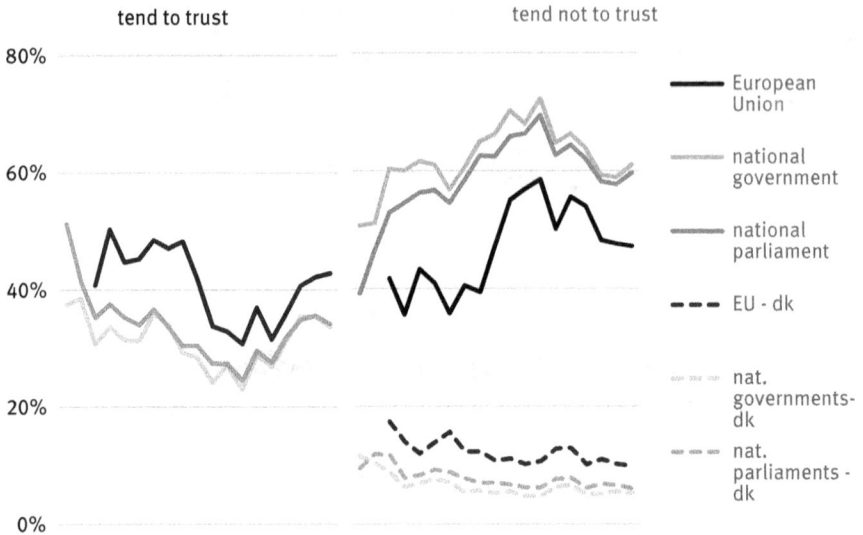

Figure 13.3: Trust in political institutions (2001–2019 · EU28).
Source: Eurobarometer data.

institutions. Additionally, levels of trust or distrust follow similar trends, meaning that public support of institutionalized politics tends to be exposed to similar forces. Finally, the share of respondents that do not know how to answer the question is decreasing, both in regard to the EU and national institutions, thus showing that respondents are more opinionated since the turn of the millennium.

On breaking down these figures by country (see Figure 13.4), we see that the deterioration in terms of trust is particularly evident for the southern European countries. The levels of distrust are remarkably high among Greek, Italian and Spanish respondents, and affect national institutions much more forcefully than the European Union. In the Netherlands, levels of distrust are much lower across all institutions, and differences are less marked, even though respondents were less confident about the EU between 2010 and 2015. In Poland, levels of distrust are much higher regarding national institutions, when compared to the EU – a picture that applies to most accession countries from eastern Europe.

The surveys show, in sum, that citizens seem to adapt their assessments and opinions to the socio-economic and political developments in their countries and the EU at large. Europeans are more critical of the EU and significantly more disillusioned about their national institutions in times of crises, and even if they are willing to be more supportive in better times, they seem to maintain

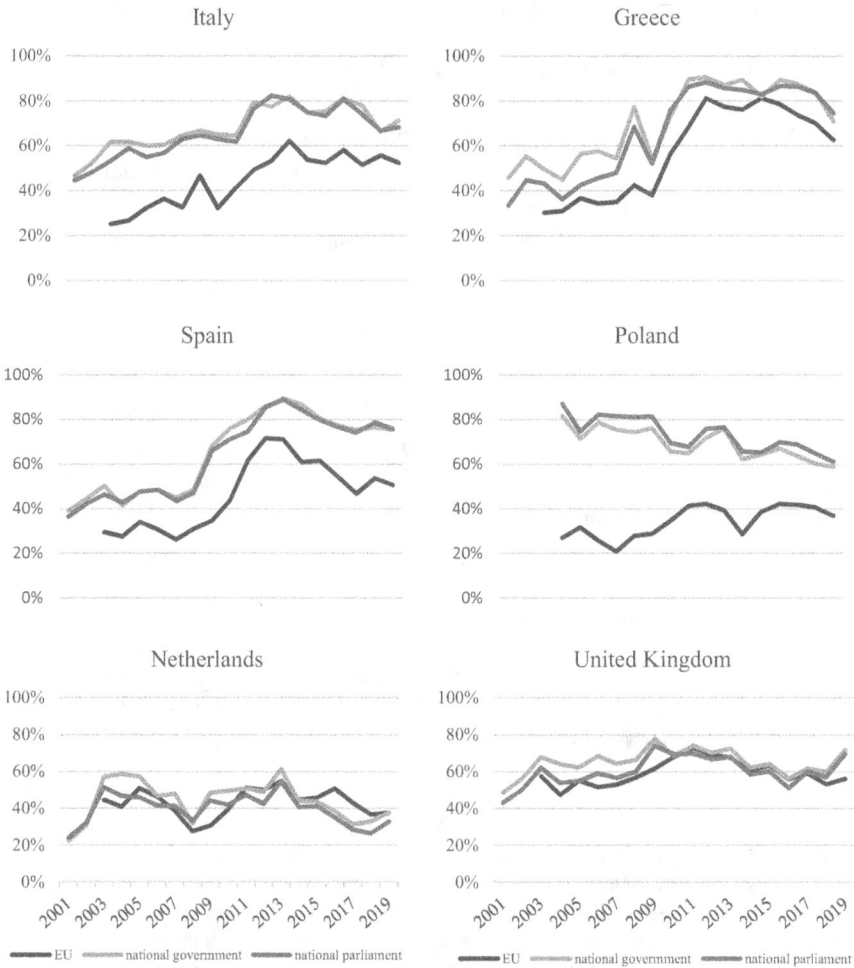

Figure 13.4: Levels of distrust in political institutions (2001–20019, in per cent).
Source: Eurobarometer data.

a more critical posture towards institutionalized politics. This is particularly true for those populations that have experienced considerable hardships during the past crises, while the public mood is more sympathetic in countries less affected by the turmoil of the last decades. Europeans are thus more divided in their political opinions, and these divisions seem to be related closely to the socio-economic cleavages between and within European member states.

Political Cleavages and Social Divisions: Political and Sociological Explanations

These descriptive observations raise questions about the factors that influence public opinion about the EU and thus help to explain the divisional lines between supporters and opponents. Research in the social sciences has been committed to this task for more than three decades, with a particular emphasis on the analysis of so-called **Euroscepticism** (Hooghe & Marks 2007; Krouwel & Abts 2007; Leruth et al. 2018). The privileged attention paid to EU-critical citizens has allowed us to take a closer look at the growing contentiousness of the EU by highlighting the large number of citizens with feelings of unease about the European Union, expressing doubts, criticism and/or even rejection. Studies have been particularly interested in unveiling the social and political profiles of EU-sceptic citizens, and the societal contexts that feed Euroscepticism. A great number of factors at the citizen and country levels have proven to be relevant.

Info-Box 13.2: Public opinion research: concepts and tools, risks, and side-effects

Public opinion research is a fully established field at the cross-roads of scientific, political and commercial interests. While highly professionalized, it is confronted with noteworthy limitations. On the one hand, the development of valid and reliable measurements is a challenging enterprise. Against politically commissioned surveys, which are primarily interested in individual opinions, academic research has tended to centre on surveying political attitudes, which are defined as individual preferences and orientations towards a political entity (an issue, a policy, a person or an institution) that are claimed to be the basis on which citizens develop issue-specific opinions (Erikson & Tedin 2001: 6). Scholars distinguish between cognitive and emotional dimensions either targeting specific persons or policies or more general entities, such as political institutions or political systems (Easton 1975; Dalton 1999). Surveys interested in political support thus ask respondents a battery of questions that aim to measure the approval of specific politicians and policies, the assessment of governmental performance, the satisfaction with or trust in various institutions, the feeling of attachment or pride, and general democratic values and beliefs. However, responses and response rates are not self-evident and always require interpretation. Decreasing levels of public support in terms of shrinking approval or trust, for instance, might not necessarily be a sign of democratic disengagement, but can also be interpreted as an expression of increasing public mobilization and democratic ambitions (Dalton 1999; Norris 2011).

On the other hand, sociological research has become increasingly sceptical about public opinion research because mass surveys might reify what we conceive as 'public opinion'. Mass surveys gather data on individual responses not necessarily reflective of a population's opinion. Social inequalities and existing power relations need to be taken into consideration. In fact, significant proportions of people are without a (firm) opinion, and opinions and omitted statements ("don't know" or missing values) are unevenly distributed within society, when considering **social class** or gender (Francis & Busch 1975). Hence, public opinion polls selectively mobilize a 'public opinion' that is an aggregated product of social inequalities. Additionally, 'public opinions' are more often than not rather a consequence of mass-mediated and elite-driven public debates. What survey analysis does is provide us with a picture of a prefabricated, mobilized and demobilized aggregation of individual opinions (Bourdieu 1991; Weakliem 2005; Lahusen 2021).

Overall, sociological research can make productive use of available survey data as long as it remains sensitive and controls for the hidden impact of societal divisions and power relations. Scholars should be sceptical when considering the descriptive precision of survey data, since they purport to be an accurate picture of public opinion, when in fact they are a volatile and selectively mobilized aggregation of opinions.

Explaining EU-scepticism at the Citizen and Country levels

In regard to the individual level, research has identified a series of social, political and cultural characteristics that are closely associated with EU-related attitudes. In regard to social features, it is known that lower occupational status and financial hardships boost criticism, and this is also true for educational inequalities (Kuhn et al. 2016). Political attitudes, identifications and preferences play an important role, as well. Citizens leaning towards the political extremes are more critical of the EU, but only right-wing respondents categorically reject European integration (van Elsas et al. 2016). Populist attitudes tend to fuel Euroscepticism in that they express an unease with the political system, based on the belief that the political classes are no longer committed to the needs of the people and conduct politics over which ordinary people no longer have any influence (Treib 2014; Kriesi & Pappas 2015). Collective identities are important because citizens are more likely to support the EU when they express feelings of belongingness to Europe, while respondents highly attached to the nation state are more critical of the EU (Hooghe & Marks 2004; Fligstein et al. 2012). Finally, media consumption plays a role because readers of traditional media are more supportive of the EU, while Internet and social media users are more likely to be critical (Conti & Memoli 2017).

EU-related attitudes do not only diverge between citizens, but also between countries. The British, Swedish, Austrian and Baltic populations have tended to be Eurosceptic, while people in Luxembourg, Ireland, the Netherlands and most southern European countries were among the supporters of the EU (Weßels 2007; Hooghe & Marks 2007). This picture has changed over time due to the various crises of the EU (see Figures 13.1 and 13.2 above), thus providing evidence that citizens' opinions tend to change collectively. Scholars have aimed to identify country-specific factors responsible for differing rates of Euroscepticism. Attention was paid, for instance, to the socio-economic situation. A bad economic performance and the effect of the financial and economic crisis are highly significant when distinguishing between Eurosceptical and friendly respondents and countries (Kuhn & Stoeckel 2014; Braun & Tausendpfund 2014; van Erkel & van der Meer 2016). This effect is evident when looking at unemployment rates, as they tend to fuel criticism of EU membership even among those that are not unemployed. Residents of countries with higher unemployment rates overall are more likely to express fears about the negative implications of membership, thus hinting at a perception of collective threats (Grauel et al. 2014).

These explanations detected general patterns and trends, albeit with numerous exceptions, thus highlighting that country-specific opinions about the EU are conditioned by various interconnected causes (Lubbers & Scheepers 2010). As a reaction to these limitations, a second approach became more prominent in the latter years when explaining the relevance of countries. According to these studies, citizens are more confident and used to expressing opinions about national politics, which means that the perception and evaluation of the EU is largely mediated by the perceptions and assessments of national politics. This means that citizens use the nation state as a proxy (Anderson 1998; Kritzinger 2003) or benchmark (de Vries 2018) for forming opinions about the EU. Citizens that are not very confident about the performance of their national governments will be more critical of the EU, and vice versa; this seems to apply to public opinions between countries at large. Additionally, studies argue that citizens tend to queue behind national elites in their support or criticism of the EU when public debates are controversial (Hooghe & Marks 2005; de Vries & Edwards 2009).

These general observations have inspired studies that attempt to identify the country-specific factors mediating EU-related attitudes. It was shown, for instance, that the political context of a country, measured in terms of party systems, plays an important intervening role because anti-European parties, many of whom are populist, severely criticize the EU and thus shape public opinion (Hutter & Grande 2014; Treib 2020). The stronger the political representation of overtly anti-European parties is, and the stronger the polarization between leftist and rightist parties, the higher the share of Eurosceptic citizens (de Vries & Edwards 2009; Armingeon & Ceka 2014). Additionally, countries with an exclusively national sense of belonging leave less room for European identities (Fligstein et al. 2012). However, people who identify exclusively with their country are not automatically Eurosceptics. This happens only in countries where political parties rally for and against pro-EU and anti-EU identities, polarising the population, propelling it to take sides (Hooghe & Marks 2004).

Cleavage Theory: The Role of Social Inequalities and Divisions

The previous summary of available evidence demonstrates that approval and criticism of the EU is affected by the following circumstances: household finances, occupational status, educational credentials, as well as the state of the national economy and rates of unemployment. Taken together, it suggests that social divisions between vulnerable and privileged population groups seem to be responsible for political lines of dissent – an argument that has been assigned to the so-called **cleavage theory** (Weakliem 2005; Hooghe & Marks 2018). This strand of research goes back to a long tradition of social theory and sociological research that highlights the importance of citizens' social characteristics, such as age, gender, occupation, income or education, and more generally, the relevance of stratificational divisions within societies along social classes. Against a strict materialist explanation that exclusively ties political ideologies (socialism, liberalism and conservativism) to antagonistic social classes, cleavage theory has argued for a less deterministic relation (Lipset & Rokkan 1967; Lipset 1981; Rokkan 1999). Political preferences do not only mirror material interests, but also patterns of opinion formation within personal networks and inter-generational relations that are more or less tied back to different social classes.

Cleavage theory has come in for substantial criticism (e.g., Evans 2002), as empirical evidence has shown that societal developments dilute traditional class divisions, weakening traditional party constituencies, increasing the ranks of undecided or swing voters, and reorganising established party systems. However, since the new millennium, there has been a resurgence of interest in cleavage theory (Kriesi et al. 2012; Hooghe & Marks 2018; de Wilde et al. 2019). The reawakened interest responds to the re-emergence of economic issues and conflicts in times of financial and economic crises. More substantially, it reflects ongoing processes of modernization that are responsible for considerable transformations of social reality: accelerated urbanization, technological rationalization and digitalization, liberalization of markets, pluralization of partnership and families, and cultural value change. Additionally, modernization is linked to a process of globalization, given that many of these developments transcend national borders and expose local communities and societies to globalizing markets, telecommunication systems, migration and mobility networks, international treaties or regional integration processes. The new dividing line seems to run between winners and losers of modernization and globalization (e.g., Kriesi et al. 2006), where the one side propagates societal modernization and globalization, thus stressing the benefits, while the other side aims to strengthen the nation state in order to curtail the destructive force of globalization as modernization.

This new divide has generated a new **political cleavage** where supporters of open societies and borders go head-to-head with defenders of national autonomy and closed societies (Fligstein 2008; Kriesi et al. 2012; Strijbis et al. 2020). The global scope of societal transformations nourishes new political cleavages that transcend individual countries and reshape the established ideological divide between left and right electorates and parties transnationally (Hooghe & Marks 2018; Kneuer 2019). In this context, research has been interested in the emergence of **populism** as a new political force that has contributed considerably to the reorganization and polarization of party systems in the European member states. While populism is not a new phenomenon in itself, it has gained considerable momentum due to the mobilization capacity of newly formed populist parties. Most of them rally around similar convictions, among them the strong appeal to 'the people' as a homogenous entity, a dualistic understanding that separates clearly between 'the people' and 'the elites', an outspoken belief in a fundamental crisis of the established order and an anti-systemic approach that criticizes not only established power-holders, but also the media, experts and science (Canovan 1999; Mudde 2004; Rooduijn 2014). Populism has shown a great ability to mobilize discontent to the right and left of the political spectrum (Taggart 2004; Ivaldi et al. 2017), and particularly in light of the various crises affecting European member states, it has developed as a European-wide phenomenon that has secured electoral successes and representation in parliaments at the national and European levels (Kriesi & Pappas 2015). Since the early 2000s, populist groups and parties have started to engage in an anti-European oratory that links the populist critique of modernization with Euroscepticism (Kneuer 2019; Treib 2020). However, it needs to be stressed that populism and Euroscepticism are distinct phenomena (Harmsen 2010; Rooduijn & van Kessel 2019) because populist parties and citizens are not necessarily against the EU, while critique of the EU is not in itself populist.

Social Cleavages and Divided Public Opinion about Europe

The impact of social cleavages on public opinion is easy to trace when looking at public support for political institutions at the national and European level. For this purpose, it is worth returning to the question of citizens' trust in political institution. Figure 13.5 summarizes the average rates of trust for eight countries – using data from a comparative study that asked respondents to indicate levels of trust on an 11-point scale ranging from 'do not trust at all' to 'completely trust'. The means show that there is a social divide in institutional trust, given that respondents who affiliate themselves with the lower classes are much less trusting of European and national institutions than respondents assigning themselves to the upper and/or middle classes. Levels of trust in the EU are much lower in Greece, Italy and the UK when compared to Spain, France and Poland. Only among British respondents are national institutions more trusted than European; among the lower classes, this is also true for Greece and Sweden. Other factors impinge on lower levels of trust as well, when considering multivariate analyses: distrustful respondents see themselves in an inferior social class position, perceive a deterioration of their households' financial situation, speak more often of a serious crisis affecting their country's national economy, lean more clearly towards the political right, and subscribe considerably more often to populist beliefs.

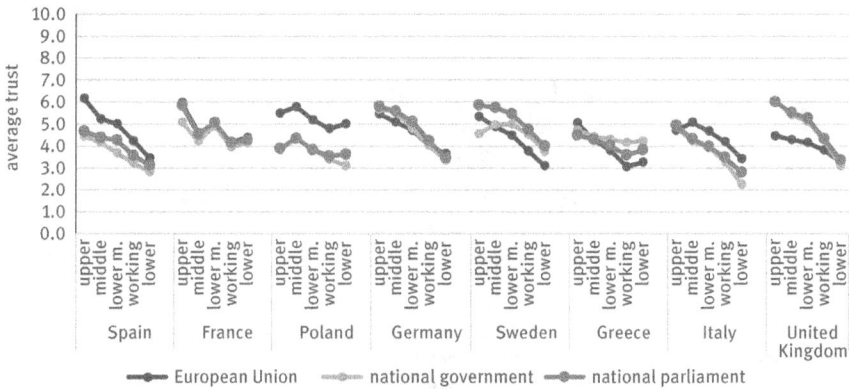

Figure 13.5: Trust in political institutions (means - 2015).
Source: Livewhat online survey.

Similar observations about the relevance of social cleavages can be made when looking at political attitudes that are more clearly related to the EU itself – in our case, the question of whether citizens assess the EU membership of their country as a good or bad thing. Compared to citizens' trust in national and European institutions, which seems to converge into a more general and interlocked form of institutional support, the question of EU membership is more apt to disentangle the potential impact of social cleavages on EU-related opinions. Sociology has important lessons to teach in this respect because the analysis of social cleavages and their potential impact on political conflicts is a demanding enterprise, once we set aside broad categorizations (e.g., winners and losers of modernization, globalization, or Europeanization). Social divisions are complex phenomena involving objective and subjective, stratification and spatial dimensions, particularly if we take a look at Europe as a whole. An impression of this complexity is provided by the relationship between occupations and EU-related attitudes. Occupations are a good starting point to determine the social dividing line of political dissent because they reflect the stratificational hierarchy of society: They are associated with a specific income, educational attainment level and professional status, and thus clearly indicate social class position in its various dimensions. Figure 13.6 summarizes the average approval of Eurosceptic statements for three occupational groups, following an Oesch-classification (Oesch 2006): managers, self-employed from the lower middle class, and low-qualified workers.

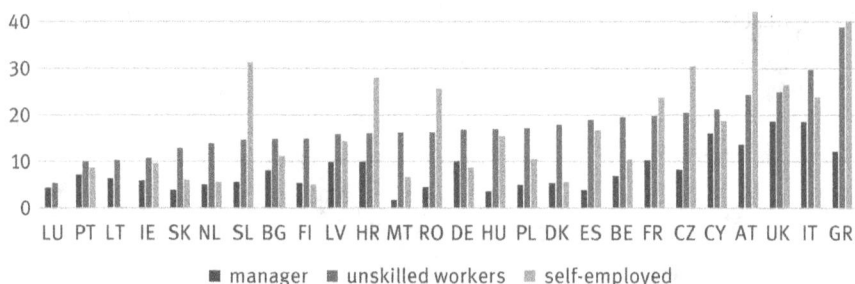

Figure 13.6: Euroscepticism and occupations (in per cent - 2016).
Source: Eurobarometer 86.1.

The first lesson to be drawn is that occupational status matters, given that only a minority of managers believes that the membership of their country is a bad thing, while low-skilled workers and the lower middle-class self-employed are much more sceptical. The second lesson to be drawn is that respondents with the same occupation do not necessarily agree across countries. Managers might be better off and more positive about the EU membership of their country, but being a manager in Greece or Italy seems to downsize this positive evaluation considerably, and the inverse is true for low skilled workers and the self-employed lower middle class. Obviously, social divisions and political disagreements maintain a rather complex relationship, once we pay attention to the EU as a whole. And this means that a thorough analysis has to disentangle the potential impact of social divisions on political cleavages in two respects. On the one hand, it is important to check whether country differences are caused by differing socio-economic contexts, while checking for the potential impact of diverging political systems. On the other hand, we need to follow conceptional and empirical lessons taught by sociology, and differentiate between different dimensions of social inequalities: objective patterns and subjective perceptions, and stratificational and spatial divisions. Such an analysis corroborates the effect of social divisions, as has been illustrated by previous studies (Lubbers & Scheepers 2010; Kuhn et al. 2016; Guinjoan & Rico 2018; Lahusen 2021).

In regard to objective structures of inequality, the analysis of survey data identified a cumulative impact of stratificational and spatial inequalities on EU-related attitudes. EU-sceptic views ('membership is a bad thing') is most dispersed among the unemployed and low skilled workers living in regions exposed to declining GDP-rates, while managers living in regions with the highest growth rates in Europe are the least inclined to support this assessment. These findings hold up even if the effect of other explanatory factors (socio-demographic traits, political parties and media systems, collective identities, etc.) are controlled for (Lahusen 2021: 170–178). In regard to the subjective perceptions of inequalities, the analysis could confirm that the self-reported household situation, class affiliation and feeling of relative deprivation matter: Among those opposed to the EU membership of their country, there are significantly more respondents indicating financial strains, seeing themselves as worse off when compared to previous times, and affiliating themselves to the lower classes. These perceptions also correlate with approval to populist beliefs and the conviction that one's own voice is not being heard. Hence, feelings of social vulnerability are paired with a sense of political marginalization.

It is important to stress that the effect of social cleavages on EU-related attitudes runs across all European member states and their regions. Vulnerable fringes of society and those seeing themselves at the lower end of the stratificational ladder are everywhere more likely to be sceptical about the EU, and there are even cumulative effects between stratificational and spatial inequality, as indicated above. What is particularly interesting is that Europeans seem to have learned how to perceive the European scope of these divisional lines. European citizens have developed a sense of what the living standards in other European countries are, and the consensus across countries is remarkable when looking at the position they assign to the various countries on a scale: Sweden and Switzerland are considered to be the best-off, France and Poland rank in an intermediate position, while Greece is relegated to the worst-off countries (Lahusen 2021: 72–91). These perceptions imply comparisons between one's own household situation and the living standards of other Europeans. What the analyses show is that these comparisons have negative implications for satisfaction levels with national politics: Citizens that see themselves as worse off than Swedish, Swiss or German citizens tend to see their countries in a serious crisis, they are more often dissatisfied with the performance of their national governments, and they are more likely to express populist believes. Hence, citizens make their own governments accountable for the fact that their own situation is below the living conditions of fellow Europeans. Conversely, it is interesting to note that these negative effects disappear once we move to those respondents who rank their own living conditions as similar as those of other Europeans. Apparently, the similarity of living conditions is a factor significantly attenuating the political discontent with national politics. And this similarity seems to be a driving factor in convincing European citizens about the merits of EU membership: Respondents that assess living conditions abroad to be better than their own are more often supportive of this membership, most probably because European integration is committed to the promise of guaranteeing comparable living standards for all EU citizens, even those who are worse off (Lahusen 2021).

Conclusions

The analysis of social cleavages is a promising endeavour for scholars and students interested in European integration and the European Union. This applies in particular to the study of EU-related public opinion because the growing politicization of the EU is patterned along these divisional lines, both within and across the various European member states. This analysis calls for sociological wisdom, given that the study of social cleavages and conflicts belongs to its core concerns and has brought about various theoretical accounts, methodological tools and empirical bodies of knowledge. Empirical findings corroborate the usefulness of this wisdom, given that social cleavages are a rather complex phenomenon that involve various analytical dimensions, i.e., objective and subjective, stratificational and spatial configurations of inequality. Available survey data highlights that societal cleavages have a clear impact on political contentions because similar living conditions nourish similar political preferences across Europe's member states. Everywhere, it is the socially privileged who are more likely to be politically satisfied with established institutions and see the merits of their countries' EU membership. And everywhere, it is the socially disadvantaged who are more likely to express fundamental criticism of established politics and are far less likely to recognize the advantages of the EU. Additionally, we see that social inequalities have a cumulative effect, given that deprived citizens living in deprived regions are more likely to be Eurosceptic, while privileged citizens living in well-off regions have a greater likelihood of being enthusiastic about the EU. Moreover, objective inequalities are augmented by feelings of subjective deprivations, which acquire a pan-European dimension as citizens compare living standards across countries and make politics accountable for these divisions.

The analysis of cleavages should make us mindful of the fact that political preferences and divisions are determined by a number of social, cultural and political factors. This also means that structures of social inequalities are responsible for one type of cleavage, besides other potential cleavages, such as cultural divisions. In all these respects, sociological accounts are indispensable. The European Union might be exposed to a gradual process of politicization, but this observation requires a better understanding of preconditions, constellations, and implications of latent and overt conflicts. The growing contentiousness of the EU is not necessarily a sign of disintegration, given that political conflicts have integrative forces, as well. What makes the analysis of societal cleavages so relevant is that political contentions develop a more problematic dynamic when social and political divisions start to converge into clear-cut and systematic fault lines. In this sense, it allows us to provide insights into the integrative and disintegrative forces of social cleavages and political conflicts.

Didactical Section

Key Learning Points

- Public opinion is an important field of research for political scientists and sociologists because it allows us to better understand what attitudes, beliefs and values are prevalent within a society, how diversified they are and the lines of dissent they nurture.
- Public opinion about the European Union and European integration is increasingly divided between supporters and opponents, thus testifying a gradual politicization of the EU within the European citizenry.
- The growing contentiousness of the European Union within public opinion is an expression of a latent political conflict strongly patterned by a social cleavage; that is, political divisions within public opinion are conditioned by social inequalities within and between European member states.
- Political preferences and attitudes are certainly affected by a series of economic, political and cultural factors. However, social divisions along stratificational and spatial inequalities, objective resource distribution and subjective perceptions play an important role in patterning EU-related attitudes and opinions, in particular the division between EU-friendly and sceptical citizens.
- Within the European Union, social divisions between privileged and marginalized citizens and regions is a fault line bisecting all member states and is thus contributing to the formation of a European political cleavage between supporters and critics of institutionalized politics at the national and European levels.

Glossary

Cleavage theory: a theory advanced in political science and sociology to explain electoral behaviour and party systems with reference to social and cultural divisions, particularly those between social classes.

Euroscepticism: a concept used to describe opposition to the EU and/or the European integration process that ranges from singular doubts to outright rejection.

Political cleavage: a division of citizens into groups with opposing political interests, preferences and beliefs that nourishes substantial political conflict.

Social class: a hierarchical division of a society based on social-economic resources and status of citizens.

Social inequalities: the unequal distribution of those social resources and goods (income, education, occupational status, profession, material goods, etc.) that determine living conditions and prospects of citizens within a society.

Further Readings

de Vries, C. E., 2018: *Euroscepticism and the Future of European Integration*. Oxford: Oxford University Press.

Hutter, S. & H. Kriesi, 2019: Politicizing Europe in times of crisis. *Journal of European Public Policy* 26(7):996–1017.

Kriesi, H., E. Grande, R. Lachat, M. Dolezal, S. Bornschier & T. Frey, 2006: Globalization and the transformation of the national political space: Six European countries compared. *European Journal of Political Research* 45:921–956.

Lahusen, C., 2021: *Political Attitudes of Divided European Citizens. Public Opinion and social Inequalities in Comparative and Relational Perspective*. London: Routledge.

Leruth, B., S. Nicholas & S. Usherwood (eds.), 2018: *The Routledge Handbook of Euroscepticism*. Abingdon: Routledge.

Lipset, S. M., 1981: *Political Man: The Social Bases of Politics*. Revised Edition. Baltimore, MD: Johns.

Rokkan, S., 1999: *State Formation, Nation-Building, and Mass Politics in Europe*. Collected Works edited by Peter Flora. Oxford: Oxford University Press.

References

Anderson, C. J., 1998: When in doubt, use proxies: Attitudes toward domestic politics and support for European integration. *Comparative political studies* 31(5):569–601.

Armingeon, K. & B. Ceka, 2014: The loss of trust in the European Union during the great recession since 2007: The role of heuristics from the national political system. *European Union Politics* 15(1):82–107.

Beyers, J. & B. Kerremans, 2004: Bureaucrats, politicians, and societal interests: how is European policy making politicized? *Comparative Political Studies* 37(10):1119–50.

Bourdieu, P., 1991: *Language and Symbolic Power*. Cambridge: Harvard University Press.

Braun, D. & M. Tausendpfund, 2014: The Impact of the Euro Crisis on Citizens' Support for the European Union. *Journal of European Integration* 36(3):231–245.

Canovan, M., 1999: Trust the People! Populism and the Two Faces of Democracy. *Political Studies* 47(1):2–16.

Conti, N. & V. Memoli, 2017: How the Media Make European Citizens More Eurosceptical. In: Caiani M. & S. Guerra (eds.), *Euroscepticism, Democracy and the Media. Communicating Europe, Contesting Europe*, pp. 121–140. London: Palgrave/Macmillan.

Coser, L., 1956: *The Functions of Social Conflict*. Glencoe. Illinois: Free Press.

Dalton, R. J., 1999: Political Support in Advanced Industrial Democracies. In: Norris P. (ed.), *Critical Citizens. Global Support for Democratic Governance*, pp. 57–77. New York: Oxford University Press.

de Vries, C. E., 2018: *Euroscepticism and the Future of European Integration*. Oxford: Oxford University Press.

de Vries, C. E. & E. E. Edwards, 2009: Taking Europe to its Extremes. Extremist Parties and Public Euroscepticism. *Party Politics* 15(1):5–28.

de Wilde, P., 2011: No Polity for Old Politics? A Framework for Analyzing the Politicization of European Integration. *Journal of European Integration* 33(5):559–575.

de Wilde, P. & M. Zürn, 2012: Can the Politicization of European Integration be Reversed? *Journal of Common Market Studies* 50(1):137–153.

de Wilde, P., R. Koopmans, W. Merkel, O. Strijbis, & M. Zürn (eds.), 2019: The struggle over borders: Cosmopolitanism and Communitarianism. Cambridge: Cambridge University Press.

Dubiel, H., 1986: Cultivated Conflicts. *Political Theory* 26(2):209–220.

Easton, D., 1975: A Re-Assessment of the Concept of Political Support. *British Journal of Political Science* 5(4):435–457.

Erikson, R. S. & K. L. Tedin, 2001: *American Public Opinion*. 6th edition. New York: Longman.

Evans, G., 2002: Class voting: From premature obituary to reasoned appraisal. In: Evans, G. (ed.), *The End of Class Politics?* pp. 1–22. Oxford, UK: Oxford University Press.

Fligstein, N., 2008: *Euroclash: The EU, European Identity, and the Future of Europe*. Oxford: Oxford University Press.

Fligstein, N., A. Polyakova & W. Sandholtz, 2012: European Integration, Nationalism and European Identity. *Journal of Common Market Studies* 50(1):106–122.

Francis, J. D. & L. Busch, 1975: What We Now Know About 'I don't Knows'. *Public Opinion Quarterly* 39:207–218.

Grauel, J., J. Heine & C. Lahusen, 2014: Who is afraid of the (big bad) European Union? European integration and fears about job losses. In: Arts, W. & L. Halman (eds.), *Value contrasts and consensus in present-day Europe. Painting Europe's moral landscapes*, pp. 19–43. Boston: Brill.

Guinjoan, M. & G. Rico, 2018: How Perceptions of Inequality Between Countries Diminish Trust in the European Union: Experimental and Observational Evidence. *Political Psychology* 39 (6):1289–1303.

Harmsen, R., 2010: Concluding Comment: On Understanding the Relationship between Populism and Euroscepticism. *Perspectives on European Politics and Society* 11(3): 333–341.

Hooghe, L. & G. Marks, 2004: Does Identity or Economic Rationality Drive Public Opinion on European Integration? *Political Science & Politics* 37(3):415–420.

Hooghe, L. & G. Marks, 2005: Calculation, Community and Cues. Public Opinion on European Integration. *European Union Politics* 6(4):419–443.

Hooghe, L. & G. Marks, 2007: Sources of Euroscepticism. *Acta Politica* 42(2):119–127.

Hooghe, L. & G. Marks, 2009: A Postfunctionalist Theory of European Integration: From Permissive Consensus to Constraining Dissensus. *British Journal of Political Science* 39 (1):1–23.

Hooghe, L. & G. Marks, 2018: Cleavage theory meets Europe's crises: Lipset, Rokkan, and the transnational cleavage. *Journal of European Public Policy* 25(1):109–135.

Höpner, M. & B. Jurczyk, 2015: How the eurobarometer blurs the line between research and propaganda. MPIfG Discussion Paper 15(6):1–26.

Hutter, S. & E. Grande, 2014: Politicizing Europe in the National Electoral Arena: A Comparative Analysis of Five West European Countries, 1970–2010. *Journal of Common Market Studies* 52(5):1002–1018.

Hutter, S. & H. Kriesi, 2019: Politicizing Europe in times of crisis. *Journal of European Public Policy* 26(7):996–1017.

Ivaldi, G., M. E. Lanzone & D. Woods, 2017: Varieties of Populism across a Left-Right Spectrum: The Case of the Front National, the Northern League, Podemos and Five Star Movement. *Swiss Political Science Review* 23(4):354–376.

Katz, R. S., 1985: Measuring party identification with Eurobarometer data: a warning note. *West European Politics* 8(1):104–108.

Kneuer, M., 2019: The tandem of populism and Euroscepticism: a comparative perspective in the light of the European crises. *Contemporary Social Science* 14(1):26–42.

Kriesi, H., 2016: The Politicization of European Integration. *Journal of Common Market Studies* 54:32–47.

Kriesi, H. & T. S. Pappas (eds.), 2015: *European Populism in the Shadow of the Great Recession*. Colchester: ECPR Press.

Kriesi, H., E. Grande, R. Lachat, M. Dolezal, S. Bornschier & T. Frey, 2006: Globalization and the transformation of the national political space: Six European countries compared. *European Journal of Political Research* 45:921–956.

Kriesi, H., E. Grande, M. Dolezal, M. Helbling, D. Höglinger, S. Hutter & B. Wüest (eds.), 2012: *Political conflict in Western Europe*. Cambridge University Press.

Kritzinger, S., 2003: The influence of the nation–state on individual support for the European Union. *European Union Politics* 4(2):219–241.

Krouwel, A. & K. Abts, 2007: Varieties of Euroscepticism and Populist Mobilization: Transforming Attitudes from Mild Euroscepticism to Harsh Eurocynicism. *Acta Politica* 42 (2):252–270.

Kuhn, T. & F. Stoeckel: 2014: When European integration becomes costly: the euro crisis and public support for European economic governance. *Journal of European Public Policy* 21 (4):624–641.

Kuhn, T., E. van Elsas, A. Hakhverdian & W. van der Brug, 2016: An ever-wider gap in an ever-closer union: Rising inequalities and Euroscepticism in 12 West European democracies, 1975–2009. *Socio-Economic Review* 14(1):27–45.

Lahusen, C., 2021: *The Political Attitudes of Divided European Citizens: Public Opinion and Social Inequalities in Comparative and Relational Perspective*. London: Routledge.

Leruth, B., S. Nicholas & S. Usherwood (eds.), 2018: *The Routledge Handbook of Euroscepticism*. Abingdon: Routledge.

Lipset, S. M., 1981: *Political Man: The Social Bases of Politics*. Baltimore, MD: Johns, revised edition.

Lipset, S. M. & S. Rokkan, 1967: *Party Systems and Voter Alignments. Cross-National Perspectives*. New York: Free Press.

Lubbers, M. & P. Scheepers, 2010: Divergent trends of Euroscepticism in countries and regions of the European Union. *European Journal of Political Research* 49(6):787–817.

Mudde, C., 2004: The Populist Zeitgeist. *Government and Opposition* 39(4):542–563.

Münch, R., 1996: Between Nation-State, Regionalism and World Society: The European Integration Process. *Journal of Common Market Studies* 34(3):379–401.

Nissen, S., 2014: The Eurobarometer and the process of European integration. Methodological foundations and weaknesses of the largest European survey. *Quality & Quantity* 48(2): 713–727.

Norris, P., 2011: *Democratic Deficit: Critical Citizens Revisited.* Cambridge: Cambridge University Press.

Oesch, D., 2006: Coming to Grips with a Changing Class Structure: An Analysis of Employment Stratification in Britain, Germany, Sweden and Switzerland. *International Sociology* 21(2): 263–288.

Pew Research Center, 2012: Pew Global Attitudes Project 2012, Spring Survey Topline Results. Washington, D.C. https://www.pewresearch.org/global/wp-content/uploads/sites/2/2012/05/Pew-Global-Attitudes-Project-European-Crisis-Topline-May-29-2012.pdf (accessed April 24, 2020).

Rooduijn, M., 2014: The Nucleus of Populism: In Search of the Lowest Common Denominator. *Government and Opposition* 49(4):573–99.

Rooduijn, M. & S. van Kessel, 2019: Populism and Euroskepticism in the European Union. *Oxford Research Encyclopedia of Politics.* https://oxfordre.com/politics/view/10.1093/acrefore/9780190228637.001.0001/acrefore-9780190228637-e-1045 (accessed March 11, 2021).

Rokkan, S., 1999: *State Formation, Nation-Building, and Mass Politics in Europe.* Collected Works edited by Peter Flora. Oxford: Oxford University Press.

Schimmelfennig, F., D. Leuffen & B. Rittberger, 2015: The European Union as a system of differentiated integration: interdependence, politicization and differentiation. *Journal of European Public Policy* 22(6):764–782.

Schmitt, H., 2003: The Eurobarometers: Their Evolution, Obvious Merits, and Ways to Add Value to them. *European Union Politics* 4(2):243–251.

Signorelli, S., 2012: The EU and Public Opinions: A Love-Hate Relationship? Study No. 93. Paris: Notre Europe, Jacques Delors Institute.

Simmel, G., 1903: The Sociology of Conflict: I, II and III. *American Journal of Sociology* 9: 490–525, 672–689 & 798–811.

Strijbis, O., J. Helmer, & P. De Wilde, 2020: A cosmopolitan–communitarian cleavage around the world? Evidence from ideological polarization and party–voter linkages. *Acta Politica* 55:408–431(2020).

Taggart, P., 2004: Populism and Representative Politics in Contemporary Europe. *Journal of Political Ideologies,* 9(3): 269–288.

Treib, O., 2014: The voter says no, but nobody listens: causes and consequences of the Eurosceptic vote in the 2014 European elections. *Journal of European Public Policy* 21(10): 1541–1554.

Treib, O., 2020: Euroscepticism is here to stay: what cleavage theory can teach us about the 2019 European Parliament. *Journal of European Public Policy* 28(2):174–189.

van Elsas, E. J., A. Hakhverdian & W. van der Brug, 2016: United against a common foe? The nature and origins of Euroscepticism among left-wing and right-wing citizens. *West European Politics* 39(6):1181–1204.

van Erkel, P. F.A. & T. W.G. van der Meer, 2016: Macroeconomic performance, political trust and the Great Recession: A multilevel analysis of the effects of within-country fluctuations in macroeconomic performance on political trust in 15 EU countries, 1999–2011. *European Journal of Political Research* 55(1):177–197.

Vobruba, G., 2012: The Social Construction of European Society. *Current Perspectives in Social Theory* 30:263–279.

Weakliem, D. L., 2005: Public Opinion, Political Attitudes, and Ideology. In: Janoski, T., R. Alford, A. Hicks & M. A. Schwartz (eds.), *The Handbook of Political Sociology*, pp. 227–246. Cambridge: Cambridge University Press.

Weßels, B., 2007: Discontent and European identity: Three types of Euroscepticism. *Acta Politica* 42(2):287–306.

YouGov, 2016: *YouGov Results – European Mega-Survey Topline Findings*. London https://d25d2506sfb94s.cloudfront.net/cumulus_uploads/document/smow6e2p43/MegaEuro trackerResults_AugustSeptember2016_Toplines.pdf. (accessed May 20, 2020).

Zeitlin, J., F. Nicoli & B. Laffan, 2019: Introduction: the European Union beyond the polycrisis? Integration and politicization in an age of shifting cleavages. *Journal of European Public Policy* 26(7):963–976

Tsveta Petrova & Susann Worschech
14 Civil Society and Social Movements

Civil society and social movement activism teach us a great deal about contemporary Europe and beyond. Why do Europeans participate in political and social life? Which formal and informal public norms are contested or infringed upon? What new norms, cleavages, and moral sensibilities are emerging? What is the current power distribution in society and how is it being challenged? How and when do activists challenge state, party, and business structures? And how and when do activists take the place of these institutions?

Civil societies, including social movements, are thus important actors in the processes of Europeanization. They address issues of local, national, European and more broadly international significance on a daily basis: civil, minority, and human rights; democracy and corruption; environmental protection; family values and religious freedom; labor and management conflicts; poverty; and war and terrorism, to name but a few.

Civil societies, including social movements, have also become increasingly significant realms of Europeanization, as they have been employed more frequently by a wider range of constituencies to represent a wider range of claims than in previous decades. And especially since the 1960s, "the doors to the streets were pushed wider than ever before" as an important forum for aggrieved citizens to press their claims (Snow et al. 2004: 4). This resulted in the social-movement form of making claims becoming largely institutionalized as part of the conventional repertoire of political participation (Tarrow 1994, Tarrow & Meyer 1998). As a result, European democracies today face a paradox: "on the one hand they are facing a profound legitimation crisis expressed by decline in citizen trust and satisfaction in electoral and institutional representative politics (Mair 2013); on the other, citizen commitment to democracy as a value is still high, and many European nations have witnessed an intense cycle of mobilizations demanding greater or 'real democracy' in the wake of the global financial crisis" (Fominaya & Feenstra 2020).

Indeed, over the past few decades, social movements and broader civic actors contesting the processes of Europeanization have been mobilizing around different visions of Europe: East/West, North/South, left/right, elite/populist, Christian/secular, open/fortress, among others. Their main area of concern has traditionally been the social and economic dimensions of European integration, with most such movements being left-wing (Dolezal et al. 2016). However, the issue of immigration has recently become increasingly salient, and far-right street activism is on the rise in the 21st century (Caiani 2019).

https://doi.org/10.1515/9783110673630-014

In summary, the processes of Europeanization cannot be understood without examining social contention and cooperation. The interplay of such social mobilization with institutional political evolution has shaped Europe throughout the modern era, with uprisings and community-building processes both alternating and remaining densely connected (Tilly 1984; 1995).

Civil Society and Social Movements: Similarities and Differences

Both civil society and social movements are not only actors and realms of public life in and beyond Europe, but also concepts for analyzing social continuity and change. Despite overlaps in the characteristics and functions of civil society and social movements, they capture different types of state-society relations.

We define civil society as "a sphere of social interaction between economy and state, composed above all of the intimate sphere (most notably family), the sphere of associations (especially voluntary organizations), social movements, and forms of public communication" (Cohen & Arato 1992: ix).

We further understand social movements as "networks of informal interactions between a plurality of individuals, groups and/or organizations, engaged in a political or cultural conflict, on the basis of a shared collective identity" (Diani 1992: 13). We find four main points of difference between social movements and civil society:

- Firstly, while social movements are likely to include more *informal* networks of interaction, civil society tends to encompass a broader range of organizational forms, from informal citizen initiatives and neighborhood networks to collective action formalized as non-governmental organizations (NGOs), civic associations, and unions (Alexander 2006: 4).
- Secondly, in building both dense and broad networks of face-to-face relationships, civil society is more likely to "cross-cut existing social cleavages" (Edwards et al. 2001: 17). In contrast, social movements tend to mobilize individuals and organizations under the umbrella of a shared collective identity and to foster *shared beliefs* that contribute to the social construction of a temporary community organized toward a particular goal.
- Thirdly, social movements are usually, and, by definition, engaged in political or cultural contestation, *conflict* or change. This is not necessarily the case for civil society, which often invests in community building, thus seeking to overcome conflict and social cleavages. It should be noted, however, that some movements seek not only to formulate political demands, but

also to affect political change by supporting alternative lifestyles and providing aid, services, and mutual help (Anheier 2004). Thus, movements often seek to impact both individuals and society at large, as well as change both institutional authority (political, corporate, religious, or educational etc.) and cultural authority (such as systems of beliefs and their resulting practices) in both conflictual and non-conflictual ways (Snow et al. 2004).

– Fourthly, given their change-oriented goals, social movements rarely have access to political elites and tend to resort to collective action, at least in part, outside of social routines and *institutionalized politics*. Nevertheless, extra-institutional action usually plays a more important role in grassroots movements and a more marginal role in interest-group movements and movements with a focus on personal and cultural change (Diani 1992: 12). Moreover, a well-developed body of research analyzes the institutionalization of movements (usually in the later part of their life cycle) and the role they play in conventional political processes, including the organizations that take part in and originate from movements. Civil society actors tend to enjoy greater access and exhibit a greater level of formality, with their collective civic action taking place in formal and institutional structures in both social and political life (Anheier 2004: 24).

In the next two sections, we examine the two concepts – civil society and social movements – and discuss their respective evolution, characteristics, and relevance for Europeanization in detail.

Civil Society in Europe

Europeanization – the 'making' of Europe – can be seen as a centuries-long process of negotiation, interaction, and interpretation of political systems and values as well as national and transnational community organization. Today, the idea of modern statehood in Europe is often linked to democracy as a politico-societal state, with our modern forms and interpretations of democracy linked to democracy's roots in ancient Athens. Most conceptions of civil society and/or democracy in Europe are thus connected to more than two thousand years of political philosophy on citizen-state relations.

From the Ancient Polis to the Medieval Ages: Civil Society as a 'Non-Concept'

Is civil society part of the political sphere? Is it a political practice itself, or is it to be found outside institutionalized politics? The term 'civil society' was introduced for the first time by Aristotle as *politike koinonia* (or *societas civilis* in the Latin translation). For Aristotle, the state was composed of two separate, antagonistic parts: the *polis* and *oikos*. They represented two different logics of social relations and governance. While the *polis* refers to the state's organizational structure, the *oikos* encapsulates the broad sphere of the private household that exists independently from the *polis*. The *polis* consisted of a self-governing community of free (male) citizens who discussed public affairs and took part in negotiations to find solutions to public problems. Therefore, *politike koinonia* can be understood as a 'political association' that relates to both modern concepts of (a) community and (b) society, while simultaneously standing for 'the political', or the state itself. Aristotle's interpretation of civil society is thus very different from today's understanding of civil society as operating on the fringes of the political sphere, yet not a state structure. However, both Aristotle's *politike koinonia* and today's conceptions of civil society are based on an assumption of the political and societal self-determination and self-organization of free citizens as the fabric of a polity (Cohen & Arato 1992: 84ff.).

Although the Latin translation of Aristotles's *politike koinonia* obviously prevailed, the concept failed to become of particular importance in Roman philosophy. Only in the 13th and 14th century, the civil society concept was rediscovered – first and foremost, in Thomas Aquinas' writings on societal and political order in the Middle Ages. Aquinas adopts Aristotle's equation of the state and civil society as being separate from the *communitas divina* – the divine community that is superior to the secular concept of *communitas civilis*. What remains significant for the evolution of civil society is its longstanding position as a public sphere outside the intimate sphere of the household, which in turn consists of a multitude of entities. Approximately two centuries later, the reformer Martin Luther preserved the theory of two realms, a divine and a worldly, yet the emergence of secularization also laid the groundwork for the separation of civil society from the state itself (Adloff 2005: 19f.).

European Enlightenment and New Thinking: The Formation of a Civic Sphere

As a consequence of the religious and political disputes and civil wars following the Reformation in Europe, absolutistic regimes were established throughout the continent in the 16th century. The concentration of power in the hands of a single sovereign ruler, and the concurrent disempowerment of once strong estates (the nobility and clergy) gave rise to a new category within society – the citizenry. However, before civil society began to take shape in the form that we understand it as today, it first disappeared entirely from the political sphere.

In the aftermath of the religious civil wars that tore through Europe, the question of how free citizens could form society and politics was not prominent – on the contrary, a state without the participation of interest groups or powerful individuals was seen as the only guarantor of peace. Thomas Hobbes, the most influential philosopher of absolutism, advocated keeping citizens out of politics, thereby depoliticizing the citizenry and creating "a state, not society" (Cohen & Arato 1992: 87). Power was given to the absolutist ruler, that is, the sovereign, who guaranteed security and peace for the individual at a price of absolute obedience and subordination. Citizens' opinions, political convictions or religious beliefs were relegated to the private sphere to minimize their (assumed-to-be-negative) influence on politics.

In the contract theory of early enlightenment liberal John Locke, however, the state's first and foremost responsibility is to ensure the protection of private property, and therefore to respect the freedom of citizens in their private economic affairs. Locke argued that even if the state managed to secure peace, in the very moment it abused its power and encroached on the private sphere, including private property, the state would lose its credibility and the privilege of citizen obedience. Locke thus introduced the idea of individual rights and freedoms and the need that they be protected from state intervention. Yet, though Locke may not have differentiated between state and civil society, his (economically based) argument paved the way for the emergence of that distinction. Locke's claim that natural law allows any citizen to own their own property implies a vision of a free individual, not only in economic, but also in philosophical and political terms.

Building on Locke's arguments, in the 18th century, Scottish enlightenment thinkers such as Adam Smith and Adam Ferguson specified civil society as a sphere of free economic forces that had to be defended from state intervention. Public goods and welfare would not be provided by the state, but by the help of the 'invisible hand of the market' and non-commercial interests of free citizens. Although this construction of the common good as an aggregation of individual preferences has long been disputed, these liberal thinkers helped define a core feature of today's understanding of civil society —; the independence of the citizenry as a pre-political, safe and self-organized realm.

A decidedly political conception of civil society was advanced at about the same time by the French monarchist, Montesquieu (1748, *The Spirit of Laws*). Concerned about the alienation of the people from the monarchy, Montesquieu argued for an intermediate sphere between the administration of the absolutist ruler and the citizenry. This sphere would function as a buffer and transmission belt between rulers and ruled; an institutionalized 'broker' between the monarchy and an increasingly autonomous, assertive citizenry (Cohen & Arato 1992: 88f.) The intermediate sphere would be largely run by the nobility in a society.

This transmission of interests became an even more important question in the transition from monarchism to republicanism, although the way in which interests would be aggregated, communicated, and integrated into the political sphere remained underspecified. One of the first radical republican philosophers, Jean-Jacques Rousseau promoted the idea that the people were not only required to obey the law but also to author it themselves (1762, *The Social Contract*). However, Rousseau did not specify how individual citizens' interests might be translated into the *volonté générale* of the people; furthermore, in his contract philosophy, Rousseau did not envision an institutionalized broker aggregating and translating citizen interests.

Enlightenment philosophers played a key role in promoting the idea that there should be a sphere of politically relevant civic interest aggregation, yet it would neither be 'political', nor part of recognized political structures. In this period, civil society emerged as the result of the negotiation of state-citizen relations and the social contract. Two distinctive civil society conceptions were promoted which the modern philosopher Charles Taylor conceptualized as the 'L' and 'M' strands of civil-society thinking (Taylor 1991). The 'L' concept can be traced back to Locke and subsequent liberal thinking; it emphasizes civil society as a pre-political, self-organized space with its own structures and rules, focused on the protection of the private sphere and property. Though the private sphere may be dominated by economic activities, it also includes space for public debate and interest formation. The 'M' concept is founded on Montesquieu and underlines the role of *corps intermédiaires*, connecting the spheres of rulers and the citizenry. These intermediary bodies constitute their own political force that both influences and limits state power. Both perspectives lay the foundations of our contemporary understanding of civil society as a sphere of both protection and intermediation.

Civil Society and the Role of the 'Buergerliche Gesellschaft' in Modern Europe

As a consequence of the Enlightenment debates, the concepts of society and the individual increasingly gained attention in the 18th and 19th century – and thus, debates on interest aggregation, individual rights (and their protection) and social integration gained prominence. Civil society came to be understood as a sphere outside both state and private affairs, yet its characteristics and goals were still to be defined.

In his *Philosophy of Rights* (first published in German in 1821), the German philosopher Georg F.W. Hegel defined the *Buergerliche Gesellschaft* – the bourgeois society – as a third realm originating from the dualities of *oikos/polis* and state/society, thereby combining the 'M' and 'L' functions of civil society. Civil society was understood as the space between the family and the state; however, as a space it cannot exist without the existence of the state. Although bourgeois society is viewed as primarily consisting of *homo oeconomicus* and business-related activities, its main social and integrative relevance arises from corporations and associations that form the core of this third sphere and provide for a connection between the *citoyen* and the bourgeois – and consequently between individuals and aggregated interests.

The most famous adoption of the idea of a bourgeois society was that of Karl Marx, who reduced the term from a complex social realm to a part of a class-based society. Bourgeois society was thus unequivocally linked to capitalism and the main actor of the political economy that came in for criticism by Marx. Cultural, intellectual, and communicative aspects of bourgeois society were consequently excluded. Subsequently, the term *Buergerliche Gesellschaft* remained both critical and polemic, and would never again be known for its initial aspects of self-organization, debate, and *societas civilis*. Adopting a different approach, the Italian philosopher and political leader of the Italian Communist Party in the early 20th century, Antonio Gramsci, detached the term from Marx's materialist-capitalist interpretation, and instead linked civil society to a cultural-interpretative superstructure. As a neo-Marxist, Gramsci aimed to establish a classless society; he regarded civil society as a necessary instrument to that end. Gramsci hypothesized that the stability of the capitalist system was protected by a civil society that valued capitalist ideology and provided for the cultural hegemony of capitalism. It should be noted that for Gramsci, civil society was only a means to an end: in a classless society, the state would merge with society so that intermediate associations would no longer be needed. Gramsci's most relevant contribution to civil society theory was his claim that civil society is about competing for power of interpretation. In all modern conceptions of civil society, including social movements, we see the aspects of agenda setting, framing and challenging existing interpretations as core features of civic activism.

Info-Box 14.1: Civil society and democracy theory

"Democracy is more than a form of government. It is primarily a mode of associated living, of conjoint communicated experience" (Dewey quoted by Alexander 2006: 37). With these words, the American political philosopher John Dewey described his interpretation of the foundation of any democracy: associations, community, and an evolving set of attitudes and habits within society that give space for collaborative problem solving and debate. While in the early 20th century, many thinkers – including German sociologist Max Weber – pleaded for expert-led governments and bureaucratic organization, Dewey called for the public space as a realm for the self-organization of citizens. The state itself would be a secondary form of association, deriving from public organizing. In the second half of the 20th century, 'communitarianists' such as Amitai Etzioni elaborated on Dewey's ideas and argued that democratic societies should be based on a core of mutually shared values, incorporated into social institutions and public dialogue.

What of the nexus of public debate, active civic community, and democracy? To understand how civil society is to strengthen democracy, we must refer to the work of the French aristocrat, publicist, and politician Alexis de Tocqueville, who is often seen as the founding theoretician of the civil society-democracy nexus. He travelled across the United States in the early 19th century and observed the American implementation of self-organization and public debate, establishing power without a royal ruler. Tocqueville was fascinated by the way local communities, as the smallest entities of the state, organized everyday life. To Tocqueville, the eagerness of Americans to join and engage in various associations, clubs, and communities as a form of self-governance stood as the central aspect of American democracy.

From Tocqueville's perspective, the link between civil society and democracy does not primarily concern institutional intermediation, but rather the creation of democratic morals, practices and customs. These practices are learned by those who engage in local self-organization, while upholding the bedrock of the rule of law. Therefore, Tocqueville regards democratization as a process of socialization that takes place in everyday negotiations on the common good and how to solve problems collectively (Tocqueville 2014 [1835]). The civil society sphere is not an economic one, but a decidedly social and political sphere, and a conjoint lifestyle and governance mode.

In the second half of the 20th century, the question of democratic practices and community as serving to strengthen democracy was explored by communitarians such as Etzioni and Robert Putnam. In his seminal books *Making Democracy Work. Civic Traditions in Modern Italy* (1993) and *Bowling Alone: America's Declining Social Capital* (1995), Putnam discussed how democratic socialization at the local level translates into abstract solidarity at the national level. Putnam used a term, coined by Pierre Bourdieu (1983) – social capital, as distinct from economic, cultural or symbolic capital. According to Putnam, social capital "refers to features of social organization, such as trust, norms, and networks, that can improve the efficiency of society by facilitating coordinated actions" (Putnam 1993: 168). Putnam differentiates between two forms of social capital: bonding social capital can be found within social circles and supports mutual assistance and cohesion between members of a particular social group; bridging social capital connects otherwise separate social clusters or groups without personal familiarity (Putnam et al. 1995; 2000). Bonding social capital could encourage particular groups – for example, ethnic or religious communities – to forge networks within their own communities and, hence, to segregate from society. Bridging social capital supports democratization as it facilitates democratic negotiation in socially heterogeneous contexts.

Today, civil society's contribution to democracy is understood to be twofold (Diamond 1999; Hahn-Fuhr & Worschech 2014): Building on Toqueville's ideas, civil society can support democratic socialization, fostering social negotiation and trust among people from different backgrounds. Building on Locke's liberal thinking, civil society can act as a 'watchdog' of democratic rights and freedoms vis-à-vis a potential authoritarian regime, providing space for (alternative or free) information, communication and association.

Civil Society in the 20th and 21st Centuries

In the timeline of civil society history, the totalitarian systems that were established in the 20th century in Europe represent both a serious fracture and a turning point in civil society theorization. As Gramsci had forecasted, these totalitarian systems sought to absorb all activities in the intermediate sphere into the state in order to build up an institutional 'ring of protection' around their own state power centers. Thus, in countries that fell under totalitarian rule – from Nazi Germany to the Stalinist USSR – existing associations and organizations such as sports clubs, women's organizations or scouts were incorporated into the totalitarian systems and new organizations were founded to strengthen the ideology and practices of the totalitarian systems themselves. In other words, civil society formed the backbone of the totalitarian state. At the same time, civic resistance and opposition to authoritarian and totalitarian power became the epitome of civil society. For example, in the case of the Polish anti-communist Solidarity movement, the juxtaposition of "society *against* the state, nation *against* the state, social order *against* the political system, [. . .] public life *against* the state" emphasized civil society as a realm of "protection and/or self-organization of social life in the face of the totalitarian or authoritarian state" (Cohen & Arato 1992: 31; italics in original). In the wake of the successful democratic revolutions in Central and Eastern Europe, civil society was theorized as a key player in democratization processes.

Civil Society, the European Union, and the Process of Europeanization

In the context of democratization in the post-communist world after 1989, civil society was studied primarily as an actor. In contrast, the debates on civil society in democratic Western Europe conceptualized civil society as a public sphere and centered on questions such as how to "democratize democracies" (Offe 2003) and whether a European transnational public sphere exists. In these debates, 'the public' refers to an intermediate sphere of processes of communication and opinion formation, consisting of speakers, the communicative content, forms of communication and an audience that is responsive to that communication (Trenz 2017). Therefore, the public sphere is a understood as a social space that allows for the expression of opinions and experiences, discussion concerning key questions and the collective negotiation of solutions to problems relevant for the community (Wessler & Rinke 2013). As noted by Habermas (1992: 435f.; English translation 1998), the public is a network of permeable and potentially open-ended communication that filters, synthesizes and condenses issue-specific public opinions. In summary, the public sphere is understood by this school of thought as a social realm that provides opportunities for the thematization, mediation, and control of public issues.

With the European unification process and the groundbreaking establishment of the European Union in the Maastricht treaty of 1993, the question of the existence of a European public sphere emerged. In response, scholars such as Klaus Eder (2000) described the transnationalization of the public sphere as a process of delimitation and the de-bordering of social spaces, which in turn led to overlaps of national and supranational spheres of communication, interaction and resonance. Hans-Joerg Trenz (2015) further emphasized the diversity of actors in the European public sphere, the notion of the Europeanization of political communication, and the formation of a shared foundation of knowledge provided by the media. The European public sphere came to be understood as a heterogeneous, fragmented, overlapping and interconnected communicative structure within and between different realms of European societies.

This perspective points to another key aspect of European civil society. As civil society and public debates address a complex transnational governance system that is multi-layered, civic communication and interaction are also multi-layered. Trenz (2009) argues that European civil society takes its initial form as a collective act of political representation, which is more than a mere aggregation of interests and the empowerment of delegates. European civil society can rather be understood as a "dynamic and reciprocal polity-constituency relationship, based on deliberation (or political discourse)" (Trenz 2009: 44). From this perspective, civil society is a transmitter of social and cultural capital in a dynamic European policy field rather than an agent or a (re)source of supranational governance.

The particular 'European' aspect of transnational civil society or transnational public sphere is rooted in the multiple levels of political or societal action; local conflicts on ecological issues or discrimination, for example, might be transmitted to the European Parliament or the European judiciary, while conflicts arising in European policies or between national and European political actors may be condensed into a debate at the local level. The Europeanization of the public sphere therefore includes the internalization, externalization and transnationalization of conflicts. Often, (a) transnational conflicts are brought up by national public actors, (b) conflicts and issues originating at national level are picked up by a transnational public, or (c) transnational issues are brokered by an equally transnational public.

Moreover, Beate Kohler-Koch (2009) introduces three different perspectives of European governance and the respective functions of civil society. First, in the classical version of the EU as a polity structure, civil society is understood to be involved in political processes in the form of organized groups, interest coalitions, and lobbying actors. Civil society is equated with organized interest representation and intermediation in the EU's political system and is considered to be a remedy to the EU's perceived lack of democratic legitimacy. A second perspective touches upon debates on the multi-level networks of governance in the European Union, in which civil society makes up one group of 'stakeholders' or actors in a participatory political process. The third perspective views civil society as being included in political processes since European politics are part of the emergence of a political-social constituency, and, consequently, a European society. In this perspective, together with an evolving European public sphere, civil society inclusion reflects active citizenship, increasing social cohesion and public deliberation (Kohler-Koch 2009: 53).

Turning from theory to practice, the European Neighborhood Policy (ENP) of the European Union explicitly sought to build upon the idea of constructing a public sphere that would provide for the thematization, mediation and control of public issues. Based on the decisions of the European Council in Copenhagen in 2002, the ENP was designed to secure stability at the borders of the EU, to counter any potentially negative implications of EU enlargement on so-called 'outsiders', and to define an endpoint of enlargement by presenting neighboring countries with an alternative to EU membership (Sasse 2007). The difficulty facing the ENP was centered on how to promote good governance within the EU's geographical vicinity "without offering the golden carrot of [EU] membership" (Börzel 2010). Supporting civil society initiatives is seen as part of a deliberate EU foreign policy and an effort to improve governance and respect for human rights in the EU's neighborhood (Youngs 2008). A vibrant civil society is still considered a necessary, though not sufficient, condition for democracy (Henderson 2002), and consequently, civil society support has become a core aspect of the EU's neighborhood policy since the turn of the century. Such support has focused on the development of civil society as both a 'school of democracy' and a 'watchdog', with many donors preferring to invest in correcting non-democratic state structures (Worschech 2018).

An unintended negative consequence of this instrumental support for civil society in the EU's neighborhood was the emergence of an 'engineered' or professionalized civil society that has lost much of its grassroots orientation, spontaneity, volunteerism and self-organization (components that are usually considered to be the core characteristics of civil society). Instead, 'political service providers' who conformed to the criteria of the European donor's program criteria but were somewhat alienated from society itself, profited from this policy in many cases, such as in Georgia after the 'Rose Revolution' in 2003 and in Ukraine after the 'Orange Revolution' in 2004 (Ishkanian 2007; Lutsevych 2013; Hahn-Fuhr & Worschech 2014). In recent years, and especially since Ukraine's Euromaidan, new movements and grassroots initiatives have emerged independently from Western funding in certain post-socialist countries, addressing local issues and seeking solutions through local community organization. For example, local culture and arts organizations, curatorial initiatives, self-aid groups for internally displaced persons and citizens' initiatives were founded independently in the Ukraine, most notably in the eastern Ukrainian regions that have been particularly affected by war, conflict, and displacement. In this disadvantageous situation, a grassroots civil society has emerged, organized around day-to-day problems, culture activities or a necessary perspective for the region, signifying the potential for increasing societal and political self-organization (Worschech 2017; 2020).

Simultaneously, the phenomenon of 'uncivil society' (Kopecký & Mudde 2003; Ruzza 2009), currently gaining increasing recognition and influence in Europe, should not be forgotten. Nationalist, populist and reactionary movements and organizations are seeking to counter European integration and transnationalization, and to establish their own concepts of a 'Europe of nations', including a cultural hegemony of socially conservative – often catholic or Christian orthodox – values and norms (Wodak et al. 2013). The chapters of this volume underline that non-state actors and movement organizations are also a core feature of a European 'uncivil society' constituted by conservative, reactionary, and right-wing extremist political actors and parties.

The contemporary processes of Europeanization, as a multi-layered and multi-directional development of a transnational society 'in the making', suggest the need for new perspectives on civil society. Even non-political issues addressed by transnational civil society may be transformed into European political claims and transnational political demands, which in turn strengthen existing and new European civil-society networks. The transnationalization of Europe implies a certain vibrancy of societal networks across borders and regions, rooted in small-scale local-level activism. These networks often include civil society organizations, local communities, and individuals from different regions that may be organized into social movements or act relatively independently. The various Europeanization and European integration processes have themselves become increasingly politicized along multiple fault lines, as diverse national and transnational social movements respond to and contest various EU policies (Fominaya & Feenstra 2020). Moreover, the concept of democracy, and the many ways in which it can be effectuated, is a central theme of discussion, experimentation, and innovation in many of these social movements (Fominaya & Feenstra 2020). As the social-movement form of civic activism has come to play an increasingly important and institutionalized role as part of the conventional repertoire of European political participation, we turn to it in the next section.

Social Movements: Drivers of Social Changes. What are they?

Many European social movements have their origins in 19th century associationism – as Europe emerged from estate-based societies, its peoples attempted to organize their own lives, challenging feudalism, monarchism, and Christian orthodoxy and paving the way for modern mass societies (Berger 2014). Such social organizing contributed to and was aided by the creation of new political parties that represented these emerging social forces, and later, by the extension of suffrage to new social groups (Tormey 2020). Some of these social movements, which irrevocably shaped Europe's pre-WWI history, include the labor, women's suffrage, and nationalist movements. Struggling to realize their interests in the workplace and through the market alone, workers in Europe's modern industries began to organize strong national union confederations capable of mobilizing mass solidarity, representing workers in political bargaining with the government, and often working with socialist and social democratic political parties in opposition to conservative, Christian or more secular liberal parties representing the nascent middle-class. More radical currents such as anarchism and communism generally lay outside or beyond the electoral process. Women within and across European countries also began to mobilize their claims to social and political rights. While the first voices to demand political participation for women were heard during the French Revolution and the 1848 Revolutions, the sustained efforts of women's movements only drew wider recognition towards the end of the 19th century, finally gaining a long-lasting foothold in Europe after WWI, and even more so after WWII. Moreover, in response to imperial competition between the major European powers towards the end of the 19th century, a number of nationalist movements emerged in Europe: some were self-determination movements such as the Serbian nation movement that directly sparked the outbreak of WWI; others, such as the German nationalist movement, were developmentalist, lamenting having missed out on the spoils of colonial conquest and expansion, and mobilizing towards more effective industrial and military organization (Tormey 2020).

The second half of the 20th century saw further growth in social-movement activism, which transformed the socio-political history of Europe. Post-WWII politics was primarily driven by an aspiration to promote economic growth and the modernization of the welfare state meant to maintain a competitive workforce. 1968 marked a moment of worldwide social unrest, expressing the generalized feeling that the old left-right ideologies were exhausted – a stark reminder of the power of ordinary citizens to unite for a shared purpose. Often working with labor unions, environmentalist, civil-rights, feminist, anti-war, and anti-nuclear mobilization – the so-called 'new social movements' – focused on overcoming specific injustices and laid the foundations of a style of politics in Europe; they aspired to be less bureaucratic and to permit alternative and more participatory styles of political engagement (Tormey 2020). In Eastern Europe, mobilization to delegitimize communism had begun in 1956 in Poland and Hungary, been reignited in 1968 in Czechoslovakia, and would continue throughout the 1970–80s, especially in the Visegrad countries and the Baltic republics of the Soviet Union. These movements, which created independent civic spaces where alternative civic and political institutions, activities, and discourses would be able to develop, eventually brought down communism. Meanwhile, in the West, a wave of neoliberalism and the acceleration of globalization were transforming European politics and societies, while the left capitulated to the logic of the free market (Tormey 2020). Still, what began as a peaceful protest against a meeting of the World Trade Organization in Seattle in December 1999 exploded into a fully-fledged confrontation; other anti-globalization protests erupted at the majority of meetings featuring international economic organizations in the following decade. The so-called Global Justice Movement, which petered out in the 2000s, spawned continental, national, regional, and city-level forums of disenfranchised citizens to develop new forms of mobilization and post-ideological, dialogical, interactive, and participatory political activism (Sen 2007).

Key Elements of Social Movements

To explore the nature of such historical and contemporary social movements, we need to start by developing a clear definition of what a social movement comprises. Several such definitions have been offered. These can be grouped by their broad correspondence to the four theoretical approaches in the study of social movements (Diani 1992). These different conceptualizations of social movements have been the cornerstone of the main theories that have been established, providing researchers with guidance on classifying certain social phenomena as social movements, as well as examining and explaining various aspects associated with them.

1) *Collective behavior*: Early studies of social movements in this tradition were preoccupied with disruptive protest, often contrasting it with 'organizational' or 'institutional' behavior; they also regularly examined protest as an instance of the successful overcoming of the collective-action problem. Scholars in the collective behavior school of thought define movements as "a *collectivity* acting with some continuity to promote or resist a *change* in the society or organization of which it is a part. As a collectivity, a movement is a group with indefinite and shifting membership and with leadership whose position is determined more by *informal* response of adherents than by formal procedures for legitimizing authority" (Turner & Killian 1987: 223, *emphasis added*).

2) *Resource mobilization*: Other scholars, also regarding social-movement activists and organizations as economically rational actors, similarly define movements as a "set of opinions and *beliefs*, which represent preferences for *changing some* elements of the social structure and/or reward distribution of a society" (McCarthy & Zald 1977: 1217–18, *emphasis added*). Yet, in their research these scholars also emphasize the role played by the leaders and structures that translate shared beliefs into action; this literature thus tends to examine the advantages enjoyed by strong organizations, leaders with previous experience, and robust networks of cooperation.

3) *Political process*: A third group of social-movement scholars quickly recognized that the state was involved, not only as the target but also the adjudicator of social grievances; accordingly, their research pays attention to the political-institutional environment that creates opportunities for mobilization. In this body of work, social movements are understood to be "a sustained series of *interactions* between *power holders* and persons successfully claiming to speak on behalf of a constituency lacking formal representation in the course of which those persons make publicly visible demands for *changes* in the distribution or exercise of power, and back those demands

with *public demonstrations* of support." (Tilly 1984: 306; Tarrow 1998, *emphasis added*) This framework was subsequently complicated by the recognition that movements are capable of having global reach and do not necessarily interact with a single national state. The overall focus, however, remained on the political process through which excluded actors and interests attempt to gain access to the establishment in a polity.

4) *Mobilization culture/New social movements*: A fourth mainstream of research set out to explore the cultural dimension of social movements – namely, the work that goes into creating movement symbols or mobilization 'frames'. They serve to present grievances publically so that they resonate with the public and elites, while establishing solidarity among movement participants and a 'collective identity' to create loyalty to the movement and its cause. In this tradition, social movements are "the organized *collective behavior* of [an] actor struggling against his [. . .] adversary for the *social control* of historicity in a concrete community" (Touraine 1981, 81, *emphasis added*). Such scholars relate social movements to large-scale structural and cultural changes, and identify social movements with processes of identity formation within the dominant conflict in a given society.

A synthesis of these definitions adopted in this chapter highlights that social movements entail: 1) networks of *informal* interaction of individuals, groups, and organizations (including organizers, constituents, adherents, and publics; 2) a set of (perceived and at times externally defined) *shared beliefs,* and a sense of belonging/ identity and/or solidarity; 3) collective action on political and/or cultural conflictual issues, meant to promote or oppose *change* at the individual, community or systemic level; and 4) sustained action that takes place at least in part *outside the institutional* sphere and the routine procedures of social life. (Diani 1992, 7)

The four dimensions of the definition of social movements help us differentiate social movements from other forms of collective action and civic activism. For instance, as discussed above, in comparison with civil society or interest groups, movements tend to be less formal (dimension 1), less embedded within a political arena (dimension 4), and less focused on community building (dimensions 2 and 3). Further, the collective action that makes up movements can take many forms, from brief to sustained, and from institutionalized to disruptive. However, it clearly differs from other extra- or non-institutional collective behavior such as crowds, panics, and fads, for instance, which lack the organizational and symbolic infrastructure and continuity of social movements (dimensions 2 and 4 above).

Research Traditions: Themes and Theory

In addition to helping researchers classify certain phenomena as social movements, the main theories of social movements offer descriptive and analytical lenses that can be used to gain a greater understanding of social movements. Accordingly, we continue to introduce these main theories by discussing how they have sought to address the three main questions most frequently answered on social movements: 1) their emergence; 2) participants; and 3) impact and evolution. These theories have evolved over time, at times challenging or complementing each other. They are presented here as most commonly used, rather than with a focus on their evolution or variants. To provide guidance for an understanding and explanation of social movements, these theories make certain critical assumptions and suggest constructs and variables to help researchers describe and interpret the observed social phenomena, formulate hypotheses, and choose research methods to answer 'what, how, and why' questions (and thus generalize on social movements). We provide a general discussion of these theories and then illustrate them with examples, presenting the ways in which they have been used to examine some of the main post-WWII social movements in Europe.

The Emergence of Social Movement – an Ideal-typical Description

The question that may have caused the greatest preoccupation for social-movement scholars concerns the reasons for which social movements appear; that is, why and how certain grievances emerge and/or translate into collective action. While early theories viewed movements as being rooted in discontent and unusual moments in a specific polity, social movements today are typically understood as a conventional means of political participation. Theories on social movement origins have focused on the characteristics of participants, the conditions in the broader socio-political environment, and the cultural symbols that link these two aspects. The majority of such social movement research has thus emphasized the importance of mobilizing structures, political opportunities, and movement frames (McAdam et al. 2001). Please note their different focus and approach in the examples below.

Resource mobilization: Some researchers argue that there are always disgruntled citizens in any society and that a certain level of personal and organizational resources is necessary to sustain the formal organizations that underpin many social movements (McCarthy & Zald 1977). These authors emphasize the importance of resources, the availability of leaders, money/ funding, and pre-existing networks to galvanize contentious action as well as provide participants with the opportunity to join movements. This research stream has found personal and organizational experience with protest and ties to the movement to be an especially significant resource for mobilization (Oberschall 1973). In summary, the emergence of social movements in this tradition is a function of the variation of the resources available for mobilization over time and space.

Consider, for example, the rise of the Polish Solidarity movement, which survived brutal repression and eventually contributed to the collapse of communism in 1989 in Poland and the entire Soviet Bloc. One exploration of the movement's emergence focuses on the importance of: 1) the structures underlying the earlier mobilization of the Catholic Church, and 2) the Church's development of a powerful symbolic vocabulary and protest tactics – cultural resources and experience that could be co-opted by the Solidarity movement's leaders (Osa 2003). This research highlights that the Polish Church decided to undertake pastoral mobilization in the 1950s to counteract the atheism, secularism, and social atomization of the communist regime; it took the form of programs designed to strengthen the link between church and society by encouraging believers to partake in intense religious activities, such as an annual pilgrimage sanctioning Catholic values. Those initiatives served to expand parish social networks. The impact was twofold. First, important resource generation took place, which improved the Church's institutional and communicational effectiveness, and second, the initiatives led to an accumulation of experience with protest and the integration of urban workers and intellectuals into moral communities together with rural workers and farmers. Both were resources that would later be mobilized in the 1970s in the development of the Solidarity anti-communist movement, which managed to unite both workers/farmers and intellectuals and reach millions of Polish citizens.

Political process: Another stream of work on social movements (Tilly 1978, McAdam 1982, Tarrow 1994) has primarily focused on the political environment in which movements emerge and operate. For these scholars, the emergence of social movements is a function of the so-called *political opportunity structure*, including the degree of openness of formal political access, stability of political coalitions, availability of political allies, and divisions among ruling elites (Tarrow 1994). These scholars also see movements as being closely linked, as the same political opportunity structure facilitates the formation of several movements almost simultaneously – the so-called waves or cycles of protest in which leaders and participants of contemporaneous and successive movements often overlap (Tarrow 1998).

For example, upon examining the anti-austerity protests across the EU in the wake of the 2008 global financial crisis, some find a general shift away from the counter-summits and world social forums of the Global Justice Movement and toward the emergence of *Indignados* movements or Occupy camps, rooted in everyday life and addressing local and national institutions (Della Porta & Parks 2016). According to these authors, this shift away from Brussels was a strategic choice in light of the increasing lack of political opportunities at EU level. In the mid-2000s, these opportunities were found to be complex and varied. An information-hungry Commission that drafts legislation and is thus generally *open* to dialogue with stakeholders, had lent itself to lobbying, even if the institutional and policy *divisions* within the Commission had tempered that openness to social movements. Similarly, given the increasing powers of the European Parliament, it had increasingly become the target of grass-roots mobilization along relevant ideological and geographical *cleavages*. With the EU's management of the 2008 financial crisis, however, power at EU level shifted to more unaccountable and *opaque institutions* – the European Central Bank, the IMF, and the European Commission. As a result, the post-2008 anti-austerity protests have tended to see 'Europe' as an issue to be addressed through and at both national and local levels.

Mobilization culture: In the cultural approach to social movement formation, mobilization is examined as an effort to influence the direction of social change by controlling a society's symbols and self-understanding. The focus is on the goals of protestors, the production of mobilization frames, and constructions of collective identities (Benford & Snow 2000), which are understood to be the essential mechanisms that allow actors to (re-) define their claims as worthy of collective action and themselves as bearers of collective goals.

To examine the *gilets jaunes* movement that emerged in France in the late 2010s, some have considered how the protest movement is constituted in and through its social media communication. The spontaneous "neither-left-nor-right", fragmented, and leaderless movement grew in opposition to perceived excessive taxation, especially on fuel, holding regular demonstrations with up to 1.3 million participants. Eventually, the movement also made a range of demands, including the resignation of the French president, a general reduction in taxes, and increases in public services and state pensions, among others. In order to examine how the movement was enacted/discursively constructed, some authors (Clifton & de la Broise 2020) have analyzed the movement's YouTube videos that comment on what it is to be a *gilet jaune*; these scholars note that the legal authority of the state was challenged by a moral authority that had been mobilized in order to be made clear to French President Emmanuel Macron the 'hard way' that he needs to step down (burning a toll booth in some of these videos). Such communication (mobilizing networks of human commentary and non-human actors (space, buildings, and clothing) accounts for the actions of the *gilets jaunes*, *talking them into being* as a political movement, entering dialogue with and resisting the French President.

Movement participation: Another foundational question in the study of social movements has been the issue of recruitment; that is, how movements grow by enlisting and retaining individuals (and organizations) to their cause. Some scholars have surveyed the general population (Walgrave & Rucht 2010); others have examined the life stories and decisions of individual activists involved in social movements (Della Porta 1995). While much of this work seeks to understand the calculus of why, when, and how individuals choose this costly and high-risk form of political participation, other studies have instead focused on the emotions and identity of participants and leaders (Jasper 1997; Goodwin et al. 2001). The discussion below highlights some of the types of analysis produced by different schools of thought, as well as certain key findings in the research on social movement participation.

Collective behavior: In the 1960s, arguments were expressed centering on the fact that most individuals are free-riders – they will not join protests or otherwise participate politically if they think they can benefit from the actions of the group/movement without taking the time to be involved personally (Olson 1965). Since to these scholars willingness to participate in a social movement is a function of the perceived *costs and benefits* of participation, movements could potentially provide 'selective benefits' to attract participants; an example of such selective benefits would be access to insurance available only to labor union members. In addition to such public goods incentives, collective behavior research has discussed moral and social incentives for participation (perceived moral obligation to participate and the expected or actual reactions of socially significant others, respectively). On the cost side, there are many barriers to participation, but repression is understood by this school of thought to be one of the more significant ones. The relationship between *repression* and participation, however, has been documented to follow an inverted U-shape curve – repression increases the cost of participation and thus depresses it until its heightened level begins to generate social and/or moral incentives to participate, as social networks begin to reward protest very highly, leading in turn to increased participation (Opp 1994).

Resource mobilization: In the 1970s and 1980s, the resource mobilization perspective instead began emphasizing the biographical availability of potential participants – for instance, few family and work obligations giving young individuals greater availability to devote time to movement activities (McCarthy & Zald 1977; McAdam 1986). Another important factor highlighted within this research tradition is based on connections to the movement – whether an individual knows someone who is already in the movement or is part of an organization that joins the movement, is found to be one of the best predictors of movement participation (Oberschall 1973). Others have qualified this finding by pointing out that it is rather a strong commitment to a particular identity, reinforced by ties to participants, whether of an organizational or private nature, that encourages participation (McAdam & Paulsen 1993).

Yet others document how different *networks* perform different functions: for example, (1) information – the capacity of networks to create opportunities for participation; (2) identity – the fact that social ties to significant others create and reproduce solidarity; (3) exchange – informal circulation of social approval, rewards, and sanctions through networks (Kitts 2000).

Generally, stronger, denser, more specific, and more centralized (formal or informal) networks are found to facilitate more costly political participation (such as protesting or demanding religious cults). Moreover, the number and intensity of ties as well as the homogeneity of networks have also been found to have a positive influence on participation. (Diani 2004) Lastly, individuals with memberships in multiple organizations are viewed as key channels for the circulation of information, resources and expertise among organizations mobilizing on issues of common concern (Curtis & Zucher 1973), as well as for the diffusion of protest across space (Sandell 2001).

Cultural mobilization: Starting in the 1980s, some scholars also began to emphasize the messages transmitted through social networks and to examine phenomena such as "suddenly imposed grievances" (Walsh 1981) – namely, events that highlight a social problem – and as "cognitive liberation" (McAdam 1982), that is, the combination of perceived injustice and collective efficacy. According to this research tradition, successful recruitment occurs when organizers offer a *frame* – a way of seeing a social phenomenon – that resonates with the views and experiences of potential recruits. Moreover, to devote time and effort to protests, people must usually collectively define their situations as unjust and subject to change through group action, while sharing the *collective identity* of the movement and expressing excitement at being part of a larger group they believe they can contribute to (Melucci 1996). Collective action involves the identification of a collectivity with common values, interests, and goals. Collective action also involves identification with a collectivity that includes a sense of mutuality and solidarity, which in turn imply a sense of loyalty and emotional interest, give rise to social cohesion, and encourage participation (Benford & Hunt 1992). In summary, to scholars in this tradition, protest is an effort to impose meaning on the world, to define and pursue collective interests, and to forge a personal and collective identity while creating and reinforcing affective bonds with others (Snow et al 1986; Goodwin et al. 2001).

While early social movement research contrasted rationality and emotionality, recent research revisits emotions in a new light. For example, injustice frames have been highlighted, in which righteous anger is central (Gamson et al. 1982), and 'moral shocks' which represent events or information that trigger outrage in citizens, inciting them to political action (Jasper 1997). Others have found affective bonds to be especially important in keeping organizations together that endorse high-risk political participation, such as underground terrorists (Della Porta 1995).

Success and Decline

A third key foundational question in the study of social movements has been the issue of the array of intended and unintended effects that social movements have on their polities. The four most-studied categories of such impact are: policy, culture, biographical, and social impact. We proceed by discussing some of the key findings on each. For all impact categories, scholars have tended to argue that *collective action/* mobilization can lead to change both in and of itself; that certain types of mobilization strategies (*frames*) and *organization* (formal vs. informal, and so on) are more effective than others; that more beneficial *political opportunities* allow for more impactful mobilization; and that combinations of specific strategies, organization, and political conditions influence the impact of social movements (Amenta & Neal 2004).

1) *Policy* – some movements succeed in persuading, compelling, or coercing businesses and/or states into enacting substantive change (by revising their policies, including by securing benefits and broader legal changes) or procedural change (by achieving gains in terms of access to the state) and representation wins (Gamson 1975, 1990; Kitschelt 1986; Amenta 1998; Cress & Snow 2000). Gains in the democratization of state processes, such as franchise and authoritarian defeat, have been among the most sought-after by the most prominent social movements, such as the women's, workers, and anti-communist movements in Europe (Amenta & Neal 2004).

2) *Culture* – movements contribute to changes in the broader culture and public attitudes at various moments, creating favorable conditions for further future change. The literature establishes three types of cultural outcomes (Earl 2004): a) social-psychological – change in attitudes, values, and beliefs; b) cultural products and practices – change in the discourse and production of art, music, media, science, and so on; c) subcultures – development of collective identities and subcultures. Some have argued, for instance, that the so-called New Social Movements that have focused on post-material issues

rather than economic well-being, have been especially concerned with contesting values, and have regarded collective identity change as their main goal (Melucci 1994).

3) *Biographical* – movements usually bring about personal transformations in protestors themselves, including in their life courses (Hareven 1994), and their political socialization and participation (Conover 1991). Examples of such transformations documented on participants in the 1960s movements of the left have been in their work history ('helping' professions), income levels (lower than age peers) and their political attitudes (decidedly leftist), party identification ('liberal' or 'radical'), and activism levels (active after and beyond the movement) (Giugni 2004).

4) *Social* – movements often leave behind experienced activists, networks, tactical innovations, and organizational forms from which other/future movements can benefit. Their impact can be generative in that they shape subsequent waves of the same struggle, create new/spin-off struggles, or spark counter-movements. For instance, the fact that mobilization occurs in waves that grow, peak, and decline speaks to the significant generative effects of movements on each other (Whittier 2004). Spillover effects can also be observed, with movements influencing the frames, collective identities, organizations structures, and relations with the state of other movements at the same time or over time (Meyer & Whittier 1994). Both generative and spillover effects spread throughout shared personnel and organizational networks that overlap, while responding to the external political environment and to changes in the social movement sector itself.

In terms of life cycles, and irrespective of the nature or size of the impact, some movements eventually 1) disband, 2) institutionalize, or 3) diffuse, or scale up or down. Firstly, consider that both the success or failure of a movement in affecting change may undermine the motivation of many participants. Movements can also become victims of their internal dynamics and evolution, such as in events of organizational, ideological and identity-reconstruction conflicts, among others. Secondly, many movements become institutionalized, reducing their reliance on extra-institutional actions. Thirdly, some movements diffuse; in other words, their collective action is emulated in other places in the same country, or in others. Diffusion travels through well-connected networks of trust (relational diffusion); through traditional and social media (non-relational diffusion); and through movement brokers (mediated diffusion); see Tarrow (2005). While diffusion is a horizontal process, movement scale shifts are vertical processes that involve the coordination of episodes of contention on the part of new collectivities against new targets at new levels of interaction. The transnationalization of protest occurs when diffusion takes place across state borders, whereas the internationalization of protest occurs when protest rises to the international level, rather than downwards towards the sub-national level.

Towards the European Movement Society

Contemporary European 'movement society' is emerging around an array of Europeanization processes of harmonization and alignment, as well as processes of pluralization, diversification and differentiation in and across European societies. European civil society, including European social movements, is a key actor and a constitutive medium of contention and debate between both rulers and society, and between other parts of society. These European civic networks offer a platform for broad discussion and the foundation of a "rational dissent" (Miller 1992), thus providing a framework for negotiation around contentious issues. However, contention at times also leads to polarization and division within or across regional or national borders; a good example of this is the destructiveness of so-called 'uncivil society'. Therefore, civil society, including social movements, often contribute to, but should not be equated with democracy and the societal integration of different groups. The relationship between civil society and Europeanization is similarly ambivalent, as these actors and their contentious actions support neither ever-lasting harmonization, nor re-nationalization, but are instead simultaneously and inconsistently comprised of both integrative and disintegrative elements. Civil society, including social movements, represents a framework for transnational negotiation and dissent, which in turn form a core feature of Europeanization.

Didactical Section

Key Learning Points

– Both social movements and civil society are rooted in social networks that unite individuals, groups and/or organizations between the economy and the state and are established or appropriated for particular issues. While such civic networks are usually more formal, institutionalized, and crosscutting, social movement networks tend to be more political and conflict-oriented.

- Civil society plays two central roles in a polity, which can be defined as: 1) 'corrective' or 'watchdog' civil society, defending citizens' rights, and 2) 'community' or 'school of democracy' civil society, building social capital and trust.
- Social movements have been examined by exploring three main questions: 1) what are the **opportunity structures** for movement emergence? 2) which *resources* do movements draw on to mobilize participants? 3) which **diagnostic, prognostic and motivational frames** contribute to a movement's emergence, development, and impact?
- Civil society, including social movements, contributes significantly to the various processes of Europeanization, and in particular horizontal Europeanization, as contemporary social networks often cross regional or national borders, bringing actors together from different realms of society based on issue-centered cooperation.

Further Readings

Alexander, J. C., 2006: *The civil sphere.* Oxford: Oxford Univ. Press.

Almond, G. A. & S Verba, 1989: *The civic culture. Political attitudes and democracy in five nations.* Newbury Park, California: Sage Publications.

Cohen, J. L. & A. Arato, 1992: *Civil Society and Political Theory.* Studies in contemporary German social thought. Cambridge, Mass. [u.a.]: MIT-Press.

Della Porta, D. & M. Caiani, 2009: *Social movements and Europeanization.* Oxford, New York: Oxford University Press.

Della Porta, D. & M. Diani, 2006: *Social movements. An introduction.* 2nd ed. Malden, MA: Blackwell Pub.

McAdam, D., S. Tarrow & C. Tilly, 2003: *Dynamics of contention.* Cambridge: Cambridge Univ. Press.

Putnam, R. D., R. Leonardi & R.Y. Nanetti, 1993: *Making democracy work. Civic traditions in modern Italy.* Princeton, NJ: Princeton Univ. Press.

Additional Web-Sources

The CIVICUS Monitor: Tracking Civic Space is a project run by a global alliance of civil society organisations and activists (CIVICUS). It provides the Monitor and Reports on the state of civil society world-wide:https://monitor.civicus.org/https://www.civicus.org

The Global Protest Tracker, run by the Carnegie Endowment for International Peace, provides data for analyzing and comparing the triggers, motivations, and other aspects of many of

the most significant antigovernment protests since 2017.https://carnegieendowment.
org/publications/interactive/protest-tracker

The Global Nonviolent Action Database provides free access to information about cases of
nonviolent action. The database is a project of Swarthmore College:https://nvdatabase.
swarthmore.edu/

References

Adloff, F., 2005: *Zivilgesellschaft: Theorie Und Politische Praxis*. Frankfurt, New York: Campus.

Alexander, J. C., 2006: *The Civil Sphere*. Oxford: Oxford Univ. Press.

Amenta, E., 2000: *Bold relief. Institutional politics and the origins of modern American social
policy*. 2nd ed. Princeton, NJ: Princeton Univ. Press.

Amenta, E. & C. Neal, 2004: The Legislative, Organizational, and Beneficiary Consequences of
State-Oriented Challengers. In Snow, D.A., S.A. Soule & H. Kriesi (eds), *The Blackwell
Companion to Social Movements*. John Wiley & Sons Incorporated: John Wiley & Sons
Incorporated.

Anheier, H., 2004: *Civil Society: Measurement, Evaluation, Policy*. London [u.a.]: Earthscan.

Berger, S., 2014: Social Movement in Europe since the End of the Second World War. In Hesse,
j.-O., C. Kleinschmidt, A. Reckendrees & R. Stokes (eds.), *Perspectives on European
Economic and Social History*. ProtoView, 1. 47:14–46.

Benford, R.D. & D.A. Snow, 2000: Framing Processes and Social Movements: An Overview and
Assessment. *Annual Review of Sociology, 26 (1)*, 611–639.

Boerzel, T. A., 2010: The Transformative Power of Europe Reloaded. The Limits of External
Europeanization. Research College "The Transformative Power of Europe", Freie
Universität Berlin. Berlin (KFG Working Papers, 11).

Boerzel, T. A., 2010: The Transformative Power of Europe Reloaded. The Limits of External
Europeanization. Research College "The Transformative Power of Europe", Freie
Universität Berlin. Berlin (KFG Working Papers, 11).

Bourdieu, P., 1983: Ökonomisches Kapital, Kulturelles Kapital, Soziales Kapital. In: Kreckel,
R. (ed.), *Soziale Ungleichheiten*. Göttingen: Verlag Otto Schwartz & Co.:183–198.

Caiani, M., 2019: The Rise and Endurance of Radical Right Movements. In: *Current Sociology
67 (6)*:918–935.

Cohen, J. L. & A. Arato, 1992: *Civil Society and Political Theory*. Studies in contemporary
German social thought. Cambridge, Mass. [u.a.]: MIT-Press.

Clifton, J. & P. de la Broise, 2020: The yellow vests and the communicative constitution of a
protest movement. In: *Discourse & Communication 14 (4)*:362–382.

Conover, P. J., 1991: Political Socialization: Where's the Politics? In: Crotty, W. (ed.): *Political
Science: Looking to the Future. Volume III, Political Behavior*. Evanston, IL: Northwestern
University Press:125–152.

Cress, D. & D. Snow, 2000: The Outcomes of Homeless Mobilization: The Influence of
Organization, Disruption, Political Mediation, and Framing. In: *American Journal of
Sociology 105(4)*:1063–1104.

Curtis, R. & L. Zurcher, 1973: Stable Resources of Protest Movements: The Multi-Organizational
Field. In: *Social Forces 52 (1)*:53–56l.

Della Porta, D. & L. Parks, 2016: Social movements, the European crisis, and EU political opportunities. In: *Comparative European Politics 16 (1)*:85–102.

Della Porta, D., 1995: *Social Movements, Political Violence, and the State: a Comparative Analysis of Italy and Germany.* Cambridge: Cambridge University Press.

Diamond, L., 1999: *Developing Democracy: Toward Consolidation.* Baltimore [u.a.]: Johns Hopkins Univ Pr.

Diani, M., 1992: The Concept of Social Movement. In: *The Sociological Review 40 (1)*:1–25.

Diani, M., 2004: Networks and Participation. In: Kriesi, H., D. A. Snow & S. A. Soule, *The Blackwell Companion to Social Movements.* John Wiley& Sons Incorporated.

Dolezal, M., S. Hutter & R. Becker, 2016: Protesting European Integration: Politicization from Below? In: Hutter, S., E. Grande & H. Kriesi: *Politicising Europe: Integration and Mass Politics.* Cambridge University Press.

Earl, J., 2004: The Cultural Consequences of Social Movements. In: Kriesi, H., D. A. Snow & S. A. Soule, *The Blackwell Companion to Social Movements.* John Wiley& Sons Incorporated.

Eder, K., 2000: Zur Transformation nationalstaatlicher Öffentlichkeit in Europa. In: *Berliner Journal für Soziologie 10 (2)*:167–184.

Edwards, B., M. W. Foley & M. Diani, 2001: *Beyond Tocqueville: Civil Society and the Social Capital Debate in Comparative Perspective*: Univ Pr of New England.

Etzioni, A., 1968: *The Active Society. A Theory of Societal and Political Processes.* New York: The Free Press.

Fominaya, C. F. & R. A. Feenstra, 2020: *Routledge Handbook of Contemporary European Social Movements.* Taylor and Francis.

Gamson, W. A, B. Fireman & S. Rytina, 1982: *Encounters with Unjust Authority.* Homewood, Ill.: Dorsey Press.

Gamson, W. A., 1975: *The Strategy of Social Protest.* Homewood, Ill.: Dorsey Press.

Gamson, W. A., 1990: *The Strategy of Social Protest.* 2nd ed. Belmont, Calif.: Wadsworth Pub.

Giugni, M., 2004: Personal and biographical Consequences. In: Kriesi, H., D. A. Snow & S. A. Soule, *The Blackwell Companion to Social Movements.* John Wiley& Sons Incorporated.

Goodwin, J., J. M. Jasper & F. Polletta (eds.), 2001: *Passionate Politics: Emotions and Social Movements.* Chicago: University of Chicago Press.

Habermas, J., 1992: *Faktizität und Geltung. Beiträge zur Diskurstheorie des Rechts und des demokratischen Rechtsstaats.* 1. Aufl. Frankfurt am Main: Suhrkamp.

Habermas, J., 1998: *Truth and Justification.* Hoboken: Wiley.

Hahn-Fuhr, I. & S. Worschech, 2014: External Democracy Promotion and Divided Civil Society – the Missing Link. In: Beichelt, T., I. Hahn-Fuhr, F. Schimmelfennig & S. Worschech (eds.): *Civil Society and Democracy Promotion.* Basingstoke, Hampshire: Palgrave Macmillan (Challenges to democracy in the 21st century):11–41.

Hareven, T., 1994: Aging and Generational Relations. In: *Annual Review of Sociology (20)*: 437–461.

Henderson, S. L., 2002: Selling Civil Society. In: *Comparative Political Studies 35 (2)*:139–167.

Huntington, S. P., 1991: *The Third Wave: Democratization in the Late 20th Century.* University of Oklahoma Press.

Ishkanian, A., 2007: Democracy Promotion and Civil Society. In: Anheier, H., M. Glasius & M. Kaldor (eds.): *Global civil society: communicative power and democracy, 2007/8.* London: Sage Publications:58–85.

Jasper, J.M., 1997: *The art of moral protest. Culture, biography, and creativity in social movements*. Chicago: Univ. of Chicago Pr.

Jasper, J., 1998: The Emotions of Protest: Affective and Reactive Emotions in and around Social Movements. In: *Sociological Forum 13 (3)*:397–424.

Kitts, J., 2000: Mobilizing in Black Boxes. In: *Mobilization: An International Journal, 5(2)*: 241–257.

Kitschelt, H., 1986: Political Opportunity Structures and Political Protest. In: *British Journal of Political Science 16*:57–85.

Kohler-Koch, B., 2009: The Three Worlds of European Civil Society – What Role for Civil Society for What Kind of Europe? In: *Policy and Society 28 (1)*:47–57.

Kopecký, P. & C. Mudde, 2003: *Uncivil society? Contentious politics in post-communist Europe*. London, New York: Routledge.

Koselleck, R., 1988: *Critique and crisis: Enlightenment and the pathogenesis of modern society*. Cambridge, Mass: Mit Press.

Lutsevych, O., 2013: *How to Finish a Revolution: Civil Society and Democracy in Georgia, Moldova and Ukraine*. Chatham House: Independent thinking on international affairs, http://www.chathamhouse.org/publications/papers/view/188407.

McCarthy, J.D. & M.N. Zald, 1977: Resource mobilization and social movements: A partial theory. In: *American Journal of Sociology 82*:1212–1241.

McAdam, D., 1986: Recruitment to high risk activism: The case of freedom summer. In: *American Journal of Sociology 92*:64–90.

McAdam, D., 1982: *Political Process and the Development of Black Insurgency, 1930–1970*. Chicago: University of Chicago Press.

McAdam, D. & R. Paulsen, 1993: Specifying the relation-ship between social ties and activism. In: *American Journal of Sociology 99*:640–667.

McAdam, D., S. Tarrow & C. Tilly, 2001: *Dynamics of contention*. Cambridge [u.a.]: Cambridge Univ. Press.

Mair, P., 2013: *Ruling the Void: The Hollowing of Western Democracy*. London: Verso Trade.

Melucci, A., 1994: A Strange Kind of Newness: What's 'New' in New Social Movements. In Laraña, E., H. Johnston & J. R. Gusfield (eds.): *New Social Movements: from Ideology to Identity*. Philadelphia: Temple University Press.

Melucci, A., 1996: *Challenging Codes: Collective Action in the Information Age*. Cambridge: Cambridge University Press.

Meyer, D. & S. Tarrow (eds.), 1998: *The Social Movement Society: Contentious Politics for a New Century*. Lanham, Md.: Rowman & Littlefield Publishers.

Meyer, D. & N. Whittier, 1994: Social Movements Spillover. In: *Social Problems 41 (2)*: 2772–98.

Miller, M., 1992: Rationaler Dissens. Zur gesellschaftlichen Funktion sozialer Konflikte. In: Giegel, H.-J. (ed.): *Kommunikation und Konsens in modernen Gesellschaften*, Frankfurt am Main: Suhrkamp:31–58.

Oberschall, A., 1973: *Social Conflict and Social Movements*. Englewood Cliffs: Prentice-Hal.

Offe, C. (ed.), 2003: *Demokratisierung der Demokratie: Diagnosen und Reformvorschläge*. Frankfurt, New York: Campus-Verl.

Olson, M., 1965: *The Logic of Collective Action*. Cambridge, Mass.: Harvard University Press.

Osa, M., 2003: *Solidarity and Contention: Networks of Polish Opposition*. Minneapolis: University of Minnesota Press.

Opp, K.-D., 1994: Repression and Revolutionary Action. East Germany in 1989. In: *Rationality and Society 6(1)*:101–138.

Pishchikova, K., 2010: *Promoting Democracy in Postcommunist Ukraine. The Contradictory Outcomes of US Aid to Women's NGOs.* Boulder: Lynne Rienner Publishers.

Putnam, R. D., R. Leonardi & R. Y. Nanetti, 1993: *Making Democracy Work: Civic Traditions in Modern Italy.* New edition. Princeton: Princeton University Press.

Putnam, R. D., 1995: Bowling Alone: America's Declining Social Capital. In: *Journal of Democracy* 6 (1):65–78.

Putnam, R. D., 2000: *Bowling Alone: The Collapse and Revival of American Community.* New York: Simon & Schuster.

Ruzza, C., 2009: Populism and euroscepticism. Towards uncivil society? In: *Policy and Society* 28 (1):87–98.

Sandell, R., 2001: Organizational growth and ecologicalconstraints: The growth of social movements in Sweden, 1881 to 1940. In: *American Sociological Review (66)*:672–693.

Sasse, G., 2007: Conditionality-lite: The European Neighbourhood Policy and the EU's Eastern Neighbours. In: Casarini, N. & C. Musu (eds.): *European foreign policy in an evolving international system. The road towards convergence.* Basingstoke: Palgrave Macmillan (Palgrave studies in European Union politics):163–180.

Sen, J., 2007: *A Political Programme for the World Social Forum.* New Delhi and India: CACIM.

Skocpol, T., 1994: *Social Revolutions in the Modern World.* Cambridge studies in comparative politics. Cambridge [England], New York: Cambridge University Press.

Snow, D.A., E. B. Rochford Jr., S. K. Worden & R. D. Benford, 1986: Frame Alignment Processes, Micromobilization, and Movement Participation. In: *American Sociological Review 51 (4)*:464–481.

Snow, D.A., S. A. Soule & H. Kriesi, (eds.), 2004: The Blackwell Companion to Social Movements. John Wiley & Sons Incorporated.

Taylor, C., 1991: Die Beschwörung der Civil Society. In: Michalski, K. (ed.): *Europa und die Civil Society. Castelgandolfo-Gespräche 1989.* Stuttgart: Klett–Cotta.

Tarrow, S., 1994: *Power in Movement: Social Movements, Collective Action, and Politics.* Cambridge [England]: Cambridge University Press.

Tarrow, S., 2005: *The New Transnational Activism.* Cambridge University Press.

Tilly, C., 1978: *From mobilization to revolution.* 1st ed. New York: McGraw-Hill Publ.

Tilly, C., 1984: *Big Structures, Large Processes, Huge Comparisons.* Russell Sage Foundation 75th anniversary series. New York: Russell Sage Foundation.

Tilly, C., 1995: To Explain Political Processes. In: *American Journal of Sociology 100 (6)*: 1594–1610.

Tocqueville, A. d. 2014 [1835]: *Über Die Demokratie in Amerika.* Edited by J.P. Mayer. Stuttgart: Reclam.

Tormey, S., 2020: Visions of a good society. In: Fominaya, C. F. & R. A. Feenstra: *Routledge Handbook of Contemporary European Social Movements.* Taylor and Francis.

Touraine, A., 1981: *The voice and the eye. An analysis of social movements.* Cambridge: Cambridge Univ. Press.

Trenz, H.-J., 2009: European civil society. Between participation, representation and discourse. In: *Policy and Society 28 (1)*:35–46.

Trenz, H.-J. 2015: Europeanising the Public Sphere – Meaning, Mechanisms, Effects. In: Liebert, U. & J. Wolff (eds.): *Interdisziplinäre Europastudien. Eine Einführung.* Wiesbaden: Springer VS:233–251.

Trenz, H.-J., 2017: Europäische Öffentlichkeit. In: Bach, M & B. Hönig (eds.): *Handbuch Europasoziologie*. Nomos Verlagsgesellschaft Mbh & Co:359–368.

Turner, R.H. & L.M. Killian, 1987: *Collective behavior*. 3rd ed. Englewood Cliffs, N.J.: Prentice-Hall.

Walzer, M., 1992: Equality and Civil Society. In: Chambers, S. & W. Kymlicka (eds.): *Alternative Conceptions of Civil Society*. The ethikon series in comparative ethics. Princeton University Press:34–49.

Walgrave, S. & D. Rucht, 2010: *The World Says No to War: Demonstrations against the War on Iraq*. Minneapolis: University of Minnesota Press.

Walsh, E.,1981: Resource Mobilization and Citizen Protest in Communities around Three Mile Island. In: *Social Problems 29 (1)*:1–21.

Wessler, H. & E. M. Rinke, 2013: Öffentlichkeit. In: Mau, S. & N.M. Schöneck (eds.): *Handwörterbuch zur Gesellschaft Deutschlands*. Wiesbaden: Springer VS:637–650.

Whittier, N., 2004: The Consequences of Social Movements for Each Other. In Kriesi, H., D. A. Snow & S. A. Soule, *The Blackwell Companion to Social Movements*. John Wiley& Sons Incorporated.

Wodak, R., M. Khosravinik & B. Mral (eds), 2013: *Right-wing populism in Europe: Politics and discourse*. London: Bloomsbury.

Worschech, S., 2017: New civic activism in Ukraine: Building society from scratch? In: *Kyiv-Mohyla Law and Politics Journal 3* (Special Issue: Civil Society in Ukraine: Building on Euromaidan Legacy):23–45.

Worschech, S., 2018: *Die Herstellung von Zivilgesellschaft. Strategien und Netzwerke der externen Demokratieförderung in der Ukraine*. Wiesbaden: VS Verlag für Sozialwissenschaften.

Worschech, S., 2020: *Deutsch-ukrainische Kulturbeziehungen. Veränderungen nach dem Euromaidan. ifa-Edition Kultur und Außenpolitik*, Stuttgart: https://publikationen.ifa.de/out/wysiwyg/uploads/70edition/deutsch-ukrainische-kulturbez_worschech.pdf.

Youngs, R., 2008: What Has Europe Been Doing? In: *Journal of Democracy 19 (2)*:160–169.

Notes on Contributors

Timm Beichelt is a professor of European Studies at the European University Viadrina Frankfurt (Oder), Germany.

Manuela Boatcă is a professor of sociology at University of Freiburg, Germany.

Stefanie Börner is a junior professor of sociology at Otto-von-Guericke-University Magdeburg, Germany.

Sebastian M. Büttner is a senior lecturer of sociological theory and cultural sociology at the Institute of Sociology, Friedrich-Alexander-University Erlangen-Nürnberg (FAU), Germany.

Emanuel Deutschmann is an assistant professor of sociological theory at the Europa-Universität Flensburg (EUF), Germany, and an external collaborator to the Global Mobilities Project at the European University Institute's Migration Policy Centre in Florence, Italy.

Monika Eigmüller is professor of sociology at the Europa-Universität Flensburg (EUF), Germany.

Sabine Frerichs is a professor of economic sociology at Vienna University of Economics and Business, Austria.

Günter Hefler is a is a senior researcher at 3s (3s.co.at) in Vienna, Austria.

Zsófia S. Ignácz is a researcher and lecturer at the Institute of Sociology at Goethe University Frankfurt (Main), Germany.

Niilo Kauppi is a research professor at the French National Center for Scientific Research (CNRS).

Christian Lahusen is a professor of sociology at the Department of Social Sciences, University of Siegen, Germany.

Fernando Losada is a research fellow of the Academy of Finland and affiliated to the Faculty of Law at University of Helsinki, Finland.

Camille Noûs is an interdisciplinary collective researcher at the Laboratoire Cogitamus. See for more information: https://www.cogitamus.fr/camilleen.html

Susanne Pernicka is a professor of sociology at Johannes Kepler University Linz, Austria.

Tsveta Petrova is a Lecturer in the Discipline of Political Science at Columbia University, United States.

https://doi.org/10.1515/9783110673630-015

Ettore Recchi is a professor of sociology at Science Po Paris, France and a part-time professor with the Migration Policy Centre of the European University Institute in Florence, Italy.

Fabio Santos is a postdoctoral researcher and lecturer at the Institute for Latin American Studies at Free University of Berlin, Germany.

Nikola Tietze is a research fellow at the Centre Marc Bloch Berlin and the Hamburger Stiftung zur Förderung von Wissenschaft und Kultur. She is also associated to the Laboratoire interdisciplinaire pour la sociologie économique (Lise) at the Conservatoire national des arts et métiers (Cnam), Paris.

Hans-Jörg Trenz is a professor of sociology at the Scuola Normale Superiore in Florence, Italy.

Eleonora Vlach is a postdoctoral researcher at the Institute of Sociology at Goethe University Frankfurt (Main), Germany.

Susann Worschech is a senior lecturer at the European University Viadrina Frankfurt (Oder), Germany.

List of Figures

https://doi.org/10.1515/9783110673630-016

List of Tables

https://doi.org/10.1515/9783110673630-017

Index

https://doi.org/10.1515/9783110673630-018

www.ingramcontent.com/pod-product-compliance
Lightning Source LLC
Chambersburg PA
CBHW071729270326
41928CB00013B/2606